highly recommended for sociologists, historians, psychologists, psychotherapists, group therapists, group analysts, and anyone who is interested in understanding more about unconscious social processes."

Haim Weinberg, *PhD, psychologist and group analyst in California and Israel, past President, Israeli Association for Group Psychotherapy, and former Director of International Programs, Professional School of Psychology, California*

"Carla Penna puts at our disposition her encyclopedic knowledge on phenomena involving large numbers of persons. She approaches the context of masses with psychoanalytic and group analytic tools, first 'mapping the field' of the unconscious life of crowds, illuminating the darkness of the twenty-first century crowds and masses."

Robi Friedman, *PhD, group analyst, past President of the Group Analytic Society International*

"This book represents an impressive tour de force. The author takes us on an exciting journey into a transdiciplinary analysis and investigation of the psychodynamics of the larger group, starting with Durkheim and Le Bon over Freud to the Frankfurt School, the Northfield experiments, Bion and Foulkes, ending up with Hopper's fourth basic assumption of Incohesion. It is an outstanding achievement and it is warmly recommended."

Gerda Winther, *MA, psychologist, former Associate Professor at the Faculty of Medicine, University of Copenhagen, and past President of the Group Analytic Society International*

"Carla Penna's particular view from Brazil, combined with her many years of experience as practitioner, teacher, and academic of psychoanalysis and group analysis, enables a full study of where we are now in understanding large groups. She provides an expansive perspective with access to writers from Latin America and Europe often with her own translations."

Dr Jale Cilasun, *BM FRCPsych, consultant psychiatrist, specialist in medical psychotherapy and group analyst*

"This is a much-needed book – in time and on time. In a world where crowds take many different forms globally and virtually, transcending lives everywhere, this transdisciplinary study investigates crowds as social and psychological phenomena historically and contemporary based on an impressive command of knowledge. However, the focus turns to the social unconscious as the most important tool for the understanding of the complicated and often incomprehensible processes that go on in the large groups that forms the crowds. The author is a psychoanalyst and group analyst and is drawing on theories and clinical experience of large group dynamics where the interaction in the social unconscious between the individual and the large group takes place."

Anne Lindhardt, *psychiatrist, trained group analyst, former Director of Mental Services, Copenhagen, and Chairperson of Institute of Group Analysis Copenhagen*

From Crowd Psychology to the Dynamics of Large Groups

From Crowd Psychology to the Dynamics of Large Groups offers transdisciplinary research on the history of the study of social formations, ranging from nineteenth-century crowd psychology in France and twentieth-century Freudian mass psychology, including the developments in critical theory, to the study of the psychodynamics of contemporary large groups.

Carla Penna presents a unique combination of sociology, psychoanalysis, and group analysis in the study of social formations. This book revisits the epistemological basis of group analysis by introducing and discussing its historical path, especially in connection with the study of large groups and investigations of the social unconscious in persons, groups, and societies. It also explores early work on group relations and contemporary research on the basic-assumption group in England, particularly Hopper's theory of Incohesion as a fourth basic assumption. *From Crowd Psychology to the Dynamics of Large Groups* enables the reader to map out the field of the unconscious life of crowds illuminating the darkness of twenty-first century collective movements.

The reflections in this book present new perspectives for psychologists, psychoanalysts, group analysts, sociologists, and historians to investigate the psychodynamics of contemporary crowds, masses, and social systems.

Carla Penna, PhD, is a psychoanalyst and a group analyst in Brazil. She is a member of the Psychoanalytic Circle of Rio de Janeiro and the Group Analytic Society International.

The New International Library of Group Analysis
Series Editor: Earl Hopper

Drawing on the seminal ideas of British, European and American group analysts, psychoanalysts, social psychologists and social scientists, the books in this series focus on the study of small and large groups, organisations and other social systems, and on the study of the transpersonal and transgenerational sociality of human nature. NILGA books will be required reading for the members of professional organisations in the field of group analysis, psychoanalysis, and related social sciences. They will be indispensable for the "formation" of students of psychotherapy, whether they are mainly interested in clinical work with patients or in consultancy to teams and organisational clients within the private and public sectors.

Recent titles in the series include:

Psychoanalysis, Group Analysis, and Beyond
Towards a New Paradigm of the Human Being
Juan Tubert-Oklander and Reyna Hernández-Tubert

An Introduction to Psychotherapeutic Playback Theater
Hall of Mirrors on Stage
Ronen Kowalsky, Nir Raz and Shoshi Keisari with Susana Pendzik

Psycho-social Explorations of Trauma, Exclusion and Violence
Un-housed Minds and Inhospitable Environments
Christopher Scanlon and John Adlam

Sibling Relations and the Horizontal Axis in Theory and Practice
Contemporary Group Analysis, Psychoanalysis and Organization Consultancy
Edited by Smadar Ashuach and Avi Berman

From Crowd Psychology to the Dynamics of Large Groups
Historical, Theoretical and Practical Considerations
Carla Penna

From Crowd Psychology to the Dynamics of Large Groups

Historical, Theoretical and Practical Considerations

Carla Penna

Routledge
Taylor & Francis Group

LONDON AND NEW YORK

Cover image: wildpixel / Getty Images

First published 2023
by Routledge
4 Park Square, Milton Park, Abingdon, Oxon OX14 4RN

and by Routledge
605 Third Avenue, New York, NY 10158

Routledge is an imprint of the Taylor & Francis Group, an informa business

British Library Cataloguing-in-Publication Data
A catalogue record for this book is available from the British Library

Library of Congress Cataloging-in-Publication Data
A catalog record has been requested for this book

ISBN: 978-0-367-02449-9 (hbk)
ISBN: 978-0-367-02450-5 (pbk)
ISBN: 978-0-429-39953-4 (ebk)

DOI: 10.4324/9780429399534

Typeset in Bembo
by Taylor & Francis Books

To the continued presence of Carlos and Renato

Contents

Tables

Acknowledgements

This book would not have been written without the collaboration of esteemed masters and colleagues, who, throughout my professional career, have been sharing their interest in the understanding of human suffering in various contexts.

I am forever grateful for having met Earl Hopper. Attentive, sensitive, and generous, he shared with me his passion for the challenging dialogue between sociology, psychoanalysis, and group analysis. I am also indebted to Haim Weinberg, Malcolm Pines, Bob Hinshelwood, Juan Tubert-Oklander, Dieter Nitzgen, with whom I had inspiring encounters. In the Brazilian milieu, I am deeply appreciative of the support of Claudia Amorim Garcia, Luis Claudio Figueiredo, and Flavio Ferraz.

However, not all my achievements would have been possible without the love of my parents, Maria Cecilia and Fernando Penna, and the support of my dear masters Julio de Mello Filho, Jose Vasco, David Zimerman, Luiz Carlos Osório, especially Roberto Bittencourt Martins.

My thanks to Raluca Soreanu, Carmen O'Leary, Clare Gerada, Julie Howley (*in memoriam*), Miriam Iosupovici, Martha Gilmore, Göran Ahlin, Svein Tjelta, Marta Gonçalves, Cristina Amendoeira, Alba Senna, Magali Amaral, Maria Theresa Barros, Regina Aragão for their friendship. I am also grateful to Marina Mojovic, Zaven Dordevic, Christopher Scanlon and the Serbian colleagues for sharing dreams in the group work.

To Dr. José Maurício Carmo, Gerson Lamenza and Vanessa Braga, I express my gratitude for their invaluable skills.

I thank Mônica Saddy Martins for her continuous support, devotion and careful revision of the English version and Branka Bakic and Daria Lavrennikov for their collaboration.

Series Foreword

I have decided not to write my usual Foreword to a book in the New International Library of Group Analysis, partly because I have contributed a chapter about my own work on Incohesion. It seems sufficient to draw to the attention of readers the engaging and enthusiastic endorsements by leading figures of Group Analysis, Psychoanalysis, and Psychosocial Studies. For example, Haim Weinberg writes "(This book) is highly recommended for sociologists, historians, psychologists, psychotherapists, group therapists, group analysts, and anyone interested in... unconscious social processes". Gerhard Wilke writes "At last a helpful and scholarly account of the history of Large Group Theory... Large Group phenomena can only be comprehended in an interdisciplinary way...". Robert Hinshelwood writes "Her book... comprises a comprehensive survey of the political and sociological nature of groups, communities and societies...This multi-dimensional picture shows human beings within the matrix of the societies which humans have created, and how that matrix can heal us as well as form us...". And Stephen Frosh writes "Moving with great clarity and energy through the history of hordes, herds, masses, and crowds, and drawing from her deep understanding of group psychologies and group analysis, Carla Penna offers both a balanced and well-informed guide to group theory...". I would add that during the last few years I have learned from my frequent discussions with Carla, who I am pleased to introduce to an English readership.

Dr Carla Penna has a highly developed appreciation of the well-known adage that the group and the individual are two sides of the same coin, and, therefore, that Sociology and Psychoanalysis should be deeply intertwined with Group Analysis. She understands the paradox in the statement that large groups are dynamic open-systems. She recognizes that in so far as in any group there is a war between the forces of regression and the forces of progression, studies of large groups are likely to emanate from the fields of both Group Relations and Group Analysis.

As a psychoanalyst and group analyst, Carla keeps in mind the tripartite matrix of any particular group. This includes the personal and interpersonal matrices of its participants, at least in terms of role suction, valence, and personification. She knows how to play the popular children's game "Where is

Wally?". She is comfortable reading Walt Whitman's *Leaves of Grass:* "I am large, I contain multitudes". She listened when in 1958 the Rio de Janeiro Group Analytic Society was founded, and Walderedo Ismael de Oliveira insisted: "… (We must eliminate) the barriers that arbitrarily separate the personal from the social…". And she knows that at the base of the Statue of Liberty in the harbor of New York it is written: "Give me your tired, your poor, your huddled masses yearning to breathe free, the wretched refuse of your teeming shore". In other words, she understands that the study of large social formations is inevitably a political project, even if not explicitly so.

Carla has shared with me some of the steps of her biography: Since early childhood, she was interested in history and books. Listening to the stories of her mother's Brazilian ancestors, she decided to study history. However, during her adolescence, she shifted to sociology. At the last-minute, perhaps influenced by her father and grandfather's careers as physicians, she began to study psychology. Working in hospitals, she spontaneously started to see disabled patients in groups. In 1988, she started her group analytic training at the Group Analytic Psychotherapy Society of the State of Rio de Janeiro (SPAG E. Rio), and in 1996 she became a training group analyst. Carla was privileged to work with the psychoanalysts Walderedo Ismael de Oliveira, Roberto Bittencourt Martins, Julio de Mello Filho, José Vasco, José Carlos Carpilovsky, Luis Carlos Osório and David Zimmerman, who were not only pioneers of group analytic work in Brazil, but also active in international professional organisations, such as the International Association for Group Psychotherapy. In parallel with these activities, she started her psychoanalytic training at the Círculo Psicanalítico of Rio de Janeiro, becoming a full member in 1997. From 2002–2008 Carla was the president of the SPAG E. Rio, and from 2004–2006 the president of the Brazilian Association for Group Psychotherapy (ABPG).

In 2006, she decided to do a PhD in the study of group analytic psychotherapy in Brazil. She wanted to understand why there had been such a marked decline in interest in group work, which was disappointing and painful both to her own generation and to that of her senior group analytic colleagues in Brazil. Slowly she turned to the question of why group analysis had continued to develop in England and in Europe more generally. It is likely that this was facilitated by the centrality of the concept of the social unconscious within the general theory of group analysis, and by building relations with our colleagues in Europe. The work of mourning has been crucial. The transdisciplinary perspective of group analytic theory has allowed Carla to combine her childhood passion for the study of history, and her unfulfilled desire to study sociology, with her experiences as a psychoanalyst and group analyst.

Dr Carla Penna is now a member of the Management Committee of the Group Analytic Society International. Her participation in the Society and in the Committee has been highly transformative. Carla often acknowledges the warm welcome given to her, especially by Marina Mojovic, Malcolm Pines and Haim Weinberg, which has allowed her to improve her knowledge and interest in groups, as well as to hone her clinical and training skills. In this context, she was herself able to mourn the loss of the highly creative and hopeful Bra-zilian situation, while honouring this tradition and the pioneers of it. This has allowed her to develop new perspectives and new colleagues in England and elsewhere in Europe. For the last three decades, she has been publishing articles and book chapters on topics such as personal and collective trauma, mourning processes, and psychosocial psychoanalysis. We have been collaborating on the study of the social unconscious.

I have little doubt that her new book will help to satisfy the need for better understanding of large groups. I am confident that she will be involved in further publications in this field. I am sure that this new book will soon be found on the reading lists of our training organizations and academic disciplines.

Earl Hopper, PhD
Series Editor

Introduction

Phenomena involving large numbers of persons have permeated history for centuries in the form of mobs, crowds, masses, riots, and other experiences in which people, even when not in the presence of each other, shared collective beliefs as rumours, panics, crazes, and mass hysteria. From the earliest recorded cases – like the dancing plague in Strasbourg (1518) or the Loudun possessions (1632–1634) – to French Revolution mobs and to crowd manifestations at the end of the nineteenth century in France, different hypotheses have been formulated to explain people's unexpected behaviour in various social formations.

In the nineteenth century, Hippolyte Taine was the first to draw attention to the modern phenomenon of crowds (Van Ginneken, 1992). At that time, the idea of the individual was already part of the social body, mixed with the history of modern ideology. However, in the last decade of that century, when deep socioeconomic transformations were taking place in France, especially different forms of collective manifestations, the intellectuals developed an interest in deciphering the psychology of crowds. Also, in the late nineteenth century, the study of social formations gained weight, setting the stage for the birth of sociology – with works by Durkheim, Weber, Tönnies, Simmel, and Tarde – and also of psychology, statistics, and criminology as scientific disciplines. These new research fields revealed the importance of collective frames of analysis and were in tune with the debates on the sociocultural and political questions of the time, facilitating the study of "texts inserted in contexts" (Mucchielli, 1998).

Therefore, from the end of the nineteenth century onwards and under contextualized frames of analysis, sociologists, social psychologists, anthropologists, social psychiatrists, psychoanalysts, group analysts, historians, and epidemiologists devoted their attention to the study of the *question du nombre* (Reynié, 1988). Previously, witchcraft, demonic possession, and hysteria (Penna, 2019) had been associated with these manifestations, but in the nineteenth century, the connection between the public and the crowd (Tarde, 1890, 2005) and ideas on collective consciousness (Durkheim, 1895) and group mind (Le Bon, 1895) prompted the investigation of crowd psychology. Nevertheless, these first analyses seemed to ignore the importance of unconscious affections.

DOI: 10.4324/9780429399534-1

In the twentieth century, at the dawn of mass society, with the emergence of mass-men (Ortega y Gasset, 1930), individuals were transformed into atomized masses fascinated by the illusory power of their leaders. Within this context, just after World War I, Freud (1921) revolutionized the nineteenth-century crowd psychology, converting it into the twentieth-century mass psychology. Freudian psychoanalysis transformed the conservative views that used to give importance to the hypnotic-suggestive features of crowds, replacing them with unconscious processes, identifications, libidinal ties, and ideal agencies. Psychoanalysis has built a new framework for the study of the masses, which, from then on, would intertwine anonymous individuals with powerful leaders. Moreover, Freud's mass psychology, together with the traumatic socio-historical and political events of the early twentieth century, foreshadowed the way unscrupulous leaders would influence and rule the masses. The concern with collective behaviour thus converted into the need to find ways to control and govern the masses (Moscovici, 1985).

Some of these concerns found new expressions in the socio-political atmosphere of the 1920s and 1930s through the Freudo-Marxist movement and after the establishment, in 1923, of the Frankfurt Institute for Social Research. The critical dimension of psychoanalysis was associated with Marxism to conduct crucial investigations into social theory and philosophy (Jay, 1973). The Frankfurt School's research covers a period that blends with the history of the twentieth century itself, to which World War II left a traumatic legacy to be worked through by the generations to come (Bohleber, 1995, 2010; Frosh, 2013a). The investigations undertaken by the Frankfurt School and other intellectuals, such as Hannah Arendt (1948, 1958), tried to cope with this complex "inheritance". Through transdisciplinary critical thinking and haunted by the horrors of two world wars, the Frankfurtians sought to analyse modernity with a special interest in studies on ideology, fascism, and mass culture (Horkheimer & Adorno, 1944; Adorno, 1951). Their research aimed at warning society and ensuring that civilization would be able to prevent barbarism (Adorno, 1947).

Later, the year 1968 entered history as a culmination of the sociopolitical and cultural transformations that triggered protests all over the world against the shackles of modernity, struggling to replace hierarchical authority with ample democratization to guarantee individual rights, equality, and freedom. These shifts, in the middle of the Cold War, led to the emergence of the sexual revolution, feminism, and social movements against the Vietnam War and for civil rights in the United States – all actions with a strong sociocultural appeal (Penna, 2020). They supported social identities that gave birth to identity politics in the following decades (Hall, 1992; Butler, 2015; Fukuyama, 2018). However, their psychodynamics seems distant from the Freudian model for mass psychology built on mutual identification, through which the masses project their ego ideal on an idealized and omnipotent leader. Indeed, social identity movements are generally supported by horizontal identifications, in which homogeneity and the illusion of fusion/merge seem to amalgamate the members of a mass around a common goal or claim.

The psychodynamics of social identity movements with a large number of persons attires attention. First, because they bring perspectives to the analysis of social formations that go beyond the features of crowd psychology and the model of mass psychology. Second, because they make us wonder what happened to the Freudian mass psychology classical model in the last decades of the twentieth century. Have contemporary Western societies succeeded in replacing the verticality of the Freudian model of mass psychology with more horizontal and equal relationships between people, as observed in social identity configurations? If so, what is their psychodynamics? What is the nature of identification processes and bonding? What is the role of illusions, ideal agencies and ideology in these social formations?

The last decade of the twentieth century brought unexpected new challenges, especially after the end of the Cold War and the reconfiguration of the European borders. Since the early years of the twenty-first century, neoliberalism and increasing socioeconomic problems have become an undeniable reality. Associated with the emergence of ethnic conflicts, neo-ideologies, fundamentalism, terrorism, racism, unemployment, and massive emigration, this reality has been a source of global concern. Moreover, the resurgence of right-wing politics, populism, and nationalism left no doubt that in the fragmented and polarized social world "democratic leadership" is being challenged by "authoritarian leadership" (Armstrong & Rustin, 2012, p. 61). The debate also points to the transgenerational psychic transmission of traumas the populations experienced during the twentieth century, and to the role of traumatic experience in the unconscious life of groups (Hopper, 2003b). These observations show a new socioeconomic, psychological, and political panorama for the twenty-first century social systems, a matter that requires investigation. Additionally, and unexpectedly, the twenty-first century brings with it ecological concerns and the "syndemic" of COVID-19 (Horthon, 2020), both of which are life-threatening to social systems throughout the whole world. The psychosocial and political-economic impact of the syndemic is yet to be determined, but is already transforming the twenty-first-century panorama.

As a Brazilian psychoanalyst and group analyst tuned to the Aristotelian idea that man is by nature a social animal, I have always been interested in inter-subjective and trans-subjective perspectives to develop my understanding of human suffering in connection to the reality of the social world. Notwithstanding the contemporary psychoanalytical, sociological, and psychosocial approaches, relationships between the individual and society, even inadvertently, remain influenced by modern dichotomies and by the individualistic paradigm (Simmel, 1908; Dumont, 1986). Yet, in the 1940s, S. H. Foulkes (1948, 1964, 1975a), a German-British psychoanalyst contemporary of Freudo-Marxists and Frankfurtians conceived group analysis as a new epistemology for individual-society relations. Prioritizing the social nature of persons, Foulkes states that the individual is "part of a social network, a little nodal point, as it were, in this network, and can only artificially be considered in isolation" (Foulkes, 1948, p. 14). In 1952, Foulkes founded the Group Analytic Society in London. Combining psychoanalytic and sociological theories, group analysis enables the exploration of the interdependencies between intrapersonal, inter-personal, and transpersonal processes through the work in groups.

Therefore, within the group analytic framework, my research acquires new contours. Moreover, my contact with the work in large groups and with Earl Hopper's (2003b) Incohesion theory added to my collaboration with Hopper and Weinberg (2011, 2016, 2017) in the international research on the concept of the social unconscious, allowing me to contextualize my investigations his-torically, in time and space.

This book proposes a transdisciplinary research on the history of the study of social formations ranging from nineteenth-century crowd psychology in France and twentieth-century Freudian mass psychology to the study of the psychodynamics of contemporary groups and social systems. This research relies on the group analytic theory for individual-society relations and on the study of the social unconscious as its background. To accomplish this task, we revisit the epistemological basis of group analysis by introducing and discussing its historical path, especially in connection with the study of large groups. In this route, we also explore the early work in group relations and contemporary research on the basic-assumption group, especially Hopper's theory of Incohesion as a fourth basic assumption.

Chapter One begins with a critique of modern individualism (Simmel, 1989) and its influence on thinking from the eighteenth to the twentieth century. The impact of individualistic theories and the birth of sociology associated with sociopolitical changes in France in the late nineteenth century provide the context for the earliest studies on crowd psychology. It also explores the socio-historical and psychological analyses of the phenomenon conducted by Gabriel Tarde (1890) and Gustave Le Bon (1895). Although having a conservative bias, these authors paved the way to the emergence of twentieth-century mass psychology.

Chapter Two concentrates on the emergence of mass society and the anon-ymous mass-men described by Ortega y Gasset (1930), along with Trotter's (1919) herd instinct and McDougall's (1920) organized groups. Freud's (1921) mass psychology, the relationship between the masses and their leaders, its role in the twentieth-century thinking about mass movements, and the Freudian developments related to psychoanalysis and culture are examined as well.

Chapter Three deepens the debate on mass psychology, associating it with the Freudo-Marxist attempts to integrate Marxism and psychoanalysis in the 1920s and 1930s. Next, we present the early years of the Frankfurt School and some of their developments in mass psychology, fascism, demagogic propaganda, and authoritarian personality (Adorno, 1950 et al., 1951).

Chapter Four discusses Georg Simmel's (1908) sociology in the study of forms of sociation, as well as Norbert Elias's (1939, 2001) analysis of individualization processes and his concept of figuration (Elias, 1984). These contributions leave behind the dichotomies that had polarized the relationships between individual and society for centuries. The framework provided by Simmel's and Elias's process sociology favours thinking in terms of interdependencies in individual-society relations, pointing to a necessary shift from a society of individuals to a society of persons, endorsing the idea that persons interact with one another from conception to death. This epistemology was fundamental for Foulkes to conceive group analysis.

Chapter Five discusses two experiments with groups during World War II at the Northfield Hospital in England. The first experiment was undertaken by John Rickman and Wilfred Bion and the second by Tom Main, Harold Bridger, and S. H. Foulkes (Harrison, 2000). These experiences became a foundation for different psychodynamic approaches to group work, such as group analysis, group relations, therapeutic communities, social and cultural psychiatry, socio analysis, sociotherapy, and art therapy (Hinshelwood, 1999). The tendencies outlined in the Northfield experiments point to the post-war emergence of two main different streams of psychoanalytically oriented groups in England. The first experiment is connected to Rickman and Bion's (1961) work with the Army and their experience with leaderless groups at the hospital. The second relates to the development of therapeutic communities and to Foulkes's approach to small-group work, which led to the creation of group analysis. Chapter Five also introduces the intertwining of psychoanalytical, philosophical, and sociological influences that allowed Foulkes to outline the benchmarks of group analytic epistemology while he was living in Germany, before emigrating to England in 1933.

Chapter Six presents the legacy of the first Northfield Experiment, leading to the establishment of the Tavistock Institute of Human Relations in 1946 in England. It introduces the early work in group relations, the establishment of the Leicester Conferences as of 1957 and the development of the A. K. Rice Institute (Rice, 1965) in the United States, which underpinned the experiential and educational learning about leadership in groups, paying special attention to the development of large-group work in group relations conferences.

Chapter Seven explores the connection between the 1960s and the 1970s sociocultural effervescence and the advances in group work in England, especially the emergence of large-group work. It highlights the importance of Bion's basic assumptions theory to the analytic thinking about groups. With this in mind, we discuss the attempts to conceptualize new basic assumptions mainly through the theories of Pierre Turquet (1975) and Lawrence, Bain and Gould (2000) in the group relations field.

Chapter Eight introduces S. H. Foulkes's (1948, 1964) work and the creation of the group analytic theory that replaced the dichotomies between individual and society by conferring value to the intrinsic relationality of human beings. It also examines the development of the social unconscious theory from its roots in Foulkesian group analysis to its contemporary developments, mainly through the extension and reconfiguration of the concept of matrix – personal, dynamic and foundation matrices (Hopper & Weinberg, 2017).

Chapter Nine focuses on the investigation of large groups in group analysis in hospitals, training, clinical and organizational settings, as well as in conferences and workshops as of the 1960s. Large-group work provides an in-depth comprehension of the primitive processes that take place in personal, interpersonal and transpersonal interactions in groups (Kreeger, 1975), offering the possibility of humanizing society and developing citizenship through dialogue (de Maré, 2012b). The study of large groups in group analysis can be considered as a theoretical and technical research tool to broaden the contemporary understanding of the psychodynamics of persons when gathered in large numbers.

The twenty-first century socioeconomic and political situation has been revealing acute dimensions of personal and social suffering, along with new struggles for recognition (Honneth, 1996) for marginalized and excluded groups and populations. We have been observing the proliferation of social identity movements to cope with these new challenges. The investigation of these processes points to the relevance of Hopper's (2003b) theory of Incohesion, especially to the traumatic experiences of failed dependency and defences associated with them in both the psychological and social spheres. In this direction, Chapter Ten discusses the importance of traumatic experience in the unconscious life of social systems by presenting the latest version of Earl Hopper's fourth basic assumption – Incohesion: Aggregation/Massification theory or (ba) I: A/M, which the author especially prepared for this book.

Trauma is privileged in Hopper's Incohesion theory. Incohesion is a manifestation of the intra-psychic phenomenology of the fear of annihilation and a defensive response to experiences of failed dependency, such as loss, abandonment, and damage in interpersonal relationships. Hopper's fourth basic assumption is important in clinical work in groups, mainly with difficult patients, and in the work conducted in traumatized organizations. It allows investigations on sociopolitical processes in societies and is relevant to explorations on identity as well. For these reasons, Hopper's contribution to Chapter Ten is followed by my critical comment on the significance of his theory for the study of identity and social identity in the contemporary social world.

Anchored in a group analytic framework and in the study of the social unconscious, my research has evolved. In these theoretical and clinical perspectives, I have found new tools for investigating the psychodynamics of crowds, masses and social systems. We hope this book engages the reader with information, insights, and reflection on the path taken by the social formations discussed here.

1 Nineteenth-century crowd psychology

Modernity and the construction of the concept of the individual

Modernity represents a profound shift in Western thought, thanks to the notion of progress and the importance given to the idea of the individual that replaced ancient traditions and medieval dogmas. It is a consensus that the Renaissance created individuality and that the modern notion of the individual was influenced by humanism, romanticism, and the Enlightenment, which emphasized the human being as the centre of the universe, endowed with autonomy of spirit and reason, freedom, and psychological subjectivity (Ariès & Duby, 1992).

The idea of the individual emerges as part of a historical shift from a worldview grounded on religion, the transcendent, and on less powerful traditional institutions to secularized conceptions and Cartesian rationalism focused on individual potentialities. The boundary separating modern society from traditional societies can be traced from an individualistic revolution that produced a change of values within societies. The Church's loss of political-ideological supremacy, the emergence of modern states, and the formation of a political sphere separated from religion were complementary events that gave rise to individualism as an ideology. Thus, the concept of the modern individual was gradually constructed and historically determined. It stems from Renaissance humanism and Enlightenment ideals and represents a clear break with the past (Dumont, 1981).

The individualistic revolution changes the emphasis from the society as a whole – holism – to the human individual, who begins to be considered as the embodiment of humanity itself – individualism. In traditional societies, values focus on order, hierarchy, and tradition, orienting human beings to act in accordance with social ideals, contributing to the overall development of society as collective beings (Tönnies, 1887). In this case, man is conceived as a social being who derives what makes him human from society and is an integral part of it, whereas in societies characterized by individualism the emphasis is on the attributes, demands, and well-being of each individual. Thus, human beings come to be seen as primary and indivisible, at the same time that they become biological and thinking beings. Each human being, as an "individual of

DOI: 10.4324/9780429399534-2

the species (*individuum*) embodies the whole of mankind, which is composed of individuals" (Figueira, 1981, p. 60; translation mine).

It was only with Alexis de Tocqueville (1835) that individualism – formerly tied to selfishness as a blind egotistical instinct, a vice of the heart – lost its pejorative connotation. Individualism became part of a body of knowledge linked to liberal democratic thinking. According to de Tocqueville, individualism has a democratic origin and is a widespread idea that evolves with the increasing equality between individuals in society and configures itself as something intrinsic to the individuals' nature.

Dumont (1986) states that individualism has made modern ideology distinguishable from all other ideologies, underlining that the components that characterize the now familiar ideas and values behind individualism did not always exist, nor did they arise overnight. From a historical perspective, Dumont points to transformations in the idea of the individual:

> ... something of modern individualism is present with the first Christians and in the surrounding world, but that it is not exactly individualism as we know it. Actually, the old form and the new are separated by a transformation so radical and so complex that it took at least seventeen centuries of Christian history to be completed, if indeed it is not still continuing in our times.
>
> (Dumont, 1986, p. 24)

To understand Dumont's point of view, we need to consider two distinct types of society that demonstrate a shift in their value system, from society as a whole – holism – to a society in which the human individual begins to embody humanity as a whole – individualism. However, Dumont's analysis stresses that the modern world turned the whole system of traditional values upside down. A society formerly organized around a collectivity was transformed into what we understand as modernity, an organization of autonomous individuals. In pre-modern societies, the idea of the individual was something of the order of the unthinkable and nonhuman, whereas in the modern world individual achievements were transformed into the highest goal of human existence within society. The structure of modern ideology, based on the principles of equality and freedom, took on as its foundational principle the prized representation of the idea of the individual, that is, human beings represented humanity, and each human being, despite their characteristics, carried with them the essence of humanity. Thus, the individual acquired an almost sacred, absolute status, and was conceived as a monad. This observation led Dumont (1981) states that every human group was made up of monads, and that society was nothing less than an alliance and, in a way, a mere collection of monads. In these terms, Dumont's analysis moved in the direction of a critique of the antagonism between individual and society, affirming that this perspective was an integral part of modern ideology, and less than satisfactory for observing society as a whole.

To criticize this antagonism, Dumont states:

> The contemporary ideological world is like a fabric woven by the continuing interaction of cultures at the least since the end of the eighteenth century; it is made up of the actions and reactions of individualism and its opposite.
>
> (Dumont, 1986, p. 18)

Therefore, ideas and values considered as modern are "the result of a historical process in the course of which modernity and nonmodernity or, more precisely, individualistic value-ideas and their opposites, have combined intimately" (p. 18). In this sense, Dumont's analysis of individualism consolidates the conception of the individual as a singular being, responsible for their acts, and an autonomous being in relation to the emergence of the modern citizen, the smallest cell of democratic modernity. The idea of individualism dates back to the origins of democratic thought, grounding political society on principles of equal rights for all humankind, following some of the hypotheses formulated by Hobbes, Locke, and Rousseau (Dumont, 1986, p. 19).

The study of individualism is interweaved with the history of modern ideology itself, shaped as a paradigm of social organization between the sixteenth and nineteenth centuries. However, its conceptualization has undergone a non-linear evolution over time, through simultaneous movements, versions of the same process of the constitution of modern subjectivities, engendered between the public and private spheres. Today, both human and social sciences make extensive use of the concept, and we can observe how the notion of individualism permeates human relations in the Western world.

Dumont (1986) analyses the historical process that gave rise to the modern ideology of individualism using the theoretical framework of social anthropology and applying a methodology of comparative analysis between modern Western society and traditional Indian society. Studying the hierarchy of the caste system in India and the emblematic figure of the "spiritual renouncer" – theory of renunciation (Dumont, 1981) – he investigates the Western individualistic culture from its earliest days. Dumont (1986) had to assume a methodological position to carry out his research on the Western social system and the caste system, given their ideological opposition.

Within this framework, it is impossible to understand the ideology of the caste system. Individualism is a product of modern Western culture and, for effective sociological analysis, it is fundamental to distinguish the concept of individualism at the ideological level – that is, as a system of ideas, beliefs, and values of the individual – as well as at the level of reality (Figueira, 1981). Thus, Dumont (1981) found two distinct meanings for the word individual. The first refers to the empirical subject of speech, thought, and will, a private citizen and indivisible specimen of humanity, present in all societies, and the primal matter and subject of sociology. The second meaning refers to a rational and independent moral being, essentially non-social, and a normative subject of the institutions, as defined by modern ideology, and existing in ideological

conceptions of individual and society. Dumont observed that the word individual embraced a polysemy that allowed, in a sociological analysis, to confuse
empirical agents with individuals, that is, to consider as individuals those subjects who were not individuals and did not represent themselves as such.
Therefore, in the Indian society, it would not be possible to work with the
category of individual in the same way as it can be done in an anthropological
analysis of the Western world (Figueira, 1981). Dumont sees individualism as
an obstacle to sociological knowledge, insofar as the category of the individual
is often used in social science research to describe realities in which its usage is
not justifiable, as in the study of the caste society in India (Dumont, 1981, p.
59). This typically modern view produces distortions and unsatisfactory results,
leading Dumont to assert that it is sociology's duty to "make good the lacuna
introduced by the individualistic mentality when it confuses the ideal with the
actual" (Dumont, 1981, p. 5).

It is Georg Simmel (1908), at the beginning of the twentieth century, well
before Dumont's study, who provides a crucial analysis of the individualistic
question, identifying two individualistic revolutions in Western history. The first
goes back to Rousseau's *The Social Contract* (1762), in which individuals come to
be considered equivalent units before society as a whole. In the eighteenth century, this gave rise to the "individualism of singleness" (Simmel, 1989), centred on
freedom and equality among individuals. The second occurs in the nineteenth
century, organized around freedom and inequality among individuals, generating
the "individualism of uniqueness" (Simmel, 1989). The first revolution is closely
related to the Enlightenment and points to a quantitative revolution in which the
individual emerges detached from the social body. It is represented by the ideals of
equality, liberty, and fraternity from the French Revolution. The second is a
qualitative individualistic revolution, the individualism of uniqueness, which
emphasizes the uniqueness of the modern individual, singular, introspective, along
the lines of the romantic ideology of the nineteenth century.

In the individualism of singleness, or "Latin individualism" (Simmel, 1989),
individualization derives from transformations of modernity and results in the
emergence of a singular being, albeit presented as the bearer of an archetype
characterized by a universal temperament. This idea of universal is linked to a
concept, a form, a law that determines what is understood as a singular existence
that each individual represents, by both nature and will. Thus, in this model of
individualism, the individual tends to be in a state of individuality that has its own
freedom, but considers itself representative of a human archetype. Therefore, it is
the universal man

> who occupies the center of the interest for this period instead of histori-
> cally given, particular, and differentiated man. The latter is in principle
> reduced to the former; in each individual person, man in general lives as
> his essence, just as every piece of matter, peculiar as its configuration may
> be, exhibits in its essence the pervasive laws of matter in general.
>
> (Simmel, 1971, p. 219)

At this point, freedom and equality can be seen to belong together by right from the very outset, allowing Simmel to state that the individualism of the Renaissance man is a sociobiological individualism based on a "natural equality of individuals" (Simmel, 1971, p. 219).

By the eighteenth century, the individual was tied to a series of political, corporate, agrarian, and religious oppressions devoid of meaning. Faced by such restrictions, the cry of freedom that emerged through the idea of equality, based on the belief of the full autonomy of the individual, forged a significant change in society as regards social and intellectual relationships (Simmel, 1903, p. 414). Thus, in the political and economic conceptualization of the individualism of singleness, society has valued and promoted "the free competition of individual interests as the natural order of things" (Simmel, 1971, p. 218). Rousseau, for whom the source of all decay and evil comes from violence exerted on men by the historically constituted society, has also contributed to affirm the individual vis-à-vis the civil society. In political terms, the egalitarian ideals of the French Revolution were present and the influence of Kant's and Fichte's philosophy produced a notion of the self as a support for the world. This has made of absolute autonomy a moral value *par excellence* (Simmel, 1971, p. 218).

However, throughout the nineteenth century, the synthesis that upheld the reciprocal creation of the notions of equality and freedom dissolved, resulting in a second individualistic revolution (Simmel, 1971). Therefore, the idea of freedom was maintained, but the notion of equality was no longer sustainable, and the need for difference emerged, giving rise to the individualism of uniqueness, also known as "Germanic individualism" (Simmel, 1989). It refers to an idea of individuality based on a singular and irreplaceable unit. This individualism develops alongside the economic liberalism of the seventeenth century, the influences of German romanticism in the nineteenth century, and the consequences of the economic division of labour. Liberated from the hierarchical bonds of the past, the individuals wish to distinguish from each other. What becomes important is no longer the free individual as such, but the fact that they are a unique and distinct being. The scale of human values ceases to be determined by the general human being who exists in each individual. The individuals begin to value the qualitative uniqueness (singularity) and irreplaceability of each human being.

Both Schopenhauer's philosophy and Schleiermacher's metaphysics influence the individualism of uniqueness; however, perhaps as a result of romanticism (Goethe), German individualism enters the nineteenth-century consciousness (Simmel, 1971). Indeed, the romantic ethos creates the basis for an awareness of the experience of this individualism, which finds its strongest expression in the romantic soul of the absolute, complete, and self-sufficient individual. In this way, German individualism decomposes the eighteenth-century synthesis of the individualism of singleness, based on equality and freedom, and introduces inequality. Therefore, Simmel's analysis of the two individualistic revolutions is supported by the observation of a progressive emphasis on inequality between individuals, unlike the equality advocated in the slogans of the French Revolution. The second individualistic revolution tried to put more emphasis on inequality between individuals than on the egalitarian proposal of the individualism of singleness.

In sum, modern European culture has produced the concept of the individual as an equation between the self and the world. The individualism of singleness allowed for freedom and equality between individuals, determining the rationalistic liberalism of France and England, whereas the individualism of uniqueness fostered uniqueness and the non-comparability between individuals from a Germanic perspective. The two variations of individualism certainly merged in the nineteenth-century economic principles. The doctrine of freedom and equality is based on free competition, while the idea of unique and differentiated personalities is the foundation for the division of labour. Moreover, these two key principles, competition and division of labour, became simultaneously and inseparably responsible for the economy and the social constitution of individuals in the twentieth century (Simmel, 1971).

From the individual to the crowd in the nineteenth century

The idea of the individual is intrinsic to the development of liberal democratic thought in modernity. Individualism spread all over the social body in the seventeenth, eighteenth and nineteenth centuries, blending with the very history of modern ideology, and finally becoming intrinsic to human nature. For Moscovici, it is "the most important invention of modern times" (Moscovici, 1985, p. 13). Simmel (1908, 1971), identified two forms of individualism that followed social, political, and ideological changes in Western history. Influenced by the ideals of the French Revolution, by the social contract, the emerging liberalism, and later by romanticism, individualism established itself as the ultimate by-product of modernity.

During its socioeconomic development, modernity was based on the necessary idea of the individual, whereas the transformations the modern world went through led to a new concern: the *question du nombre* (Reynié, 1988). In medieval times, the individuals conformed to feudal or communal collective solidarities in which the ideas of public and private mixed up without much distinction between private and public life (Ariès & Duby, 1992), which means that many acts of daily life happened in public, in the communal space. After the emergence of the bourgeois thinking and later, in the eighteenth century, of the cultivation of privacy, intimacy, and authenticity, typical of the individualistic model, the private experience of individuals began to be valued and opposed to the entirely different public sphere (Sennett, 1974). It was precisely in the public sphere, especially after the transformations brought about by the French Revolution, that the issue of crowds was first considered as an isolated phenomenon and began to be studied from different angles by historians like Carlyle, Michelet, and Taine (McClelland, 1989).

In his investigation of the behaviour of mobs, Girondists and Jacobins in several events of the French Revolution, Hippolyte Taine – today known as a pioneer scholar in French psychohistory (Van Ginneken, 1992) – revolutionized nineteenth-century historiography as regards crowd psychology. Taine wrote *Les Origines de la France Contemporaine* (1874–1893) – translated into English by John Durand as *The Origins of Contemporary France* (1880) – in a fresh style that blends a historical analysis with the evolutionary psychology of the time. His works exerted a determining influence on the emerging field of crowd psychology (Van Ginneken, 1992). Throughout the nineteenth century, especially in its last quarter, scholars' concerns and investigations turned to that new focus of interest. The idea of the individual was already embedded in the social body at that time; however, it was only then that the notion of crowd took shape. It means that, although the crowds had been a reality since classical Greece, when Plato worked out some ideas close to the modern theory of crowds, and since the Roman historians who discussed the populace (McClelland, 1989, p. 34), today we know that pre-modern crowds found different ways to deal with collective rights (Rudé, 1964). In the Middle Ages, epidemics involving crowds were usual (Rudé, 1964; Penna, 2019) and, in early modern times, Shakespeare highlighted the role of the mobs in *Coriolanus* (Shils, 1975). However, the idea of the crowd as an entity with its own behaviour and features emerged only in the nineteenth century, associated with urban development, industrial progress, capitalism, and the advent of the working classes (Moscovici, 1985).

Just as, before the Renaissance, it was impossible to think of the isolated individual, it was only in late modernity that the idea of the group arose, underlying the idea of the crowd, considered as a spontaneous, unorganised assemblage. Based on Anzieu's (1984) research on the origins of the word *group*, we can reflect on the emergence of this idea. *Group* is one of the most recent words in Western languages. It was imported from Italy to France at the end of the seventeenth century to designate every gathering of living people. Earlier, ancient languages did not have a word to name an association or assemblage of people. Fernández (2006) adds that the word *groppo*, or *gruppo*, originated in the Italian Renaissance, that is, in modern times, when it was used to define a *gruppo scultoreo*, a group of sculptures in a patio or garden that acquires harmony and plastic or aesthetic meaning when circled or seen from afar. Only from the nineteenth century – when society started to observe and worry about the crowd phenomenon – did the word group begin to be used more colloquially, expanding the concept. However, it remained as one of the most confusing words in modern languages – so far, there is no lexical equivalent to the idea of a small group, for instance. The idea that, until so late in civilization, there was no word to name groups makes us think that assemblages of people only late in culture acquired enough relevance to be part of social world representations. This evidence seems to prove the hypothesis that the ideas of group and crowd developed late in history. Indeed, modern transformations, the individualistic paradigm, and the resulting Cartesian oppositions, especially those that oppose individual and society, gave representation and prominence to the crowd after the French Revolution, when the phenomenon took on a sociopolitical meaning in the modern world (McClelland, 1989).

The nineteenth century and the zenith of European civilization: perspectives and fears

The nineteenth century was marked by the socioeconomic impact of the Industrial Revolution in Great Britain (1780) and by political and ideological changes resulting from the American Revolution (1776–1783) and the French Revolution (1789–1799). The Industrial Revolution was responsible for the beginning of the economic modernization, the consolidation of capitalism, and the projection of Western power on the world. The American and French revolutions, inspired by the liberal side of the Enlightenment, created and spread the ideal of freedom, equality of rights, popular sovereignty, and democracy, altering the economic, social, political, and cultural foundations of the West (Hobsbawm, 1975a).

In terms of historical analysis, the nineteenth century spans from 1815 to 1914 (Schnerb, 1968). Even though the conflicts between the Old Regime and the ideology of 1789 had not ended yet, the Europe of the Restoration in the nineteenth century experienced a phase of unprecedented growth and reached its peak. After the revolutionary and Napoleonic era, manufacturing and transportation techniques improved gradually, favoured by eighteenth-century inventions, changing significantly the commercial, industrial, and financial activities that consolidated the European hegemony in the modern world. The bourgeoisie started to enjoy advantages provided by the industrial and liberal economy, and the debate heated up between the traditional order and the bourgeois liberalism, in part because of the anxiety produced by poverty among the growing urban population. The Industrial Revolution revealed the rise of capitalism, but the terrible social conditions in which it developed gave birth to a working class that opposed the bourgeoisie. The nineteenth century also marked the foundations of American progress and independence. On the one hand, it favoured the emergence of the European colonial policy in Africa and Asia; on the other, it reached its highest point with the end of slavery in the Americas (Hobsbawm, 1975b).

Since the eighteenth century, the European population had grown at great rates, and increased throughout the nineteenth century, mainly as a result of advancements in medical and scientific research (Schnerb, 1968). Concerning research on mental disorders, the nineteenth century was also fundamental to reduce the prejudice against the alienated, opening the way to the studies conducted by Kraepelin, Janet, Charcot, and Krafft-Ebing. In the Western world, the cultural atmosphere in Vienna at the end of the nineteenth century concentrated a fascination for mental illness and sexuality, leading to the emergence of psychoanalysis (Bettelheim, 1956). The nineteenth century was also influenced by romanticism, which emerged in Germany as an expression of disquiet and an idealistic reaction to the rationalistic culture of the Enlightenment.

The fierce conflict between, on one side, the Old Regime and its colonial extensions and, on the other, the new bourgeois and popular forces, has marked the nineteenth century. Indeed, that century has seen a profound metamorphosis in the individual, who, subsumed in the crowds in the streets of growing cities, in the workshops, in the factories, and in political agglomerations, gave rise to new subjects. The rapid mechanization of industry, represented by the steam engine and the concentration of salaried workers, transformed cities into battlefields where popular classes fought the bourgeoisie, opening the way to a "virulent and massive" (Moscovici, 1985, p. 21) working class. The classic work by Tönnies (1887), describing the transition from community (*Gemeinschaft*) to society (*Gesellschaft*), reports the changes under way and creates a metaphor about it. Tönnies's analysis defines the moment when a spontaneous collectivity, based on blood alliances, fraternal relations, and cohesion of beliefs, gives way to a cold, artificial, and coercive collectivity, based on agreement of interests, mutual advantages, and the logic of science. Modernity became thereby responsible for the end of old communities. From the nineteenth century, cities and provinces tended to homogenize, resembling each other concerning values, tastes, and language (Shils, 1975).

In this process, nation-states arose and played an important role in the nineteenth century, bringing about the patriotic spirit and the nationalism. The idea of national sovereignty and autonomy as an expression of freedom, together with a romantic notion of the people (*Volksgeist*), contributed to the concept of nation, providing new bases for the modern state. Nationalism revealed one of the main ideologies of the century and, by strengthening ethnographic, linguistic, religious, and geographic factors, it eventually favoured a policy of greater respect for religious minorities, promoting, among other actions, Jewish emancipation. Yet, from a democratic and progressive ideology, it gradually became a reactionary force in Europe (Stackelberg, 1999). The decline of traditional faith, the expansion of institutions and public education, advancements in freethinking, and fights for universal suffrage marked the consolidation of liberal developments in the nineteenth century. Nevertheless, these developments were not without problems, and republican ideals took long to consolidate in European countries (Visentini & Pereira, 2008).

The situation of England in the nineteenth century was different from that of other European countries, and it was through its "splendid isolation" that England consolidated both its hegemony in Europe and the *Pax Britannica*, especially with the advantages derived from its Industrial Revolution, economic liberalism, and colonial policy. England watched the continental balance and exerted its influence on the seas and other continents, constructing a liberal world order and an informal empire (Hobsbawm, 1975b). However, historians such as Carlyle (1980) called the society's attention to changes in English culture after the French Revolution: the struggles of the labour movement and the activities of the English industrial bourgeoisie were pointing to new times when leaderless crowds would become a threat (Rudé, 1964). Pines (2009, p. 9) highlights:

> The French Revolution had legislated for the maximum freedom of the *abstract* individual. This had led to the dominance of privileged groups; liberty, equality and fraternity had simply become slogans, in reality, illusions.

It means that such status was unreachable for a huge number of people.

On the other hand, Germany entered the nineteenth century with a structure different from that of France or England. Like the Italian states, Germany was behind other Western European countries concerning its economic development. The Holy Roman Empire, immensely powerful in the seventeenth and eighteenth centuries, had been crushed by new economic centres in Western Europe, and disintegrated into many independent states, among which Austria and Prussia stood out. Notwithstanding different projects to unify the country, Germany brought together many ethnic groups and remained rural and dominated by a land aristocracy. German unity depended on the political and economic strengthening of a state in which liberal ideals were little known and the defence of the principle of nationalities would prevail. Even though Prussia had rejected the ideology of the French Revolution and opposed France, it took an active part in the modernization of the state. With Bismarck and the support of military and conservative forces, Prussia underwent rapid industrial capitalist development, consolidating the primacy of the German Empire, or Second Reich (Stackelberg, 1999). Austria developed differently, and Vienna, at the end of the nineteenth century, was a prestigious cultural centre, where music, theatre, and other arts flourished (Bettelheim, 1956).

The consolidation of capitalism gave Europe a new socioeconomic configuration with visible effects on nineteenth-century society. Among the main changes, the advent of the working class represented a social problem, because the rest of the population felt insecure and feared rebellion. This era is thus characterized by a chronic effervescence and a constant threat of popular insurrection that found expression in street demonstrations, union struggles, riots, the revolutions of 1830 and 1848, and in the Paris Commune (1871) (Visentini & Pereira, 2008).

Those events had profound effects and influenced the thought of that time, as we can see in nineteenth-century literature. The writers' ability to capture and predict the crowd phenomenon and the fear and social conflicts the crowds caused reveal the *Zeitgeist* of the century. Alessandro Manzoni, in *The Betrothed* (1827), seems to have been the first to portray the features of a crowd in a novel – he describes a violent event in which a starving and protesting crowd, inflamed with passion, destroys Milanese bakeries and flour warehouses, prefiguring descriptions the scholars who studied the crowds would use at the end of the century (Nye, 1995). Flaubert, in *Sentimental Education* (1869), describes the connection between the actions and statements of crowds and their claims around ideals such as democratic sovereignty. It is also in Flaubert's work that we can read about the magnetism of crowds and their irrational states of mind. In England, Charlotte Brontë's *Shirley* (1849) is set against the backdrop of the Luddite uprisings in the Yorkshire industry, and Charles Dickens describes crowd behaviour in some passages of *A Tale of Two Cities* (1859). Ibsen, in turn, depicts the relationship between crowds and politics in his play *An Enemy of the People* (1882).

However, it was Émile Zola, in *Germinal* (1885) and *La Débâcle* (1892), who highlighted hysterical women and savages in literature, comparing their behaviour to that of the crowds, and showing in many of his novellas the dynamics between the leader and the crowd (Nye, 1995). Some literary critics, as Torres (2007), confirm how important Zola is to understand the matter, for having been able to penetrate crowd psychology. Crowd behaviour is described in *Lourdes* (1894), a novella in which a pacific and generous crowd gathers around the promise of a fairer religion, ready to be conducted by a conservative leader. In *Lourdes*, Zola analyses creatively a religious crowd, capable of showing cohesion and noble ideals, and offers for the first time a more positive view of the crowd, opposed to ideas that emphasized only the crowd's negative features (Torres, 2007).

In the nineteenth century, the enemy seemed to be in the "revolutionary hydra" represented by the proletarians (Schnerb, 1968). The working class was inflamed with ideals of justice and seeking greater social equality. At that moment, Marxist ideas played a fundamental role, suggesting a transformative social order. In Marx's words about nineteenth-century insurgent movements, "barbarism reappears, but created in the lap of civilization itself and belonging to it" (Marx, 1847, p. 434). Later, Engels (1908, p. 89) stated that "the class struggle between proletariat and bourgeoisie came to the front in the history of the most advanced countries in Europe".

Conflicts between capital and labour escalated in Europe from 1815 to 1848. Revolutionary movements as conspiracies, secret societies, and barricades derived from the tension between progressivism and conservatism, aiming at solving the increasing discontent of the salaried classes. The purposes of these movements were strongly affected when Marx published the *Manifesto of the Communist Party* in 1848. The Marxist theory produced a revolution in modern thought, and Marx, together with Durkheim and Weber, is considered an architect of modern social science. Marx made a profound critique of capitalist societies when he used a materialistic idea of history to understand dialectically the interrelationships among social processes (Hobsbawm, 1975b).

It was then that Socialism emerged when both romanticism and anarchism – to which Marx was radically opposed (Schnerb, 1968) – were representing the nineteenth century. In that context, socialist ideas spread, having as background the migration from rural to urban areas. Although socialism was capable of coming to power peacefully, the nineteenth-century revolutions crowded the streets with agitators and demonstrators calling for changes that threatened the *status quo* of the ruling classes.

Also during the nineteenth century, the anarchist movement gained momentum, becoming the "worst enemy" of the monarchies. Around 1880, through the writings of the Russian political activist Kropotkin, anarchism spread fast across Europe. Active in Italy, France, and Spain, where they initially joined the socialists, the anarchists despised private property and parliaments, and nursed a grudge against national leaders. Their weapons consisted of fomenting general strikes and killing many national leaders. In texts by Gabriel Tarde (Clark, 2010) and Gustave Le Bon (1895), as well as in Scipio Sighele's (1891) analyses of criminal crowds, questions regarding anarchists' behaviour are formulated either as a background for investigations of crowds and crime or as a threat to late nineteenth-century society.

Consequently, it was in nineteenth-century France, in the opposition between liberals and conservatives, when popular movements gained power, that the research on crowd psychology expanded. On the other hand – from the same psychohistorical perspective of analysis (Van Ginneken, 1992; Löwenberg, 1996) – we can see that the differences and singularities of the antiliberal and antidemocratic development in Germany and parts of Italy (Stackelberg, 1999) allow us to understand how the nineteenth-century crowd psychology transformed into the twentieth-century mass psychology. It means that, in Western Europe, the effects of the policy of nationalities on the nineteenth century eventually became responsible, in the twentieth century, for the outbreak of two world wars and the genocides that transferred the study of crowd psychology to the sphere of mass psychology (Canetti, 1960).

Therefore, it is clear that Freudian psychoanalysis, Marxist theory, and the Frankfurt School encouraged the development of new instruments of analysis to understand crowd behaviour, conferring a new status on what would become mass psychology in the course of the twentieth century. From this same new perspective, the focus of analysis changed and concentrated on the study of the role of the leader, as well as on the need for controlling and subjugating the masses. In this respect, nineteenth-century crowd psychology, through Tarde's and Le Bon's ideas, has contributed significantly to the twentieth-century mass psychology to take shape.

Thus, that which the conservative forces have initially considered as a threat to their *status quo* resulted in the formation of a new relevant focus of interest and study in the twentieth century, making authors like Moscovici (1985) to state that, in the beginning of the century, the victory of the masses was certain.

Crowd psychology in the nineteenth century

The history of confrontations between crowds has been calling the attention of historians since the French Revolution, either because of impressive manifestations of collective violence or because the vision of barbarism caused horror and fear among the historians and intellectuals of the rising nineteenth-century sociology (Rudé, 1964). Still, it was a long time until the crowd became an object of theoretical reflection and the *question du nombre* (Reynié, 1988) acquired importance. With the revolutionary movements of 1789, this issue entered the political scenario and inaugurated new disciplines such as statistics, the theory of law, and political theory, inspiring literature as well, which gave an identity to human beings gathered in crowds. However, the nineteenth century was the century of pessimistic number theories that used to associate the crowd with barbarism, violence, and irrationality.

In the period before the French Revolution, the *question du nombre* was only an administrative problem related to the division of population masses, urban balance, hygiene, or simply to statistical evaluation. After the revolutionary upheaval at the end of the eighteenth century, this question entered the political scene once and for all; since then, politics has not been possible without taking the role of crowds into account (Reynié, 1988).

Before the crowds became an object of scientific research, many questions about their behaviour had been asked, which may be summarized in a single one: what is a crowd? (Moscovici, 1985, p. 71). Three answers have been produced, generating three lines of thought that Moscovici considers insufficient at first, but whose outcome was the advent of crowd science.

The first attempt to define a crowd says that "a crowd is a mass of individuals on the fringe of the establishment who have taken a stand against the establishment … crowds are asocial and their members are asocial" (Moscovici, 1985, p. 71). In this sense, the crowds were the result of the disaggregation of groups and social classes and corresponded to the plebs, the populace, the *lumpenproletariat*. They were men and women with no known identity, on the fringe of the social fabric, taken from ghettos, living as outlaws, as outcasts. They represented disturbances, ruptures in society's functioning, social disorder, and hostility. Thus, they could not be a matter of science or a new or important phenomenon to be investigated; they were seen as epiphenomena, at most (Moscovici, 1985, p. 72).

The second answer to the question states that the crowds were insane and fomented obscure dreams, gathering crazed fans or frenzied people around a leader. Extravagant crowds revealed feats or criminal acts, and their unusual, delirious, and pathological character fascinated society. However, apart from this spectacular character, they did not arouse any other interest (Moscovici, 1985, p. 73).

As to the third answer – the one that says the crowds were criminal, capable of destroying anything in front of them or committing the most terrible crimes, resisting to authority and law – it deserves emphasis because it was from this idea that the study on crowds developed into a new science (Moscovici, 1985, p. 74). In the nineteenth century, the crowd phenomena multiplied, frightening authorities and prompting intellectuals to search for universal laws to underpin the psychosocial crowd phenomena.

The word crowd has served a complex, shifting, albeit generally reactionary function in Western political thought. In fact, crowds were one element in a much wider critique of the Enlightenment and classical liberalism (McClelland, 1989). Here, the connections between crowds and power are obvious (Canetti,

1960; Nye, 1995) and the study of crowd psychology explores not only inter-connections between power and knowledge, but also how the crowds were used to convey conscious and unconscious discourse and political agendas. Through more contemporary lens, under the influence of Weber and Mannheim, Simmel and Elias, Merton and Kuhn, as well as through Foucault's analysis of power apparatuses (Foucault, 1979), we can gauge how knowledge was used to exert power. In this vein, it is important to highlight that the *fin-de-siècle* European context intertwines personal stories, groups, and societies – in what group analysis later called "tripartite matrices" (Hopper & Weinberg, 2017) – to produce conscious and unconscious discourses about the crowds. This knowledge reveals the importance of place and *Zeitgeist* (*Ort und Zeitgeist*) (Van Ginneken, 1992, p. 13) to understand crowd psychology.

Therefore, a new discipline came to give meaning to ideas that, for almost a century, had been known and discussed both by historiography and literature, but that, in the nineteenth century, developed a "singular language" in the heart of society (Pick, 1989b). The importance and seductive power of crowd psychology thus derive from the complicity of nineteenth-century tripartite matrices (Nitzgen & Hopper, 2017) in the co-creation of this "unconscious language" that ascribed to the crowds frightening tendencies and seemingly inexplicable behaviours.

In this context, especially in France (with Henri Fournial, Gabriel Tarde and Gustave Le Bon) and in Italy (with Cesare Lombroso and Scipio Sighele), a generation of intellectuals emerged that would devote to the theoretical study of the crowds. The investigative vein centred on crowd psychology has also coincided with the birth of social sciences in France (Mucchielli, 1998) and with the study of criminology (Sighele, 1891; Pick, 1989a), initiating a creative and valuable period in the field of collective psychology. The characterization of the crowds as irrational or savage has dominated the thought of the first generation of scholars, leading them to create a crowd science initially centred on the interpretation of collective behaviour as a pathological phenomenon.

Although today studies on crowds are formulated with respect to different parameters, especially after Canetti's (1960) *Crowds and Power* – in which the phenomenology of crowds (masses) are classified – the tendency to highlight their irrational, anomic and pathological character (Nye, 1995) remains the same. The seductive LeBonian idea of group mind still finds its followers in the contemporary world. However, in the twentieth century, the pessimistic current and the fear initially associated with the crowds were replaced by political exploitation and by the control of charismatic leaders. Thus, what was feared in the nineteenth century started to be manipulated, controlled, and disciplined (Foucault, 1979) in the twentieth century.

Notwithstanding so many investigations on the subject, it is not easy to define what a crowd is nor to determine the differences between mobs, crowds, hordes, and masses, mainly because these definitions often overlap, revealing through their "protean quality" (McClelland, 1989) how difficult it is to grasp what happens when a substantial number of persons gather.

According to the *Webster's Dictionary*, a crowd is "a large number of persons, especially when collected into a somewhat compact body without order". In turn, a mob is "a large and disorderly crowd of people, especially bent on riotous or destructive action", and a horde is "a large unorganized group of individuals: a teeming crowd or throng". Though differently from crowds, mobs may also describe fans or a criminal set, such as the gangs (McClelland, 1989). As to the words *crowd* and *mass*, they are used by different authors either as synonyms – as Canetti, Moscovici, and McClelland have done – or different words, when authors opt for using one of the terms. The word crowd can be seen in analyses by Sighele, Tarde, Le Bon, Moscovici, and McClelland. The word mass, in turn, was used by Freud (*Massen* in German, translated into English as crowd), Ortega y Gasset, and the Frankfurtians. This seems to reveal that the word crowd was used in the first investigations carried out at the end of the nineteenth century, whereas the word mass started to appear in analyses made from the twentieth century, when the topic was associated with the figure of the leader. Nevertheless, it is difficult to precise the use of both terms.

Gabriel Tarde: the laws of imitation, the science of opinion and the crowd

Jean-Gabriel de Tarde (1843–1904) was a French jurist, philosopher, sociologist, and one of the first influential thinkers within the field of modern criminology. His academic trajectory reveals his talent as a brilliant student whose poor health left him with time to study Leibniz, an author who influenced his thinking profoundly. Parallel to his magistral career, Tarde developed and researched criminology. Initially, a supporter of Lacassagne and Lombroso, although further along opposing their propositions, Tarde strongly rejected the theories that referred to the psychic and biological origins of crime, choosing to highlight its sociological and psychological aspects (Clark, 2010). Lombroso stated that crowds were composed of people with delinquent tendencies, postulating for the inclusion of crowd psychology as part of criminal anthropology (Pick, 1989a). Tarde (2005), in turn, insisted on the importance of the social environment to explain crime, to the detriment of the value given to biological attributes, and examined the behaviour of crowds using a more analytical approach.

Contemporary to Durkheim, his interlocutor and opponent, Tarde took part in the first debates that gave rise to the birth of French sociology. His work *The Laws of Imitation* (1890), in which he describes the relationship between social behaviour and individual psychological tendencies, made him one of the great actors in the intellectual debates of the second half of the nineteenth century. Although Tarde's sociological thinking remained eclipsed in the twentieth century, his work is now considered as a forerunner of modern sociology and has been lately rediscovered and re-edited in France (Mucchielli, 2000). Tarde influenced profoundly the authors working on the boundaries of sociology and psychology. In the United States, the Chicago School has seen Tarde as one of the founders of social psychology (Clark, 2010). In France, he was rediscovered by Deleuze and Guattari in the 1960s, and more recently by Bruno Latour (Reynié, 1988).

Consolim (2008a) points to the central role Tarde played in Parisian intellectual life around the 1890s. Even though Tarde did not have disciples, he occupied a prominent position in the social sciences, still considered as social psychology. At a time when access to the institutions depended on intricate power relations and political positions, Tarde established a career in which his intellectual and social conservatism was decisive. The legitimacy of his opinions stemmed from his commitment to scientific and republican values in opposition to socialism, social Darwinism, and to Durkheim, with whom he engaged in a historical debate on the nature of sociology and its relation to other sciences (Clark, 2010).

According to Tarde (1890), the psychological diversity of individuals is the basic stage of collective aggregations. Social reality is not a homogeneous construction imposed on the individual, but the result of dynamic social ties such as invention, imitation, resistance, and adaptation, the outcome of interactions between individuals. In this sense, social reality and democratic consensus are constructions of individuals based on processes of imitation and personal conduct. Tarde proposed two notions to explain social movements: imitation and invention. Imitation would be the constitutive principle of human communities, which could be defined as a collection of individuals insofar as they are imitating each other (Tarde, 1890, p. 76). His inspiration for the idea of imitation came from Leibniz's philosophy, from the concept of the monad to think about individuals as a large ensemble of reflections that interact as if in a game of mirrors:

> Each individual sees and mirrors himself in that which is akin, judges and is judged by the other, so that one naturally observes and recognizes oneself in the other, doing as the other does.
>
> (Reynié, 1988, p. 5; translation mine)

Tarde believed that history was a succession of imitative flows, that is, a succession of specular models leading to the phenomenon of imitation by large numbers of people.

For Tarde, then, "imitation is the very social bond" (Reynié, 2005, p. xxi; translation mine), created through public opinion and not by a determined *a priori* truth. That is, the opinion would be created within the society, and conveyed, transmitted, and legitimized by it, together with its whole system of beliefs and values. One individual's opinion, idea, or desire would gradually become the opinion, idea, or desire of a large number of people. Thus, the future of an innovation would be its universal propagation, facilitated by the concept of suggestion and the phenomenon of imitation of one individual by another and then by the crowd. It comes from this proposition that it is not a form of sleepwalking, of hypnotism (Tarde, 1890). In this respect, Tarde was attuned to the thinking of his time, when research on hypnosis conducted by

Bernheim, Richet, and Binet gained ground and the suggestibility of crowds acquired prominence (Moscovici, 1985).

However, it was through the idea of imitation that Tarde's work approached the emerging field of psychoanalysis. In this sense, imitation is fundamental to understand the phenomenon of crowds, and the way the author conceives imitation resembles the concept of identification postulated by Freud in *Group Psychology and The Analysis of the Ego* (1921) (Pines, 2009). The similarity between the concepts of imitation in Tarde's work and identification in Freud's led Fischer (1961 *apud* Moscovici, 1985, p. 256) to suggest a continuity between the two concepts. The importance Tarde gives to imitation, considering it as the "social bond itself" (Reynié, 2005, p. xxi; translation mine), can be linked to the identification Freud presents as "the most remote expression of an emotional tie" (Freud, 1921, p. 105), that is, as the origin of the social tie *par excellence*. Freud was aware of Tarde's ideas, coming even to the point of quoting him in 1921. However, he was categorical when he said that what Tarde called imitation, he referred to as suggestion (Freud, 1921, p. 88). Nonetheless, after a closer investigation of Freud's later work, we can see that imitation and suggestion are not equivalent in meaning, as Freud supposed.

In *The Opinion and the Crowd* (Tarde, 2005; Clark 2010), we find a collection of Tarde's texts that represent a milestone in the sociological *question du nombre*. In general, Tarde's work brings together reactions against the fear of a life-threatening disorder that the crowds could produce in the nineteenth century. Tarde points to the importance of public opinion and the growing education of the public, topics that mobilized the intelligentsia of the period (Reynié, 2005). This is illustrated in the emblematic "Dreyfus affair" (1894–1906), which stirred up debates and divided public opinion and the French intellectual elite. Political battles, as well as the responses to opinions about the affair, gave birth to modern anti-Semitism, favouring a public dispute between left-wing agitators and conservative politicians, who, after the episode, began to use a rhetoric of their own to mobilize and manipulate large crowds (Van Ginneken, 1992). Nye (1995, p. 13), reflecting on the affair, claims that, "Modern mass politics – stinking of race, class, and national hatred – was born in the crucible of the Dreyfus affair". For Behr (2018), the "Dreyfus affair" gives an eloquent example of scapegoating, a recurrent group phenomenon. In addition, we may say that Dreyfus himself "personified" (Hopper, 2003b) the main concerns and prejudices regarding race, gender, and social class embedded in the social unconscious of *fin-de-siècle* European persons.

An opinion propagates thanks to the social movement of imitation, even when it is imperceptible. Thus, all social life and, therefore, all opinion are reduced to suggestion (Tarde, 2005). It is as if the laws of imitation corresponded to an ideal of nineteenth-century progress in which the acceleration and circulation of opinions were accompanied by fewer social barriers, as if ideas spread above and beyond beliefs, across clans or social classes. Therefore, if earlier opinions or ideas were imposed in an authoritarian way, after Tarde's contribution they started to be presented persuasively to the public. Tarde's conceptions criticize modern individualism, revealing the impossibility of the existence of the individual without a social context, delivering a lethal blow to beliefs in the freedom and equality of men propagated during the Enlightenment.

Tarde (1890) contributed to the emergence of a modern theory of public opinion. He gave to public opinion a sociological content by transforming it into a new form of mass social relations that he named and referred to as *the public*. For the first time in history, crowds no longer needed to meet in one location in order to be considered interrelated. Through the notion of the public, it was possible to imagine crowds dispersed without physical contact, but sharing characteristics similar to those of gathered crowds. Therefore, for Tarde, as a result of the invention of the press and increasing speed in communications, a completely different type of public began to appear. This type of public continued to grow and its indefinite extension was one of the markers of its time, configuring what was no longer denominated psychology of the crowds, but psychology of the public. For Tarde, at that moment, the difference between public and crowd was established. This observation led him to the conclusion that the nineteenth century constituted the era of the public, unlike Le Bon (1895), who imagined the nineteenth century as the era of crowds.

Tarde's perspective on the similarities and differences between audience and crowd supported his ideas and offered an analysis of the public that managed to enrich and add detail to the study of crowds (Reynié, 2005). Although Tarde was a forerunner in the development of the science of public opinion, propaganda, and studies of the masses in the twentieth century, the most interesting points to single out from his work are the analyses of imitation, contagion, suggestion, and hypnosis. These are crucial phenomena to be considered in the investigation of crowds, and we will now discuss them in Tarde's work.

With the coming of the Modern Age, a different kind of public appeared that multiplied indefinitely, creating currents of opinion. To describe this phenomenon, Tarde (2005) named it the crowd and, in his view, it seemed to be constituted of a bundle of psychic contagions produced by physical contact. Thus, the relation established between individuals in the crowds would be of the order of simultaneity of convictions or passions, of shared wills simultaneously transmitted by contagion to a large number of people. The crowd is the most natural form of grouping and is considered different from other social agglomerations. From this perspective, passers-by in a busy street, travellers gathered in a train station or a passenger car, and farmers at a fair are physically, but not socially, grouped. Although they do not know each other nor show any degree of cooperation among them, these people bring along with themselves the possibility of a social grouping. Therefore, if the occasion demands, these people can associate spontaneously and form a crowd. Thus, through a series of intermediate degrees, a rudimentary, fleeting, amorphous aggregate can become a crowd that, further along, could also become a structured group, if it is sufficiently organized.

By Tarde's (2005) standards, the members of a crowd are considered inferior in intelligence and morality, and predictable and unstable in behaviour. Tarde (2005, p. 172) perceives the crowd as feminine, capricious, moody, and easily suggestible. This comparison seems to be linked to biased social representations of the female sex at the end of the nineteenth century by attributing to women a suggestible and unpredictable behaviour, as observed in hysterical persons or in the suffragettes. Moreover, crowds have characteristics of primitive peoples and neurotics and their behaviour can be similar to the behaviour of psychiatric patients with collective hallucinations and paranoia (Tarde, 2005, p. 52). The crowd is extremely sensitive to a type of collective hypnosis fostered by suggestion, credulity, and contagion. These statements echo Le Bon's (1895) considerations on contagion, hypnosis, and madness.

Tarde highlights especially the individual's predictable behaviour in the crowd in the form of obedience to the leader and a tendency towards homogenization that can be determined by race and nationality. Initially, this perspective, adopted by both Tarde and Le Bon, is conservative and outdated, a result of views in vogue in the nineteenth century, influenced by social Darwinism. However, from a contemporary perspective, it may evoke reflections on the social unconscious of persons (Hopper & Weinberg, 2017) in different cultures, whose behaviour is affected by the unconscious restraints and constraints that characterize the *habitus* of a specific foundation matrix. Therefore, in the nineteenth century, the differences found in the behaviour of crowds are attributed to race, whereas in the twenty-first century they revolve around the features of tripartite matrices in social systems.

Tarde (2005) went on to define crowds in terms of love and hate. Crowds of love are capable of incredible prodigies and altruistic achievements. On the other hand, crowds of hatred can unleash their fury and commit the worst atrocities. Generally speaking, a criminal crowd does not act based on revenge, a need for punishing real crimes, or a sense of social justice. It is fired up by a "justice of the primitive times" (Tarde, 2005, p. 50; translation mine). When a person trusts a leader, he/she is capable of actions founded on a credulity that borders on a dream state or hypnosis. In this sense, Tarde's comments on crowds being not just credulous, but crazy, help us understand the attributed hypnotic fascination that drives a criminal crowd.

Tarde responded to a reality still linked to the importance of the leader. The nature of the bond between the crowds and their leaders and the communion of beliefs or desires that unite crowd members affect their behaviour. This led Tarde to conclude that "the proud sensation of their numbers intoxicates the assembled men and makes them despise the isolated man who is speaking to them, unless he manages to dazzle or charm them" and that "the crowd attracts and admires the crowd" (Clark, 2010, p. 39). The question of the leader's intention, albeit still restricted to the phenomena of imitation, contagion, and hypnotic influence, was already prominent in Tarde's work, foreshadowing the importance leadership would have in the twentieth-century mass psychology.

From the notion of crowd, Tarde slipped into an analysis of what he named "corporations", later studied as organized groups. This led Tarde (1893) to examine the behaviour of anarchists, religious sects, and criminal groups. In other words, Tarde's investigation reveals that, behind the activities of a corporation or an organized crowd, we can always find the belief in a leader. A leader can transform the spontaneous, anarchic crowd into the structured and artificial crowd that is at the foundation of organized groups and social life.

Tarde's work initiated important ideas in the history of social sciences. He defined the relationships between the public and the crowd, providing the dimension of the investigation carried out on crowds in the nineteenth century. His theories are in tune with the main concerns of that time: anarchism, the socialist threat, strikes, the revolt of the proletariat, debates on race and nationality, the role of women, and the public opinion. Moreover, Tarde's concept of imitation, as well as the importance it grants to suggestion and the role of the leader, allowed contemporary thinkers to perceive the kinship between Tarde's theory and that of Freud (Moscovici, 1985).

Ultimately, in Tarde's work, through imitation and suggestion, crowd psychology was responsible for expanding communication phenomena. His ideas were central to the developments of crowd psychology in the twentieth century, when politics, propaganda, and the media erected a new culture, transforming crowd psychology into mass psychology. Tarde and Le Bon, with whom Tarde has countless similarities, allow us to dive into the spirit of an era that marks the beginning of the study of psychology and mass society.

Gustave Le Bon and crowd psychology

Charles-Marie Gustave Le Bon (1841–1931) studied medicine at the University of Paris. He did not graduate, but even so wrote on a variety of subjects. Le Bon's academic life was marked by scarce economic resources and an ambition to cultivate arts and culture, which characterized his disposition as a free intellectual of contradictory professional choices (Nye, 1995). After his experience as a physician in the Franco-Prussian War (1870–1871), his interest seems to move away from medicine towards sociology and the emerging field of psychology.

Le Bon's career evolved in opposition to the tendencies of specialization in the scientific world that dominated the France of his time. He followed a singular path that provided him with financial resources, prestige, and prominence, but, on the other hand, closed off all doors to a coveted academic position (Nye, 1995). Despite his modest social position, Le Bon was ambitious and sought public success, even at the cost of being despised by the experts and the academia. McClelland (1989) states that there is something furtive about plagiarism in his career, and Van Ginneken (1992) points to Le Bon's "presumed ignorance" of Henry Fournial's pioneering ideas on crowd psychology developed in the 1890s. Yet, Le Bon's prestige was immense among statesmen, literati and scientists such as Théodule Ribot, Henry

Bergson, Henri Poincaré, Paul Valéry, and the princesses Marthe Bibesco and Marie Bonaparte (Moscovici, 1985).

Le Bon seems to have predicted with precision the aspirations of his time. His longing for answers led him to work ceaselessly as an *outsider*, even when that meant being on the fringes of the official circles with a reputation of scientific vulgarizer. His works achieved great success and have been read widely and translated into at least sixteen languages. From the 1890s, Le Bon published his works on psychology, which came to be considered fundamental to the birth of psychology in France (Nye, 1995).

Le Bon's political and social success was fuelled by academia's resistance to his work. His talent seemed to be connected with his ability to capture and translate into words the spirit of his time, that is, the social circumstances of the late nineteenth century, among them the disturbing phenomenon of crowds and the fear displayed in response to threats of socialism and anarchism. Le Bon's work reflects the encounter of new and progressive ideas with the old literary tradition (Moscovici, 1985, p. 36); however, it was ostracized in the social sciences (Consolim, 2008b) after his death and in the second half of the twentieth century. Yet, we can state that he contributed to the advancement of crowd psychology as a science.

Le Bon's *The Crowd* (1895) revolves around nineteenth-century conservative theses attuned to the political and intellectual vanguard of the time, influenced by Spencer's evolutionism, Bernheim's psychiatry, and Ribot's experimental psychology (Moscovici, 1985). Therefore, the new discipline Le Bon tried to develop was not an original creation. Its premises adopt scientific concepts and theories from other medical, psychiatric, and anthropological discourses. Many of the concepts Le Bon used – such as imitation, suggestion, hypnosis, and contagion – were imported from Charcot's École de Salpêtrière and Bernheim's École de Nancy (Van Ginneken, 1992). Theses on social hierarchies, the inheritance of race, and collective beliefs influenced his postulations on the behaviour of crowds, exactly as they did with Tarde's. For this reason, Le Bon is considered an evolutionist who attributes a fundamental role to inheritance in individual and collective psychology (McClelland, 1989). Influenced by Bernheim, Le Bon advocated for the idea that hypnosis was a process of suggestion a physician would carry out by manipulating patients' imagination and leaving them suggestible to ideas or acts, especially in the case of women, savages, or children, who, at Le Bon's time, were considered as "inferior forms of evolution" (Le Bon, 1895, p. 55). In this way, hypnotic suggestion is a phenomenon that occurs in a hierarchical relationship, that is, in a relationship of power that associates superior and inferior creatures (Nye, 1995).

Le Bon places crowds at the core of his interpretation of the modern world. His theses acknowledge a social conflict between the elite and the population represented by the crowd. His perception of the threatening reality France was immersed in led him to seek an antidote against the disorders that the crowds caused using embryonic psychology. Le Bon formulated the hypothesis of the existence of a group mind shaped by elemental impulses and organized around

beliefs insensitive to experience or reason. To underlie the general characteristics of crowds, Le Bon proposed the study of the psychological law of their
mental unity (LeBon, 1895, p. 43), that is, the study of the crowds' ways of
feeling, thinking, and acting.

In most cases, crowds consist of individuals who gather, feel, reason, and
relate amongst themselves on a specific psychic field, that is, they express a
group mind. Just as the soul of an individual obeys a hypnotist, the crowd
obeys the suggestions of a leader or conductor who imposes their will, making
the group, as if in a state of trance, execute orders that otherwise would never
be executed by the individual. Along this line, intellectual skills and individuality disappear in the crowd, which then shares ordinary qualities and a
feeling of invincibility. These characteristics are related to the idea of mental
contagion associated with hypnosis and suggestibility (LeBon, 1895, p. 50).

Both contagion and suggestion resemble the state of fascination of the individual in relation to the hypnotist. Therefore, the psychic changes that happen
to an individual in a crowd would be analogous to what occurs when an
individual is hypnotized (Le Bon, 1895). It means that collective states of mind
are analogous to hypnotic states. The individuals in a crowd seem to be in a
twilight state, between waking and sleeping, less actively conscious, which
allows them to be carried away by mystical ecstasy, as if in a dream, a nightmare, or in a state of panic. Therefore, the idea of suggestion explains why a
person in a crowd is different from a single person, in the same way, that a person
is different when seen awakening or in hypnotic sleep (Le Bon, 1895, p. 51). In
this sense, suggestion merges the individual and the crowd, and hypnosis functions
as a model for the relationship with the conductor.

Crowd psychology deals with a series of transformations in individuals: the disappearance of the conscious mind; the predominance of unconscious mechanisms;
self-orientation through suggestion and the contagion of feelings and ideas; and
the hypnotic influence of the conductor on a crowd. Intolerance, authoritarianism, and conservatism play their role as well. Unable to reason and devoid of
judgment and critical awareness, the crowds' typical actions are instigated by
ambivalent and exaggerated thoughts and feelings. All these transformations in a
crowd are described as a man descending "several rungs in the ladder of civilization" (Le Bon *apud* Nye, 1995, p. 14). Here, we can see that suggestibility and
credulity, in addition to an automatic mode of thinking, may cause the individuals
in a crowd to be affected by collective hallucinations.

Disillusioned with French parliamentary democracy, Le Bon highlights that
national leaders failed to engage and cope with crowds. For him, this is one of
the reasons for the social and political problems Europe faced in the nineteenth
century. As far as these problems are concerned, the idea is that it was enough
to know the laws of crowds and how to recognize them in order to control
them. This idea captivated the elites, which saw there as a conceptual tool to
validate their deepest fear of the crowds and provide them with a set of rules to
manipulate and dominate the crowds' violent potential (Rudé, 1964; Nye,
1995).

Unfortunately, Le Bon's recipe offered to state leaders in French salons was not followed only by military circles and the early nineteenth-century democracies; it also served as an inspiration for totalitarian leaders. It is well known that both Mussolini and Hitler were dedicated readers and enthusiasts of Le Bon's ideas (Moscovici, 1985). Horkheimer and Adorno (Frankfurt Institute for Social Research, 1956) claim that *Mein Kampf* is characterized by Hitler's adherence to Le Bon's ideas about the crowd turned into cheap copies, full of clichés, of supposedly scientific value. Throughout the twentieth century, Le Bon's work also affected the way world wars were fought. His work persuaded Democrats such as De Gaulle, but also unscrupulous dictators who transformed it into inflexible rules of action and are considered proto-fascists (Moscovici, 1985).

How can an author with such a controversial reputation – elitist, conservative, supported by outdated scientific assumptions – still be a reference in a study as complex as crowd psychology? Why then did his ideas – based on long-abandoned undemocratic premises – not lose interest or importance in the study of crowd psychology? Nye (1995) is accurate in stating that all subsequent commentators on the subject, from Freud and Park to Adorno and Canetti, could absorb or refute Le Bon's ideas, but not ignore them. In fact, after being restructured by Freudian psychoanalysis, and harshly manipulated by right- and left-wing dictators, they could seem exhausted or overanalysed, without much novelty to the unsuspecting reader. Nevertheless, the most recent theories on the topic, even inadvertently, pay tribute to Le Bon.

Le Bon's originality is not simply in linking suggestion to politics. Above all, his main contribution was to transpose a strictly legal perspective that used to deal with the issue of the crowd from an exclusively criminal point of view and look for a plausible psychological explanation for the disturbances the crowds caused (Moscovici, 1985; McClelland, 1989). He showed the crowd is neither a disease nor an excrescence of the existing social order. It is, primarily, a social phenomenon whose understanding requires a new perspective, no longer from law or political economy, but from psychology, where its unconscious character stands out.

Although Le Bon (1895) states that consciousness can be individual, he does not refer to the unconscious as an individual unconscious. Le Bon relies on a biological view of the unconscious, the "racial unconscious", and says that the substrate of the unconscious is formed by hereditary influences containing the ancestral residues of the soul of a race. However, Le Bon's notion of the unconscious represents much more than an ancestral residue of a nation or race. The unconscious would derive its strength from each particular addition made to it by a long succession of generations (Moscovici, 1985). Le Bon refers to "historical race" (Le Bon, 1895, p. 100) as something constructed from successive generations' experiences that determine a people's behaviour through particular traditions and institutions. Thus, the culture, history, and traditions of a race can imprint singular features on crowds, conveying expressions of their group mind. In this process, time is the terrain where crowds' opinions and beliefs germinate, accumulating residues of experiences from a distant past upon which the ideas of an epoch will be born.

Le Bon seems to speak about a type of crowd, one in which unconscious factors are governed by a phylogenetic heritage. Then, qualitatively different crowds exist, revealing the unconscious manifestations of a social group. Le Bon's analysis addresses the crowd seen as a people or a nation in which the transversality of its history combines with the horizontality of the here-and-now in determining differences of behaviour. His conception of the unconscious, albeit distinct from the Freudian individual unconscious (Freud, 1921, p. 75), seems to hold on to intuitions that resemble those of Freud's phylogenetic unconscious. McClelland (1989) states that Le Bon's racial unconscious is similar to what we would call now national culture. In this regard, we can associate some of the LeBonian outdated formulations on racial unconscious with twentieth-century studies on national character. Moreover, this discussion is useful for the study of *habitus* (Elias, 1989) in connection with research on the social unconscious (Hopper & Weinberg, 2017).

Even though Le Bon's idea of the unconscious is different from Freud's, his perception of the unconscious nature of the behaviour of crowds allows for an analysis of its psychological characteristics. Moscovici (1985) highlights that Le Bon's brilliant idea is to assert that the main feature of the crowd is the merging of individuals into a group spirit that blurs individual differences in favour of collective behaviour. The universal nature of these effects may bring about a transformation that affects people gathered in a crowd. Thus, from a psychological perspective, crowds are an autonomous reality, organized as a collective form of life. For Le Bon (1895), the crowd represents the raw material of political institutions, the synergy of social movements, and the primitive state of all civilizations.

In a crowd, suggestion is always an illusion. Ideas and emotions are shared with others by contagion and suggestion. Illusions are related to beliefs transmitted within crowds, and both illusions and beliefs guide their actions. Yet, the conductor can still construct and manipulate them (Moscovici, 1985). A leader dictates the course of action for the crowd, but beliefs play their role as well. This is especially true concerning religious beliefs, when religious sentiment and blind submission to the leader dominate the crowd. A crowd's intolerance and fanaticism make it impossible to discuss dogmas and those who oppose beliefs and convictions conveyed by the group mind or by leaders are considered as enemies. Moreover, leaders can renovate the racial soul when guiding crowds and nations. Thus, based on Le Bon, we can infer part of the fascination for authoritarian leadership in the twentieth century.

In the nineteenth century, the focus on criminal crowds left virtually no room for other analytical perspectives to emerge; however, as the twentieth century approached and the psychological analysis of crowds developed, research on crowds shifted towards the political sphere (McClelland, 1989). At that moment, the idea that crowds could be controlled and manipulated by a charismatic leader was beginning to take root. Closely observed, they could be transformed into objects of study and scientific research on methods of governing to be employed by men of action or heads of state. Le Bon's ambition was to establish a new science to provide a solution and a method to the governance of mass society (Moscovici, 1985). He was convinced that the nineteenth century predicted the emergence of an age of crowds. Indeed, the masses triumphed in Western society, as Ortega y Gasset (1930) examined years later in the tendency towards homogenization, the collectivization of modern life, and the concept of "mass-man". Moscovici (1985) states that the nineteenth century entered the era of crowds.

Like other nineteenth-century theorists, Le Bon (1895) claims that the role of the leader is fundamental; however, his view of the leaders is not flattering at all. He emphasizes their despotism, little clairvoyance, and stubbornness in defending their ideas, to such a point that these ideas seem to be professions of faith. The greater or lesser influence of a leader depends on the power of their words and to their capacity to change ideas and beliefs into images that acquire a magical and transformative power. The issue at stake is the power of manipulation, the prestige of leaders: "To know the art of impressing the imagination of crowds is to know at the same time the art of governing them" (Le Bon, 1895, p. 92). It echoes Machiavelli's and Hobbes's ideas. Through contagion, a leader or an idea invested with prestige is imitated and imposes ways of feeling and expressing thoughts. Although Le Bon has elaborated on the phenomenon of leadership in the crowds by emphasizing the effects of contagion, suggestion, hypnosis, and prestige, his analysis remained superficial. It was only after Freud (1921) advanced the notions of libido and identification as responsible for the social tie that the reflections on the masses took on new directions.

The confluence of the interest of late-nineteenth-century theorists' research on the phenomena of crowds is remarkable, maybe because that century represents the apex of a time when Positivism "learned to speak the language" of the Enlightenment and fed the imaginary of people. However, the second half of the nineteenth century brought disillusionment and societal shifts that transformed pride and progress in social fears and violence. The study of crowds grasped conscious and unconscious transformations and pointed to new expectations at the dawn of a new century. Therefore, it was necessary to wait for the twentieth century to precise the meaning of the crowd psychology endeavour and to confer to the study a "less tacit and a more systematic meaning" (Nye, 1995, p. 18). In this direction, the triumph of crowd politics was attained with the rise of National Socialism in Germany, which enabled Canetti (1960) to discuss "the whole experience of the crowd from its anthropological beginnings and to re-work the whole tradition of crowd theory" (McClelland, 1989, p. 293). In fact, what Canetti provides is a broad analysis of the history of humankind, favouring a deep understanding of twentieth-century mass psychology through the investigation of the genealogy of power. Shils (1975) confirms this reflection and says that a "theory of mass society" had to wait for National Socialism in Germany and the Weimar Republic to acquire its modern form.

The transformation of crowds in masses is not easily conceptualized. Thus, it is probably not only marked by conscious and unconscious processes that historically configured imprecise distinctions between the terms crowd, mass, and mob; it is also shaped by ideology and loses meaning in translation (Tubert-Oklander, 2014). However, Consolim (2008b) clarifies the question that permeates this discussion and leads to the widespread use of the term mass in the twentieth century, instead of the term crowd. A crowd is typical of "biologically or psychologically inferior groups" – such as the plebs or the populace in the nineteenth century, when, especially in the 1890s, the word mass became a prerogative of left-wing thinking and was excluded from any republican reference or analysis that characterized Tarde's or Le Bon's investigations. Thus, it was only as a result of the research on nineteenth-century crowd psychology that twentieth-century mass psychology and its leaders were possible.

In this process, the little-noticed nineteenth-century religious crowds (Torres, 2007) played a transitional role, for they displayed features based on a shared faith and organized around a leader or powerful idea. Freud's mass psychology thoroughly analysed that later. Therefore, the type of crowd that had gone almost unnoticed by nineteenth-century crowd psychology contributed to reframing the topic by replacing the study of the turbulent crowd with the study of masses artificially organized around an ideal and a charismatic leader. Consequently, religious crowds contributed to the shift from crowd psychology to mass psychology. Indeed, religious crowds and fervent followers have crossed history with manifestations that range from faith and wisdom – easily identified in religious processions or pilgrimages to Mecca – to intolerance, fanaticism, and terrifying behaviour – as in religious wars, the Inquisition, or during the massacre of St Bartholomew. However, more than updating crowd psychology features, this unveils the importance of ties and illusions between leaders and followers, prefiguring what Freud and other mass psychology theorists would explore in depth in the twentieth century.

Le Bon (1895) also devoted to enumerating the criteria of heterogeneity and homogeneity that were important to define different types of crowds. His categorizations predicted differences that would be decisive for understanding different group formations throughout the twentieth century. Therefore, in the nineteenth century, the study of the psychology of spontaneous crowds prevailed, with low levels of organization, whereas in the twentieth century, mainly after McDougall (1920) and Freud (1921) examined organized groups, the analysis focused on groups structured around a leader. Thus, the influence of leadership played a fundamental role in the psychological, sociological, and philosophical studies on the masses in the twentieth century. However, the extreme circumstances of the sociopolitical context in the twentieth century, with two world wars, totalitarian regimes, and barbarianism (Adorno, 1946, 1947; Arendt, 1948), demanded new perspectives of analysis, leading to interdisciplinary research with special emphasis on the work of the Frankfurt School.

The beginning of the twenty-first century brings forth uncertainty regarding the *question du nombre*, renewing perspectives and fears. Contemporary sociopolitical conjunctions show unexpected contours; the old and the new are revised interdependently, renovating the interest in understanding the behaviour of crowds and the phenomenon of the masses. Therefore, a seemingly distant Le Bon's statement is updated, renewing an enigma so familiar to psychoanalysis and fostering the ongoing debate:

> Crowds are somewhat like the sphinx of ancient fable: it is necessary to arrive at a solution of the problems offered by their psychology or to resign ourselves to being devoured by them.
>
> (Le Bon, 1895, p. 124)

2 Twentieth-century Freudian mass psychology

After introducing the study of crowd psychology in the context of modernity and studies on individualism (Simmel, 1908), this chapter draws on the investigation of twentieth-century mass psychology. Initially, it focuses on the emergence of mass society and mass-men presented by Ortega y Gasset (1930), then on the early ideas Wilfred Trotter (1919) formulated on herd instinct and William McDougall (1920) on organized groups. Freud's work *Group Psychology and the Analysis of the Ego* (1921) is comprehensive and includes the collaboration of different scholars, aimed at highlighting that mass psychology and the idea of the leader were acquiring importance in the twentieth century. Psychoanalytic concepts as narcissism, ego ideal, libido, and identification are discussed here, as well as the debate on the psychic economy of life and death instinct in groups. Much of what will follow in the analysis of Freud's contributions to mass psychology opens new avenues of inquiry in the study of group formations. This chapter underlines the role of illusion in groups as a key concept to understand twentieth and twenty-first-century sociopolitical processes.

From crowd to mass psychology in the twentieth century

As the twentieth century approached, the weight of crowds on political and historical events began to produce profound changes in society. Either by vote or by insurrection, or even by the population's growing awareness of its transforming power as an organized crowd, the society little by little produced new outlines and new forms for political organization (Van Ginneken, 1992). However, in the twentieth century, especially between the two world wars, crises in sociopolitical life led the world to face new problems, including radical changes in political thinking. The period beginning with World War I marked the irruption of masses with their ways of thinking and their own beliefs. On the other hand, socioeconomic transformations and the growing industrialization gave rise to new forms of collective life, to a new society, the mass society (Ortega y Gasset, 1930). Individuals experienced a metamorphosis that transformed them into anonymous beings, into the public (Tarde, 2005), influenced by propaganda, means of communication, and suggestion and manipulated by

DOI: 10.4324/9780429399534-3

their leaders. This pressure to conform to a collective model resulted in a tendency to homogenization, which converted individuals into mass-men:

> Today this treasure threatens to be devoured by a form of homogeneity that has triumphed over the entire continent. Everywhere there has arisen the mass-man, a type of man built hurriedly, mounted on a few poor abstractions ... He is a man emptied of his own history, with no inward past, and so given over to any so-called "international" discipline. He is less a man than the shell of one, made of plain *idola fori*: he has no insides, no inalienable privacy of his own, no irrevocable "I".
>
> (Ortega y Gasset, 1930, p. 56)

Literature and crowd psychology had already predicted these changes. Differently from what had been thought previously, they did not generate the proletarization of man or the socialization of economy. On the contrary, the twentieth century has seen a mixture of heterogeneous social categories, majorities and minorities, proletarians and capitalists, all forming a homogeneous human complex: a mass composed of mass-men who became the "new protagonists of history" (Moscovici, 1985, p. 25). Baudelaire's poetry and his concept of *flânerie*, as well as Simmel's descriptions in *The Metropolis and Mental Life* (1903) and his *blasé* individual, have prefigured such changes since the end of the nineteenth century. Another author who captured some of those new tendencies was H. G. Wells in his novel *A Modern Utopia* (1905), where, in a planet exactly like the Earth, all men and women existed in duplicate, sharing the same language, customs, and laws.

In the early twentieth century, but still linked to crowd psychology, Boris Sidis (1903) explored the role of hypnosis and suggestion in crowd behaviour in America (McDougall, 1920). Sidis's approach offered new contributions to the study by highlighting the importance of modernity shifts in crowd phenomena. For him, modernity promoted a new social order in which technology and velocity include different forms of mental strain on the masses (Pick, 1995). These transformations became a source of fantasies and fears in the twentieth century. Inspired by the works of H. G. Wells, Aldous Huxley in some way portrayed such transformations and their effects on average men in his *Brave New World* (1931).

However, it was José Ortega y Gasset, in a series of articles published from 1926 in a Madrid newspaper and collected in *The Revolt of the Masses* (1930), who emphasized the importance of such shifts in his critical analysis of mass-men and the rising phenomenon of mass society. Concerned with the course of individualistic liberalism, he wondered about a modern society in which the valuation of collectivism was threatening individualism, the individuals' *status quo*, with the proposal of new forms of sociopolitical organization to lead the masses to power. The individuals transformed into mass-men were eventually subject to the influences of mass culture in the production and communication of opinions:

> There is one fact which, whether for good or ill, is of utmost importance in the public life of Europe at the present moment. This fact is the

accession of the masses to complete social power. As the masses, by definition, neither should nor can direct their own personal existence, and still less rule society in general, this fact means that actually Europe is suffering from the greatest crisis that can afflict peoples, nations, and civilisation ... It is called the rebellion of the masses.

(Ortega y Gasset, 1930, p. 11)

The beginning of the twentieth century was then characterized by the rising of the masses and the average man, who seemed to have taken over modern civilization. Influenced by nationalist ideals, average men tried to reach a more homogeneous form of political organization, whose logic was to disalienate human beings from anything that could prevent them from recognizing themselves as subjects in the mass. Yet, this is a typical modern problem that has brought dramatic consequences to the study of the masses in the twentieth century, since thinking of the mass as a subject is in itself a contradiction.

The birth of mass society and mass-men inspired scholars to advance hypotheses about equivalences between individual and collective consciousness in different theoretical fields. These ideas have resonated with philosophical traditions since Hegel's metaphysics, as well as thoughts from sociologists such as Durkheim and psychologists such as McDougall. The biological outlook on these reflections enabled analogies that convey the idea that the "individual consciousness of any man or animal is the collective consciousness of the cells of which his body, or his nervous system, is composed" (McDougall, 1920, p. 44). It means that, "all these cells continue to enjoy a psychical life and that the consciousness of the individual man or animal is the collective consciousness of some or all these cells" (McDougall, 1920, p. 45). Today, ideas as collective consciousness, mental life of crowds, and group mind may seem in line with some contemporary analysis; however, they remain attached to those analyses of mass psychology phenomena that inadvertently amalgamate body, mind, personal, and collective processes (Hopper, 2003b).

Ortega y Gasset (1930), like the nineteenth-century conservative theorists, did not believe in the capacity of the masses for self-government – "masses reign but do not rule" (Moscovici, 1985, p. 52) – and wondered about the future of a mass society where differences seem to have been abolished and the individuals have given up their own opinions and felt at ease with being identical to the others. In that respect, Ortega y Gasset foretold chain-like crises, precisely because of society's tendency to create homogeneity, and also because he knew by intuition that bringing culture to the masses would threaten society and its control.

Although Ortega y Gasset had a reactionary and elitist outlook on the issue of masses, his thoughts point to the fact that the masses transformed into ubiquitous elements of society and played a key role in modern politics and culture. This is why the study of crowds, by capturing these profound shifts in society, lost interest in the phenomenological description of the behaviour of masses and developed a wish for knowing them in order to exorcise and rule them as a form of action and control over their effects. Consequently, the question asked of men of science in the nineteenth century about crowds broadened in the twentieth century to include men of power learning what to do with the masses (Van Ginneken, 1992).

The psychology of crowds had then to answer two basic questions from the twentieth century: how did mass society emerge? How to teach the ruling classes to rule mass society? Thus, the apparent mystery that surrounded the understanding of crowd behaviour in the nineteenth century became an attempt, in the twentieth century, to decipher not only the enigma of its origin, but also ways to rule the masses. The study of nineteenth-century crowd psychology would give rise to mass psychology in the twentieth century, and "this radical shift of intellectual perspective has thus meant that crowd psychology has put the masses at the very centre of an overall view of the twentieth-century history" (Moscovici, 1985, p. 27). Crowd psychology scholars were convinced that they had found in mass psychology "the Ariadne's thread of the labyrinth of power relationships" (Moscovici, 1985, p. 30), hence, without the knowledge of mass psychology, the rulers and the ruled were subject to the irrationality of crowds. Consequently, crowd psychology moved on from being an instrument to investigate a frightened nineteenth-century society to an object of research and political exploitation in the twentieth century, for everything led to the belief that "politics is the rational form to exploit the irrational substance of the masses, and its psychology confirms it" (Moscovici, 1985, p. 35).

In much the same way that crowd psychology portrayed the end of the nineteenth century, mass psychology tried to answer twentieth-century issues, concerned as it was with mass-men and their control. It was from the heart of modern conservatism, from nineteenth-century liberal democracies that society saw the height of the masses in the twentieth century. From this perspective, it seemed that the solution for mass rebellion depended mainly on the knowledge of mass psychology, and twentieth-century sociopolitical movements and leadership pinned all their hopes on this investigation. Foreseeing this idea, which seems to have encompassed the whole investigative spirit of the twentieth century, Freud wrote *Group Psychology and the Analysis of the Ego* (1921), an essay that revolutionized the understanding of mass psychology, because, from a psychoanalytic perspective, among the contributions to the topic that will be discussed below, he was faithful to the spirit of his time, focusing his investigations on the figure of the leader, a phenomenon that seems to summarize the key question about the masses throughout the twentieth century.

Sigmund Freud's mass psychology

Mass psychology's influence on society has been continuous since it exists as a phenomenon to be investigated – by philosophy, psychology, literature, or politics. Among all contributions that built the twentieth-century sociopolitical body, crowd psychology was the one that transformed sociological research by revealing the power of unconscious factors. Although Tarde and Le Bon referred to an idea of the unconscious very different from Freud's, they were fundamental for Freud to take his great leap forward from crowd psychology to mass psychology.

Two other authors, Trotter (1919) and McDougall (1920), who contributed to the foundations of social psychology in England, also influenced Freud's study of the masses. In the early twentieth century, controversies over the identity and scientific status of sociology, psychology, and social psychology were at the centre of debates (Swanson, 2014). Trotter was a prestigious surgeon who devoted his time to investigating the psychological foundations of social/collective behaviour and exploring the existence of a herd instinct. Trotter was also interested in psychoanalysis and introduced his friend Ernest Jones to Freud, which resulted in their collaboration on the development of the British psychoanalytic movement (Harrison, 2000). However, it was Nietzsche, in 1882, who first used the concept of the herd instinct to highlight the negative influence of social constraints on individual freedom, arguing that "the state maintains its power over individuals through a Judeo-Christian moral code that represses natural instincts oriented towards individual expressiveness" (*apud* Swanson, 2014, p. 23).

Trotter's work on the concept of the herd instinct was formulated to point to the human capacity for association and to its discomfort in loneliness:

> All human psychology, it is contended, must be the psychology of associated man, since man as a solitary animal is unknown to us, and every individual must present the characteristic reactions of the social animal if such exists.
>
> (Trotter, 1919, p. 12)

Trotter's observation reveals human dependency and vulnerability; moreover, as Freud suggested, Trotter thus exposes the Aristotelian features of man as a "political animal" (Freud, 1921, p. 112). Based on William James's psychology, Trotter postulates the existence of a fourth human basic instinct – gregariousness – to be added to self-preservation, nutrition, and sex. That is, actions towards the preservation of the group derive from instinct, and the inherent human capacity for association depends on the environment and the context. Gregariousness has been observed since the passage from unicellular to multicellular organisms and to social animal life. It also permeates all psychological activities. Hence, the gregarious instinct is "the foundation of social life", that is, "a metaphor for associated life" (Swanson, 2014, p. 24).

At this point, before exploring Freud's mass psychology, it is important to discuss continuities and discontinuities between nineteenth-century crowd psychology and Trotter's investigation of the herd instinct. The *question du nombre* continued to gather attention in the early twentieth century. Both developments were grounded on the dawn of psychology, sociology, and social psychology, supported by biology, too; however, they led to different perspectives, according to cultural and sociopolitical contexts in France and England. Trotter's (1919) idea of gregariousness is connected to concepts such as association, homogeneity, suggestibility, all of which are features of crowd psychology. By extension, the herd instinct is also used to account for the individual's susceptibility to an irrational form of imitative behaviour. In that respect, in a historical continuum, Trotter's herd instinct could be inadvertently associated with the development of crowd psychology. However, he rejected this association and conducted his research following the Anglo-Saxon sociological tradition, which saw collective life as a context for human thriving. Trotter was not inclined to discuss Le Bon's group mind. On the contrary, he was interested in an understanding of gregariousness as a mentality and in the way it affected the structure of the mind (Swanson, 2014, p. 28).

Trotter also postulated that, in its highest manifestation, human sociability is linked to the capacity for altruism, given that human fulfilment is realizable only through association (Trotter, 1919, p. 32). This more positive outlook contrasts with Le Bon's investigations of crowd psychology, especially concerning the role the theory of crowd psychology played in the social unconscious of persons in France in the nineteenth century. Perhaps, because of these contextual differences, Trotter considered the theoretical side of crowd psychology incomplete and relatively sterile (Trotter, 1919, p. 26). Moreover, we can suppose that his homogeneous herds may be associated with Ortega y Gasset's (1930) contributions, later described as the homogeneity of mass-men, which indicates mass psychology's new shape in the early twentieth century, when it began to flourish.

Discussing the influences of mass psychology on individuals, Freud (1921) brought about Trotter's (1919) concept of the herd instinct and the notion of group mind to object to the idea that it is difficult to attribute to the group a significance so important as to make it capable of arousing a new instinct in mental life. It means,

> that the social instinct may not be a primitive one and insusceptible of dissection, and that it may be possible to discover the beginnings of its development in a narrower circle, such as that of the family.
>
> (Freud, 1921, p. 70)

Therefore, early on, the individual is marked by the group in a double sense: early in evolutionary history and early in individual development (Pick, 1995). For Freud, circumscribing the ontogenesis of the herd instinct was complex and would not give space for the development of leadership (Freud, 1921, p. 119). Perhaps, it would have been more successful "to correct Trotter's pronouncement that man is a herd animal and assert that he is rather a horde animal, an individual creature in a horde led by a chief" (Freud, 1921, p. 121). Building on this statement, Freud joined the 1921 developments on mass psychology and the reflections of *Totem and Taboo* (Freud, 1913) on the "myth of origin" of the social. In 1913, Freud put forward the hypothesis of the primal horde, stating that the fortunes of the horde have left indestructible traces upon the history of human descent (Freud, 1913, p. 17). Totemism comprises in itself the dawn of religion, morality, and social organization, and it is connected with the assassination "of the chief by violence and the transformation of the paternal horde into a community of brothers" (Freud, 1921, p. 122). In this sense, mass psychology corresponds to a state of regression to a primitive mental activity similar to the one we are inclined to ascribe to the primal horde, of which the mass seems to be a revival (Freud, 1921, p. 123).

Although overlooked for decades or erroneously enmeshed with Le Bon's crowd psychology, Trotter's herd instinct and the idea of "humankind as a horde animal" (Bion, 1961, p. 132) are mentioned, in England, not only in the Northfield Experiments (Harrison, 2000) but also in Bion's (1961) theoretical developments in groups and in the work on group relations (Torres, 2003).

To proceed with the analysis of Freud's mass psychology, it is fundamental to outline his concerns and the historical context that set the scene for him to build his theory on mass psychology, which was different from that developed in France at the end of the nineteenth century. Soon after the end of World War I, throughout 1919, a series of treaties, especially the Treaty of Versailles, marked the end of Central European empires. Despite its considerable territorial losses, Germany became a "geographic monstrosity" (Gay, 2006, p. 379). In Austria, the situation was no different: territorial concessions, precarious economy, and a starving population were part of a formerly splendorous Vienna. Moreover, as Freud himself wrote in 1920 in a letter to a former Hungarian patient, "the reactionary wave should be setting in here, too, after the revolutionary one had brought nothing pleasant" (Freud, 1920, p. 387), offering a glimpse of the dark times to come after the rise of totalitarianism and the recrudescence of anti-Semitism (Bettelheim, 1956).

Post-war impact on an already sexagenarian Freud was decisive in making him, in maturity, shift his concerns to social phenomena (Mezan, 1985; Gay, 2006). In a post-script to his autobiography, Freud mentions another reason for this change, directly linked to the previous one, when he reveals that he had taken up some of his interests as a youth again in old age:

> Threads which in the course of my development had become intertangled have now begun to separate; interests which I had acquired in the later part of my life have receded, while the older and original ones become prominent once more ... My interest, after making a lifelong *détour* through the natural sciences, medicine and psychotherapy, returned to the cultural problems which had fascinated me long before, when I was a youth scarcely old enough for thinking.
>
> (Freud, 1935, p. 71)

Freud's interest in crowd psychology meets his concerns with the sociopolitical situation of his time. The illusion nurtured by part of twentieth-century intellectuals – among them, Freud himself – as regards the reach of civilization achievements gave rise to despair after World War I when they saw that neither political regimes nor optimism or pacifism could prevent humankind from being swept up in hate, destruction, and demagogy. Likewise, the promises made by movements of oppressed masses did not materialize, and hopes formerly pinned on liberal democracy gave rise to totalitarian and anti-Semitic movements (Moscovici, 1985).

There is also an intellectual motivation in the attention Freud (1921) gave to mass psychology that involves the relevance of hypnotic suggestion in the history of psychoanalysis and in crowd psychology. Suggestibility and hypnosis, ubiquitous in crowd psychology, demanded that Freud renewed previous investigations of the enigma of suggestion. However, in his research, Freud moved away from both Tarde's imitation (1890) and Le Bon's (1895) mutual suggestion and the prestige of leaders, as well as from McDougall's (1920) principle of direct induction, when he associated suggestion with libido (Freud, 1921, p. 89). The second meeting of Freud with hypnotic suggestion in mass psychology was fundamental, because his reflections moved from the individual sphere to the collective universe. Questions about the father of the primal horde, about how a group is formed, or what the origin of culture would be became a focus of interest, revealed previously unknown manifestations of the human psyche (Costa, 1989). Transferring the importance formerly attributed to suggestion and hypnosis to the libido, Freud revolutionized the reflection on mass psychology, stating that loving relationships, that is, libidinal cathexis, through the aggregating power of Eros, is the essence of the group mind. Thus, the idea that suggestion would be an irreducible and primitive phenomenon of human psyche is replaced in Freud by the concept of libido and suggestion "is not based upon perception and reasoning but upon an erotic tie" (Freud, 1921, p. 128).

In *Psychical or Mental Treatment* (1905), Freud summarized his interest in the study of collective phenomena for the first time, pointing, albeit rudimentarily, to the influence of human groups on the individuals' beliefs. It was only fifteen years later that he resumed the topic of masses in *Group Psychology and the Analysis of the Ego*, [1] written between 1919 and 1920, at the height of the post-Great War crisis, when he was going through "the impact of general misery on his own household" (Gay, 2006, p. 381). Freud wrote it during one of the worst Viennese winters, mourning the loss of his daughter, and submitted to "really a starvation diet" – *Hungerkost* (Gay, 2006, p. 382) – with no electricity or heating, working by the light of candles (Martins, 1986).

Although living in unfavourable circumstances, Freud transformed the view on the topic of crowds with an optimistic interpretation of the creation of libidinal ties, based on identifications among individuals and on the ego ideal in place of the leader. For Semprún (2002), Freud's 1921 essay inaugurates the twentieth century and is a fundamental book to understand it. To a certain degree, it is also a premonitory book, if we take into account what was to come in Europe in the following years. Produced soon after the end of World War I, it describes Freud's thoughts about replacing personal libidinal cathexis, initially favourable to the Austro-Hungarian Empire, with the astute reflections on war and death on which he had been working from 1915, in *Thoughts for the Times on War and Death* (1915b), to 1933, when he published *Why War?* (1933c), his correspondence with Einstein. Freud's investigations on war and death paved the way to the work on mass psychology, written in a historical moment in which "a series of Germanic passions were coming to an end, and the democratic values were threatened by the insurgence of a new law, the law of masses" (Semprún, 2002, p. 20).

The mass, the unconscious, and the libidinal tie

In 1921, from a psychoanalytic perspective, Freud introduced the study of mass psychology, imbued with the desire to carry out an analysis of the collective life of individuals, stressing the conflict between instinctual life – and the resulting need for narcissistic gratification of individual desires – and group ties. With a critical and transforming view, he analysed the Ego within the context of collective psychology, borrowing descriptions from nineteenth-century crowd psychology. Freud's analysis of the masses developed along two different lines. The first aimed at explaining mass psychology based on shifts operating in the individual, whereas the second resumed his metapsychological investigations started in *On Narcissism: An Introduction* (1914) and *Mourning and Melancholia* (1917), which he continued in *The Ego and the Id* (1923a).

In the introduction of *Group Psychology and The Analysis of the Ego*, Freud (1921) is revolutionary when he refers to the contrast between individual and social psychology:

> … only rarely and under certain exceptional conditions is individual psychology in a position to disregard the relations of this individual and others. In the individual's mental life someone else is invariably involved, as a model, as an object, as a helper, as an opponent; and so from the very first individual psychology, in this extended but entirely justifiable sense of the words, is at the same time social psychology as well.
>
> (Freud, 1921, p. 69)

In Enriquez's words (1990), Freud's essay starts controversially, as a "bomb", when he challenges the opposition between individual and social psychology, since his description eliminates the characterological typologies discussed in the nineteenth century – which used to associate personality traits with biology (Pick, 1989a) – confirming the idea that individual psychology is connected to the context in which the individual is inserted into the fabric of social relations. Thus, Freud seems to have fired a fatal shot into the anthropological tendencies that tried to ignore the relationship between individual and collective when explaining social phenomena, pointing to the need of alterity in the subjective constitution and establishment of social relationships. In that respect, Freud's work on the masses contributed to creating social psychology, tracking the link that binds the individual and the social and necessarily involves the other "as a model, as an object, as a helper, as an opponent" (Freud, 1921, p. 69).

Freud offered a new starting point to explore psychoanalysis and culture, combining interpretation of individual and social processes and trying to position himself exactly where their essential imbrication is. In that respect, "individual processes started to connect in an incontestable way with the social dimension of existence, that is, with the vast, complex, and diverse field of the relationships with the other" (Figueiredo, 1999, p. 36; translation mine). Freud presented the family as the first group formation, referring to relationships established from childhood and ratifying the influence of the other in the subjective formation. Although Freud's view on the interconnection between individual and social processes has taken years to be understood and acknowledged in psychoanalysis, it was through this view that he developed his work on the masses.

Using nineteenth-century crowd psychology, but borrowing the theoretical framework of individual psychoanalysis, Freud aimed at sorting out mass behaviour and understanding the influence of the masses on individuals by asking the following questions:

> What, then, is a "group" [mass]? How does it acquire the capacity for exercising such a decisive influence over the mental life of the individual? And what is the nature of the mental change which it forces upon the individual?
>
> (Freud, 1921, p. 72)

To answer these questions, he built primarily on the work of Le Bon (1895), even knowing both Sighele's (1891) and Tarde's (1890) research. From the beginning, Freud criticized the existence of a collective mind and did not find in Le Bon's analyses an element to explain his postulation. For this reason, he opposed to his predecessors' idea of a collective mind and turned to the primacy of unconscious factors in crowd behaviour (Freud, 1921, p. 82).

The individual in the mass is thereby under the influence of unconscious tendencies responsible for individual psychic aspects and for mass behaviour as well, in which suspended repression produces instinctual manifestations and intensified affections. In the mass, individuals are led to psychic and intellectual regression, and plunge into a state resembling that of the fascination the hypnotized finds in the relationship with the hypnotist (Freud, 1921, p. 114). Freud corroborates some of Le Bon's descriptions of crowd psychology, especially those that emphasize unconscious processes, regression, lowered intellectual ability, as well as the influence of beliefs and illusions. For Freud, as for Tarde (2005) and Le Bon (1895), the association of group mind with mental life in primitive people, children, and the neurotic is crucial; however, Freud dissociates himself from these authors by refusing to attribute this link to biological and evolutionist factors, or even to racist and elitist views, thus ratifying the primacy of unconscious aspects (Costa, 1989).

Freud believed that the way Le Bon (1895) described the importance of the leader was somewhat inconsistent. Although Le Bon made countless points about the prestige and influence of leaders, Freud did not observed in his account the formulation of an underlying principle that could define its relevance, and took the opportunity to criticize nineteenth-century scholars for not having understood the real importance of the leader for crowds, despite having given relevance to the leader's role. Thus, instinctively grouped under the influence of a leader, fascinated by a profound faith, taken by the mysterious, illusory, and fascinating prestige of the leader, the crowds were hypnotized by this figure. Although, for Freud, Le Bon's work was a "brilliantly executed picture of the group mind" (Freud, 1921, p. 81), he is firm when he points out that Le Bon's descriptions have not brought anything new to what other authors and nineteenth-century literature had already said (Freud, 1921, p. 83).

Drifting away from the analysis of what he considers ephemeral, such as the transient crowds studied by Sighele, Tarde, and Le Bon, Freud (1921), based on McDougall's reflections in *The Group Mind* (1920), turned to the investigation of artificial crowds, which were stable in the form of permanent associations called organized groups. Reasoning like Tarde (1890) when he separates transient crowds from artificial crowds, Freud plunged into his research on organized crowds. Initially, he demonstrates the difference McDougall defined between an occasional crowd (McDougall, 1920, p. 27), without any sort of organization, and a crowd that, albeit apparently unorganized, reveals the rudiments of an organization, enabling the observation of fundamental facts of collective psychology (Freud, 1921, p. 85). The condition for a shift from an occasional crowd to an organized group was that group members should have something in common, such as an interest, or an emotion, or a reciprocal influence, even if unexpected (McDougall, 1920). Therefore, the higher the degree of homogeneity found among the members of a crowd, the more merged these individuals are in the crowd and the more their individuality loses its limit, making it easier for the group to transform from an unorganized crowd into a psychological crowd. In McDougall, emotion exacerbation or intensification seems to have defined how an organized crowd forms and how the individuals are led to share a common and intensified feeling that could be explained by a "direct induction of emotion" (McDougall, 1920, p. 37). It means that, in a crowd, individuals tend to lose their critical judgement, allowing themselves to experience an emotional contagion and an increasing mutual interaction.

McDougall (1920) corroborates some of Le Bon's ideas about the features of crowds and also ascribes to them lowered intelligence, suggestibility, and impulsiveness; however, McDougall contrasts such features with those of the organized group. In an attempt to define the distinctiveness of collective mental life, he focused on the analysis of the concept of collective consciousness (McDougall, 1920, p. 43). Influenced by Comte's and Spencer's positivism and by analogies between animal life and life in society, McDougall tried to prove the existence of a collective consciousness that would encourage cooperation and experience sharing within the group. Although he did not find enough evidence to support his hypothesis, his analysis of the Army set the scene from which Freud started to present the psychoanalytic view on the organized group. For McDougall, the goals the Army partakes as an organized group would lead to a rise in ethical and moral standards and group intelligence, directing actions and achievements, always in obedience to the leader (McDougall, 1920, p. 70). McDougall's anthropological studies also led him to infer the existence of a "group spirit" (McDougall, 1920, p. 87) – responsible for the individual's involvement and responsibility in the face of the community – that results from the value given to the feeling of belonging. In this sense, McDougall's descriptions of the organized group, in contrast with the crowd's features, seem to be his highest merit (Harrison, 2000). Certainly, his research contributed to the study of small groups in the twentieth century, revealing a more optimistic view on organized groups and also underlining their intrinsic characteristics, especially the homogeneity that leads to group cohesion. However, his arguments are beneath Freud's analysis of group formation.

After the analysis of artificial crowds, especially the Church and the Army, Freud (1921) moved away from nineteenth-century research and revealed new distinctive features in the functioning of groups: an emotional relationship between group members and the leader, shared values or beliefs, and interaction through either collaboration or rivalry with other groups. These are fundamental conditions for creating organized groups in which stability, continuity, and internal structuring prevail (Freud, 1921, p. 86). That was how, with libido and the aggregating force of Eros as allies, Freud conducted his analysis of organized groups, making use of the illusion nurtured by group members that the leader – were he Christ, the commander, or the chief – loves all group members equally, believing in a "myth of egalitarian love" (Pick, 1995, p. 61). This idea is

> an idealistic remodelling of the state of affairs in the primal horde, where all of the sons knew that they were equally persecuted by the primal father, and feared him equally.
>
> (Freud, 1921, p. 125)

Therefore, the core of the 1921 study is the statement that the heart of group functioning is in the libidinal tie formed between group members and the leader. Consequently, a group remains united by the aggregating power of Eros, which makes individuals abandon individuality and instinctual demands to identify horizontally with other group members, harmonizing with them to the point of preventing individual initiatives from competing when the group meets and leading to the formation of a "group individual" (Freud, 1921, p. 117).

Now, the concept of identification becomes essential to understand the nature of group libidinal ties and acquires a central value in Freud's works, since individuals are constituted as subjects through identification. Although Freud had already referred to identification – in letters to Fliess, in a description of the relation between identification and hysterical phenomena and the dream, or in studies on narcissism and homosexuality – it was only in 1921 that he focused on its investigation and presented it as "the original form of emotional tie with an object" (Freud, 1921, p. 105). In that work, Freud stressed the role of identification in the resolution of the Oedipus complex, when the abandonment of libidinal cathexis to parents gives rise to identifications and to the relation with culture. In group psychology, identification is of capital importance, for it allows us to understand that the ego of a person can be moulded "after the fashion of the one that has been taken as a model" (Freud, 1921, p. 106). It means that the mutual tie formed in a group is based on identification among its members, who, once identified with themselves, would take the leader as a model.

Considering the nature of group libidinal ties, in artificial groups erotic ties develop along two axes. In the horizontal axis, group members are libidinally tied to each other with the same degree of intensity. In the vertical axis, the members are tied to the leader, to the chief, to the substitute primal father of the primal horde – an elaboration on articulations carried out in *Totem and Taboo* (1913) (Figueiredo, 1999). For Freud (1921), mass psychology involves a state of regression to a primitive mental activity like that of the primal horde. In a group, there is a revival of the primal horde and individual acts are eventually abolished and make room for collective functioning. However, although group members are subject to shared emotional ties, the chief is free, that is, the demand for equality is attributed only to group members. The leader is allowed a different status and all wish to be led by them. The leader of the primal horde has few libidinal ties, does not love anyone but themselves, that is to say, their nature is dominating, absolutely narcissistic (Freud, 1921, p. 123).

Nevertheless, to preserve the libidinal tie in the organized group, a balance between horizontal and vertical forces is necessary, along with a good deal of illusion against the irruption of psychic forces that oppose group cohesion and favour the construction of group defences to avoid the destruction of these ties. In that respect, Freud (1921) calls attention to the consequences of ignoring libidinal ties in an organized group. He takes the Army as an example, and attributes part of the failure of the Prussian militarism in World War I and the increase in war neuroses – treated in group for the first time by Ernst Simmel (Freud, 1919a, 1921), who used abreaction in caring for war neurotics – to the frailty of the emotional tie that united that Army, submitted to a hard treatment on the part of its officers (Freud, 1920). Therefore, Freud believed that, subject to fear or collective panic, individuals worry only about their existence, and the group is left to disorganization. In such occasions, the libidinal ties that keep a group united loosen, and the very illusion of being loved by the leader is destroyed (Freud, 1921, p. 96). In reality, the idea of libido introduced by Freud changed the conceptions about the matter, since for a group to remain united and for its members to give up their individuality while in the group it would be necessary that, besides being libidinally tied to the group and to the leader, group members should hold the illusion that they are equally loved by their leader.

The drive circuit in group ties: an economic point of view

Although Freud (1921) relies on the nature of libidinal ties in group formations, its greater or lesser degree of cohesion, or even its disintegration, depends not only on the degree of identification between members and leader, but also on a balance between individuals' libidinal cathexes, either in their own selves or in the group tie. Thus, within a group, a collective narcissism will follow, because the individual identifies with the others and invests their ego ideal in the group. In this respect, the individual's identification within a group is always ambivalent, given that a close emotional relationship between two persons contains feelings of aversion and hostility (Freud, 1921, p. 102). In groups, it is no different, and Freud borrowed Schopenhauer's porcupine metaphor to demonstrate the need for an optimal distance between group members to guarantee a peaceful coexistence, since, even in groups, ambivalent tendencies concur to lead individuals sometimes to preserve individuality, sometimes to bind with the group. The balance, the optimal distance between these two tendencies, their psychic economy then seems to be the key to group coexistence. Bion (1970) investigates this oscillation through the pair narcissism/socialism. However, as Freud (1921) observes, in the formation of a group a possible hostility among its members tends to disappear and individuals start to behave as if they were identical, likened to each other. Therefore, the basic condition for joining a group would depend on the possibility that individuals invest part of the individual narcissism in the identification with the group and with the leader, so that – from that moment, limited in their individual narcissism – they could attain a collective narcissism that would favour cathexes in group activities. It follows that the issue of the relationship between individual and group seems to be linked not only to libidinal ties, identifications, or ambivalence but also to the psychic economy that permits a balance of forces, an optimal level of libidinal cathexis that may or may not guarantee group cohesion.

Narcissistic limitations within groups are produced by libidinal ties among its members; however, such limitation of narcissism – contrary to the expectations that point to the maintenance of the tie just to take advantage of collaboration among people – would tend to encompass relationships among individuals through tie strengthening in the social sphere. This led Freud to state that, in the development of humankind, only love acts as a civilizing factor, transforming egoism into altruism (Freud, 1921, p. 103).

In this vein, the relationship between narcissism and mass psychology is clear, since in group formations the limit for individuals' narcissism is, therefore, connected to the idea that "love for oneself knows only one barrier – love for others, love for objects" (Freud, 1921, p. 102). Thus, Freud's main goal in mass psychology seems to be finding limits for individuals' narcissistic expansion in the social sphere:

The condition for the possibility of renouncing to narcissism is the social state of the mass; on the other hand, [Freud] suggests that, in the mass, the individuals lose their individualities, alienating them to the leader's benefit.

(Costa, 1989, p. 67; translation mine)

It seems that, for Freud, there is an opposition between "the state of individual and the state of mass" (Costa, 1989, p. 67; translation mine) that can be understood as a polarization between libidinal cathexis in the self or in the group, or even between individual narcissism and collective narcissism. This dichotomy is underpinned by traditions of modern rationalism that oppose mind and body, individual and society. However, instead of reflecting on the issue in dualistic terms, the economic point of view of psychoanalysis allows examining the subject in a quantitative *continuum*. It means it is clear that part of individual narcissism has to be put aside when it comes to belonging to any kind of group, that is, the mass is the greatest antidote to narcissism. In the masses, individuals suffer a limitation to satisfy sensual love and replace it with identifications and with the choice of a leader who stands in place of the ideal to which the ego subjects itself (Freud, 1921, p. 116). Libidinal cathexes based on mutual collaboration among group members – those that make cooperation possible, as well as the greatest human accomplishments and the most terrible atrocities – are acquired by limiting part of individual narcissism with the aid of identification, ideal agencies, sublimation mechanisms, and idealization. The ego ideal then emerges in the group as a substitute for narcissism, and that which the individual "projects before him as his ideal is the substitute for the lost narcissism of his childhood in which he was his own ideal" (Freud, 1914, p. 85).

However, even though individual narcissism seems to have been replaced with collective narcissism, the problem of ideals confirms once again that the question is economic, for libidinal cathexes, either in the individual himself or in the group, are always grappling with the narcissistic sphere. In this sense, it seems that only a transformation of individual narcissism occurs; a narcissism that, in the mass, finds itself committed to the collective. It is by this transformation that groups remain cohesive. Still, the balance of group formations is delicate and involves internal tensions that try to neutralize within the group the ambivalence of feelings, aggressiveness, and suspended repression, which are constant threats to group cohesion.

In group formations, given the need for preserving identification among group members, ambivalent feelings seem out of place and the group is invested with positive features that favour cohesion. Hostile and aggressive feelings, in turn, are projected outward. Thus, in the expression of antipathies or aversions that people feel for strangers, we can identify the expression of self-love, that is, of narcissism (Freud, 1921). Undeniably, libidinal cathexes in the group guarantee the preservation of the individual at the expense of a quickness to hate and aggressively reject the other or whatever may be different. Therefore, if, on the one hand, the narcissism of minor differences (Freud, 1921, 1930a) functions as an amalgam for the illusion of group cohesion, on the other, it encourages the projection of everything that, albeit antagonised and rejected, is fundamental for group preservation. The narcissism of minor differences in Freud rests on a fusion of instincts that involves life and death instincts and contributes to both preserve group cohesion and project aggressive instincts onto the external world. In this respect, the concept is essential to understand the psychodynamics of ethnic/national groups and contemporary masses, in which ancestral hatreds intensify and are massively projected onto rival groups (Volkan, 2006).

A reflection on the narcissism of minor differences refers to another of Freud's texts, *The Uncanny* (1919b), contemporaneous with mass psychology, in which Freud states that feelings of uncanniness are rooted in childhood complexes. Accordingly, although ordinarily the word "uncanny" – *unheimlich* – means what might seem non-familiar, Freud associates the problem of the uncanny with "something which is familiar [*heimlich*] and old-established in the mind and which has become alienated from it only through the process of repression" (Freud, 1919b, p. 238). If that which has caused uncanniness is something familiar that had been repressed, the reflection on the opposition among groups develops new forms of understanding. It means that, in human groups, keeping cohesive often happens at the expense of a need for opposition or hostility toward the other. Driven by the narcissism of minor differences, which expresses itself in feelings of uncanniness, repulsion, hatred, or indifference, the members of a group create rivalries with other human groups. However, the affections they find "uncanny", transmit to and project onto other groups may be exactly those that one day belonged to themselves, but had been repressed before coming back modified. The research on "the uncanny" is important for the analysis of group phenomena – especially as far as its relations with narcissistic and mirroring phenomena (Zinkin, 1983; Pines, 1998) are concerned – through the study of the double (Rank, 1927) and in the relation with the narcissism of minor differences, the compulsion to repeat, and the death instinct/death drive (*Todestrieb*).

Although Freud, when approaching the narcissism of minor differences, has paused to analyse aggressiveness and death instinct expressions – which he had formulated one year earlier in *Beyond the Pleasure Principle* (1920) – in mass phenomena, his discussion has evolved around the aggregating force of Eros in group formations when the individuals, limited in their narcissism and influenced by an illusion, invest in the affirmation of libidinal ties with other group members. At this point, Freud seems to put aside the opportunity to discuss what he has conceptualized as the death instinct and choose to endorse the importance of love and libidinal ties as civilizing factors. Moreover, "what form would his [Freud's] theories concerning the death drive and mass psychology have taken after Auschwitz and Hiroshima?" (Gampel, 2001, p. 131). This is something we cannot determine.

Considering the preservation of stability and the permanence of artificial groups, the idea that sexual instincts, which usually unite and strengthen artificial masses, may also produce disruptive and disintegration effects, draws attention to issues that Freud put aside in 1921. In this sense, Figueiredo (1999) proposes reconsidering the role that death instinct plays in the preservation of artificial groups, either in the inhibition of sexual aims, fundamental to social ties among group members, or in the reduction of intragroup tensions and neutralization of affective tendencies, indispensable to consolidate the life of organized groups.

In mass psychology, Freud (1921) points to inhibited sexual aims in groups and to different forms of object cathexis and libidinal tie. In this respect, every libidinal tie is sexual in its origin and sexual aims are inhibited in group formations with the main intention of stabilizing and preserving social ties. Thus, when sexual aims are attained and libidinal instincts are satisfied in the group, the libidinal decathectization becomes inevitable and ties weaken temporarily, leading to a period of rest, refractory to new excitations. However, when sexual aims are not inhibited, the group may form a pair – later described by Bion (1961) in the basic assumption of Pairing – which eventually hinders and weakens horizontal and vertical libidinal cathexes. The pair formed moves away from collective and altruistic commitments with the group thereby finding an outlet for its egotistic pleasures (Figueiredo, 1999).

This phenomenon may also involve the whole group, leading members to invest their libido heavily in each other to obtain pleasure through the group. It means that the excess of erotic ties within the group produces a high cathexis in collective narcissism, stopping the circulation of libidinal energy and concentrating only on the narcissistic achievements derived from group ties. This excessive internal tie points not only to an economic issue but it also reveals a tendency to detach from the external world, which is harmful to social achievements. In this way, closely identified, group members move away from the external world and collective life to concentrate on libidinal satisfaction, which is reached exclusively through group ties. This seems to be a marked tendency that Anzieu (1984) described as "group illusion". Here, we can see that the conflict between individual narcissism and collective narcissism actualizes in the group:

> Therefore, it is necessary to inhibit sexual aims and, at the same time, give rein to libidinal circulation along the two axes (horizontal and vertical) mentioned above, so that there is enough energy in the mass to keep it united and organized, but not so much energy as to produce, on the contrary, its disintegration, either by uncontrollable eroticism or increased aggressiveness.
>
> (Figueiredo, 1999, p. 39; translation mine)

Thus, in economic terms, the optimal balance of a group requires sufficient investment of a quantum of energy to preserve horizontal and vertical ties. At the same time, this energy must be stable, so that it does not jeopardize group vitality nor cause disintegration.

Therefore, in Freud's work, the question of group ties seems to be always oscillating between identification among group members and control of narcissistic expansion, still an economic aspect in the sense of a need for avoiding excessive erotic ties in groups through the preservation of their collective narcissism by identification (Costa, 1989). The relevance of identifications is then emphasized, since they promote similarities by reducing or even eliminating differences among group members. It means that the inhibition of sexual aims becomes easier in identified groups. However, if, on the one hand, erotic libidinal cathexis gives rise to identifications in the group and these identifications, in turn, are responsible for preserving group ties, then, on the other hand, they favour the construction of an environment suitable for the illusion of equality among group members, causing homogenization and, sometimes, leading to disastrous consequences.

In economic terms, homogeneity guarantees the inhibition of sexual aims by identification, survival, and mutual attraction among group members; from a contrasting point of view, it increases the tendency to leave out, to send out all that is different or opposes the cohesion and the desire for homogeneity. In this respect, the narcissism of minor differences contributes to the process of homogenization, which, in order to preserve a group, needs to project the primitive anxieties, hatred, and ambivalence produced in the group continuously onto the external world or onto a stranger or a stranger group who is not like us. Therefore, the most intense non-sublimable erotic impulses are sent out, and this mechanism contributes to the balance of libidinal energies within the group, ensuring its internal cohesion as well.

In Figueiredo's (1999) analysis, homogenization is a necessary condition for artificial group cohesion, since it contributes to inhibiting erotic ties, besides promoting an illusion of stability in the libidinal circuit of group formations. However, this balance is delicate, for it involves the drive circuit as well. If, as Freud stated in 1921, Eros is responsible for creating group libidinal ties, the life instinct exists in both group cohesion and group achievements and interventions in the external world. However, considering that life instinct preserves identifications and group cohesion, with excessive cohesion, a decathectization in the environment may occur, together with the stagnation of the group that is turned exclusively to egotistic interests, more inclined to the death instinct. In 1920, based on erotic life, Freud underlined that the encounter of differences can generate excitations and tensions and that, in this case, the erotic tie would be against tension reduction, against the tendency to rest, opposing the return to an inorganic state, to death. In this sense, the tendency to homogenization tries to eliminate differences through identifications, then, when equality sets in, bonding gives rise to detachment, and the death instinct prevails. Here, we should remember that "beliefs such as are held by Born Again Christians, and similar groups, reveal almost nakedly the death instinct … the aspect of nirvana of the death instinct, as described by Freud" (Segal, 1997, p. 122).

In a more classic reading of psychoanalysis, it would be essential to analyse the influence of the death instinct on the preservation of group ties and on mass phenomena. We observe groups formed around an illusion of homogeneity and equality, and horizontal identifications, but not necessarily invested in relation with the leader. Interactions are established regressively around idealizations of the group itself (Anzieu, 1984), and identifications are, at most, of the adhesive (Meltzer, 1975), addictive – clinging dependence – or imitative kind, leaving no room for differentiation among group members (Zimerman, 1993). The wish for belonging and the undifferentiated fusion to a homogenized group seems to be the only objective sought (Turquet, 1975; Chasseguet-Smirgel, 1984). In such group formations, the death instinct is indelibly and silently present in its ceaseless task of making the libido return to the state of absolute, primary narcissism, in which the encounter with difference and alterity is abolished. On the other hand, for this kind of narcissistically identified group to survive, the degree of repulsion and projected aggressiveness to the external world must be high. The psychoanalytic understanding of such questions, based on drive theory, should take into account death narcissism as postulated by Green (1988) when referring to the tendency to "an undifferentiated" that reveals the search for an absolute narcissism that pursues the zero, the neutral. In this sense, the rest in the unity of the neutral is something sought by all means, including love, and involves not an Eros that promotes ties and movement, but "the Eros that seeks and promotes difference ... the platonic Eros that seeks a supposed lost unity" (Figueiredo, 1999, p. 41; translation mine).

In sum, through Freud's lens, group formations have features that vary according to a greater or lesser balance between the group members' libidinal and instinctual cathexes in the group. Once again, Schopenhauer's porcupine metaphor can be useful, this time to state that the intermediate distance reached in the balance of the drive circuit is fundamental for the group's future. If its members are too close, they will be led to fusion, undifferentiation; if they keep an optimal distance, they will be able to preserve their individuality and be led to committed activity. Thus, it seems that, as regards mass psychology and organized groups, the economic issue is always part of the debate.

The illusory nature of group formations

In the texts Freud dedicates to culture (1921, 1927, 1930a), he emphasizes the conflict between the need for narcissistic satisfaction of individual desires and the civilized life that requires the renunciation of instinctual satisfaction to guarantee a safe existence, protected from the dangers of civilization. Instinctual gratification has always been an obstacle to create lasting social ties, and stable group formations expect individual demands to be replaced by the group's ideal (Freud, 1921). However, in order that individuals renounce to full instinctual gratification and internalize cultural rules, civilization should provide them with "narcissistic consolation" (Costa, 1989, p. 71; translation mine). It was then, in *The Future of an Illusion* (1927), that Freud introduced three species of compensation for individuals' life in civilization, resuming the narcissism of minor differences and explaining the function of religion and art. The narcissistic gratification provided by the fulfilment of cultural ideals operates as an antidote to hostility against civilization or even against the cultural group itself; however, these are outlets that Freud considered neurotic, the inevitable price to pay for living in civilization. Only art and intellectual work are seen as satisfactory compensations for human beings, although they are not a possible outlet for the masses. With their notorious intolerance and ambivalent attitudes, the masses, fascinated by and subject to their leaders, albeit important to social ties, are also the cradle of fantasy life and illusion as a result of their regressive and narcissistic nature.

Consequently, a reflection on the relationship between group formations and illusion becomes essential. The concept of illusion has been used in Freud's texts since *The Interpretation of Dreams* (1900) and was initially related to wish fulfilment. In *Creative Writers and Day-dreaming* (1907), the reader can infer the concept from the relation established between playing, adult fantasy, and literary creation when Freud states that both childhood games and adult fantasy are wish fulfilment. Considering *On Narcissism: An Introduction* (1914), the idea of wish fulfilment is introduced in its relationship with the formation of the ideal, because the ego ideal represents an attempt to re-encounter the mythical experience of completeness, typical of the primary narcissism, and also functions as a defence against the acknowledgement, on the subjects' part, of their state of helplessness. For Freud, the wish fulfilment that characterizes what has been conceptualized as illusion emerges associated with a defensive manoeuvre and with a protection against the inevitability of dependence and helplessness. Therefore, on an essentially narcissistic register, the first formation of an ideal in Freud represents a defence, a protection against helplessness (Garcia, 2007).

In *Beyond the Pleasure Principle* (1920), the antagonism between individual and culture is described as instinctual, and repression is the factor responsible for including individuals in the social. Hostility and opposition involve a conflict between individual narcissistic issues and the demands imposed by life in society. After 1920, the defensive character of illusion starts to occupy a central place in Freud's theory, inasmuch as the dialectic between repression and instincts had taken shape with the formulation of the second topic and the interplay between life and death instincts. In 1920, Freud introduces the benevolent aspect of illusion, which, as a defence, protects individuals against the inevitability of death and the tendency to return to the inanimate, typical of the death instinct (Freud, 1920, p. 60). Illusion thus begins to function as an attempt to deny the instinctual order, especially concerning repetition compulsion and the death instinct, described as "benevolent illusion" (Garcia, 2007, p.107), differently from what Freud had introduced in his work on narcissism in 1914, in which the desire was the return to a state of narcissistic wholeness.

In *Group Psychology and the Analysis of the Ego* (1921), wish fulfilment and the need for protection were articulated in the concept of illusion, for the attempt to preserve the pleasure principle and the belief in the love of the leader would prevail in group's functioning. Therefore, illusion represented not only an attempt to resist the establishment of the principle of reality and, consequently, the narcissistic wish for preserving the pleasure principle, but also the possibility of supporting the social tie through the belief of being loved by the chief.

(Garcia, 2007, p. 170; translation mine)

Illusion, through its protective and defensive aspect, may be seen as the locus of the origin of cultural formations. In mass psychology, the illusory nature of group formations can be guessed, because groups demand limitations to individual narcissism by proposing a collective life. However, they also provide illusory protection through social ties and the supposed love of the leader.

In *The Future of an Illusion* (1927), illusion is a defence against the acknowledgement of life's ephemeralness, as well as the place where cultural formations come from in the form of ideals, art, and religion. In that respect, the discussion about illusion advanced and Freud defined that what was typical of illusion was the fact that it derived from "the oldest, strongest and most urgent wishes of mankind" (Freud, 1927, p. 30), from a need for protection against helplessness in childhood. Ideals and art represent the preservation of the most sublime human achievements in life in culture, seeking reconciliation with the impositions of civilization, whereas religions are compensations that protect against helplessness, promoting and nurturing illusory gratifications through the preservation of an infantile psychological life and collective neurosis. For Freud, religious illusion threatens humankind, although he points to wish fulfilment and to the inevitability of beliefs and illusions in the preservation of the social tie since the *bedrock of illusions* protects against psychic illness.

The idea of illusion found a new place in Freud's work as of 1927. In 1921, belief – charged with desire in the love of the leader – was fundamental to form groups, which made it a necessary element to the theory of object, ego, and ego ideal, whereas, in 1927, illusion became the essential element to start the civilizing process, offering protection against structural helplessness (Enriquez, 1990, p. 94). Collective formations then acquired a key role in the struggle against individual neurosis, although, in some cases, it had been replaced by collective neurosis, participating actively in the construction of civilization itself (Enriquez, 1990, p. 81). Therefore, illusion and its corollary – belief – became key concepts to understand collective psychology and individual mentality.

Observing collective formations, be they ephemeral crowds or organized groups, gathered or not around a leader, we may consider that they do not differ in their relationship with illusion. It means that, despite their greater or lesser commitment to life in civilization or to the different levels of limitation for individual narcissism, we can see in the masses the same need for believing in the love of the leader (or in an ideology) in place of the ego ideal. From this perspective, illusion is crucially important in the discussion about the masses and, in general, about the formation and preservation of group cohesion. As illusion functions as a defence against the original helplessness, and is at the foundation of collective and cultural formations, it is possible to state that, although libido is the main aggregating element in the masses and identifications are the most remote forms of social tie, without illusion no group lasts for long. Eizirik (2001) seems to corroborate this idea when he states that, although Freud has privileged the psychological point of view in his analysis of the masses, almost ignoring the biological, social, and anthropological tenet, the main idea put forward in 1921 was the idea of illusion.

In the same vein, Adorno (1946) associates fascist propaganda with the illusion related to gratifications and wish fulfilment for the followers of a fascist agitator. Semprún, playing with words in the title *The Future of an Illusion*, points to the "illusion of a future" and observes that charismatic leaders, more than encouraging identification between group members and idealization, try to use illusion to keep the promise of a future for its followers, thereby promoting the perpetuation and crystallization of intragroup relationships (Semprún, 2002, p. 22).

The legacy of Freud's mass psychology

While closely related to nineteenth-century culture and society, crowd psychology has not addressed conflicts between instinctual needs and life in culture. It was only after mass psychology that these conflicts were brought about and contextualized. In both nineteenth-century crowds and twentieth-century masses, the individuals are subject to the influence of the unconscious and instinctual desires, but this does not seem to cause, at first, a conflict with life in civilization. On the contrary, through identification ties and narcissistic limitations, the masses eventually play their role in the civilizing game, when they unite to each other through loving ties, choosing a leader as object, and putting them in place of the ego ideal. From a Freudian perspective, the masses become fundamental parts in the constitution of social ties as the cradle of the narcissistic transformations required for life in civilization, with a leader as their conductor and main aggregating factor.

The ideas Freud developed about the masses do not represent just a contribution to the theory of culture; they are a true revolution in psychoanalytic theory. Freud's analysis of the masses enabled investigations on the origin of culture and humankind and favoured the emergence of new ideas about twentieth-century totalitarianism. This also sheds light on the problem of love, oppression, and voluntary human servitude in an allusion to La Boétie (1577) (Costa, 1989). Years later, Canetti (1960) masterfully developed these topics.

Although – as Freud himself wrote in a letter to Romain Rolland in 1923 – *Group Psychology and the Analysis of the Ego* was a "little book" dedicated to the initial study of topics Freud would never approach again, Semprún (2002, p. 22) states that it was fundamental for the understanding and development of twentieth-century history. Theses defended by Arendt, Broch, Elias Canetti, Adorno, and Sartre could never have been formulated without the work on the masses, in which Freud, in a unique way, brought together critical judgement, modesty, and clarity.

Post-World War II literature is full of dystopian romances that confirm Semprún's thesis, such as *Animal Farm* (1945) and *1984* (1949) by George Orwell; *Island* (1962) by Aldous Huxley; *Fahrenheit 451* (1953) by Ray Bradbury; *Clockwork Orange* (1962) by Anthony Burgess; and *The Man in the High Castle* (1962) by Philip Dick. Differently from nineteenth-century literature, which highlights the frightening power of crowds, twentieth-century novels approach the masses and their leaders with dystopian and science-fiction narratives. These novels and their heroes try not only to work through the recent past, but also to face a socially unconscious task: preventing, in the middle of the Cold War, the rise of new forms of totalitarianism. Ultimately, by presenting the daily life of the masses and their leaders under dystopian totalitarian social systems, these novels illustrate mass psychology features introduced by Freud and further developed by other authors, such as Hopper (2003b), for instance.

Enriquez (1990) states that the work on the masses awakens in most analysts a polite interest that does not match its magnitude. Collective formations stem from illusions and function as collective neuroses, also diverting individuals from their direct sexual aims, in a constant conflict between the ego and the ego ideal (superego) (Enriquez, 1990, p. 77). On the other hand, the nature of the libidinal tie is original, pointing to the intersubjectivity of human nature. However, the twentieth century had to run its course so that *Group Psychology and the Analysis of the Ego* (1921) could enjoy its deserved status within the Freudian work. Therefore, through a contemporary look that bets on the expansion of psychoanalytical research in the twenty-first century, Enriquez (1990, p. 78; translation mine) writes:

> … the message of this book could only be denied or concealed. The time of disillusion had to come so that this lucid text could finally be read without taking sides and be considered for what it is, the introductory (fascinating, obscure, and uncertain) text of a new discipline: psychosociology, the science of groups, organizations, and institutions.

Note

1 Freud's German title is *Massenpsychologie und Ich-Analyse*, therefore, the word "group", chosen by the editors of the *Standard Edition*, is inadequate to translate *Masse* (Gay, 2006, p. 394). However, we must emphasize that Freud agreed to translate the word *Masse* into both McDougall's *group* and Le Bon's *foule* (Freud, 1921, p. 69). As Eizirik explains, Strachey translated the German word *Massen* as *group*, instead of *mass*, because Freud had used *Masse* both for Le Bon's *foule* and McDougall's *group*; however, that was not a good decision, since "crowd psychology would have been more faithful to Freud's views" (Eizirik, 2001, p. 156). French translations were not precise either. Freud chose the word *Massen*, and not *Menge*, to translate the French *foule* used by Le Bon, favouring the political connotation carried by *Massen* in German (Roudinesco & Plon, 1997, p. 613).

3 Twentieth-century left-wing mass psychology

From the first discussions about nineteenth-century crowds to the most astute analyses carried out in the twentieth century, mass psychology is related to explanations for psychological phenomena and political, historical, and cultural topics. If, at the end of the nineteenth century, crowd psychology represented frightened reactions to sociocultural transformations, during the twentieth-century the analyses would turn into pointed critiques of society. From conservative and liberal, mass psychology turned into an important instrument for the study of fascist and left-wing revolutionary ideological manipulation (Moscovici, 1985, p. 232). The first generation interested in crowd psychology in the nineteenth century showed its conservative view in studies aimed at safeguarding a threatened social order by way of a protective shield against the revolutions that were drawing near. According to Horkheimer and Adorno (Frankfurt Institute for Social Research, 1956), this type of reflection on the crowds put aside a philosophical tradition that dated back to Plato and reached Bacon and Nietzsche, who, despite placing the enemy of truth in the crowd, believed in the individual's power and ability to avoid the worship of collective idols. In that respect,

> crowd psychology stressed the opposition between individual and mass, which is made clear in the use of Le Bon's concepts of "soul of the race" and "soul of the class" or McDougall's "organized group" and "unorganized group".
>
> (Frankfurt Institute for Social Research, 1956, p. 77)

This polarization brought remarkable consequences for crowd psychology, since, by ascribing to the masses an inherent evil, it created the need for controlling them, passing this urgency on to the twentieth century. At the same time, this urgency provided a powerful instrument for totalitarian corruption (Canetti, 1960), associating mass with power for good.

The following generation of researchers was concerned with the masses for believing that, thanks to their power of influence, they could represent a break on revolution and demagogic forms of domination (Adorno, 1946; Löwenthal, & Guterman, 1949). That was how a revolutionary and left-wing mass psychology was born in the twentieth century, intending to investigate the questions around

DOI: 10.4324/9780429399534-4

which mass psychology revolved at the time: why cannot the masses be led to revolution, if their economic and social situation leaves a lot to be desired? How is it possible that the majority accepts being oppressed by the minority? Which psychological obstacles deter them? (Moscovici 1985, p. 230). These questions date from the reflections on voluntary servitude proposed by La Boétie (1577) centuries earlier.

During the years in which Freud concentrated on psychoanalysis and culture, all major topics related to crowd psychology had already been approached – the fusion of individuals in the mass; the power of leaders; the origin of beliefs and religion and their preservation in the unconscious of the groups involved; the enigma of the submission of men and the art of ruling them (Moscovici, 1985, p. 232). Moreover, Freud's associations between psychoanalysis and culture, especially between the world wars, gave rise to a philosophical strand in socialist countries known as Freudo-Marxism. This is the reason why, in that initial period, the essays that sought for a synthesis between Marxism and psychoanalysis were inevitably situated in the field of mass psychology.

Freudo-Marxism

Freudo-Marxism is an intellectual current that traverses the history of psychoanalysis from 1920 to 1975, from both a doctrinal point of view – in the relationships between Freudianism and Marxism – and a political point of view – in the relationships between communism and psychoanalysis in several European countries (Roudinesco & Plon, 1997). At its onset, mainly in the 1920s and 1930s, Freudo-Marxism aimed at "using psychoanalysis in its critical dimension, associating it with Marxism, conceived as a critique of ideology" (Rouanet, 1986, p. 18; translation mine). The main protagonists of Freudo-Marxism, albeit from different perspectives, were Wilhelm Reich, Otto Fenichel, Ernst Simmel, Siegfried Bernfeld, Erich Fromm, Paul Federn, Edith Jacobson, and Marie Langer. From different thinking traditions, these intellectuals agreed that both Freudianism and Marxism were liberation doctrines that could be linked to the paradigm of the socialist revolution (Jacoby, 1983).

According to Zaretsky (2004), the first attempts to combine Freud's thoughts with Marx's were marked by historical events: the Bolshevik Revolution in 1917 and Hitler's rise to power in 1933. After the storming of the Winter Palace by the Bolsheviks in 1917, the confluence of a series of political manifestations in Europe, and the communists' rise to power in Hungary, psychoanalysis started to be used as an explanatory phenomenon for questions related to the bourgeois ideology and the culture of the time (Jacoby, 1983). In the first phase of the Revolution, psychoanalysis was viewed with sympathy in the USSR and, in Hungary under the rule of Béla Kun, it developed rapidly. Driven by the need to treat war neuroses, the 1918 Budapest Congress opened the way for the organization of state-funded mass therapy. Moreover, reflecting changes brought about by World War I, psychoanalysis took on a social character in the 1920s and 1930s, after the nationalization of uncountable healthcare services in Hungary and the establishment of mental health centres of a social nature, such as the Tavistock Clinic in London, the sanatorium Schloss Tegel, run by Ernst Simmel (Jacoby, 1983), or the Berliner Poliklinik, run by Max Eitingon, both in Berlin (Zaretsky, 2004). Freud even stated that low-cost psychoanalysis was a social necessity and that patients "especially prone to neurosis are sinking irresistibly into poverty" (Freud, 1923b, p. 285). The "mass use" of analysis involved psychoanalysts in a function that was more than analytical, it was truly pedagogical, and included the distribution of psychoanalytic primers to the working classes. The enthusiasm and the desire to attach psychoanalysis to bolshevism were so great that "Lenin complained that Freudianism had become a fad" (Zaretsky, 2004, p. 130). However, after Lenin's death, cultural experiences came to an end, and notwithstanding Trotsky's efforts, psychoanalysis was banned and completely replaced by Pavlov's reflexology.

As to the West, lines of reasoning emerged that used psychoanalysis to understand the socialist view of the world. Aiming at investigating what was going on at the confluence of the psychological with the social, the first line of thought to take shape, with Federn and Fromm, was left-wing revolutionary mass psychology (Moscovici, 1985). Federn (1919) examined the collective behaviour of the Austrian post-World War I generation, which, in a reaction to the ruin of aristocracy and monarchy, and driven by utopic projects and by an "unconscious parricide", wanted to create a fatherless society, without noticing the risk of becoming a victim of conformism, alienation, and totalitarianism. Works like this favoured the emergence of a new ethics to gather individuals in a fraternal society, organized as a mass and based on an idealized model of the parent-child relationship.

However, psychoanalysis followed different paths in the Bolshevik and social-democratic regions of a post-World War I world. In Western European social democracies, experiences of a social-psychoanalytical nature carried out in the 1920s and 1930s were fundamental for developing psychoanalytical theoretical strands and techniques in the following years (Zaretsky, 2004). On the other hand, the fate of Freudo-Marxism in the socialist world – it was "repressed" after the exile of its main representatives (Jacoby, 1983) – is now virtually unknown in the psychoanalytic milieu, as Rouanet (1986, p. 63; translation mine) remarks:

> One of the strangest phenomena in the history of knowledge is the deathly silence that seems to have been brought upon the Freudo-Marxists of the twenties and thirties, and to which especially the theory of ideology and the process of ideologizing have succumbed.

Roudinesco & Plon (1997) claim that Freudo-Marxists have been persecuted by both the International Psychoanalytical Association – especially during the term of Ernest Jones, who chose to favour policies to "preserve psychoanalysis" in Nazi Germany – and the communist movement itself, which, after initial enthusiasm, would eventually, under Stalin's rule, consider psychoanalysis as a bourgeois science.

In fact, even at the height of the Soviet Union's New Economic Policy, psychoanalysis and bolshevism showed differences and a fundamental contradiction. In bolshevism, the concept of personal life did not exist, it "was an illusion, a mere diversion from the dream of a communal society" (Zaretsky, 2004, p. 132). Although Marxist theses considered society and not the individual as the ultimate reality, they believed in relations between psychoanalysis and Marxism; more than that, they glimpsed the utopic possibility of attaching psychoanalysis to Marxist theoretical assumptions and worldview (Rouanet, 1986). However, psychoanalysis was anything but utopic; on the contrary, Freud had a pessimistic view on life in civilization and made the conflicted individual its cornerstone. In his personal life and in his works, Freud (1927, 1930a) revealed an astute rationality and an urgent need to stay away from any kind of illusion, whether ideological or not. Consequently, he remained reticent about any ideological association between psychoanalysis and Marxism or other political system and faithful to the view of man as an individual. Zaretsky stresses that Freud tried to escape all attempts of associating psychoanalysis with a political system, because "analysis was Freud's only motherland" (Zaretsky, 2004, p. 133). Moscovici (1985) recalls Freud's words in a letter to Arnold Zweig:

> In spite of all my dissatisfaction with the present economic systems, I have no hope that the road pursued by the Soviets will lead to improvement. Indeed, any such hope that I may have cherished has disappeared in this decade of Soviet rule. I remain a liberal of the old school.
>
> (Freud, 1930b, p. 21)

Roudinesco & Plon (1997) went further by asserting that Freud even nurtured certain hostility to communism and Freudo-Marxism.

Both in Germany and in Austria, the threat of a socialist government at the beginning of the century contributed to the growth of National Socialism, meaning that the revolution had failed and the anti-revolution was approaching. Freudo-Marxism was discussing exactly this topic in an attempt to explain the efficacy of ideologies and their demobilizing effect on the workers' conscience. Ideologies have settled along the socialization process by successive drive deprivations that family and other social institutions imposed on individuals (Jacoby, 1983). In this view, the dissolution of the Oedipus complex results in identification not only with the father figure, but also with the whole system of values it embodies. Therefore, in the development of the superego, the authority is internalized and gives rise to ideology. In this sense, "repression is the key element that ensures the penetration of ideology and determines the vulnerability of human psychism to its influence" (Rouanet, 1986, p. 24; translation mine). Moreover, Freudo-Marxists were capable of identifying the reciprocal influence between ideologies and psychic processes, producing the idea that "the drive apparatus ... is completely plastic and can be modified to be restructured by ideology" (Fenichel, 1934, p. 303). This restructuring would be attained by a network of institutions that, later, Althusser (1971) named as "ideological state apparatuses".

Although the Freudo-Marxist movement has dispersed over time, it was extremely important in the history of psychoanalysis. Many Freudo-Marxist ideas have been assimilated into Reich's and Fromm's theoretical systems, and played a fundamental role in the Frankfurt School's later analyses on psychoanalysis and culture. Attempts to integrate Freudian and Marxist doctrines – together with works by Bernfeld, Federn, Simmel, Fromm, and Reich – belong to this first phase and are relatively well-known – many years later, they were revived by the American New Left. However, most of what was produced during those years remain unknown (Rouanet, 1986).

Reich's (1933) contributions are among the main initiatives that tried to associate psychoanalysis with Marxism. Reich used psychoanalysis, dialectical materialism, and historical materialism to investigate the roots of the ideologizing process and its effects on the workers' conscience, reformulating the Freudian theory in such a way that his revision eventually resulted in a theory of genitality and a theory of character. Nevertheless, Reich's excessive concern with the idea that sexual repression was a fundamental instrument of power in the ideologizing process radicalized to such an extent that, besides moving him away from traditional psychoanalysis, led him to reject Marxism (Rouanet, 1986).

In *The Mass Psychology of Fascism* (1933), Reich used his theory on sex-economy to investigate fascism, which he considered to be an expression of the irrational character of man, whose primary, biological needs and impulses had been repressed for millennia. Therefore, instead of considering fascism as the result of politics or socioeconomic oppression, Reich saw it as the expression of an unconscious structure that encompassed the collective and derived from the masses' sexual dissatisfaction (Reich, 1933, p. 104). Roudinesco and Plon (1997) state that Reich resumed the issue of mass psychology in opposition to both Le Bon and Freud, providing it with a radically new content underpinned by the repression of sexuality. Moscovici (1985), in turn, says that Reich tried to understand Hitler and the Nazi movement based on mass psychology. In his work of 1933, Reich considers the Nazi ideology as a manifestation of the patriarchal order and sees National Socialism as a German bourgeoisie's panic reaction to the Bolshevik danger. Reich ignored that the movement he tried hard to criticize using mass psychology had used the same psychology, via Le Bon, to engender itself. It means that, "Reich was interested in mass psychology to explain social reality, on the other hand, Hitler had used it, applying it to the same reality" (Moscovici 1985, p. 235). In that respect, it seems that mass psychology has been an instrument of power for both the Right and the Left to construct discourses and manipulate reality at the same time as it has been employed in the critical analysis of the essence of the socio-historical process.

Another important collaborator in the Freudo-Marxist debate was Erich Fromm (1930, 1932), especially in the 1920s and 1930s, when he sought to understand ideologies as the result of interactions between the instinctual apparatus and the socioeconomic situation. For Fromm, ideology was at the crossroads between the psychic, the social and psychoanalysis, and its function was to explain how real socioeconomic situations are represented in the individual mind. By this logic, the societal context pervades the history of an individual; consequently, the character of individuals or cultures is historically determined. According to Jay (1973, p. 93), "when the socioeconomic base of a society changed, so did the social function of its libidinal structure".

Using Reich's idea of character, Fromm postulated the existence of a social character that would be the sum of features common to all individuals living in the same social condition. However, this social character is not contingent, but, rather, a normative standard that, formulated as an ideology, moulds individual personalities across the socialization process and the internalization of culture (Rouanet, 1986). In 1934, Fromm settled in the United States to escape Nazism. His reflections on the influence of ideologies and social order on the individual led him to glimpse the idea of a social unconscious (Fromm, 1930, 1932, 1962, 1963), a concept group analysis would rework in the twenty-first century (Hopper & Weinberg, 2011, 2016, 2017).

The Freudo-Marxist movement was a reference for the Frankfurt School, which eventually became one of the most marked influences on Western thinking in the twentieth century. Rouanet (1986) reminds us that many theses supported by the Frankfurt School and also by Althusser and Gramsci were, in fact, repeated ideas first suggested by Freudo-Marxists. Indeed, the differences between the Frankfurt School and Freudo-Marxism are not radical and, from 1923 to 1933, both schools of thought engaged in a fruitful dialogue, precisely when Reich and Fromm made their main contributions. However, after this initial period, the Frankfurtians' critiques to the psychoanalytic revisionism represented by Fromm's culturalism, together with an intensification of Reich's Sex-Pol after 1934, moved Fromm and Reich away from the Frankfurtians permanently. It means that many of the main exponents of Freudo-Marxism ended up separated from the roots of the thought that aimed at combining psychoanalysis and Marxism. Moreover, changes in Marxism itself, which consolidated as a political system after the 1930s, placed its focus elsewhere (Jay, 1973).

The Frankfurt School and mass psychology

The Frankfurt School was an initiative of a group of German thinkers. They founded the Frankfurt Institute for Social Research in 1923, supported by Felix Weil, aimed at conducting Marxist research as an alternative to the theoretical conflicts that divided Marxism at the time. Although its name has been associated with the city of Frankfurt throughout its existence, the Institute remained linked to the city only during the Weimar Republic (1919–1933). In

1929, the Frankfurt Psychoanalytic Institute was established in the same building of the Institute for Social Research, fostering their scholar's relations with psychoanalysis. However, after Hitler was appointed as chancellor in 1933, the Institute went through changes and many of its collaborators fled Germany. At first, the Institute settled in Geneva, then in Paris, and finally in New York City, where it remained until the end of World War II. After exile in America, the Institute went back to Germany, but some of its members remained in the United States. The Institute for Social Research continued to produce expressive results, such as the critical theory, a theoretical-methodological framework that initially joined authors such as Theodor Adorno, Herbert Marcuse, Friedrich Pollock, Erich Fromm, Walter Benjamin, Leo Löwenthal, and others in a common interdisciplinary program under Max Horkheimer's supervision (Jay, 1973).

The Frankfurt School has conducted discussions of psychoanalysis, politics, society, culture, and art. Its goal was to examine society critically about economics, culture, and the production of knowledge from a renewed Marxist perspective, that is, detached from historicism and materialism (Rouanet, 1986). It seemed as if traditional Marxist theory could not explain adequately the socialist society's unexpected development in the Soviet Union, the emergence of National Socialism, or the growth of capitalism in the twentieth century. For this reason, the first Frankfurtians' analyses pointed to an investigation of sociopolitical development, historical context, mass culture, and aesthetic modernism. Guided by a critical and dialectical reflection centred mainly on the contributions of psychoanalysis and also on Weberian sociology and existentialism, the Frankfurtians tried to transform the social through a new *praxis* (Jay, 1973). In Ortiz's opinion (2016), the Frankfurt School analyses were marked by a reflection on a disenchanted world, typical of the political circumstances of the 1930s. The totalitarian movements, especially fascism, lent a pessimistic tone to such analyses and, even during its time in America, the Frankfurt School carried out studies on American society committed to theses that had been developed to grasp mechanisms of domination in Germany.

Critical theory focused on society as a whole, in its historical specifics, aiming at helping forward the critical understanding of its assumptions to favour individuals' emancipation. Therefore, the Frankfurtians intended a philosophical and psychological critique of society underpinned by reason and nature through several intertwinements of rationality and social reality and of nature and its forms of domination. They were also opposed to positivist, scientistic, or observational worldviews. Based on Weber, Horkheimer argued that the social sciences are different from the natural sciences, because generalizations or general laws from experience are not possible, given that ideologies shape both thinking and the historical context. Summarizing all contributions from the Frankfurt School in a single specific definition is difficult. The movement stretches from the orthodox Marxism of the 1930s to the negative dialectics of the end of the 1960s. Its history covers a period so long that it blends with the history of the twentieth century itself (Jay, 1973).

In reality, the historical changes of the first half of the twentieth century – from the integration of workers to society and the Great Depression to post-World War II transformations in the United States – have been thought, experienced, and debated by the Frankfurt School (Musse, 1999). These changes eventually reflected on the theoretical mutation of the Frankfurt School's object of study and its relation with psychoanalysis. However, we can state that its essence was in the dialogical relationship between Freud and Marx, and that both their doctrines functioned as negative limits to each other, relativizing each other and relativizing their totalizing intentions. It means that "if the Frankfurt School is the critique of ideology and the critique of culture, it is so, mostly, through Marx and Freud, but also against Marx and Freud" (Rouanet, 1986, p. 76; translation mine). In its pointed critique of society, critical theory has thereby not only found in psychoanalysis a means of expression, but also its intrinsic characteristics, its own style, its own way of thinking (Rouanet, 1986). In that respect, the Frankfurtians have been able to criticize culture without criticizing psychoanalysis, since both were in a dialectical relation:

> Freudianism is not an influence on the Frankfurt School: it is a constitutive interiority that inhabits its theoretical body and allows critical theory to think its object, to think itself, and to think Freudianism as a moment of culture.
>
> (Rouanet, 1986, p. 11; translation mine)

Consequently, the theoretical body of psychoanalysis helps critical theory think of itself, think of the whole, and think of the individual as a singular being mediated by the whole. Psychoanalysis influenced most studies conducted at the Institute for Social Research, especially as of the 1940s. Even after the Institute went back to Germany, this relation persisted in both theoretical and empirical work and, in 1956, a special edition to celebrate the centenary of Freud's birth was published (Jay, 1973).

The influence of leaders on the masses, though known since the nineteenth century, has acquired new perspectives and critical depth after the Frankfurtians started to use Freud's mass psychology in their analyses, among which stand out: investigations into the psychological techniques of American demagogues and fascist agitators (Adorno, 1946; Löwenthal & Guterman, 1949) and research on latent fascism (Adorno, Frenkel-Brunswik, Levinson, & Sanford, 1950) and anti-Semitism (Horkheimer & Adorno, 1944).

Reflections on ideology and on individuals' affiliations with groups were important for the Frankfurtians. They believed the masses supported the development of fascist ideology (Adorno, Frenkel-Brunswik, Levinson, & Sanford, 1950), that is, fascism – as it emerged in Europe after World War I – had objective, historical, political, economic, and social determinants; however, people's support to fascist ideology and its leaders was inevitably a phenomenon of mass psychology (Carone, 2012).

In the study on fascist agitators, submission and active cooperation between individuals combined in a conjuncture that, manipulated by a fascist leader, would mobilize individuals' unconscious emotional needs and primal fears. Fascist propaganda promoted gratifications, illusions, and idealizations of leaders, as well as paranoid suspicions directed towards the external world. Fascist agitators' techniques also used rhetorical skills and ritualistic performances that, repeatedly and standardized in their speeches, endowed the leaders with a tremendous persuasion power over the mass (Adorno, 1946). It means the success of fascist ideological propaganda, its "wish-fulfilment" (Adorno, 1946, p. 127), was based on the manipulation of people's psychology, of the unconscious yearning of the masses, and of the way ideologies ingrained in the psyche.

The Authoritarian Personality (Adorno, Frenkel-Brunswik, Levinson, & Sanford, 1950) is an extensive field research project conducted at the University of California from 1944 to 1947 that involved an interdisciplinary team led by Adorno. Aimed at examining latent social prejudice and discrimination, combining concepts from the industrial society with irrational beliefs deep-rooted in the individuals, the authors analysed the rise of an "anthropological species" they named *the authoritarian type of man*. Looking into psychosocial predispositions to fascism, they tried to identify fascist features and a conscious or unconscious fascist mentality in modern democratic societies such as the United States.

By analysing predispositions to anti-Semitism, they also observed that this behaviour tends to idealize a certain group with which people identify – the "in-group" – and to project negative aspects onto groups with which people counter-identify – the "out-group" – and which are objects of prejudice (Löwenthal & Guterman, 1949). In this sense, the object of prejudiced representations is exchangeable and fulfils a function in the prejudiced individual's psychic economy. In 1921, Freud pointed to many of the psychological mechanisms involved in this psychodynamics, but Carone (2012) states that the studies for *The Authoritarian Personality* improved the knowledge of prejudice dynamics. Therefore, after an investigation that congregated cross-fertilization between social sciences and psychology, it was possible to circumscribe the psychosocial factors that enabled the rise of the authoritarian type in modern society. Then, the name *authoritarian personality* or *authoritarian syndrome* was given to personality traits attributed to a type of subject potentially capable of developing a fascist mentality (Adorno, Frenkel-Brunswik, Levinson, & Sanford, 1950). Once formed, the *authoritarian syndrome* operates as a more or less permanent personality structure that acts upon the way subjects select the ideological stimuli provided by the cultural atmosphere of their time, as well as their political options and behaviours. The research on the *authoritarian personality* reveals an influence of psychosocial context and historical processes on the construction of individuals' minds (Jay, 1973). It also represents the first scientific attempt to study the problem of ideology and to investigate its relation with individuals' personality using instruments from social psychology and psychoanalysis (Carone, 2012).

Overall, Freud's mass psychology played a fundamental role in the subsequent analyses of the masses and their leaders. From a Left political viewpoint, mass psychology knew how to take part in the most important debates of the twentieth century. Accordingly, the research proceeded in two critical analyses of Freud's *Group Psychology and the Analysis of the Ego* (1921), produced by György Lukács and Theodor Adorno, who demonstrated how Marxism and the Frankfurt School used mass psychology in a pointed critique of psychoanalysis and on a reflection on fascist ideology, respectively.

Two critical contributions to Freud's mass psychology: Lukács and Adorno

György Lukács was an important Hungarian Marxist philosopher in the intellectual scene of the twentieth century. Initially, he focused on the development of Leninist ideas about philosophy and produced the emblematic *History and Class Consciousness* (1923), a seminal work for Western Marxism, which exerted an inspired influence on the Frankfurt School. In that same year, Lukács took part in the "Marxist Work Week" organized by Felix Weil. Although Lukács had never been a member of the Frankfurt School, his position in 1923 was very close to the spirit of the Frankfurtians. However, even being a contemporary of both Freudo-Marxists and Frankfurtians, he remained independent of these two influences, stabilizing as a convinced Marxist, a severe critic of psychoanalysis and of the Marxist thought of his time (Musse, 1999).

One year after the publication of *Group Psychology and the Analysis of the Ego* (1921), Lukács, in the review "Freud's Mass Psychology" (1922), gave strong critiques of psychoanalysis in his reading of the Freudian text, asserting that, when psychoanalysis turns to the analysis of culture, it does not take into account the totality of social phenomena and is always based on "the human being artificially insulated, isolated – through capitalist society and its production system" (Lukács, 1922, p. 33). This way, psychoanalysis would be mistaken and, therefore, turn the essence of things upside down by explaining

> man's social relations from his individual consciousness (or sub-consciousness) instead of exploring the social reasons for his separateness from the whole and the connected problems of his relations to his fellow-men.
>
> (Lukács, 1922, p. 33)

In Lukács's opinion, in mass psychology Freud makes the same mistakes he made in his theories on individual psychology, disregarding the importance of economic, social, and historical influences, focusing solely on the individual. Lukács tries to prove that the social composition of masses is not important for Freud's psychology. Concerning the analysis of artificial crowds in Freud's work, Lukács (1922, p. 35) stated:

> Needless to say, he does not distinguish between one army and another: in his view the peasant armies of ancient Rome, the medieval armies of

knights (...) and the crowds mobilised in the French Revolution are exactly the same "psychologically".

Lukács (1922) believed that Freud understood the masses based on the individuals and their love relationships, always observing the mass in the same way, regardless of social composition, number of members, or state of organization. For this reason, Freud would not have grasped the true meaning of the problem; on the contrary, he underestimated it and remained tied down to a bourgeois and reactionary view. In an attempt to escape a derogatory interpretation, typical of the nineteenth-century intellectuals who diminished the moral or intellectual value of crowds, Freud fell into an equally imprisoning trap when he overvalues the relationship between the mass and the leader, lapsing into an "overestimation of leaders" (Lukács, 1922, p. 34). It meant that, in placing the central issue of masses in their relationship with the leaders, explaining the phenomenon through his theory of sexuality and the primary relationship between parent and child, Freud disregarded the historical and social determinants of the problem, especially the fact that the masses have features inherent to class struggle in a bourgeois society. Lukács believed that "Freud, in a totally uncritical way, comprehends the emotional life of man under late capitalism as a timeless 'primal fact'" (Lukács, 1922, p. 35). In this regard, Freudian psychology is essentially bourgeois, because it

> neglects the most simple and basic facts of history in order to arrive at "interesting" and "profound" theories through fanciful generalising from superficial phenomena or even from purely invented and contrived "spiritual facts".
>
> (Lukács, 1922, p. 36)

For Lukács (1922), psychoanalysis remains stuck in a circle of pseudo-problems and false answers for not perceiving the social, class-governed character of its paradigms. In Lukács's critiques, we understand that his view of social reality and subjectivity is very different from the view of traditional psychoanalysis. From the classical Marxist perspective to which Lukács belonged, social reality and subjectivity are crossed by subjective and objective dimensions and formed along dialectic processes that encompass the relationship between individual and society (Silva, 2008). Moreover, Lukács's concept of the subject is directly linked to what he called the consciousness-raising process, introduced in *History and Class Consciousness* (1923). In fact, in classical Marxism, there is no concept of subjectivity that may be reduced to an individual, psychological, or personality dimension, because these dimensions are always determined by critical and socio-historical perspectives (Silva, 2008). Therefore, it seems there is no psychic and individual autonomy as regards macrosocial determinants.

Lukács's (1922) harsh criticism of mass psychology is a striking example of how, at that time, the analyses, especially those of a political and ideological nature, was influenced by psychoanalysis. Although today they can be valued as instruments of reflection on the contributions and limitations of classical psychoanalysis about topics that go beyond the individual sphere, these critical studies reveal, above all, the paradigmatic incompatibility between psychoanalysis and Marxism at the time.

However, contemporary psychoanalysis – in theories of object relations and field theory, as well as in group analytic studies and in the Argentine school of analytic groups (Tubert-Oklander, 2017) – relativized some of Lukács's critiques. This is not about updating the premises of the Freudo-Marxist movement; it is about analysing the matter using intersubjective and trans-subjective thinking and the process sociology of Georg Simmel and Norbert Elias, which will be discussed in the next chapter. The debate will proceed within a contemporary analytic framework that replaces the conflict between insulated individuals and their societal constraints with analyses based on forms of sociation (Simmel, 1908) and figurations (Elias, 1984) co-created by persons (not insulated individuals) and their social systems (Hopper, 2003b).

In the beginning of the 1950s, at the height of the Frankfurt School's expansion, Adorno wrote *The Freudian Theory and the Pattern of Fascist Propaganda* (1951), based on Freud's text of 1921. There, Adorno provides astute considerations on the relations between mass psychology and fascism, linking their distinctive features to the main political events of the twentieth century. In a reflection on the liberation and resistance of the masses to authority, he claims the repressions that restrained rebellion against totalitarianism and the social order can be overcome.

Initially, Adorno's (1951) analysis shows how mass psychology has been used by fascist agitators to create situations whose main goal was to control the masses. Fascist propaganda, therefore, was directed to the masses, which, seen as a structural unity subject to a political ideal and a massive and calculated psychological propaganda, would eventually be controlled in a rational way. Although Freud's original concern was not political, but psychoanalytical, he perceived the nature and the rise of fascist mass movements in their psychological aspects. Adorno attributes this feeling to the fact that Freud might have captured unconsciously the scenery of his time and brought about tendencies that would remain latent until much later in the century (Freud, 1921, p. 119). For Adorno, the problem with mass psychology is related to social changes in the twentieth century, which witnessed the rise of the masses and the fall of the individual, a crisis that Freud (1930a) had discerned in the relations of individuals with the civilized world. Moreover, he has foreseen in the individual "the traces of its profound crisis and willingness to yield unquestioningly to powerful outside, collective agencies" (Adorno, 1951, p. 120).

Based on Le Bon's descriptions of the crowd, Adorno (1951) calls attention to the fact that Freud has not despised them nor displayed the traditional contempt most nineteenth-century researchers had for the masses. Instead, moving away from usual accounts, Freud wondered about the conscious and unconscious mechanisms that determine the constitution of masses (Adorno, 1951, p. 122). Psychoanalytical research also rejects Trotter's hypothesis on the gregarious instinct, and tries to investigate the psychological forces that transform an individual into a mass-man. In that respect, Adorno points to Freud's important finding that regressive and unconscious aspects are involved in mass behaviour, instead of endorsing that primitive and irreducible psychological mechanisms are ubiquitous in the crowds, as was believed in the nineteenth century. Based also on Freud's finding of the emotional tie that holds the members of a group together, Adorno confirms that fascist manipulation involves a libidinal tie.

Therefore, using psychoanalysis, Adorno (1951) was able to talk about how fascist manipulation, in the service of charismatic leadership, has used libidinal ties to control the masses demagogically by way of an illogical and pseudo-emotional rhetoric. Fascism sought to keep the libidinal energy of the individuals at its disposal, so that it could lead the masses to fulfil its political goals. More than defending an ideal, the goal of fascism was to manipulate with ritualistic performances, authoritarian means, and unconscious mechanisms a mass that was regressed, homogenized, and therefore prone to domination. Besides being a manifestation of destructivity, a reoccurrence of the archaic or of primitive parent-child relations, fascism is the very reproduction of the archaic "in and by civilization itself" (Adorno, 1951, p. 122).

Although Freud described the masses bound by love ties and love for the leader, even when sublimated, this connection is not so clear in fascism, that is, a reference to love seems excluded in artificially integrated fascist masses. Adorno (1951) exemplifies his argument referring to the fact that Hitler did not played the role of a loving father, but rather that of a threatening authority (Adorno, 1951, p. 123). Using techniques similar to those of a hypnotist, fascism reveals a fascinated individual, though submitted to the awakening of an archaic inheritance that reproduces in the mass the relations between the primitive individual and the dreaded father of the horde. Fascist agitation is centred on the idea of the leader, because the image of the leader is at issue. It could "reanimate the idea of the all-powerful and threatening primal father" (Adorno, 1951, p. 124). Therefore, the fascist agitator uses the skilful awakening of a passive-masochistic attitude of the masses towards the image of the leader to reproduce the relationship of the mass with the threatening primal father of the horde. In contrast, the followers' irrationality emerges as a conviction based on the needs of their erotic life. The psychological mechanism involved in this relationship is then erotic-libidinal and the tie is based on identification. Moreover, the innermost desires and prejudices of fascist followers are actualized and accomplished in the fascist leader's speech and action. For his purpose, Adorno (1951) examines the narcissistic and primitive nature of identification processes aiming at finding the passive-masochistic roots of relationships of submission to the leader in pre-identification stages. In these stages, the leader's image "seems to be the enlargement of the subject's own personality, a collective projection of himself, rather than the image of the father" (Adorno, 1951, p. 125).

Adorno furthers his analysis of fascism and the relationship of the mass with the leader by stressing the importance of idealization and ideal instances. He confirms that a fascist community and the psychology of its leader act similarly to what Freud (1921) presented in his psychology of the masses: the individuals project their ego ideal onto the figure of the leader. The masses are thereby transformed by identification and idealization into a picture of themselves, but free of "the stains of frustration and discontent" (Freud, 1921, p. 126). The fascist leader's irrational image, by psychological manipulation and the externalization of their unconscious, gratifies "the follower's twofold wish to submit to authority and to be the authority himself" (Freud, 1921, p. 127).

One of the main Freudian statements about mass psychology refers to the topic of individuals in the group putting the leader, and the group itself, in place of the ego ideal. In *The Authoritarian Personality*, Adorno, Frenkel-Brunswik, Levinson and Sanford (1950) observe that, through a narcissistic identification, a prejudiced individual tends to submit to a group ego at the expense of their own ego ideal, which becomes virtually merged into the culture's external values. In this sense, the fascist personality deals with the extinction of the individual superego by replacing it with a group ego, that is, it deals with the "substitution of a collective ego for paternal imagery" (Adorno 1946, p. 126). Individuality is thus replaced with identifications between the members of a fascist community and the collective authority; consequently, what is good for the group is good for its members. This mechanism reveals how, through identifications, a tendency may arise in the group towards a "malicious egalitarianism", an excessive fraternity within the "in-group", which can lead to the loss of critical judgement in favour of a created conformity to the group's ideals. This tendency of mass psychology, discussed in Chapter Two through its psychic economy, is also an important element of the homogeneity sought by fascist propaganda and by fascism itself. These features will be discussed through a contemporary lens in the next chapters.

As in the psychodynamics of organized groups, in which there is a marked distinction between those who are loved within the group and those who are rejected for being outside, in fascism, too, a cohesive group strongly identified with an ideal tends to project hostile feelings outside of the group. Consequently, aiming at preserving group cohesion, homogeneity, and survival "people love what is like themselves and hate what is different" (Adorno, 1951, p. 128). Adorno defines this tendency to love the leader and reject and eliminate the external group as a "negatively integrating force" (Adorno, 1951, p. 130) that finds support in the social context, using differences in religion, gender, or race. At this point, as Figueiredo (1999) will do decades later, Adorno observes that, in mass psychology, Freud does not approach the "negative integration" that feeds on destructive drives. Instead, Freud chooses to use the concept of narcissism to understand them. However, Adorno states that it was only in *Civilization and its Discontents* (1930a) that the role of the death instinct is recognized as fundamental in the process (Adorno, 1951, p. 130).

Adorno's investigation of Freud's mass psychology is a thought-provoking example of the use of psychoanalytical theory to understand culture, history, politics, and ideological manipulation. Adorno's main goal seems to have been an attempt to answer questions that left-wing mass psychology proposed about human relationships in mass society. Certainly, mass psychology provided the Frankfurtians with elements to analyse the sociopolitical context of the twentieth century, allowing them to observe the psychological and the critical dimensions of power relations.

Moreover, observing the history of humankind, Adorno warns of the danger of the "appropriation of mass psychology by the oppressors" (Adorno, 1951, p. 135). Therefore, it is up to the individuals to become aware of what is leading them to convert into a mass, so that they can consciously oppose the processes conducting to massification (Frankfurt Institute for Social Research, 1956, p. 87). Especially after World War II, Frankfurtian studies revolve around ideologies, forms of totalitarianism, and the danger of mass manipulation. Such studies evolved, investigating Nazism as a "frightening manifestation of the collapse of Western civilization" (Jay, 1973, p. 142), and had as a background a strong fear that what has happened in Europe could repeat, reverting an enlightened society to barbarism. In that respect, the ghost of Auschwitz, which Adorno introduces in *Education after Auschwitz* (1947), seems to guide the Frankfurtians' efforts. They see in education for autonomy and in the development of the power of reflection key instruments to never allow that nightmare a chance to repeat itself.

Ortiz (2016) states that the Frankfurtians' critique of culture replaces the idea of class with that of mass in Marxism, emphasizing domination processes and power relations, but underlining that the concept of mass has not been invented by the Frankfurt School. Until then, this concept was marked by a conservative tradition based on Le Bon (1895), Tarde (Clark, 2010), and Ortega y Gasset (1930). Influenced by Freud, the Frankfurtians rejected such tradition, pointing to the fact that it concealed ideological positions of a conservative nature regarding the working class. Nevertheless, Ortiz (2016) argues that the Frankfurtians, Le Bon, and Ortega y Gasset have points in common. The first point concerns the analysis of the suggestibility of crowds and their manipulation by charismatic leaders, which found a parallel in the Frankfurtian studies on fascism. The second prompts common reflections on the tendency of the masses to homogenization, a feature that Ortega y Gasset (1930) mentioned as prevailing in mass societies and in the personality of the mass-man. Therefore, in the twentieth century, the claims to equality traditionally ascribed to Marxist working classes were also being made by liberals to undifferentiated crowds and to the homogenized mass-man. Although stemming from opposed theoretical positions, conservative contributions about the masses acquire new connotations that are integrated to the Frankfurtians' critical views.

Consequently, after a conservative phase in the nineteenth century and a later phase marked by the consolidation and affirmation of mass society in the twentieth century, mass psychology suffers a true swing to the left in the second half of the century, converting into a critical instrument to capture the movements of mass society and their leaders. Thanks to Freud and his followers' influences, as well as those of philosophers and sociologists, mass psychology was able to carry on making history, undertaking a trajectory linked to sociopolitical changes in the twentieth century. Further, we can observe and confirm historically that the phenomenon of masses, more than reproducing the *Zeitgeist* of a historical period in either the nineteenth or twentieth century, represents, manifests, and embodies the restraints and constraints that are at the heart of the social unconscious of persons living at a certain time.

The Frankfurtians' investigations improved discussions about the *question du nombre*. In the twentieth century, up until World War II, the rise of the masses and their leaders was clear. It was urgent to find theories to explain the functioning of the masses, as we explored here and in Chapter Two. In this regard, classical psychoanalysis seemed perfect to intertwine psychoanalysis and politics – as the Freudo-Marxists have done – as well as psychoanalysis and philosophy, in the case of critical theory. Therefore, understanding individuals, culture and society, and processes related to the internalization of social objects was a challenge to twentieth-century philosophers and social theorists, as we can infer from early analyses of the masses to contemporary investigations of the social unconscious.

However, as Hopper (2003b) reminds us, some of these early investigations are marked by the misleading idea that the properties of a body or a person can be used to describe the properties of a social system. Though, as the twentieth century progressed, different possibilities of analysis emerged. Post-modernity, transdisciplinary thinking (Lyotard, 1984), intersubjective psychoanalysis, interpersonal and transpersonal processes, and group analytic studies (Foulkes, 1964, 1975a), all allowed for replacing the isomorphism pointed by Hopper with perspectives that take into account interdependencies between persons and society, which will be explored in the next chapters. For now, it is important to retain that the Frankfurtians' analyses touched on core issues of the psychodynamics of the masses and their leaders. Next, we will see how such investigations proceeded with respect to their complexity.

4 Reflections on a society of individuals

Interweaving theories

As presented in Chapter One, the study of individualism helped to create the philosophical, political, economic, and religious character of modern ideology, permeating human relations in the Western world. Simmel's (1908) study of the two individualistic revolutions was fundamental to understand early twentieth-century social transformations, when increasing industrialization, fast-growing metropolises, and intense social life served as a stage for the consolidation of the idea of the individual. Moreover, the individualism of uniqueness (Simmel, 1971), insofar as it refers to a subjective and singular dimension of the individual, was essential to the birth of psychoanalysis and the construction of the idea of the subject. It was through the individualism of uniqueness that the Enlightenment ideal of the individual's autonomy reached its peak in the twentieth-century "psychological society" (Jay, 1973) and the culture of narcissism (Lasch, 1979).

In parallel with the birth of psychoanalysis, by the end of the nineteenth century Le Bon (1895) was pointing to the rise of the era of crowds and Tarde (1890) had already glimpsed the dawn of the era of the public. In this sense, as Moscovici (1985) states, in the early twentieth century, the triumph of the masses was certain. However, the analysis of these emerging phenomena was permeated by the Western individualistic paradigm and by the modern dichotomy that for centuries opposed individual and society. Despite Freud's (1921) work on the masses and his investigations on psychoanalysis and culture (Freud, 1927, 1930a), the conflict between the subject and the restraints life imposes on life in civilization prevailed in the psychoanalytic mainstream (Mezan, 1985; Gay, 2006). Thus, embedded in this dichotomy, psychoanalysis brought to Modern thinking a particular approach to history, morality, and culture, in which "the idea of the unconscious marked a lived sense of disjuncture between the public and the private, the outer and the inner, the sociocultural and the personal" (Zaretsky, 2004, p. 6).

In the sociopolitical atmosphere of the 1920s and 1930s, the Freudo-Marxists tried to synthesize Marxism and Psychoanalysis in clinical work, and the Institute for Social Research introduced psychoanalysis in its nèo-Marxist critical

DOI: 10.4324/9780429399534-5

theory. The Frankfurt School investigated the social conditions that Marx left unexplored in his theory, recovering the philosophical dimension of Marxism and distancing from "vulgar Marxism" (Jay, 1973, p. 42). In this sense, unlike classical Marxism, critical theory was not focused on class consciousness. It turned its attention to the connections between research and praxis, as well as to the investigation of negative forces in the world, especially during World War II (Jay, 1973, p. 84). This shift represented a detachment from material concerns and an interest in the superstructure of modern society by focusing on the structure of authority and studies on mass culture. However, to proceed with the analysis, it was necessary to fill a gap in the classic Marxist model of the substructure and superstructure. The missing link was the psychological; therefore, psychoanalysis was the theory chosen (Jay, 1973, pp. 85–86) to play this role.

If, on the one hand, that "unnatural marriage" (Jay, 1973, p. 86) ended up relegating the Freudo–Marxist movement to oblivion in psychoanalysis, on the other, the Frankfurt Institute for Social Research could absorb from Freudian psychoanalysis not only its analytical tools, but also its style, which shaped the contours of critical theory (Rouanet, 1986, p. 99). In this sense, the affinities between psychoanalysis and critical theory's self-reflection are located at the meeting point of epistemological, methodological, and philosophical questions. In epistemological terms, both theories refused positivism. In methodological terms, they were supported by an immanent criticism of its object. Yet, its philosophical view is based on the "principle of non-identity", related to an ambivalence between the particular and the universal, the whole and the parts, the individual and society, fundamental for both critical theory and Freudian psychoanalysis debates (Rouanet, 1986, p. 110).

In this research, the "principle of non-identity" is important for allowing us to intertwine psychoanalysis and philosophy and the discussions carried out in Chapters Two and Three, enabling the introduction of sociological developments in this chapter. In psychoanalysis, the question of non-identity brings to light the impossibility of reconciliation between the interests of the individual and those of civilization (Freud, 1930a). The "principle of non-identity" reveals Freud's Cartesian dualism, his instinctual theory, and Adorno's negative dialectic that refuses a utopian synthesis, and ends up "condemning the socialized individual to renunciation and repression" (Rouanet, 1986, p. 111; translation mine). In this sense, the malaise (*Unbehagen*) of life in civilization and the idea that the civilizing process dooms the individual to the instinctual sacrifice point to the natural condition of the individual's interaction in society. However, the reconciliation between individual and society, although necessary (in theory and praxis), is impossible, utopian. Adorno and Horkheimer, on the other hand, relativize the discontents of the individual in society and are more receptive to a historical explanation of the *Unbehagen*, and describe the formation of the individual through culture and the reproduction of culture through the individual as part of the same movement (Rouanet, 1986, p. 120).

In *Aspects of Sociology* (Frankfurt Institute for Social Research, 1956) – a more recent work, prefaced by Horkheimer and Adorno – the collaborators of the

Frankfurt Institute for Social Research underlined that, although classical sociology was more inclined to the study of social totality than to the individual, individual-society relations have been inseparable from Nature since Aristotle, pointing to the social nature of human beings. However, relations between the universal and the particular, the individual and the society have always been marked by tensions and complexities. For Horkheimer and Adorno, "The pure concept of society is just as abstract as the pure concept of the individual, and abstract too is the allegedly eternal antithesis between the two" (Frankfurt Institute for Social Research, 1956, p. 46). Therefore, to understand these interactions it is necessary to give up on generalizing definitions and focus on "the analysis of concrete social relations and of the concrete forms the individual takes on within these relations" (Frankfurt Institute for Social Research, 1956, p. 46). Influenced not only by a philosophical tradition that dates back to Plato but also by the sociopolitical experiences of the first half of the twentieth century, the Frankfurtians state that a good enough interaction between individual and society can only be achieved when the existence of human beings, as individuals and citizens, occurs in a fair and humane society (Frankfurt Institute for Social Research, 1956, p. 48). Today, from a neoliberal perspective, the antagonism between individual and society seems intensified and human interactions are no longer marked by recognition and cooperation. Instead, we see a growing gap between them, as Elias identified in the parable of the "thinking statues" (Elias, 2001, p. 114), depicting the indifference and isolation that arise from individualization in the modern world – *Homo clausus*.

Thus, to reflect on the current reality of the prevailing society of individuals, it is essential to investigate how modern polarities can be dissolved and transformed in the name of a more integrated individual-society interaction. For this purpose, we need to go back to the end of the nineteenth century, when sociology emerged as a new discipline derived from the ascendancy of the masses over the interests of individuals, exploring forms of human sociality (Levine, 1971). This deviation – when introducing the sociology of Georg Simmel (1908) on forms of sociation, as well as the ideas of Norbert Elias in *The Civilizing Process* (1939), *The Society of Individuals* (2001) and through the theory of figurations (1984) – allows the revelation of a different paradigm in the study of the individual-society relation. In this sense, the non-positivist perspectives that process sociology has presented eliminate modern dichotomies, enabling us to think in interactions/interdependencies between individual and society. This fundamental change allows us to revise the investigations on crowds and masses and paves the way to the establishment of the group analytic paradigm conceived by the German-British psychoanalyst S. H. Foulkes (1948, 1964, 1975a) in the interface of psychoanalysis and sociology, as we will discuss in the next chapters.

The sociology of Georg Simmel

Simmel's (1908) work dates from the early twentieth century, when Sociology had not yet acquired an official status, when intellectuals shared an eclectic background and their work focused on a range of different areas – philosophy, psychology, history, sociology, and economics (Mucchielli, 1998). Simmel was a prolific writer and brilliant lecturer who studied the most diverse subjects. However, his university career was difficult, for he lacked academic rigour and was of Jewish descent. Simmel founded the German Society of Sociology with Weber and Tönnies (Waizbort, 2001). After his death, his work was somewhat overshadowed, largely due to the sociological formalism that consecrated Marx, Weber, and Durkheim as the founding fathers of sociology. Nevertheless, in the last decades, the relevance and topicality of Simmel's approach to subjects of interest to the contemporary world – such as the philosophy of money, life in the metropolis, and studies on individualism – have attracted attention to his work. Moreover, his early work on the sociological aspects of secrecy and the sociology of music (Simmel, 1908) became important to contemporary investigations on interpersonal relationships and to the social unconscious research.

It is not an easy task to point out Simmel's theoretical affiliations, considering that he rarely referred to his sources (Levine, 1971). However, we can say that Kant's influence was key to Simmel's thinking. The dualism between form and matter is always present in his writings, as well as psychologism and vitalism, topics he discussed until the end of his life. Already ill, Simmel turned his attention to reflections on the philosophy of life. His philosophy is a sophisticated synthesis of neo-Kantianism that opposes forms, content, and vitalism through the idea of interaction (Vandenberghe, 2005).

The study of socialization (Vergesellschaftung) or sociation in individual-society relations

One of Simmel's main concerns in *Sociology* (1908) was to provide guidelines for the construction of sociology. At that time, the main difficulty was to find a set of singular issues that, within the concept of society, shared a common component from which to envision a point where sociology could establish as a science, but that would still be issues left at the margins of other sciences (Durkheim, 1895). However, even when these issues pointed to the possibility of a thematic unity, a more in-depth investigation would always collide with the idea of society, leading Simmel (Levine, 1971, p. 6) to ask: how is society possible? His search for an answer led to the idea of the individual, since it was evident that only individuals exist; achievements and experiences can only be attributed to them. From this perspective, society is an indispensable abstraction for practical purposes and for a possible synthesis of phenomena, but not an actual object that exists beyond individuals and the processes they experience. In this sense, Durkheim's sociology is different from Simmel's tenets (Lukes, 1973). For Durkheim (1895), sociology is a science of social facts, defined as every way of acting, fixed or not, capable of exercising an external constraint on the individual; or, again, every way of acting that is general in a given society, while, at the same time, exists in its own right, independent of its individual manifestations, its individual consciousness. In this sense, social facts cannot be reduced to individual facts and are defined as ways of acting, thinking, and feeling that are exterior to an individual and, hence, endowed with a power of coercion over them. It is not dependent on one individual; it concerns society as a whole. It is a general, external, observable phenomenon with some control over the individual. Durkheim believed that social facts should not be treated as concepts, but as things to be observed objectively. In this vein, social facts are seen as effective guides and controls of conduct only to the extent that they become internalized in the consciousness of individuals and continue to exist independently of the individual. Therefore, in Durkheim's sociology, the combination of social facts ultimately represents the social or the *conscience collective* (Durkheim, 1893) as opposed to the individual (Lukes, 1973). Simmel (1908) does not share the positivism that stands at the centre of Durkheim's method. For Simmel, society is a complex web of multiple relations between individuals who are in constant interaction with one another. For him, society is merely the name for a number of individuals connected by interactions and sociation forms. "Forms" are to Simmel what "facts" are to Durkheim.

Picking up Simmel's (1908) thread of reflections, if only individual existences are considered real, one could not refer to phenomena that happen in reality in collective terms and, therefore, society would become an abstract concept. However, not all groupings and collective configurations submitted to an investigation can be constituted solely by the characteristics of individual forms of existence. Society is not a mere representation, although it exists thanks to unique elements in relation to which it assumes an independent position. In fact, what can be known about human individuals are only the specific and unique traits that appear in situations of reciprocal influence and require independent understandings and deductions. Meanwhile, only in interaction is it possible to understand these elements.

Therefore, society is the result of actions and reactions of individuals among themselves, that is, of their interactions. These are "intermental processes, whose holders, as subjects of action, are the individuals, their awareness, and the totality of their psychic life" (Moraes Filho, 1983, p. 20; translation mine). Thus, society means that individuals are linked to each other by mutual influences and by the reciprocal determination they exercise on one another, forming a unity. Society is not something static and finished. On the contrary, it is something that has always happened and is happening, constantly coming into being. Simmel (1908) refers to this fundamental process as *Vergesellschaftung* (socialization), which means more than society; it refers to social interactions within society (Simmel, 1908, p. 10). Simmel's North American followers translate *Vergesellschaftung* as sociation to avoid confusion between socialization and association (Moraes Filho, 1983). In this book, we use the term sociation.

Simmel (1908) proposes three types of sociology as scientific disciplines that complement one another: general sociology, philosophical sociology, and pure or formal sociology. General sociology is a by-product of formal sociology and has as its object of analysis specific processes at different stages of development, as well as the foundations of social institutions and historical life at a social and individual level (Simmel, 1908, p. 16). Philosophical sociology concerns the epistemological and metaphysical aspects of society and rethinks the methodological assumptions of the discipline, fostering a method of analysis based on a trans-sociological perspective of the individual (Simmel, 1908, p. 23). Pure or formal sociology, which receives greater attention here, has as its main object of study the social forms as organizers of social matter, insofar as they give it structure and continuity. Therefore, it is a question of identifying irreducible and independent relationships, that is, those forms that differ from a specific, infinitely variable content that appears in the universe of intersubjective relations, be that the family, the school, the army, or the church (Moraes Filho, 1983). The goal is always to reach the final form.

Formal sociology is then established as an autonomous discipline, different from other social sciences, specialized in the analysis of forms of sociation. As a systematic study of the structuring forms of interaction processes, formal sociology is an interactionist sociology that analyses not only inter-individual interactions but also institutions and organizations as interactions of interactions (Simmel, 1908, p. 21).

The basic process of sociation is made up of individuals' impulses, interests, and aims, as well as of the forms these motivations assume. In the process of sociation, it becomes necessary to distinguish between form and content. However, just as empty forms do not exist, there is no content without form. With these notions in mind, Simmel (1908) tried to find the form through which sociology is made, that is, the forms of sociation that make up society, instead of searching for the substance that makes up social life. The objective of formal sociology is the inductive abstraction of forms of sociation from their content, to be precise, abstracting living materials from the content that fills these forms to find structured interactions (Vandenberghe, 2005). In other words, sociation is a form achieved in several ways. In it, individuals constitute a unit through which they can accomplish their goals. Therefore, one can conclude that resolving the question of what society is only happens when the forms of human sociation are established.

Throughout the ten chapters and thirteen digressions organized and published in the two volumes of *Sociology* (1908), Simmel analyses and exemplifies these formal conditions, revealing combinations and interactions between individuals, as well as methodological distinctions between form and content in the domain of social life. Levine (1971) points out six hundred forms of sociation in Simmel, organized, on the whole, around social processes (division of labour, meetings), social types (the stranger, the mediator, the poor, the adventurer, the renegade), and developmental formations (interactions between social circles, personality development etc.).

In some chapters of *Sociology* that illustrate certain forms of sociation, Simmel (1908, p. 87) mentions a quantitative determination of social groups, through which he examines different types of interaction between members of smaller and larger groups to identify features produced in accordance with collective numerical conditions. Concerning smaller groups, Simmel gives examples of interactions in both small socialist societies and religious sects or aristocratic interrelationships. As for larger groups, his analysis refers to the masses and to questions about interactions and group size, as well as cohesion and radicalism (Simmel, 1908, p. 93).

Domination and subordination processes related to the dynamics of interactions between the dominant and the dominated in society are also under analysis in the Simmelian forms of sociation. Domination is a specific form of interaction, directly linked to subordination, and factors of inclusion and exclusion, coercion and dominance, authority, prestige, and leadership in social interrelationships (Simmel, 1908, p. 181).

Another important pure form of sociation is conflict as an interaction, fundamental to collective life (Simmel, 1964). A conflict aims at resolving divergent dualisms among the components of society and functions as a way to achieve some sort of unity, even if through the annihilation of the adversary. For Simmel, conflict is an inherent part of human relations and means the negation of unity, although functioning as an integrative force in the group. Conflict is neither pathological nor harmful to social life, as often thought outside the social sciences. On the contrary, conflict is a condition for maintaining social life, as well as a fundamental process to transform forms of organization (Moraes Filho, 1983).

On analysing competition, Simmel (1964) takes it as an indirect form of conflict and attributes a form of sociation and a civilizing function to it. That is, if, on the one hand, there is hostility in a conflict motivating the dispute and leading to the competitors' mutual annihilation, on the other hand, from the point of view of society, competition offers a subjective motivation that produces objective social values. In a competition, each competing party seeks to get close to the other, to know more about the other party, which eventually creates new links and connections that will produce an associative effect (Simmel, 1964, p. 61).

There is also another form of sociation considered as an important tool for analysing the forms of social interaction represented by games (Simmel, 1908, p. 45). In fact, for Simmel, the forces, shortcomings, and real impulses of life produce modes of behaviour that can be expressed through this model, in which forms become autonomous as regards the content. By way of eroticism and the art of seduction and flirtation (Simmel, 1908, p. 50), it reveals an interaction that involves a dynamic game of approximations and withdrawals from the object of desire through cohesive behaviour and polar oppositions, composed of actions and interactive reactions. In the case of flirtation, the most important are the forms of the seduction game and not the content that they convey. These forms are forms of sociation that refer to another important Simmelian concept in the study of formal sociology, that of sociability.

Sociability (Simmel, 1908) functions as a playful form of sociation, that is, it shows a process in which content and form of social existence are separated. In sociability, forms acquire a life of their own, free from material content.

Through actions and reactions, they reveal pure figurations without any objective purpose (Simmel, 1908, p. 42). In sociability, everything that can be defined is understood as based on the sociological form of the game. In this way, societal games (Simmel, 1908, p. 49) are constituted as free expressions of forms of sociability. Thus, all forms of sociation established among human beings – such as the desire to win or surpass the other, exchange, party formation, opposition and cooperation, deception, revenge – give us the possibility of glimpsing the dynamics of a game. In this case, the components gain life and are propelled by reactions of attraction and repulsion, movements that are part of an interaction of individuals.

Therefore, for Simmel, sociation results from the interaction of the individual with their peers, and the game of interactions (*Wechselwirkung*) between them is the living substrate of the social. In this way, interactions and reciprocity of action between individuals are the necessary and sufficient condition of society, and the network of established interactions is a kind of labyrinth. Interaction is always a mutual, multiple, and mobile relationship, like a piece of fabric continually woven. Thus, just as society entails the individual, the individual society and the connection between them occur through interaction. Therefore, it serves as a vehicle of sociation. It means that, when individuals form a unit in interaction and in socialization, it is only through actions among them that they become producers and products of a society.

At this point, the question Simmel raised in the beginning of *Sociology* (1908) reappears: how is society possible? Many years later, Norbert Elias attempted to answer it.

Norbert Elias and the interdependent individuals

The place of Norbert Elias in intellectual history is not easily defined, given the originality and diversity of the subjects he studied. Of Jewish descent and born in Germany in the late nineteenth century, after studying medicine and philosophy, he graduated in sociology. His life can be confused with the history of the twentieth century itself, marked by world wars and anti-Semitism. Perhaps, his troubled biography took his thinking process beyond the usual boundaries of a single science, encompassing contributions from several knowledge areas. Throughout his intellectual production, Elias showed an analytical approach that rethought the divisions between the micro-and macro-sociological dimensions established in the field of social sciences. It took some time for Elias' thinking to be recognized, but the diversity of themes he explored certainly expanded the field of research in the human and social sciences (Heinich, 2002). Concerning his reflections on modern individualism, Elias gave important contributions to the analysis of the relationship between individual and society. On conceiving the social world as a network of relations, he envisioned the collective dimension of individual identities.

Elias's approach to sociology was directly influenced by Simmel, Weber, and Marx (Garrigou & Lacroix, 1997), connected to the sociology of culture that,

in the twentieth century, was in a process of development and institutionaliza-
tion in Europe (Neiburg & Waizbort, 2006). Although his contributions have
not been frequently used in psychoanalysis, Freud's influence can be seen in
many of Elias's ideas. Thus, Elias contributed to the construction of the theoretical framework of Group Analysis. With Foulkes, he was one of the founders
of the Group Analytic Society London in 1952.

In 1938, still living in Germany, Foulkes prepared a review of the first
volume of Elias's *The Civilizing Process* (1939) – having also revised the second
volume in 1941 – to draw the attention of psychoanalysts to sociological
thinking (Foulkes, 1990, p. 79). At that time, as a psychoanalyst, Foulkes was
already concerned with the study of the processes of introjection (Foulkes,
1990, p. 57). Moreover, that review shows that Foulkes, before conceiving
group analysis, had already stated that the "content and object of our mental
life" is influenced and transformed by "external circumstances" (Foulkes, 1990,
p. 80). In his book, Elias reveals how individuals end up internalizing the regulations of society's living conditions until they become their second nature
(*habitus*). In this sense, instead of pointing to the conflict between instinctual
life and society, as Freud did in 1930, Foulkes highlights, through Elias's study,
the processes involved in the individual internalization of external conflicts
(Foulkes, 1990, p. 81).

The connection between psychoanalysis and sociology was very important
for Foulkes. However, in 1973, he stated that, when he began his work in
group analysis, except for the ideas of Norbert Elias and Franz Borkenau, he
did not find in sociology any work "helpful about small groups" (Foulkes,
1973, p. 72 *apud* Foulkes, 1990, p. 79). This comment may explain how Simmel's (1908) work on forms of sociation, as well as his explorations on the
quantitative determination of social groups, the investigations on socialist
societies, religious sects and aristocracy, remained unnoticed by Foulkes.

The individualization and the we–I balance in The Society of Individuals

Centuries of Cartesianism and a deep-rooted notion of the individual – free,
singular, and autonomous – ground the experience of the modern human
being, making of the idea of the individual a paradigm of Western modernity.
What in the past was seen in a more integrated way was transformed into
dualistic oppositions. For that matter, based on three essays written over fifty
years and gathered in *The Society of Individuals* (Elias, 2001), Elias gives a contribution for the sociology of the twentieth century with a reflection on the
opposition between individual and society that results in part of the contemporary Western discomfort.

For Elias (2001), the traditional opposition between individual and society
conveys a misperception of this relationship, seeing that it would not be
through antinomies, but rather through interdependencies between individuals
and society that the analysis should be guided. Elias's primary goal is to

understand the social process that leads to the development of individualization in modern societies. He undertakes what he, himself, refers to as a "Copernican revolution" when dealing with issues involving the individual and society not as closed relationships, but as contextualized and historicized relational processes (Heinich, 2002).

In *The Society of Individuals*, Elias states that the relation of the plurality of people to the single person, called the individual, and the relation of the single person to the plurality of individuals do not seem clear in the modern world. Although analyses on the subject use concepts such as individual and society, they are antagonistic and dichotomous. The first concept conceives the human being as an entity that exists in total isolation, whereas the second oscillates between two opposing poles. Thus, if on the one hand society is a mere accumulation of individual persons, on the other, it can be seen as an object that exists beyond individuals. It means, "the single human being, labelled the individual, and the plurality of people conceived as society, were two ontologically different entities" (Elias, 2001, p. vii). Society exists only because it brings together a large number of people and only works because in isolation people make it work. However, its structure and its great historical transformations are independent of the intentions of any particular person. From this definition, Elias states that the answer to these questions led to "two large opposed camps". On the one hand, there is the idea that "socio-historical formations as if they had been designed, planned and created, as they now stand before the retrospective observer, by a number of individuals or bodies", as if they were "the rational and deliberate creation of a work – such as a building or a machine – by individual people" (Elias, 2001, p. 4). From a different point of view, the individual does not play any part in these transformations. In this case, the conceptual models used to explain the question come from the natural sciences, especially from biology, and aim at interpreting and explaining long-lasting social processes through a scientific approach to thought. From this perspective, "society is conceived, for example, as a supra-individual organic entity which advances ineluctably towards death through stages of youth, maturity and age" (Elias, 2001, p. 4), that is, these conceptions see as inevitable a single path of ascension and decline for societies. They are approaches that seek to explain socio-historical formations and processes through the influence of "anonymous supra-individual forces" (Elias, 2001, p. 5) and consider that social processes are constituted as life cycles inescapably repeated in the same way (Elias, 2001, p. 71).

From psychological perspectives on the subject, Elias (2001) also points to controversies. Some attempts to understand human relations view each individual as something that can be isolated and elucidated within the structure of their psychological functions, disconnected from other individuals. On the other hand, trends in social or mass psychology do not reserve any place for individual psychological functions. They attribute a supra-individual origin to society and, to the masses, a soul that transcends individual souls, considering that social formations possess a collective anima or a group mind, and that society is a mere additive accumulation of individuals (Elias, 2001, p. 6).

Next, Elias (2001) critically claims that "it appears as if the psychologies of the individual and of society were two completely separable disciplines" (Elias, 2001, p. 6), as if there was an insurmountable abyss between individual and society, pointing to the fact that the gap between individual and society does not exist in reality, because "no one can be in doubt that individuals form a society or that each society is a society of individuals" (Elias, 2001, p. 6). In these terms, the words individual and society designate, for Elias, inseparable processes. Therefore, the reflection on the question must shift from a substantialist point of view to a relational mode of thought. However, reflecting on such antinomies is complex, since human beings traditionally perceive themselves as individuals and have a sense of what society is, even if their ideas about these concepts never coalesce (Elias, 2001, p. 4).

In 1939, when the first essay of *The Society of Individuals* was written, the Gestalt theory was gaining importance in psychology, founded on the idea that the whole was greater than the sum of its parts (Lewin, 1947). Gestalt theories had been around in Germany since the 1920s and it was also in the Gestalt theory that Elias (2001) found the background for a deeper understanding of the phenomenon of individual-society relations. With examples taken from dance and music, he analyses the relationship between the part and its whole in both musical compositions and dance steps and choreography. He was thus able to create conceptual models that enabled reflections on the interdependencies between individual and society. Based on these analogies, Elias shows that society is more than a mere agglomeration of individuals and "it is necessary to give up thinking in terms of isolated, single substances and start thinking in terms of relationships and functions" (Elias, 2001, p. 19).

Thus, starting from the premise that it would be a mistake to accept unquestioningly the antithetical nature of the concepts individual and society, Elias began to investigate the origin of these concepts. The terms individual and social can be found in all European languages and have a common origin in medieval societies (Elias, 2001, p. 153). However, they are not always part of the vocabulary of Western society, and there are times in history when the notions of individual and social do not exist or do not make sense.

Therefore, the concept of individual is recent, having been constructed through a process in which the "I-identity" and the "we-identity" (Elias, 2001, p. 193) merge and differentiate in a socio-historical and evolutionary continuum from primitive to modern societies. It conveys the idea of them being ontologically different. In more primitive societies, the sense of we-identity is more pronounced, and life and work in community, traditions, and religious pantheism lead to a life centred on collectivity. A sense of I-identity is of little importance, but the community's survival is vital. The human self and the world, concepts once grounded on religion and hierarchical power, give rise to modernity, to secularized conceptions, and to new forms of autonomous and individual self-consciousness, which also relate to the emergence of modern individualism and the increasing individualization in the social process (Elias, 2001, p. 110). These transformations derive from a growing commercialization, the emergence of nation-states, and the rise of aristocratic and urban classes in modern societies, in which the division of functions and the monopoly of goods and social values eventually established, producing a major change in the economic and psychological character of human behaviour and favouring a process of individualization (Elias, 2001, p. 67). In this way, Elias (1939) can state that the individual formation of each person depends intrinsically on the historical modifications to social patterns and human relations structures. For him, individualization is contingent on the civilizing process. Seen from this point of view, advances in the process of individualization during the Renaissance are not the result of isolated changes, but social events deriving from a profound transformation in society, instigated by the breaking up of old hierarchical groups and by changes in these groups' position and social stratum. In sum, it results from a specific restructuring in human relations. Thus, the concept of individual is gradually constructed:

> … our image of man emerges late in the history of mankind, at first slowly and for a relatively short period in limited circles in ancient society, and then in the so-called Renaissance in occidental societies.
>
> (Elias, 2001, p. 92)

Thus, what today resembles a universally valid concept can be seen as something that has been instituted through a relatively recent historical process. The image that humans have of themselves as individuals should not be presumed, but considered as the result of specific transformations that, according to Elias (2001), affect the three basic coordinates of human life: the development and positioning of the individual within the social structure, the social structure itself, and the relation of social human beings to the events of the nonhuman world (Elias, 2001, p. 95).

The relationship between the I-identity and we-identity, to which Elias (2001) refers as the we–I balance, has never been decisively established in the course of history and is subject to specific transformations. Today, the primary function of the word individual conveys the idea that every human being is an autonomous entity, different from others. Therefore, it is typical of the structure of Western societies that differences between people, their I-identity, are more valued than what they have in common, their we-identity. In the simplest societies, the very opposite occurs, for the we-identity outweighs the I-identity. The ancient Roman republic is a classic example of a historical moment when a sense of belonging to the family, the tribe, and the state, that is, the we-identity of each individual person, was much more important than it is today in the we–I balance. Thus, the we-identity is virtually inseparable from the image of the individual person. The idea of an individual without a group, of a person devoid of reference to a sense of "we" would have made very little sense at that time (Elias, 2001, p. 154), since there was no need for a universal concept concerning the isolated person as a "quasi-group" entity or for a word in ancient languages to designate the equivalent of the concept of the individual.

The social and psychic transformations of relatively small groups – which acted in a short-sighted manner, with simple needs and uncertain satisfaction – would, in larger groups, with clearer and more specialized divisions of functions and more diversified necessities, trigger significant modifications in the we-I balance. Throughout this process, an increasing number of people begin to live within the framework of a growing mutual dependence (interdependence) and develop progressively specialized tasks, while individuals gradually differentiate from each other.

These changes culminate in the individualization of human beings in the process of social interaction and produce psychological transformations in people's interrelationships. Individualization also leads to transformations within each individual, resulting in the development of self-consciousness, containment of impulses, and postponement of needs, all described by Elias in *The Civilizing Process* (1939). However, the process of individualization and the increasing control of natural forces by human beings was possible only within an organized context and a social structure, that is, they are facilitated by new and more complex interdependencies, typical of industrialized societies that allow "a growing process of self-control of affections and short-term instincts throughout the civilizing process" (Neiburg & Waizbort, 2006, p. 225; translation mine). Thus, the civilizing process follows a given direction in which self-control begins to play an increasingly important role in the building of a civilized world, to the detriment of external coercive forces. The establishment of social patterns of behaviour through a growing internalization of habits and containment of impulses determines the psychological changes necessary to create a different social structure. It is the result of an intimate connection between social structure and the economy of affection, that is, an inter-relationship between social dynamics and psychological dynamics in the civilizing process (Elias, 1939).

Some members of the scientific community criticized the theory of the civilizing process and the idea of social process and, based on a misunderstanding, insisted on their reputed evolutionism or on the normative and teleological character of Eliasian sociology (Neiburg & Waizbort, 2006). This resistance was founded on the "difficulty in understanding the temporal dimension of social figurations, too quickly identifying 'transformation' and 'genesis' with 'evolution'" (Neiburg & Waizbort, 2006, p. 12; translation mine). Indeed, the theory of the civilizing process describes the sociogenetic and psychogenetic research on the process of civilization in a clear and interdependent way that allows the analysis of different dimensions of the same socio-historical phenomenon (Garrigou & Lacroix, 1997). We will not go further into considerations about the intrinsic relationships between the civilizing process and the individual-society relationship. Yet, it is important to point out that the idea of an evolutionary, but not linear process is central to Elias's analysis of the individual and the society (Mennell, 1997). In this sense, Mennell postulates that we cannot state that civilization evolves in a given or planned direction in a teleological sense since issues concerning the direction that society can take relate to the unpredictable processes that form the unexpected by-product of inter-weaving projects and intentions of a multitude of agents who act according to a specific dynamics (Mennell, 1997, p. 222). From this standpoint, Elias (2001) postulates that the relationship between individual and society is in constant transformation. This reflects changes occurring throughout the civilizing process in both the way societies are understood and the way the different people who form these societies understood themselves. In other words, how they related to their self-image and to the social composition of individuals – their *habitus* (Elias, 2001, p. 185).

The concept of *habitus* for Elias arises for the first time in *The Civilizing Process* (1939) before Pierre Bourdieu (1986) popularized it. It comes about to designate the relationship between the social dynamics and the structure of the personality, characterized by a "second nature" or an "embodied social knowledge" (Dunning & Mennell, 1996, p. ix). Elias uses the concept in *The Germans* (1989) as well, to investigate German social development, distancing the analysis from the notion of a national character to show how the destiny of the German nation was entangled in the *habitus* of its individual members (Dunning & Mennell, 1996).

The *habitus* emphasizes the individual's dependence on the learned and distinctive behaviours of a particular group; however, it is not related to the individual's free choice. Thus, the *habitus* encompasses a range of behaviours, from the individualized to those shared by members of the same group, who, for Elias, can be the members of the same we-identity or of a specific national identity (Elias, 2001). In Elias's work, the concept of *habitus* helps circumvent the dichotomies between individual and society, revealing that the emotions and dispositions experienced at the individual level are closely related to collective processes of unconscious embodiment of social patterns and behaviours (Heinich, 2002, p. 100). Elias believed that the social *habitus* of an individual prepares the terrain for personal and individual differences to flourish, so that the individuality of a person represents, in a sense, a personal elaboration of a common social *habitus* (Elias, 2001).

Scholars suggest that Bourdieu's and Elias's considerations about the *habitus* emphasized the importance of taken-for-granted ways of perceiving, thinking, acting and reacting to the social world that is shared, sometimes unconsciously, by the individuals of the same group/society (Elias, 1939). It means the concept of *habitus* enables the bridging of social theory with the psychological and psycho-analytical tenets that explain the interdependencies between individuals and society by illuminating how reality is, co-created by them, as postulated in group analysis. The notion of *habitus* is also connected to group analytic discussions on the concept of the social unconscious in persons, groups, and foundation matrices (Hopper & Weinberg, 2011, 2016, 2017).

The concept of figuration

Elias (2001) creates the concept of figuration as a counterpoint to the notion of *Homo clausus*, an expression that, for him, translates the stage of the social sciences at the turn of the twentieth century. The concept of figuration arises with the need for eliminating the duality between subject and object and asserting the impossibility of prioritizing the individual over the social, or vice versa. Figurations are defined as "a structure of mutually orientated and dependent people ... the network of interdependencies formed by individuals" (Elias, 1939, p. 482). Figuration dynamics transformed the investigation of dualistic oppositions, shifting the once restricted debates on issues of the individual to an established dynamics of social groups in different interwoven fields (Elias, 2001, p. 189).

In works such as *The Court Society* (1983) and *The Society of Individuals* (2001), Elias deals with the notion of interdependencies. In *The Court Society*, interdependence is associated with the organization of the French court during the Old Regime and, in the third essay of *The Society of Individuals*, it is associated with the Cold War. The sociological understanding of interdependencies is still in its initial stage because the paradigm of the Western intellectual tradition is based on the dualism subject/object, cause/effect. In this sense, the ontological dualism, the representation of a world divided into subjects and objects, gives the impression that subjects can exist without objects. Therefore, the idea is to change radically the model of representation of the social world – or sociological paradigm – by replacing the linear causality that links separated substances with the circularity of the "interdependence of functions" (Heinich, 2002, p. 90).

In *What is Sociology?* the idea "develops both as a continuation of earlier theories and yet as a critical departure from them" (Elias, 1984, p. 182), revealing Elias's conception of what would be a sociology that criticizes the polarities traditionally involved in the relationship between individual and society. As an alternative approach, he builds the theory of figurations and the model of interdependent relations between individuals, replacing the egocentric relationship of the individual with society and reorienting it towards the understanding of the concept of society through the model of representation of interdependent individuals and the theory of figurations (Elias, 1984, pp. 13–14). Elias thus promotes new forms of thought that avoid the individual's egocentricity and the tendency to anthropomorphize concepts and embraces a perception of the interconnections and figurations found in relationships between people (Elias, 1984, p. 28).

In Elias's work, interrelationships and interdependencies refer to the idea that society is a network of relationships, a relational whole in which the social is conceived as a system of relations between interdependent groups and individuals. Figurations enable this reflection to move beyond a sociological monism that dichotomizes individual and society and starts to value the connections between changes in social structure and the psychic constitution of individuals.

Using metaphors to describe the relationship between individual and society, based on Elias's work, Dalal proposes that individuals are connected to each other by a series of "elastic bands" (Dalal, 1998, p. 87). It means the individuals' activities and their thoughts are determined by the group. Reflections on interdependencies refer to power relations:

The notion of figuration strikes a fatal blow against the existentialist and humanistic idea that we are free to choose – free to choose our destiny once we have purged the ideas of others out of our heads.

(Dalal, 1998, p. 90)

What Elias proposes in the concept of figuration and in the network of inter-dependencies is not to emphasize social structure constraints as if they existed as an objective reality, above and beyond the individuals who produce them. Elias avoids reducing society to the notion of individuals or considering them as mere "puppets" of the social process. On the contrary, he seeks to demonstrate that social forces are exercised by people over one another and over themselves, which can only happen through power relations. Thus, thinking in figurational terms would be to complexify the models of domination and power relations that exist in society to the point that power can no longer be conceived as a unidirectional action that comes from outside (Dalal, 1998). Within a figura-tion, a balance of forces determines the behaviour of its components. Elias's ideas point effectively to the sociogenesis of social groups, attentive to the relations of tension and power established between and within groups. His ideas try to examine in the social field the fundamental structures that shape events with a specific orientation and morphology.

Relationships of interdependence bind individuals and constitute social groups. They can be represented by the model of the game (Garrigou & Lacroix, 1997). A game is a particular figuration in which individuals are united by interdependencies that give meaning to their actions. In a game, forces interact and each part plays a role related to the others. One can never play alone because playing is always "playing with" (Elias, 1984, p. 71). In this sense, in Elias's work, the interdependencies between humans occur as a bal-ance of power, as a game of forces directly linked to the processes of differ-entiation in society. Through an established dynamics among the players of a collective game, such as soccer, chess, or even within a hierarchical society or a nation, a didactic model can be found to analyse different levels of integration in societies (Elias, 1984, p. 90). Thus, the fabric of human relations expressed by the concept of figuration is constituted by a network of interdependent players, ranging from simpler games, such as those found at the level of primary competition (Elias, 1984, p. 76), to the more sophisticated forms (Elias, 1984, p. 101). The idea of figuration as a game permits us to distinguish between polarities that define a system of complex interdependencies, allowing the analysis of social groups in their totality. In other words, figuration is nothing more than a system of interactions, that is, the social structure observed at the individual level (Elias, 1984, p. 161).

It is within the concept of figuration that Elias shows his connection with the sociology from his training years, that is, with Simmelian sociology. Indeed, it is the formal conceptualization of something that, in Simmel's sociology, remains limited to an analytical record, as expressed in *Sociology* (1908). Although Elias, upon formulating the concept of figuration, does not refer to

Simmel's work, both Simmel and Elias belong to the same intellectual tradition. If the former remained undervalued for some decades, the latter received a delayed recognition further on in life. However, the continuity between Simmel's and Elias's thinking allows process sociology to revolutionize the conceptual language of the social sciences by offering a new dimension to the relationship between individual and society (Neiburg and Waizbort, 2006).

Approximations between Simmel and Elias

Elias's conceptualization of the social is very similar to that of Simmel. For both authors, the social is a set of relations. Waizbort (2001) defends the thesis that the founding and fundamental elements of Elias's sociology derive from Simmel's work. In this case, for both Simmel and Elias, the whole – be it a society, a group, or a community – is a relational whole constituted by the set of relations established between the elements that compose it. Therefore, the primary outcome of these two authors' sociological ideas concerns the relationship between individual and society. From this perspective, individual and society do not exist as separate or autonomous entities, that is, individuals produce society and society produces individuals.

For Simmel, the unity, the whole, consists of interactions between parts in mutual relations that extend infinitely in a process, like a fabric continuously woven. Simmel's world is, therefore, a world of relationships. He analyses forms of sociation, not of society, emphasizing the idea of process and continuity. Simmelian sociology is thus a process sociology that postulates a dynamic and relational conception of society as a form of sociation. Norbert Elias's sociology follows the same path. Thus, when Elias refers to the entanglements that co-create society through the concept of figuration, he is actually referring to Simmel's forms of sociation. In this sense, Eliasian formulations are in close continuity with the thought of Simmel. Both authors believe that interdependencies (Elias) and interrelationships (Simmel) are in a continuous movement (Waizbort, 2001).

Simmel tries to understand the genesis of human interactions and relational concepts calling into question modern conceptions of unity, whereas Elias works on relations between unity and multiplicity. This is transposed to the view of the individual and society by the concept of figuration. Thus, the idea of interaction eventually takes on a fundamental role in the relations between individual and society (Waizbort, 2001).

For Simmel (1908), the idea of game emerges as a form of sociation in the context of sociability (games of society), that is, in relations of domination and subordination and in flirtation and conflict. For Elias (1984), the game is used as a model by which the interdependence and bonding that connect individuals are performed. Therefore, the game would serve as a tool to think through the relationships between social groups, understood as sets of relationships of interdependencies. We find many similarities between Simmel and Elias in the use of the idea of game to express interrelationships between individuals and society. However, Elias (1984) went further when he stated that games reveal society's power relations. In Simmel's *Sociology* (1908), this idea, although not fully explained, may be intuited from his theory.

It seems that the further we go into Simmelian and Eliasian sociology, the more we learn about the points they have in common. For both, sociology is based on the relation between social groups and concerns relations of tension and power established inter- and intra-groups (Waizbort, 2001, p. 109). Their importance, among innumerable other contributions to the field of sociology, is to strike a deadly blow to individualism and to dichotomies from the modern era.

Towards a society of persons

Dumont (1986) examines the importance of individualism in the construction of modern ideology. He draws attention to the fact that premodern societies organize around a collectivity, but, in modernity, they represent a society of individuals. To define how this change affects political philosophy in Hobbes, Rousseau, and in the Declaration of the Rights of Man and of the Citizen (1789), or even the construction of a nascent sociology in the nineteenth century, is a relevant task in the investigation of the intellectual history of modern ideology. However, we have to emphasize, in this specific figuration, how the process sociology for Simmel and Elias offers a counterpoint to modern social theories, understanding humans as social, relational, and interdependent beings and the forms of sociation and figurations as elements leading to "the synthesis of society" (Simmel, 1908, p. 284; Elias, 1939). In effect, it is a matter of calling attention to conceptual differences and theoretical and methodological contributions, which point on a *continuum* to paradigms different from those adopted by traditional sociology or classical psychology/psychoanalysis, both influenced by the modern ideology of individualism.

In this sense, the problem is to find or rediscover the ideas that favour the emergence of epistemologies that, from the outset, prioritize the interdependence between individual and society. Group analytic theory has prioritized thinking in terms of interdependencies and matrices (Foulkes, 1964, 1975a). Moreover, Elias's influence on the creation of group analysis was vital. Elias (1939) uncovers and links the social experiences of groups by studying the fundamental economic, symbolic, political, and psychological dimensions of the development of group analysis. However, Simmel's importance in the same field and the relevance of the forms of sociation processes, as well as Simmel's influence on the thought of Elias are not well known. The study of forms of sociation – especially Simmel's essays on the quantitative aspects of the group (Simmel, 1908, p. 87), the secret society (Simmel, 1908, p. 307), the conflict (Simmel, 1908, p. 61), and the stranger (Simmel, 1908, p. 402) – contains significant reflections, still unexplored by group analytic theory.

In psychoanalysis, on the other hand, epistemological, genealogical, and paradigmatic questions have been discussed over several decades. Any opposition to the dominant paradigm has long been regarded as heresy in the face of "true psychoanalysis" (Birman, 2013). One of its consequences is the traumatic repression, condemnation, rejection of not only original ideas of authors such as Burrow, Ferenczi, Adler, and Jung, but also of styles of psychoanalytic training in the interest of standardized and internationalized patterns (Birman, 2013). At stake in this approach is what Freud used to refer to as the narcissism of small differences.

Indeed, *fin-de-siècle Zeitgeist* in Vienna, Cartesian dualism, romanticism, and individualism influenced the construction of the theoretical framework of Freudian psychoanalysis. Yet, a closer reading of his writings, especially the texts on culture, allows us to glimpse a Freud more open to the future of psychoanalysis, concerned with the investigation and understanding of the cultural community and its pathologies and illusions (Freud, 1927, 1930a). In Freud's works, this perspective may broaden the use of psychoanalysis and expand the interconnections between individuals and culture, although such possibilities, already in place since the beginning of psychoanalysis, have been obscured by decades of idealization (Eizirik, 2001) and by power relations in the psychoanalytic establishment.

Nevertheless, it seems impossible to advance contemporary research on sociology, psychoanalysis, and social psychology without renewed efforts in the theoretical construction of a bridge between individual-society relations. In this sense, a paradigm shift is fundamental, such as the one carried out by contemporary psychoanalysis and especially by group analysis (Foulkes, 1948, 1964, 1975a; Pines, 2009; Hopper, 2003b; Tubert-Oklander, 2014). This shift eliminates the emphasis on individual/individualism and on dichotomies between individual and society, giving value precisely to forms of sociation, figurations, and interdependencies between interrelated persons. In this direction, Hopper (2003a, 2003b) stresses the importance of moving from the notion of individual to the notion of person, stating that individuals are in interaction, but persons are in relationships with one another from conception to death. Indeed, persons are born into relationships, families, and groups that shape their personalities, which, in turn, shape their groupings:

> In the beginning there is no such thing as an infant, but only an infant in relationship with its mother (Winnicott, 1952); there is no such thing as an "individual", but only an individual within a society (Dalal, 1998); there is no such thing as a "first" human being, but only a person born into a breeding group.
>
> (Hopper & Weinberg, 2011, p. xxxi)

Working with categories such as individuals, persons, or subjects reveals different frames of reference, paradigmatic options, and even ideological assumptions. Therefore, the notion of person is not usual in classical psychoanalysis and may even sound strange for some group analysts. Marcel Mauss investigated it in 1938, stressing that the idea of the "I" is recent in philosophy and exploring the different development stages of the idea of a person. Mauss tried to show how, from a primitive background of indistinction, the notion of person we know and to which we erroneously attribute a universal existence, slowly moves away from its social roots to constitute a legal, moral and even logical category.

(Goldman, 1999 *apud* Spink, 2011, p. 4; translation mine)

Moreover, in *Aspects of Sociology* (Frankfurt Institute for Social Research, 1956), the Frankfurtians criticize the concept of the individual and introduce a discussion on the notion of person. They focus on the idea of the individual as a social unity, pointing to the importance of communication and relationship for human beings. The definition of human beings as persons is supported by the development of the idea of *persona* from the Roman theatre to the Protestant Reformation. However, in our discussion, we must underline the fact that the definition of human beings as persons involves roles within a range of social relations. It means that a human being in relation to their peers is always the "child of a mother, student of a teacher, member of a tribe or of a profession" (Frankfurt Institute for Social Research, 1956, p. 41). Therefore, it is impossible to find a

pure individual in his ineffable singularity, but rather at a wholly abstract point of reference. And even this itself could only be understood in the context of society … Even the biographical individual is a social category.

(Frankfurt Institute for Social Research, 1956, p. 42)

Thus, human beings can define themselves only in their relationships with other persons, and their lives acquire meaning in specific social conditions, within a context in which the social nature of humankind, the Aristotelian *zoon politikon*, can be valued and fostered.

In sum, unlike the concept of the individual, the idea of person contributes to the social sciences and to group analysis, as well as to studies on psychoanalysis and culture, enabling the development of intersubjective and transsubjective perspectives. It encourages independent thinking, free from the shackles of modernity and involving a broader and deeper understanding of interdependencies and figurations between persons, groups, and societies. Thus, in the next chapters, within a renewed framework, this reflection may find more contemporary dimensions to evolve.

5 The Northfield experiments

The cradle of group work in England

With the purpose of understanding the development of group work in England, it is necessary not only to explore the history of the two Northfield experiments carried out at the British Army's Northfield Hospital in Birmingham from 1942 to 1946 by some military psychiatrists (Harrison, 2000) but also to identify the sometimes unacknowledged theoretical influences that lie at their roots and contributed to their success.

The challenging sociopolitical context of the 1920s and 1930s that culminated in the onset of World War II motivated critical theorists to explore the major problem of their time: the rise of fascism in Europe (Jay, 1973). During the war, the resistance to this threat permeated the professionals' motivations at Northfield, inspiring innovative and creative work. After the war, the problem of the masses and the spectre of totalitarianism continued to pervade the discourse of intellectuals (Arendt, 1948; Canetti, 1960), as Horkheimer and Adorno (1944, p. xiv) have so well summarized: "… why mankind, instead of entering into a truly human condition, is sinking into a new kind of barbarism". This unanswered question has certainly remained entrenched in the social unconscious of European citizens, influencing and "haunting" (Frosh, 2013a) their reflections, discourses, and practices for many years after the war.

The tendencies outlined in the two Northfield experiments point to the emergence of two main different streams of psychoanalytically oriented groups in England. The first is connected to Rickman and Bion's first experiment with groups at Northfield, which led to the postulation of Bion's basic-assumption group theory (Bion, 1961) and to the establishment of the Tavistock Institute of Human Relations in 1946. That first experiment contributed to developing the field of group relations and its application to work with experiential and educational learning on leadership in groups, as well as to the Tavistock approach to organizational consultancy (Armstrong, 2005). The second experiment encompassed the work of Harold Bridger and Tom Main at Northfield, which interconnects to the development of S. H. Foulkes's group analysis. The second experiment motivated the establishment of the Group Analytic Society in 1952 (Foulkes, 1964). The two Northfield experiments with groups, together with Maxwell Jones's work at Mill Hill Hospital in London during the war, also created the opportunity for developing

DOI: 10.4324/9780429399534-6

democratic therapeutic communities in health care (Whiteley, 1975; Pearce & Haigh, 2017; Harrison, 2018).

After the war, Northfield became the cradle of different psychodynamic approaches to group work, such as group analysis, group relations, therapeutic communities, social and cultural psychiatry, socio-analysis, sociotherapy, and art therapy (Hinshelwood, 1999, 2018a). Over the years, the Northfield experiments achieved a legendary status in the field, becoming a turning point for the development of analytically oriented work in groups. They gathered together important pioneers at the Northfield Military Hospital, which "in the midst of war ... represented the triumph of hope and initiative", as well as "the clash of desperate originality with the forces of conservatism" (Hinshelwood, 2000, p. 7).

The Northfield experiments: some early influences

Northfield was the result of an encounter of tendencies in human sciences. It "did not happen in a *vacuum*" (Hinshelwood, 2000, p. 9). In the twentieth century, social psychology research contributed to the pioneers' work at Northfield in the form of the investigations into crowds and herds developed earlier by Le Bon, Trotter, and McDougall (Harrison 2000). However, group treatment acquired importance in wartime, when persons were forced to take on new roles in an artificial group, the Army (Martins, 1986). It had already happened in World War I, in an experiment with war neurotics conducted by Ernst Simmel (Ferenczi et al., 1921), who used a cathartic method to identify and develop knowledge about traumatic neurosis. Before World War I, in practical terms, given that little was known about the subject, physical illness, suicide, alcoholism, and discharges from the Army were invariably related to cowardice and desertion. It was only after the battle of the Somme in 1916 that pathological symptoms such as shell shock started to be associated with psychological issues (Harrison, 2000).

The psychoanalytic community recognized Ernst Simmel's interventions and Freud himself commented favourably on Simmel's work (Freud, 1921). In 1918, Abraham, Freud, Ferenczi, Simmel, and Jones discussed many psychoanalytic observations about war neuroses, later published in *Psycho-Analysis and the War Neuroses* (Ferenczi et al., 1921). Although these texts have unquestionably shown the interference of the social context in the development of neurosis, and Freud (1919a), in his introduction to the book, discussed alterations in war neurotics' subjectivity – though faithful to the sexual etiology of neurosis, their findings did not lead to immediate changes in psychoanalytic theory with regard to the relevance of the social context in psychic illness.

During the first half of the twentieth century, several pioneers contributed to developing the theory and technique of group work, especially from the 1930s, when social psychology gained in importance and the concept of group psychotherapy was in vogue (de Maré, 1972). The psychological theories of the 1920s and 1930s – among them Kurt Lewin's field theories, the *Gestalt* psychology, and works with groups by Burrow (Pertegato & Pertegato, 2013),

Slavson, Schilder, Moreno, and the English Joshua Bierer – influenced the Northfield experiments (Pines, 1999). Studies on social psychiatry, especially Peckham's and Hawkspur's experiments, as well as the works with delinquents Aichhorn conducted in Vienna after World War I, were the first examples of attempts to consider patients' well-being within institutions. In addition, at the Psychopathic Clinic, later the Portman Clinic, Edward Glover and Dennis Carrol – who became Commanding Officer at Northfield – had conducted pioneering psychoanalytic work with delinquents and criminals. Bion worked as a staff member in this Clinic before the war (Pines, 2003). Both Tavistock Clinic members, as of the 1930s, and the British Psychoanalytic Society were aware of such initiatives (Harrison, 2000, p. 69). Moreover, the evolution in the understanding of traumatic neurosis in World War I and psychoanalysis itself – through Freud's seminal influence and Melanie Klein and Fairbairn's object relations theory (Harrison, 2000), all organized in the theoretical body assimilated by analytically oriented psychiatry – flourished in the live and self-reflexive experience that was Northfield.

However, in some of these early works with groups, the sociocultural context still played a secondary role or remained obscure when compared to the problem of the individual in the group. In this sense, traditional sociological interpretations and the dichotomies typical of modernity discussed in Chapter Four marked those first incursions, opposing individual and society. Therefore, the conceptual differences perceived in group approaches may be related to the different values they confer to the individual and the group. Describing substantial differences of focus in a simple way, de Maré shows that these first-phase experiments valued the analysis *in the* group – such as those carried out in the 1930s by Wender, Schilder, Slavson, Wolf, and Schwartz, whose technique and treatment focused on the individual in the group, instead of focusing on the group *per se* (de Maré (1972, p. 70) .

The social field theory developed in Berlin from the 1920s with Kurt Lewin. In the 1930s and 1940s, using principles from the social sciences and the *Gestalttheorie* to understand social psychology, Lewin (1947), already established in the US, used experimental groups (T-groups) in his laboratory in Bethesda, Maryland. He brought about an important change of perspective on group work, advancing the central hypothesis that the group is a whole whose properties are different from the sum of its parts. Lewin's hypothesis has been fundamental to building a theoretical framework for group practices since World War II. For him, "Field does not mean an interaction between individuals in a group. It means a background out of which something emerges as a figure in the foreground" (Hinshelwood, 2018b, p. 1410). In this sense, "the field is the whole social entity, described as a system of forces acting in an interpersonal space to move each individual into specific social roles and psychological states" (Lewin, 1947 *apud* Hinshelwood, 1999, p. 472). Therefore, the social field theory added the importance of context to individual dynamics in relations between foreground and background, which operate as a single unity.

The idea of group-as-a-whole exerted a remarkable influence on the Northfield experiments, but part of these different approaches can be observed in the way each pioneer absorbed the concepts of the social field. Lewin's influence can already be seen in Rickman's (2003, p. 140) work in the War Office Selection Boards (WOSBs). As for Bion, he became acquainted with Lewin's theories at Northfield and at the Tavistock Clinic, where the social field theory had been known since Eric Trist's trip to the United States in 1934 (Trist & Murray, 1990). Lewin's theory influenced not only Rickman, Bion, and the Tavistock approach to groups, but also Foulkes's work on groups (Hinshelwood, 1999, 2007, 2018b). The notion of group-as-a-whole favoured the idea that, in the group, a social field of forces was in action. Bion transformed this premise into an object of psychoanalytic study after leaving Northfield (Hinshelwood, 1999; Torres, 2003).

On the other hand, Foulkes assimilated group-as-a-whole ideas through the influence of the Gestalt psychology, Adhémar Gelb's "psychological analysis" and the neurology of Kurt Goldstein (Foulkes, 1946). Later, Foulkes adapted these influences, referring to the figure/ground relationship when he postulated the interplay between the individual person and the group as background (Foulkes, 1990, p. 40). Moreover, before the war, Foulkes was already acquainted with Norbert Elias's sociology and the idea of the social nature of persons in a society of persons. However, the argument is getting ahead of itself; firstly, it is necessary to tell the story of the so-called "first experiment", and of Bion's contributions to it.

The Northfield experiments: 1942–1946

In 1939, at the beginning of World War II, only two psychiatrists and six medical officers trained in psychiatry were in active service in the British Army. The techniques used to select officers were based on criteria that valued individual performances and abhorred fear and cowardice, ignoring the importance of trust relationships, *esprit de corps*, and the role the environment plays in boosting the morale of troops (Harrison, 2000, p. 82). Although the Army attempted to avoid them, psychiatric events increased, posing new challenges, since the pathologies found at the beginning of World War II were significantly different from the shakes acquired in the trenches of World War I (Thorner, 1946). Consequently, during the onset of World War II, military psychiatry focused on breakdown prevention and formulated strategies to deal with the selection and rehabilitation of officers (Thorner, 1946). In the Navy and Airforce, psychiatrists of neurological-organicist orientation took the lead; in the Army, Ronald Adam assumed the general command. J. R. Rees, director of the Tavistock Clinic in 1934, was invited as a psychiatric advisor and recruited colleagues of a psychodynamic orientation, such as Ronald Hargreaves, who took over the leadership of psychiatry at the WOSBs in 1942 (Harrison, 2000). The psychiatrists' social therapeutic role at the WOSBs was to foster the development of specially adapted military institutions and to create experiments to deal with the challenges the officials were facing concerning leadership issues. Eric Trist, Wilfred Bion, Eric Wittkower, and John Sutherland were summoned up for the initial experiences in the selection boards (Trist & Murray, 1990, p. 49).

Rickman and Bion: the first experiment

John Rickman was already a seasoned psychoanalyst when he joined the army as a psychiatrist. A Quaker by origin and upbringing, he worked as a physician in a Tsarist Russian village in 1916–17 (Rickman, 1938), which certainly influenced his thinking during his work in the Army during the war. His interest in anthropology and in the interrelationship between psychoanalysis and the social context was evident early in his career. W. R. Rivers was Rickman's mentor and introduced him to psychoanalysis. Rivers also invited Rickman to join the medical section of the British Psychological Society, where he met William McDougall (Harrison, 2000). Rickman played an important role in the psychoanalytic scene in England and was in analysis with Freud in 1920, with Ferenczi in 1928, and with Melanie Klein from 1934 to 1941 (Bléandonu, 1994). He assisted Ernst Jones in the foundation of the Institute of Psychoanalysis in 1924 and in the creation of the London Clinic of Psychoanalysis in 1926. Moreover, he was an active member of the British Psychoanalytic Society, devoted to publishing activities and to public lectures in the 1930s. Just before the war, Rickman (2003) published papers and sometimes anonymous editorials that influenced professional and lay opinions. In 1938, he visited Freud in Vienna and contributed to the immigration efforts of some analysts to London (King, 2003).

When war was declared in 1939, Rickman joined the Emergency Medical Service (EMS) as a civilian psychiatrist at Haymeads Hospital and was later transferred to Wharncliffe Hospital, where he worked with Bion in 1941. By 1942, Rickman had joined the psychiatric team at the WOSBs (King, 2003). He seemed to be aware of everything that happened in the Army and played a fundamental role in the selection and rehabilitation of officers and in the theoretical-clinical orientation and inspiration of works carried out by his younger colleagues. Such was his prestige at that time that it seemed that nothing happened in the Army without his knowing (Main, 1983; Harrison, 2000). In this sense, his contribution to psychoanalysis and to the social field was seminal both during and after the war.

Bion, though younger than Rickman, had acquired valuable military experience as a tank commander and was awarded both the Distinguished Service Order (DSO) and the Croix de Chevalier of the Légion d'Honneur in World War I (Pines, 1999). He was born in India, but educated in England from the age of eight. Bion studied history in Oxford and later medicine, becoming house surgeon to Wilfred Trotter at the University College Hospital in 1930 (Bléandonu, 1994). Trotter's ideas exerted a remarkable influence on Bion's thinking, especially on his views about social groups. In Northfield, Trotter's ideas inspired Bion, who borrowed the concepts of gregariousness and man as a herd animal to shape his further work on groups (Torres, 2003, p. 89).

Bion had been a member of the Tavistock Clinic since 1932 and for seven years was under psychotherapeutic training with Hadfield. Under his influence, Bion moved to psychoanalysis, becoming Rickman's patient in 1937–39 (Bléandonu, 1994). Their encounter was transformative.

Bion was one of the first Tavistock physicians to join the Army. He began his military activities as a psychiatrist in the role of Command Psychiatrist at Chester Hospital in 1940. Bion's self-assertiveness and physical posture, allied with his military experience – which made him seem more a general than a psychiatrist in uniform (Trist, 1985) – and his aptitude for what, years later, he would call binocular vision, allowed him to be an innovator from the beginning of his career. In his interventions in the Army, we can see his constant search for truth (Hinshelwood, 2003).

In 1940, in Emergency Medical Services such as Mill Hill – where Maxwell Jones was starting his work with what would become known as therapeutic community (Pines, 1999; Pearce & Haigh, 2017) – and Wharncliffe Hospital, there was an interest in investigating how the social context could be used to assist in the treatment of soldiers (Trist, 1985, King, 2003). Rickman and Bion were working there and their experience spread and passed on to other Neurosis Centres under the EMS. At the time, they prepared a document known as the Wharncliffe Memorandum, which contained the project of a therapeutic community, aiming at using systematically the events and relationships produced in the hospital during their patients' treatment (Bléandonu, 1994; Trist, 1985). The potential use of Lewin's field theory and the influence of the "social field" on the individual as applied to the wider environment was evident in the proposal (King, 2003). The fate of this memorandum is unknown, but the ideas in it were essential for the Northfield experiments and transformed the hospital into the first therapeutic community of psychoanalytic orientation in England (Main, 1983; Bridger, 1990; Harrison, 2000).

Bion worked with Rickman at Wharncliffe Hospital, but Rees transferred him, justly disappointed, to York as a mere sector psychiatrist (Trist, 1985; Bléandonu, 1994). However, in 1942, Bion was assigned to the psychiatric team that implemented the WOSB no. 1 in Edinburgh. Among several other initiatives at the WOSBs, Bion (1961) conceived the leaderless group method, in which a group is left to its own initiative to cope with a situation. In leaderless groups, formal situations are removed and leadership patterns are left to emerge through a series of group situations, beginning with the least structured and proceeding to more structured events, in the here-and-now. Mutual introductions, free group discussion, as well as the creation of group tasks and intergroup games in spontaneous situations complete the proposed methodology (Trist & Murray, 1990). Leaderless groups unified and changed the selection of officers at the WOSBs, transforming team interaction during warfare, re-empowering the Army's trust on its own ability to recruit and train war officers (Trist, 1985).

In June 1942, the British Army appointed Rickman as major in charge of training officers and psychiatrists at Northfield (King, 2003). Following his recommendations, the hospital was divided into the rehabilitation wing and the training wing. Bion arrived at the end of 1942 and was assigned to work in the training wing, which was housing between one and two hundred patients. He yearned to put into practice, together with Rickman, the ideas of the Wharncliffe Memorandum. For this purpose, they had to transform the hospital into a new type of organization, in an integrated therapeutic community where neurotic disorders could be treated, allowing soldiers to regain abilities and morale (Whiteley, 1975; Harrison, 2000). Influenced by Lewin's ideas (Hinshelwood, 2018b, p. 1416), they aimed at studying intragroup tensions in real-life situations where patients could lay bare their neurotic behaviours and learn to face the enemy as a group, instead of using illness to run away from the enemy as individuals (Trist, 1985).

When Bion started working at the training wing, he found it dirty and disorganized, crowded with undisciplined and apathetic soldiers (Main, 1983), and identified the "enemy": neurosis. It was necessary to control it, because morale needed to be high in a regiment so that the true enemy could be fought. During six weeks, Bion and Rickman gathered patients using the leaderless group method developed at the WOSBs. One month later, the atmosphere of the training wing changed and became "self-critical" (Bion, 1961, p. 18). The group was interacting in a more constructive and integrated way, discharges dropped, and the soldiers' relocation in their units proceeded. The wing had finally acquired an *esprit de corps*: the soldiers' skills in interaction situations could be identified in the group-as-a-whole, which was essential for the war effort.

However, that was not the Army's opinion, and the experiment was terminated prematurely without explanation. Bion and Rickman were dismissed from Northfield (de Maré, 1985; Main, 1983). They were aware that their project would reintegrate patients into active service through group spirit and consciousness of their role in the Army. Both were used to working independently, ignoring the hospital organization and the bureaucracy of military administration (Bridger, 1990). Nevertheless, their activities seemed to be "subversive" (Rustin & Armstrong, 2019, p. 475) and the radical nature of the view they imprinted on the training wing eventually led to a clash of cultures with military authorities (Hinshelwood, 1999).

In the next chapter, we will explore the legacies of the first Northfield experiment, focusing on the early years of the Tavistock Institute of Human Relations and on the creation of Group Relations Conferences, aiming at highlighting the importance of Bion's theories on basic-assumption group and work group to group relations. However, first, we discuss the second Northfield experiment.

Bridger, Main, and Foulkes: the second experiment

Foulkes's early influences: paths for an epistemological turn

When S. H. Foulkes arrived at Northfield in March 1943, six weeks after Rickman and Bion left the hospital, he was a senior psychiatrist and qualified psychoanalyst. Since 1939, Foulkes had accumulated experience with therapeutic groups in Exeter. In 1944, he handed to his colleagues at the hospital an informal memorandum about the Goldstein holistic approach in neurology (Hinshelwood, 2007). He also published his first article, together with Eve Lewis, describing the early experiences with groups and introducing group analytic principles (Foulkes & Lewis, 1944).

At the beginning of his career in Germany, Foulkes was in contact with Gelb's and Goldstein's work and, already working as a psychoanalyst, with the Freudo-Marxist movement and the research carried out at the Frankfurt School. He was also influenced by what he named as "sociological analysis", or socioanalysis, through Karl Mannheim's and Norbert Elias's sociology (Foulkes, 1946). In a careful reading of Foulkes's first book, *Introduction to Group-Analytic Psychotherapy* (1948), we can identify, between the lines of group analytic theoretical and clinical principles, "the result of many years working and thinking" (Foulkes *apud* Nitzgen, 2008, p. 326) and the influence of the German intellectual tradition of the 1920s and 1930s. However, until today, it has not been easy to determine the impact that these influences exerted on his thinking. It would require an archaeological investigation of his psychoanalytical journey – especially the articles published in Germany (Foulkes, 1990) – and of his personal and professional affinities before he left for England (Nitzgen, 2008, 2014). Moreover, "for English speaking readers Foulkes' works from the 1930s are somewhat lost in translation" (Nitzgen, 2014, p. 218). It means that much of his thinking before his move to England remains unknown or unexplored by non-German readers (Nitzgen, 2014).

In the 1920s, Foulkes began his training as a psychoanalyst in Vienna and, during his formative years (1924–1926), working in Frankfurt as an assistant of Kurt Goldstein (1926–1928), he was influenced by Goldstein's holistic approach and by the ideas of his nephew, Ernst Cassirer (Nitzgen, 2011). At that time, Goldstein was investigating neuron networks in the brain and claimed that the central nervous system always reacts as a whole. It means, "disorders of the brain could not be 'localized' in local lesions, but were to be considered as dysfunctions of the nervous system as a whole" (Nitzgen, 2011, p. 6).

In 1936, Foulkes published a review of Goldstein's 1934 book, *The Organism*, summing up Goldstein's neurology and his own psychoanalytical views (Foulkes, 1990, p. 40). Those findings allowed Foulkes "to transfer Goldstein's original insights to the social field and to apply them to socio-psychological phenomena" (Nitzgen, 2011, p. 7) in Northfield. Foulkes (1948, p. 1) was thus led to value the whole organism in a total situation, widening this approach to encompass the individual as a whole in a total situation and the society as a network. From this new epistemological perspective, Foulkes was able to build his group analytic theory and state that the origins of psychic difficulties are not restricted to the individual psyche; they belong to a network of interactions – the group matrix (Nitzgen, 2011).

Foulkes was also influenced by Freudo-Marxists, especially Bernfeld, Fenichel and Homburguer-Erikson (Nitzgen, 2011, p. 9). Freudo-Marxist research has shifted the emphasis psychoanalysis once placed on individual neurosis to the role of the sociocultural dimension on shaping psychic illness. Nitzgen (2011) underlines Foulkes's connection with the Freudo-Marxists, especially with Bernfeld, stressing the importance he attributed to the "social location for the understanding of neurosis, deprivation and education" (Nitzgen, 2011, p. 9). Moreover, as Nitzgen (2011, p. 9) says, the "original German expression *der soziale Ort* can equally well be translated into English as the social *situation* or the social *location*". In group analytic theory, a social situation refers to the idea of total situation, which, for Foulkes (1946), was a benchmark in the synthesis he made of Gestalt ideas, Goldstein's views, psychoanalysis, and sociological analysis. From this standpoint, Foulkes was able to see individuals as nodal points "at the intersections of communications" (Hinshelwood, 2007, p. 347).

Homburguer-Erickson also contributed to building Foulkes's approach, when he discusses the "basic nature of social influences" such as family history in connection to the psychoanalytic theory, enabling Foulkes (1948, p. 12) to state, just after he left Northfield, that "the goal of the psychoanalytic treatment is identical with that of Group Analysis". Fenichel, too, has exerted some influence on Foulkes, for his work at the Berlin Institute used to value a model of psychoanalysis in connection to social factors (Nitzgen, 2011).

In 1930, Foulkes moved back to Frankfurt and joined the Frankfurt Psychoanalytic Institute, founded by Karl Landauer and Heinrich Meng. Erich Fromm and his wife Frieda Fromm-Reichmann had also joined the group (Foulkes, 1990, p. 10). Foulkes was responsible for the outpatient department of the Institute for Psychoanalysis and was involved in lectures, courses, and seminars. Though not a member of the Institute for Social Research, Foulkes was geographically and intellectually close to the cooperation between the Institute for Psychoanalysis and the Institute for Social Research (Rothe, 1989). This intellectual atmosphere influenced Foulkes's thinking, as we can infer from Horkheimer's, Fromm's and others' "Studies on Authority and Family" (1936) as well as from Fromm's (1941) studies on character formation. Their contributions are also connected to the study of the social unconscious that we will explore in Chapter Eight.

In Frankfurt, Foulkes was in contact with the sociological work of Karl Mannheim and his assistant Norbert Elias, as well as with the work of the Frankfurtian Franz Borkenau (Nitzgen, 2014). Mannheim and Foulkes had been contemporaneous at Frankfurt University. Moreover, the Sociology Department led by Mannheim in Frankfurt was close to the Institute for Psychoanalysis and to the Institute for Social Research (Winship, 2003). Foulkes and Mannheim's association conferred importance to psychological and socio-historical factors in the understanding of human nature. (Nitzgen, 2011). In this sense, both authors "took the sociological field into the psychoanalytic (group) consulting room" (Winship, 2003, p. 38). Foulkes (1946) attributed to Mannheim the introduction of the term group analysis in 1943, but in a more sociological way (Winship, 2003), even being aware that the American psychoanalyst Trigant Burrow had used this term for the first time in the 1920s

(Pertegato & Pertegato, 2013). In Foulkes words, Burrow "was the first person to put the group into the centre of this thinking, and that was and remains his great merit" (de Maré, 1983, p. 221).

Foulkes was acquainted with Norbert Elias's ideas, and we can surmise that he not only absorbed much of Mannheim's sociology, but also improved his sociological knowledge through Elias's work (Waizbort, 2001). Foulkes's reviews of the two volumes of Elias's *The Civilizing Process* (Foulkes, 1990) show how, before joining the Northfield staff, Foulkes's thinking was already influenced by Elias's ideas about *habitus* and interdependencies among the phylogenetic, psychogenetic and sociogenetic aspects of human life. From Elias's work, Foulkes (1948, pp. 13–14) apprehended that the individual depends on the social restrictions of their surrounding world, as well as on the conditions and claims of the community, the group in which they live. These constraints are transmitted by parents or parental figures. The individual is completely permeated by them: "He is part of a social network, a little nodal point, as it were, in this network, and can only artificially be considered in isolation, like a fish out of water" (Foulkes, 1948, p. 14). In this sense, as Nitzgen (2014, p. 221) summarizes, "the gist of what Foulkes gained from the sociologists (Borkenau, Elias and Mannheim) is the basic conviction that '*the group is a more fundamental unit than the individual*'" (Foulkes & Anthony, 1984, p. 23, italics mine).

Thus, a combination of Gestalt psychology and Goldstein's holistic approach with the Freudo-Marxist "psychoanalysis in context" and Foulkes's insights into the Freudian theory (Nitzgen, 2008), in association with the ideas of Foulkes's "sociological friends" (Foulkes, 1990, p. 79), provided the seeds to an epistemological change introduced by group analysis. The second Northfield experiment was the soil on which a new Foulkesian perspective could germinate, gaining weight and fostering further developments in the decades to come. Foulkes's work in Northfield contributed to revealing how the social nature of persons allowed individual and group-as-a-whole perspectives to be approached as totally intertwined, forming a single and integrated whole.

The second Northfield experiment: a new ethos

From 1944 to 1946, the second experiment with groups at Northfield brought together Harold Bridger, Tom Main and S. H. Foulkes (1948), among others. This second experiment was carried out under more adverse circumstances, because the number of soldiers had increased; they were coming from the second front of the war in Northern France suffering from physical and psychological problems (Harrison, 2000).

In 1944, after Rickman and Bion left Northfield, Hargreaves offered the command of the training wing to Harold Bridger, an educator with experience in the approaches developed at the WOSBs. The first experiment had terminated abruptly, but paved the way for important developments in the second experiment, which eventually attributed to Northfield an *ethos* – not always recognized in the aftermath (Harrison, 2018, p. 448) – that transformed the whole hospital into a therapeutic community (Harrison, 2000, 2018) and fostered the development of group analysis (Foulkes, 1948, 1964, 1975a).

The expression "therapeutic or camp community" was coined by Sullivan in 1939 (Pines, 1999, Harrison, 2000); however, it was from wartime experiences that it generated a "new paradigm" (Bridger, 1990, p. 69) for post-war psychiatry. The therapeutic communities revolutionized patient-doctor-staff relationships and the role of authority in treatment settings by highlighting the "living learning" and democratic experiences in the here-and-now (Whiteley, 1975; Pearce & Haigh, 2017). After the war, these experiences spread out and allowed for the use of group-as-a-whole approaches in different settings in England, such as prisons, schools, churches, addiction centres, hospitals, and communities. In these institutions, they also developed intersubjective and trans-subjective thinking by introducing the importance of the psychosocial and contextual levels in healthcare, emphasizing the figurations established between persons and groups, since "as open systems, therapeutic communities are part of, and interact with, the wider society" (Bridger, 1990, p. 69).

Bridger was influenced by the Peckham Experiments and by the work conducted in emergency hospitals such as Dumfries, in Scotland, and Mill Hill, in which physical, psychotherapeutic, and psychosocial activities were taking place (Bridger, 1990, p. 69). Since 1941, in Mill Hill, Maxwell Jones had been observing that collaboration among soldiers who were suffering in the hospital was more helpful to each of them than all staff efforts (Pearce & Haigh, 2017). With this in mind, Bridger decided to work using the dynamic of the hospital-as-a-whole, stressing the importance of the context and the settings where interactions occur. He adopted what he later called

> the "double-task" approach, with one task located at the level of the hospital as an institution and the other at the level of those parts that showed leadership in developing relevant creative work.
>
> (Bridger, 1990, p. 77)

After the war, Bridger co-founded the Tavistock Institute of Human Relations and trained as a psychoanalyst.

By that time, Tom Main, a psychiatrist and WOSB member, with battlefield medical experience gained during the Western Desert campaign (Main, 1983, p. 203), was posted as Commanding Officer at Northfield, and supported the new developments that were taking place at the hospital. After the war, in 1946, he transferred to the Cassel Hospital and, as a medical director, expanded the therapeutic community model to British psychiatric hospitals (Pines, 1999). At Northfield, Main and Bridger encouraged discussions with different staff members, aiming at learning about intragroup tensions and the hospital as a whole, including the several systems at work in the institution and their prevailing, but conflicting cultures (Bridger, 1990, p. 77). Bridger's idea was to take over the leadership of the rehabilitation unity and undertake an extensive reformulation of the hospital-as-a-whole with its mission. It happened through the organization of staff seminars, interdisciplinary discussions, and ward meetings exploring the interplay between internal stress and the wider environment, and eventually transformed the pattern of relationships between professionals and patients. In addition, incentives for social and occupational activities centred around the Hospital Club, which functioned as a transitional space (Winnicott, 1971) for personal and community growth and became a source for recovering patients, broadening the scope of their interaction with the wider society (Bridger, 1990).

For Main (1983), reflections on unconscious dimensions in the hospital's routine were vital, which can be seen in the importance given to the co-created culture of the social system as a whole, that is, "the human *folk ways* by which the systems were operated, the quality of *human relations* inside the social structure" (Main, 1983, p. 201) of the hospital. In the Northfield wards, Main observed what he later named "phantastic collusion" (Main, 1975, p. 61), a defensive dynamic in role-relations: "I found the usual hospital convention of regarding all the staff as being totally healthy ... and all the patients as being totally ill" (Main, 1983, p. 204).

Aware of these dynamics, the hospital staff, in training and staff groups, and the patients, in psychosocial activities, could identify their problems from a new angle, promoting a transition from the patients' passive and forced childlike attitudes to an active and mature participation in their own rehabilitation (Foulkes, 1948). At the end of the second experiment, the patients were sharing the hospital management, fully engaged in its affairs. Moreover, the "invisible college" – an active correspondence and exchange of experiences between Hargreaves, Rickman, Bion, Bridger, Main, and others – contributed with important orientations for developing group work in the hospital's units (Main, 1983; Harrison, 2000).

In this shifting scenario, more open to innovative treatments, many of them group-based, Foulkes (1948, p. 18) successfully managed to set up small-group weekly meetings in his ward. The hospital situation, later described as phase A, led Foulkes to initiate a small-group treatment with nine specially selected patients, facilitating the development of his technique and eventually guaranteeing the success of group therapy at the hospital (Harrison, 2000, p. 234). Foulkes was supported by Martin James, who joined Northfield in 1944, and it was just after a meeting between them that the young psychiatrist Patrick de Maré met Foulkes (de Maré, 1983, p. 220). After the war, de Maré became a pioneer group analyst devoted to the work and study of small, median, and large groups. The British pioneer in group treatment, Joshua Bierer, joined the staff and his participation is remembered by many colleagues. By that time, phase A1 of the work had started, and several psychoanalytic oriented therapists and psychiatrists were interested in group approaches (de Maré, 1983; Harrison, 2000).

Researchers point out that, in the beginning of his work at Northfield, Foulkes was more focused on the development of the theory and technique of small-group psychotherapy, and has been "counselled strongly to stick to group psychotherapy" (Hinshelwood, 2007, p. 351). Some state that it was only slowly that he came to the idea that the whole community might become therapeutic (Trist, 1985). However, when Foulkes arrived at Northfield, he was already a seasoned professional and was "gestating" his new epistemology (Foulkes, 1948, p. 1). In this direction, Nitzgen (2008) brings another perspective to the debate, saying that, differently from his colleagues, "as a German refugee, Foulkes was excluded from the executive level of these large-scale planning processes of the medico-military establishment" (Nitzgen, 2008, p. 336). It seems that Foulkes, at least when he first arrived at Northfield, was unaware of the power struggles at stake both in the hospital and in British military psychiatry. Then, more than being "restricted to the role of a specialist in group psychotherapy" – as we can read in different reports of the time, especially in Hargreaves's letter of 1945 (Hinshelwood, 2007, p. 351) – Foulkes "was meant *to be* and *to remain* in this 'restricted' role" (Nitzgen, 2008, p. 337).

Still, by the end of 1944, a military staff knowledgeable in WOSB procedures, as well as in psychologically oriented group processes was in action at Northfield. The wards started to be conducted along group lines and, inspired by Foulkes's training, group work spread across the hospital, characterizing phase B of the second experiment (Main, 1983; de Maré, 1983, p. 225). Foulkes wrote that he had the advantage of working with life groups, soldier-patients, semi-organized groups, occupations, and functions in the hospital at large. This observation allowed him to understand the effects of small-group work as if he was in a "laboratory" (Foulkes, 1948, p. 19). In fact, the application of group-analytic principles in his own ward, dealing with the dialectic duality between relationship and context, was the basis for his success, resulting in a large-scale transformation in the hospital (de Maré, 1983, p. 224). In collaboration with Bridger, Foulkes helped to break down the barriers between the psychiatric domain and the social activities. Considering the hospital as a whole, he encouraged self-governance and transformed the institution into a self-responsible environment (Foulkes, 1948). Small-group work could be found all over the hospital, involving military staff, psychiatrists, and patients.

A hospital of a new kind was born: patients and staff were able to explore their unconscious tensions and their defensive use of roles in the community. The second experiment created a democratic society at Northfield, where a culture of enquiry (Main, 1983, p. 211) was established, enabling its participants not only to foster democratic and reparative processes, but also to tackle the psychosocial problems of the wider society (Bridger, 1990, p. 87). This success also influenced post-war developments and the work of Civil Resettlement Units for repatriated prisoners of war (Hinshelwood, 2018a).

When Bridger left the hospital in 1945, Foulkes was assigned to take on group work. Phase B2, situated between VE day and the end of the war in Europe, marked the epilogue of the Northfield experiments (de Maré, 1983). Indeed, by the end of 1945, the atmosphere at the hospital had changed. Patients and staff were then focused on their reintegration into civilian life and on their own future (Foulkes, 1948). Moreover, administrative and technical problems at the different wings, combined with a large number of convoys crowded with ex-combatants, finally disrupted the service, making Foulkes himself complain about overcrowding, lack of support for group work, and conflicts with non-medical staff (Harrison, 2000). Group work started to be used for examining clinical or administrative crises involving inter-staff and staff-patient relations in the whole system; however, the "group spirit" was disappearing from the hospital (de Maré, 1983). With the demobilization of troops in the immediate post-war period, Northfield's major brains began to disperse. Foulkes left the hospital in December 1945, and Main in 1946. By the end of 1948, the Army had closed down Northfield Hospital, which, after an intense period of activity, was in a precarious state of maintenance and hygiene (Harrison, 2000).

At Northfield, Foulkes (1948) demonstrated that the individual is part of a social network and, from cradle to grave, persons belong to various groups in connection to different functions. The challenge at Northfield was to study the group's situation – a collective of human beings in a social setting – in which the group, as well as individuals in their social aspects, could be examined in a total situation. Inspired by his German influences and also by Malinovsky's anthropological fieldwork, Foulkes stated that the move from "arm chair" to "open air" anthropology fitted exactly with his developments at Northfield, where he managed to move from "consulting room" to "living open air" psychiatry (Foulkes, 1948, p. 17). The Northfield experience led Foulkes to interweave intrapersonal, interpersonal, and transpersonal psychodynamics, which became of real significance to a theoretical shift that allowed for the "handling of new dimensions: the social, cultural and political dimension in relation to neurosis and its analytic treatment" (de Maré, 1983, p. 228).

Legacies

The Northfield Hospital experiments allowed Rickman, Bion, Bridger, Main, Foulkes, and so many collaborators to transform group work in England. Leaderless groups, therapeutic communities, and small-group work left an important legacy to group practices in the following decades. Moreover, wartime initiatives in groups – along a longitudinal and socio-historical chain – are somehow connected to the efforts of the conservative nineteenth-century crowd theorists, as well as to Freud's analysis of the masses and their leaders in the first half of the twentieth century. However, in the overwhelming and traumatic context of World War II, the "band of brothers" who advanced on the almost impossible front of Northfield Hospital created theory through practice, fostering spaces where peer figurations and co-responsible leadership could flourish. In doing so, they showed the world new patterns of relationship in mental health and in live groups, becoming "one growth point in western culture with an enduring outcome" (Hinshelwood, 2018a, p. 440).

At Northfield, instead of conforming to established ways to deal with healthcare practices and the Army, the professionals captured and transformed into action the fears, fantasies, and urgent claims that were at the core of the social unconscious of the persons during wartime in Europe. Relationships in larger settings were reinvented with the creation of a new culture (Main, 1985) that was decisive for transforming human relations and acted as an antidote to the revolting masses and the malignant leadership of the time. Therefore, group work improved tremendously at Northfield, bringing answers to quests in a traumatic context in the form of new discourses, theories, and techniques. We could suggest that their endeavour connects with what Bion (1970), years later, would discuss about the interplay between individuals, groups, and society and the "flash of genius" concerning the relationship between the messiah (genius or mystic) and the establishment. Similarly, it is possible to associate the Northfield innovative shifts with some of Elias's reflections on the disruption of new figurations in *Mozart: Portrait of a Genius* (1993), which reveals how Mozart's genius challenged the Viennese court culture.

The resourceful initiatives taken at Northfield Hospital have grown like the branches of a tree, and until today the uniqueness of the developments brought about by the two Northfield experiments lights up new attempts and hopes in live groups. Moreover, in the revolutionary context of the 1960s and 1970s, an enquiring group spirit led up to the development of large-group theory and practice. Inadvertently, these two intertwined generations actively promoted, fostered, and shaped new theories for the socio-historical analysis of the phenomena of crowds, masses, and their leaders. They unquestionably contributed to contemporary research on the topic, and even today their practice acts as a *pièce de résistance* against fundamentalist thinking and massification states, as we will discuss in the next chapters.

Therefore, it is worth underlining that the Northfield experiments revealed two distinct and clashing forms of working with groups – the military culture and the caring culture – that shaped different group approaches in England to this day (Hinshelwood, 1999, p. 477). At Northfield, Bion challenged the hospital, prioritizing the individual's health. Indeed, the first experiments related to the "military culture", for their main objective was not therapeutic care, but intervention in the group-as-a-whole, as if the training wing was "a battalion at war" (Hinshelwood, 1999, p. 473). Bion's research tried to account for group phenomenon in a field of forces. His attention seemed focused on the psychoanalytic understanding of group relations and on the social morale of the troops by developing the experience of belonging to a group, to the Army. Those were activity groups embedded in a military culture (Hinshelwood, 1999, p. 476). On the other hand, Foulkes's groups, although fitting into the "hospital-as-a-whole" context, relied on other perspectives and were primarily therapeutic groups. The main concern was to rehabilitate the patient as a person through communication and facilitation of free-floating discussions in the group. In this sense, they were verbal groups inserted in a caring culture (Hinshelwood, 1999, p. 476). After the Northfield experiments, these different views of the group as an object of ontological investigation or therapeutic intervention influenced different lines of research on groups (Hinshelwood, 1999, 2007, 2018a).

Moreover, observing the early initiatives in group work described by de Maré (1972) in the beginning of this chapter, the unfolding of the Northfield experiments revealed the emergence of group techniques that put in perspective the psychodynamics *of* the group itself. Thus, after the war, Bion and the members of the Tavistock Institute of Human Relations developed group-as-a-whole approaches that emphasized the analysis *of* the group (de Maré, 1972). On the other hand, Foulkes's (1948, 1964, 1975a; Foulkes & Anthony, 1957) group analysis favoured "a form of psychotherapy *by* the group, *of* the group, including its conductor" (Foulkes, 1975a, p. 3).

The Northfield experiments brought significant transformations to the mental health scene in England. Thereafter, things changed dramatically, because an innovative "link between the deepest 'vertical', interpersonal axis with the transpersonal 'horizontal' of the social and cultural context" (de Maré, 1983, p. 108) had been established to reorient psychiatry, psychoanalysis, and psychotherapies. Although these traditions followed different paths, they shared a common postulate:

> ... it is neither the individual nor the group, neither the part nor whole which is primary, but it is the interstice of intercommunication, interaction and interrelation which play the primary role.
>
> (de Maré, 1972, pp. 38–39)

In the next chapters, we discuss the development of two important legacies initiated in Northfield, through the exploration of the emerging fields of group relations and group analysis. It is remarkable how the two Northfield experiments engendered different theoretical approaches as if the Northfield Hospital professionals have had two children, separated in infancy, who were crossed by the narcissism of minor differences in the way they learned from experience.

6   Group relations and Bion's legacy

After World War II

The Northfield experiment left an important legacy to group work in England. Although it lasted only six weeks, Rickman and Bion's first Northfield experiment was fundamental for the development of group thinking, contributing to forging new paths for psychoanalytic theory. Rickman and Bion applied in the psychiatric service a combination of ideas from different disciplines that allowed them to explore intragroup tensions in groups and foster a healthier functioning in the Army (King, 2003). However, their work faced resistance by the military establishment, making the psychodynamic oriented psychiatrists perplexed about the fate of their innovations (Sutherland, 1985). Rickman and Bion's ideas marked breakthroughs in different phases of war effort and contributed to the social transformation that took place in early postwar Britain (Trist, 1985, p. 3).

In January 1943, Rickman and Bion left Northfield and were posted to the WOSB nos 6 and 7, respectively (Trist, 1985; Bléandonu, 1994). In the same year, they published an article in *The Lancet*, titled "Intra-group Tensions in Therapy: Their Study as the Task of the Group", in which they discussed their experiences at the hospital (Bion, 1961; Rickman, 2003, p. 220). After leaving Northfield, Rickman played a relevant role in the Army's psychiatry, described in some of his papers (Rickman, 2003), but a coronary thrombosis forced him to leave the Army in 1944. Even so, he helped in the demobilization of psychiatrists and psychologists and, through a Control Commission set up by the Allies, he visited Germany officially in 1946.

After the war, Rickman returned to his professional activities as a psychoanalyst at the British Psychoanalytic Society, of which he was elected president in 1947. He also collaborated actively on the reconstruction of the legal constitution of the Institute of Psychoanalysis, participating in the extension of its training programme as well. Rickman passed away in 1951, after outstanding contributions to the British psychiatric and psychoanalytic scene (King, 2003).

As for Bion, he left Northfield in 1943, disappointed and angry with the military hierarchy. He was assigned to work with officials, applying group methods in Winchester, and was transferred to Normandy in 1944 (Bléandonu,

DOI: 10.4324/9780429399534-7

1994). In 1945, Bion's wife died after giving birth to their daughter. Devastated, he returned to England. By that time, the leaderless group method was influential in the Army, having contributed to the creation of the Civil Resettlement Units (Trist, 1985). In the aftermath of the war, Bion re-established himself at the Tavistock Clinic, where a new action-oriented philosophy, connecting psychiatry and social sciences to society, became a reality in practice (Trist & Murray, 1990; Rustin & Armstrong, 2019).

The creation of the Tavistock Institute of Human Relations

After the war, but still considering wartime experiences, the Tavistock Clinic created an Interim Planning Committee – "Operation Phoenix" – to reflect on the future of the organization and redefine its mission. This committee, chaired by J. R. Rees, met twice a week during the autumn of 1945 and prepared some reports. A memorandum was written as well, at the request of the Rockefeller Foundation, which was interested in finding out if, in times of peace, there would be a group committed to undertaking the kind of social psychiatry the Army had developed in wartime. For such a purpose, the Foundation sponsored the establishment of the Tavistock Institute of Human Relations in 1946, at first as a division of the Tavistock Clinic, with its own permanent staff, committed both to psychoanalysis and its integration with the broader social contexts (Rustin & Armstrong, 2019). This new endeavour was initially chaired by Bion, who acted as a conductor of "normative planning" activities (Trist, 1985, p. 25).

As time went on, it is possible to say that, under a democratic culture of dialogue and exchange (Rustin & Armstrong, 2019), the Institute's socio-psychological perspective became a combination of the psychoanalytic object relations theory with the Lewinian field theory, the personality-culture approach, and the open systems theory (Trist & Murray, 1990). In the following decades, the use of psychoanalytic ideas to understand social practices within institutions became an important conceptual breakthrough at the Institute from the work of leading figures as Jaques (1955) and Isobel Menzies (Menzies-Lyth, 1961). Their formulation of social systems as a defence against anxieties in organizations not only bridged Kleinian and Bionian psychoanalysis to sociology, but also provided a new paradigm for the work in organizational consultancy (Armstrong, 2005). However, in Britain, until today, the dialogue between psychoanalysis and sociology faces "resistances and blind spots on both sides" (Rustin & Armstrong, 2019, p. 487). In this sense, we can infer that, despite the interdisciplinary approach and the more inclusive conception of social science promoted by the Tavistock Institute, the broader perspectives on individual-society relationships brought about by the Northfield experiments remain a challenging endeavour in our milieu.

In the early phase of the Institute of Human Relations, Bion led a programme of multiple group projects – student group, industrial group, and patient group – in search of the role of psychiatry and psychoanalysis in the

wider society (Trist, 1985, p. 26). He was exploring group-as-a-whole perspectives, using "the group as both context and instrument for personal growth
and learning" (Lipgar, 2003, p. 41). Here, it is important to underline that, at
the Tavistock, as a "taker of groups", Bion used to make little distinction
between psychotherapeutic task groups and staff self-study groups (Sutherland,
1985). Immediately after the war, he was concerned with the role of psychiatry
in the wider society and, in 1947, in his presidential address "Psychiatry in a
Time of Crisis" (Bion, 1948) at the British Psychological Society, he highlighted that his work with groups in wartime demonstrated his hopes that
humankind, after reaching the "depths of barbarism that will ensure that our
era will go down in history as one in which all the bestialities of recorded time
have been easily surpassed" (Bion, 1948, p. 81), would be able to achieve a
further stage of emotional development.

In 1948, the Tavistock Clinic joined the National Health Service (NHS) and
had to implement a psychotherapeutic outpatient psychiatry service that met
the treatment criteria accepted by the Regional Boards. The Institute of
Human Relations was then established as an independent organization (Trist,
1985, p. 36). Bion was again a forerunner and conducted groups with regular
patients. Also, from 1947 to 1948, he held weekly professional and administrative staff group meetings at the Institute at which it was possible to study
groups in non-medical settings, including organizational contexts (Trist, 1985;
Sutherland, 1985). These pioneering activities contributed to the postulation of
Bion's basic assumptions and were fundamental for organizing group relations
conferences.

Bion's basic-assumption group and the work group

In 1948, Bion presented his first public statement on groups at the International
Congress of Mental Health, in which he investigated the equivalent of the
psychoanalytic method in a group situation. Bion's ideas "became a conceptual
and methodological break-through ... and constituted an action step" (Trist,
1985, p. 28) at the Tavistock. At that time, the Tavistock Clinic was joining
the NHS and Bion resigned. By 1950, he had abandoned his work on groups
and begun to work with individual psychotic patients, while in analysis with
Melanie Klein (from 1946 to 1953). The work with groups continued at the
Tavistock, undertaken by Eric Miller, Eric Trist, Harold Bridger and others,
who went on to develop the study of group relations.

Although his formulations about the parallels between individual and group
psychology were not always clear, Bion redefined their relationships (Hopper,
2003b). He undeniably envisaged individual psychology and group psychology
as intertwined and overlapping processes through the metapsychological notion
of protomental system, defined as "one in which physical and psychological or
mental are undifferentiated" (Bion, 1961, p. 102). For Bion, "there was one
'socio'; and all socio- had a 'psycho'- dimension, all psycho-, a social dimension" (Trist, 1985, p. 33).

For Bion, the study of groups was essential for the life of an individual and fundamental for the understanding of human psychology. The interdependence between individual and group psychology enabled him to achieve important developments in group thinking. Bion regarded the human being as a group or political animal and stated that the "individual is a group animal at war, both with the group and with those aspects of his personality that constitute his 'groupishness'" (Bion, 1961, p. 168). This assertion lends new perspectives to Trotter's ideas on the nature of groupishness and group morale (Torres, 2003) and to the irreducibility between individual and group psychology that Freud discussed in *Group Psychology and the Analysis of the Ego* (1921). Some of these considerations took different shapes in further developments of group work, both in group relations (Rice, 1965; Miller, 1990; Armstrong, 2005) and group analysis (Foulkes, 1964; de Maré, Piper, & Thompson, 1991; Hopper, 2003b). Moreover, it is important to highlight how Bion's ideas on the protomental level are akin to the Argentine psychoanalyst José Bleger's (2016) postulations of early phases of undifferentiation in the individual's development (Hinshelwood, 2003, p. 197) and Hopper's fourth basic assumption, discussed in Chapter Ten.

With these ideas in mind, Bion's papers with Rickman were published in *The Lancet* (1943) and in *Human Relations* (1948–52) and gathered in *Experiences in Groups* (1961). These publications introduced new concepts, such as group mentality, group culture, basic-assumption group, work group, among others. In his early papers, Bion put forward the idea that the group can be regarded as an interplay between group mentality, group culture and individual needs. Although individual needs are always frustrated by the group's impossibility to afford the individual a full life (Bion, 1961, p. 54). Bion asks, "How did the use of these three concepts, group mentality, group culture, and individual, as interdependent phenomena, work in practice?" (Bion, 1961, p. 61).

In Bion's experience, groups always react in a "tiresomely erratic manner" (Bion, 1961, p. 61), consequently, interpretations based on concepts of group mentality, group culture, and individual are inadequate to understand group dynamics. Re-examining his ideas, he noticed that the individual regresses to a set of assumptions about being in a group, leading him to postulate the ubiquitous coexistence, in any group, of two different forms of mental activity: the basic-assumption group and the work group. Basic assumptions emerge as unconscious and regressive manifestations of primitive nature in the progress of the work group, guaranteeing the preservation of the group (Bion, 1961, p. 63). They appear as three different alternating forms, sometimes one or the other prevails: Dependency (baD), Fight-Flight (baF/F), and Pairing (baP). The protomental system encompasses prototypes of the three basic assumptions, each as a function of the individual's membership in the group. It is "a matrix from which basic-assumption emotions flow to reinforce, pervade or dominate the mental life of the group" (Bion, 1961, p. 102).

Initially, basic assumptions seemed to Bion to be innate or instinctual, "a set of three endowed 'valences' that embodied unthought assumptions about the nature and purpose of the group and which all human individuals have available for linking with each other" (Hinshelwood, 2003, p. 186). However, in 1952, influenced by his clinical work with psychotic patients and by Kleinian psychoanalysis, he reformulated his earlier group dynamics theory. Bion (1961, p. 141) suggested that, instead of being innate, basic assumptions derived from psychological developments as manifestations of the infantile psychotic positions described by Klein. Basic-assumption groups are formed by defences that protect against psychotic anxieties – "group mentality is thus a psychotic mentality" (Hinshelwood, 2003, p. 186). Indeed, group mentality conducts the process in a manner akin to temporary psychosis and members of groups, even without noticing them, are affected by splitting and projective identification, diminution of contact with reality, lack of belief in progress and development through work and suffering (Menzies-Lyth, 1981). In this sense, in the basic assumption states:

> the group appears to have lost the non-psychotic, alpha-function of the individuals – there is no moral sense, a loss of mature judgement (all is exclusively good or bad), an absence of recognising consequences to actions, a lack of development in group thought and achievement, a failing of the sense of time, etc. What we witness is the reversion to a psychotic mental functioning – the reversal of alpha-function.
>
> (Hinshelwood, 2003, p. 187)

The basic assumption of Pairing (baP) refers to the observation that, whenever two people interact or exchange in a group, a basic assumption seems to be in action, held both by the group and by the pair concerned: "The relationship between them is sexual, as if there was no other possible reason for two people coming together, except sex" (Bion, 1961, pp. 61–62). In this respect, the anxieties inherent to primitive phantasies associated with Pairing (baP) are also related to a feeling of hope sustained by the idea of finding a saviour, "a Messiah, be it person, idea, or Utopia" (Bion, 1961, p. 152). Next, Bion (1961, p. 63) inquires:

> If the basic assumption about the pair is that they meet together for purposes of sex, what is the basic assumption in a group about people who meet together in a group? The basic assumption is that people come together as a group for purposes of preserving the group.

From this perspective, the group seems to know only two self-preservation techniques – Fight or Flight (baF/F) – that show the group is intolerant of activities other than Fight or Flight. This "leads the group to ignore other activities, or, if it cannot do this, to suppress them or run away from them" (Bion, 1961, p. 64).

In the basic assumption of Dependency (baD), the group meets together to obtain security from one individual on whom the group depends and who is perceived as the person "in a position to supply the needs of the group, and the rest in a position in which their needs are supplied" (Bion, 1961, p. 74).

Here comes to the fore what Bion (1961) defines as sophisticated group and, later, work group. The relationship between the work group and the basic-assumption group differs from the relationship among the emotional states associated with the three basic assumptions. There is no direct conflict among basic assumptions, only oscillations from one state to the next. The inoperative basic assumption remains confined to the protomental system, that is, if emotions associated with the basic assumption of Dependency (baD) suffuse the work group, the Fight-Flight (baF/F) and Pairing (baP) basic assumptions are kept within the limits of the protomental phase (Bion, 1961, p. 102). However, conflict arises just at the junction between the basic-assumption group and the work group (Bion, 1961, p. 98). Work groups recognize the need to develop and learn from experience rather than to rely upon the endless interplay among basic assumptions. A group meets for a specific task, and cooperation has to be achieved to fulfil collective aims, which implies more sophisticated means. Therefore, "work groups are different in kind from the capacity for cooperation evidenced at the basic-assumption level" (Bion, 1961, p. 99).

Groups are always subject to a basic assumption activity that interferes with the capacity of the members to work together. Basic assumptions are the basis, that is, potential group reactions activated whenever a work group fails to accomplish a task (Kernberg, 1998). Therefore, for the work group, the challenge is to use basic assumption processes in which the heterogeneity of group members may be creatively applied to accomplish a task. Basic-assumption groups have been thoroughly investigated; work group, on the contrary, tend to be taken for granted and remain underdeveloped in both theory and practice (Armstrong, 2005, p. 140).

Bion's group theory suggests a complex phenomenology of persons as both individuals and group members: "We thus have a situation in which the individuals behave as if they were conscious, as individuals, of the basic assumption, but unconscious of it as members of the group" (Bion 1961, p. 94). This brings up for discussion not only the splitting between psychotic and non-psychotic parts of the individual (Bion, 1967) but also the human dilemma between individuality and groupishness, as horde animals. This might be translated as the struggle between the need for individuality and the need for belonging, the "dilemma of the individual" (Bion, 1961, p. 118) that is so dear to Bion's tradition and its further developments. Accordingly, through Bion's lens, there is an "ongoing tension between task (work) and affiliation (maintenance of cohesiveness through shared fantasies)" (Lipgar, 2003, pp. 32–33), a tension between learning from experience and valency for the basic assumptions. In this direction, Trist's (1985) analysis of the important interlace between individual and group psychology acquires new meanings, especially regarding the "primary task" that Bion had set for the study of groups at the Tavistock: the study of intragroup tensions in the here-and-now.

The creation of the group relations conferences

Since Northfield, significant progress had taken place in the emerging field of group relations. We must underline here the relevance of group relations and the study of leadership in the "haunted", but hopeful post-war context of the 1950s, as inferred from Horkheimer and Adorno's quest in 1944, from Bion's presidential address at the British Psychological Society in 1948, and from various presentations by Foulkes in the late 1940s and early 1950s.

The group relations study on leadership and authority was established by a theoretical and technical framework initially based on Bion's insights into groups developed at the Tavistock, where experiential and educational learning on leadership in groups was fostered. Lawrence (1985) states that one of Bion's outstanding contributions to group work is the growth of group relations training conferences, known as the Tavistock method.

Since 1957, the Tavistock Institute of Human Relations, in conjunction with the University of Leicester, has been sponsoring experiential working conferences for studying the behaviour of groups as a whole in the here-and-now (Miller, 1990; Bridger, 1990). The Tavistock/Leicester Conference is organized as a "two-week residential and educational event devoted to experiential learning about groups and organizational behaviour, with an emphasis on the nature of authority and leadership" (Miller, 1990, p. 165). The endeavour was influenced by the laboratory method and the T-Groups Lewin (1947) developed in the United States and by psychoanalysis as well (Rice, 1965). According to Miller (1990), the first conferences began with small study groups (Gosling, 1981), a staff consultant, and a staff observer. The other main events were lectures, application groups, and plenary review sessions. In 1959, intergroup events and application work with participants were introduced, followed by the creation of intergroup and large-group activities (Miller, 1990, pp. 165–168).

In Washington, the A. K. Rice Institute (founded in 1969) for the Study of Social Systems took the leadership of group relations conferences in the United States. Under Rice's and Margaret Rioch's guidance and with the collaboration of Pierre Turquet and John Sutherland (Rice, 1965; Rioch, 1970a, 1970b, 1983; Miller, 1990), these conferences changed technically and conceptually. At first, they embraced as their primary task the idea of learning about leadership (Rice, 1965, p. 5). Later, they started to emphasize the study of authority and the problems in exercising it within organizations and institutions (Lawrence, 1985, p. 308). Their approach to learning about leadership, authority, and later to the study of the politics of relatedness (Lawrence, 1985) has been formulated since then. Their work in conjunction with organizations such as the Grubb Institute for Behavioural Studies in London, and the Department of Education of Bristol University improved the endeavour (Gosling, 1981). Today, numerous initiatives use the expression "group relations" in the title of their meetings (Miller, 1990); however, as Armstrong (2005, p. 146) defines:

… group relations conferences are temporary training institutions set up to explore or study the tensions inherent in group life, using a method of experiential learning. This is their manifest intention or primary task.

At the A. K. Rice Institute, the design of the group relations conference developed significantly under Rice's leadership during the 1960s, taking the shape it has now (Lawrence, 1985). Firstly, the innovative use of large group experiences with tasks was similar to those of the small study group – defined as "the study of its own behaviour as a group in the here-and-now" (Rice, 1965, p. 57) – but including conference members and two to four consultants. Secondly, the intergroup events were redefined, "now having a single task: the membership was to form itself into groups and to study their interrelatedness in the here-and-now" (Miller, 1990, p. 167). Moreover, a second type of intergroup event – the institutional event – was introduced to focus on the study of member/staff relationships within the conference institution as a whole. This last improvement relates to the development of the idea of learning from experience – "knowledge-of-acquaintance" (Rice, 1965, p. 24) – and to a decrease in formal lectures. The plenary sessions and application groups from the original framework have been retained and the use of review groups increased, offering members an opportunity to reflect on their experiences (Rice, 1965, p. 167). The design of a group relations conference provides a temporary institution and a containing structure that allows participants to learn from experience and apply the knowledge acquired to their work (Miller, 1990), that is:

> … a clear geographical map (space boundaries), an inflexible schedule (time boundaries), and a stereotyped staff (role boundaries) in which the consultant never consults to an individual and always only to the group as a whole.
>
> (Agazarian & Carter, 1993, p. 216)

Since World War II, many group relations conferences have adopted a pattern whereby speakers address the whole conference and the discussion about lectures takes place in small groups, later reassembled in large groups (Rice, 1965). It was observed that large-group settings offer an ideal and more public situation to explore leadership and authority, and also the possibility to gather conference membership as a whole. Rice (1965) reported that he and the psychoanalyst Pierre Turquet perceived that, in conferences, the plenaries are influenced by the upsurge of incomprehensible forces, so, in 1963, they decided to introduce and convene large-group meetings in the conferences, aiming at exploring their psychodynamics (Turquet, 1975). Rice (1965, p. 72) defined the large group event as one

> in which members can experience the forces that a large group brings to bear on its leaders, in a setting where the prescribed task is to study those forces.

For Rice, the primary task is to study large group behaviour as it happens, and the consultants' role is to help participants accomplish this task. Their technique is to use observations and feelings to enable them to recognize, learn, and be insightful to what is happening to the group in the here-and-now. However, accomplishing this task is more complex than in small groups, and it is clear that large groups pose special problems and demand different abilities from members and conveners. The relationship patterns, the creation of subgrouping, and the difficulty to set boundaries for the task represent additional challenges to the large group as a learning process (Rice, 1965, p. 74).

Rice underlined the importance of the psychodynamics between the individual, the small group, and the large group in the conference design. He related these elements to the concept of primary task and to a theory of organization based on open systems when tackling the problem of learning about leadership (Rice, 1965, p. 17). Rice was able to integrate the open systems theory in Bion's work on small groups and Turquet's views on large groups (Kernberg, 1998). Here, we must stress that, according to Rioch (1983, p. 253), the idea of primary task

> ...seems to be a blood-brother to the "work" of groups and organizations as conceptualized by Bion. The primary task is that task which the group or organization must perform if it is to survive.

Therefore, each part of a conference had its primary task, which was different from the tasks of other parts, but designed to contribute to accomplishing the primary task of the whole. From Rice's developments, we should retain the assumption that individual and group behaviour are affected by unconscious forces. It means that, in any group, institution or community meeting, affections, denials, and repressions jeopardize the relationship between individuals and their tasks. Consequently, the understanding of these unconscious processes and the culture they co-create may contribute to solve leadership problems (Rice, 1965, p. 10).

Indeed, experiences with groups have improved the Tavistock/group relations framework, as well as instigating psychoanalytic and group analytic studies. Over the socio-historical course of this research, we inferred that investigations into Bion's basic assumption group and group analytic work could bring new ideas to the study of the psychodynamics of crowds and masses. A deeper understanding of these theories does provide an interdisciplinary, theoretical understanding for the *question du nombre*, but it gives us tools for intervening, reshaping, and transforming interactions between larger numbers of persons in groups. Therefore, the study of group processes offers some clues to the "enigma of the sphinx" proposed in Le Bon's (1895, p. 123) crowd psychology. In this direction, it is noteworthy that, many years later, Bion (1961) explored the idea of the sphinx in his psychoanalytic investigations of group phenomena. This focus on the sphinx relates to problems of knowledge and scientific method (Biran, 2015).

Bion's perspectives on group work were taken forward in his work with groups and organizations, reaffirming the A. K. Rice's and Tavistock's traditions (Sher, 2003). In the Tavistock model and in group relations conferences, Bion's basic assumption group and work group were fundamental to formulate the underlying working hypothesis and methodology. The Tavistock model was crucial for building a "heuristic framework for identifying and understanding what conscious and unconscious processes take place within and between groups of people" (Lawrence, 1979, p. 2). In this sense, Bion's words about groups are related to "the use of the group *per se*, the dynamic of the group in the here-and-now as the instrument of therapy and learning" (Menzies-Lyth, 1981, p. 662). Bion was able to advance important hypotheses about the nature of humans in groups, observing the individual as a nodal point in a group dynamic. His theories allowed us to develop a binocular vision on individual-group tensions that leads to thinking "beyond the frames" (Lawrence, 1985, p. 307).

It would be interesting to explore the conceptual and technical framework of group relations in depth. However, this chapter concentrates exclusively on the influences the Northfield first experiment and Bion's work exerted on the establishment of the Tavistock Institute of Human Relations and on the design of group relations conferences. Bion's influence was also important in developing large-group experiences in group and seminal for postulating new basic assumptions. We will discuss such developments in the next chapter.

7 Towards new basic assumptions in groups

A new world *Zeitgeist* for group work

The first half of the twentieth century was shaped by two world wars and required personal sacrifices on behalf of nation-states and their collective goals, which took the lives of millions. In England, as described in Chapter Five, the Northfield experiments conferred new figurations to relationships between persons and their contexts, thus providing a field for developing group work. Moreover, after the end of World War II, a series of changes in the global sociocultural milieu began to take place, reaching its apex in the 1960s and 1970s. Such transformations and the ideas and new practices that came with them co-created new discourses, fantasies, and myths in the social unconscious of persons in Western societies, changing both personal and collective lives.

Post-war reconstruction in Europe, in the middle of the Cold War, produced a social democratic moment that gave rise to "a dense tissue of social benefits and economic strategies in which it was the state that served its subjects, rather than the other way around" (Judt, 2006, p. 360). Therefore, in the golden age of the welfare state, state protection seemed more effective than the unrestricted market, not only in "dispensing justice and securing the realm, or distributing goods and services, but in designing and applying strategies for social cohesion, moral sustenance and cultural vitality" (Judt, 2006, p. 361). In this sense, it is interesting to observe that the way the welfare state offered containment and care to its citizens functioned as a conscious and unconscious strategy to deal with the damage the dark times had caused them. Even illusorily, a collective feeling of cohesion and belonging seemed to prevail in the effort to reconstruct Europe, with an influence on therapeutic practices as well. On the other hand, the fear of the rise of totalitarianism, together with generational and transgenerational unmourned losses, haunted people's lives. These silenced traumatic experiences would take years to be worked through (Mitscherlich & Mitscherlich, 1975; Bohleber, 1995; Frosh, 2013a) and start to be explored in groups (Hopper, 2003a), and they are still alive in the unconscious life of European matrices.

In the 1960s, the world experienced anti-colonial wars, the Vietnam War, armed struggles in Latin America and Africa, the movement for civil rights in

DOI: 10.4324/9780429399534-8

the United States, and social movements that interwove new figurations for individuality, subjectivity, liberty, equality, and fraternity. The year 1968 entered history as a milestone of a series of sociopolitical and cultural transformations, fostering countercultural values and attempts to replace hierarchical authority with ample democratization to guarantee individual rights, equality, and freedom (Penna, 2020). Moreover, the intellectual vanguards were concerned about collective life and expressed their thoughts mainly through Lévi-Strauss's structuralism and the New Left's revival of Marxism. As of the 1960s, Foucault's post-structuralist perspectives, Lyotard's post-modernity, and Deleuze's and Derrida's deconstructions also played their role in the process (Judt, 2006).

In this sociocultural effervescence, important advances took place in psychoanalytic and analytic group theories. The nineteenth-century psychoanalytic discussion, centred on hypnosis and cathartic mechanisms, evolved in the twentieth century to adopt a metapsychology based on Oedipal configurations in the clinic of neurosis and in the drive theory. However, influenced by transformations in the 1960s and 1970s, psychoanalysis, focusing its attention on the clinic of difficult patients, started to investigate narcissistic configurations and pre-Oedipal moments of subjective development (Kohut, 1971; Green, 1974; Winnicott, 1975; Kernberg, 1975).

Following a similar path, the nineteenth-century research on groups was initially restricted to a conservative analysis of crowd behaviour, whereas in the twentieth century it started to dedicate to the psychology of masses and their leaders and the construction of the group field. Between the late 1940s and the 1970s, the legacies of the Northfield experiments began to organize and consolidate as new group traditions in England. Immersed in the *Zeitgeist* of the 1960s and 1970s, investigation in groups found a lively space to thrive in hospitals, institutions, organizations, conferences, and therapeutic communities (Foulkes, 1964, 1975a; Kreeger, 1975; Pines, 1983; Trist, & Murray, 1990; Schlapobersky, 2016; Pearce & Haigh, 2017).

However, before exploring these new developments, especially regarding explorations in large groups, we should observe that research on groups had turned, as in psychoanalysis, to the analysis of primitive anxieties and to the regressive and pre-Oedipal aspects of group psychodynamics (Kernberg, 1998). In the effort of psychoanalysts working with groups, such as Pierre Turquet (1975), Kreeger (1975), and others in England, Anzieu (1984), Kaës (1975), and Chasseguet-Smirgel (1984) in France, and José Bleger (2016) in Argentina, we can see this tendency. In this sense, group research went beyond Freud's (1921) considerations on the psychology of masses by focusing no longer on the idea of the leader as an Oedipal father – although "the collective investment of ego-ideals is, by definition, pre-Oedipal" (Hopper, 2003b, p. 27) – but on primitive and defensive aspects of group psychodynamics (Kreeger, 1975). These investigations revealed the importance of illusions, fantasies of fusion with an omnipotent mother (Chasseguet-Smirgel, 1984), the tendency for homogeneity (Turquet, 1975) or withdrawal and isolation (Lawrence, Bain, &

Gould, 2000), and Incohesion processes in groups (Hopper, 2003b). Therefore, group activity turned to "capturing very profound and archaic levels of unconscious, pre-symbolic manifestations and the possibility of symbolizing them" (Mello Franco, 2015, p. 274; translation mine).

Towards the postulation of new basic assumptions

In this chapter, our discussion focuses on important research that has stood the test of time. It has been at the heart of group experiences since Northfield and the early days of the Tavistock Institute of Human Relations, influencing until today the study on groups. It concerns the study of Bion's (1961) three basic assumptions (ba) – Dependency (baD), Fight-Flight (baF/F), Pairing (baP) – introduced in Chapter Six and other attempts to conceptualize new and ubiquitous basic assumptions in group psychodynamics. Bion's *Experiences in Groups* (1961) became a landmark in the conceptualization of unconscious group processes that concur to demonstrate the ubiquitous regressive phenomena that influence people. Psychoanalysts, together with group relations and group analytic professionals, have been discussing basic assumption group and work group configurations since Bion outlined his theory. Different perspectives on the nature of the three basic assumptions have been presented so far (Grotstein, 1981; Brown, 1985; Billow, 2003; Hopper, 2003b; Lipgar, 2003; Miller, 1998; Hinshelwood, 1999, 2003; Sandler, 2013, Neri, 2013). They aim to understand how these different forms of unconscious mental activity interfere with individual psychoanalytic treatment – psychoanalysis as a "two-body group" (Sandler, 2013) – especially in small- and large-group processes.

Therefore, we may ask why the postulation of new and ubiquitous basic assumptions is so relevant to the study of analytic group processes. This was first, because Bion gave a seminal contribution to the understanding of the unconscious life of groups. Hopper (2003b, p. 29) mentions that Bion's work may be considered as "a time marker in the psychoanalytic study of groups that should be known as 'zero', all previous studies to be dated 'BB' and all subsequent 'AB'". Second, because this remark confers meaning to Mello Franco's (2015) statement. He says that the premature abandonment of Bion's work with groups has left to his followers a difficult mourning process, then transformed into a feeling of orphanhood. This might have led to the creation of a socially unconscious claim in group professionals that oscillates between a continuous search for the absent father's theory through research on new ideas about basic assumptions and, at the same time, an unconscious wish to work through and overcome the premature loss of Bion's influence. In this sense, the search for new basic assumptions in analytic group thinking may be an attempt to appropriate Bion's legacy, similarly to what Freud, quoting Goethe, once wrote: "Strive to possess yourself of what you have inherited from your ancestors" (Freud, 1913, p. 160).

In the following sections, we discuss how the transmission of this inheritance evolved, transforming and reshaping perspectives on the basic assumption group theory and the study of large groups.

Pierre Turquet: the theory of Oneness

The Northfield experiments planted the seeds for the development of large-group work in the 1960s not only at the Tavistock/Leicester Group Relations Conferences in England and at the A.K. Rice Institute in the US, but also in the group analytic field. In 1966, Lionel Kreeger and Patrick de Maré introduced the work with large groups in hospitals such as the Halliwick Hospital, London. Indeed, by that time, therapeutic communities blossomed in psychiatric hospitals, as at the Henderson Hospital (Whiteley, 1975), setting the scene for a hospital to be seen as a therapeutic institution (Main, 1983) and its units and wards "treated as a group" (Foulkes, 1948, p. 112). Thus, the work carried out in hospitals in the *modus operandi* of therapeutic communities eventually conferred to the work with large groups a special function in the hospital as a whole. In parallel, the Institute of Group Analysis in London began to host large-group experiences in its training programs in 1971 (Kreeger, 1975).

A veteran of the War Office Selection Boards (WOSBs), a member of the British Psychoanalytical Society and of the Tavistock Clinic, Pierre Turquet was a pioneer in group relations conferences and group analytic work. In 1952, he joined the Tavistock Clinic with a special interest in group relations. From 1968 to 1973, he became Chairman of its Adult Department and took part in large-group work since its inception. First, at the Tavistock/Leicester Conferences in 1957, and just after, in partnership with Kenneth Rice, at the A. K. Rice Institute (Turquet, 1975).

The introduction of large groups in the group relations conferences organized by the training programme of the Tavistock Institute of Human Relations and the A. K. Rice Institute was a result of their staffs' observation that large plenary sessions had an especial dynamics (Lawrence, 1985). It is difficult to precise the number of participants that elicits large group psychodynamics, for this number vary with different authors. In Turquet's (1975, p. 87) opinion a large group has about forty to eighty participants. Large groups pose special problems for their members and conveners, especially concerning communication in task performance and leadership. Such difficulties produce primitive psychological mechanisms and the defences associated with them, which, in turn, influence group psychodynamics (Rice, 1965; Turquet, 1975; Kreeger, 1975). These processes have been explored in group relations and group analysis.

Turquet's observations as a consultant in large groups in conferences led to the conceptualization of what some authors called a fourth basic assumption in the 1970s: the theory of Oneness (baO), which refers to behaviour within large unstructured groups (Kreeger, 1975). Turquet proposed his theory in two seminal papers, one in 1967 (Turquet, 1974) and the other in 1969 (Turquet, 1975). His sudden death in 1975 prevented him from improving his ideas. Yet, they became a classic in the study of large groups.

From a Freudo-Kleinian perspective, the theory of Oneness shows a not always acknowledged influence of Bion's (1961) three basic assumptions.

Although Turquet (1974, p. 107) mentions it in his first paper as "a fourth basic assumption ... and [I] call it Oneness", Bion's influence is not cited in Turquet's second paper (Hopper, 2003b, p. 51). Hopper (2003b) states that Turquet did not regard Oneness as a fourth basic assumption. He was influenced by Joffe's discussions on the nature of envy and its connections to helplessness, as well as by some theoretical debates on Melanie Klein's theory (Hopper, 2003b, p. 51). Turquet's ideas were also marked by two little known public lectures Rickman (1938) gave at the British Psychoanalytical Society in 1938. Both seminal lectures were gathered in "Does it take all kinds to make a world? Uniformity and Diversity in Communities" and were recently published in the collection of Rickman's works organized by Pearl King (2003).

Rickman (1938) describes his psychoanalytic and sociocultural observations during his experience as a physician at the Friends' War Victims Relief Unit in a czarist Russian village in 1916–17, just before the outbreak of the Bolshevik Revolution. Rickman's reflections show human interactions in a deeply cohesive, homogeneous community that lived humbly on farming. It was a leaderless community that had in uniformity, that is, in homogeneity, its shared ideal. Rickman explores two episodes that reveal a strong correlation between group homogeneity, aggressive behaviour, and the need for safety. These episodes show a forbearing attitude towards a refractory member of the community and an intolerant and aggressive behaviour towards an outsider. In both situations, the community's cohesion was at risk. Rickman discusses that, in the first episode, although an offence had been perpetrated by a member of the community, the offender shared bonds of affection and kinship with the village. Moreover, the offence did not threaten the group-as-a-whole. In the second episode, in which a foreign propagandist tried to bring new ideas to the villagers, there was a risk of splitting the group into different small subgroups, because the outsider was not "one of us" (Rickman, 1938, p. 161).

The equilibrium and control of aggressive impulses are guaranteed by projective processes. They preserve the community's cohesion, leading people to be indulgent with "the good like us" and aggressive towards "the bad like them" (Rickman, 1938, p. 176). In a homogeneous community, the tendency to uniformity of thought is strong and differences between thought and deed are denied. Moreover, the possibility of independent thinking and the emergence of leadership is considered an aggression against the community's cohesion. There is no space for personal differences, and any manifestation of individuality is scapegoated or expressed by a constant flow of emigrating community members. In this dynamic, Rickman identified the features of an idealized family, in which everything is perfect and all needs can be fulfilled. However, such perfection is based on the need to be surrounded by enemies. In the psychodynamics of group members, Rickman (1938, pp. 170–171) observed that the community, "by letting the group function as the ego ideal, gave ... security to the members both against the hardships of fate and against the individual's own impulsive tendencies". By maintaining a pure culture and lacking internal aggressiveness, the group is kept through an incessant projection of aggressiveness to the outside or through its expression as a coun-terattack on external aggressiveness.

The community functions as an ideal, as a group ideal, in the manner of Anzieu's (1984) concept of group illusion, was postulated years later. Rick-man's considerations enhance the relevance of the psychoanalytic economic point of view, already discussed in Chapter Two, for the discussion about cohesion in group formations. In this regard, the interplay between homo-geneity and heterogeneity, uniformity and diversity, unity and fragmentation would shape the psychodynamics of interactions among the villagers (Hopper, 2003b, p. 51). Moreover, Rickman (1938) was a pioneer in promoting debates on jealousy and envy, using psychoanalytic concepts such as projections and splitting to discuss the interplay between the inner and outer world. His ground-breaking lectures emerged in a moment when psychoanalysis was still deeply attached to investigations on the individual's intrapsychic universe. In his investigation, the role of identifications, idealizations, and projections in connection to leadership and hero-worship enliven the discussion of these interrelations.

Rickman's lectures extended the ideas Freud expressed in *Group Psychology and the Analysis of the Ego* (1921) and broke novel ground for investigations into homogeneity and heterogeneity in communities and societies that only later have been explored in groups. Turquet (1975), Lawrence, Bain and Gould (2000), and Hopper (2003b) developed conceptualizations on basic assumptions that hold at their core some of Rickman's analysis of the Russian village psy-chodynamics. This was an innovative way of using psychoanalysis to under-stand the interdependencies between individual persons and their contexts in a moment when the psychoanalytic mainstream was still deeply attached to the investigations of the intrapsychic universe.

Turquet's (1975) perspective on large groups privileged the phenomenology of individual experiences in large group settings. His theory discusses challenges for the individual's identity, as well as defences associated to primary envy, such as the tendency to fuse and acquire homogeneity, typical of debates about cohesion in group formations.

Turquet's analysis begins by observing the participation of group relations conference members – an "I". To describe the status of an individual in the early stages of the large group, he used the term "singleton" (S.), borrowed from the card game bridge, but also coined from the observation of the indi-vidual in the large group as "an isolate duck, separated from the huddle of ducks" (Turquet, 1975, p. 316). In their search for a relationship with other participants or for a role within the group, the singleton experiences some dif-ficulties in joining the large group. It means that, in large unstructured groups, face-to-face interactions and identifications are uncertain, due in part to group size. Communication is discontinued, dialogue is impaired, even paralyzed, contributing to the failure of the singleton's efforts to make contact with other group members. The larger the group, the more participants will experience invisibility, anonymity. Then, threatened in their personal integrity and identity, taken by excessive stimuli, fearful of their annihilation, as well as of others' aggressiveness, the individuals regress, adopting homogenization as a major defence against such pressures (Turquet, 1975, p. 92). They are thus led to show a behaviour characterized by envy, projective identifications, fear of annihilation, separation anxiety, fusion, and skin phenomena.

For Turquet, one of the characteristics of the large group situation is that many participants remain in the singleton state, given their unwillingness to join a situation that challenges not only their individuality – "I" – but also their survival. Turquet named the singleton who establishes a relationship within the group-as-a-whole and with other singletons an individual member (I.M.). Thus, in the flux of large group interactions, the initial "non-role" of the singleton may evolve to an engagement in the group as an individual member who struggles to relate with other participants (Turquet, 1975, p. 94). Turquet described three different and transitory participation status for the singleton in the large group: individual member (I.M.), membership individual (M.I.), and isolate (I) (Turquet, 1975, p. 94). There is also one more state, the transitional one, in which the individual member moves between the other states (Turquet, 1975, p. 95). These different states are provisional and represent possibilities of belonging. Moreover, for Turquet, the exercise of this choice is an expression of individuality, of "I-ness" (Turquet, 1975, p. 96). However, as the large group progresses, Turquet observes its attempts to transform the individual member into a membership individual, a state in which group membership predominates over the individual, hindering the maintenance of the individual member state.

For a singleton, the chance to join the large group concerns the possibility of finding a boundary, a skin – external (skin-of-my-neighbour) and internal (my own skin) – whose limits define them and circumscribe their identity (Turquet, 1975, p. 96). The external skin distinguishes the singleton from the others – "me/not me" – guaranteeing to the singleton the possibility of recognizing themselves as an individual member. It prevents the singleton, taken by large group forces, from assuming the state of membership individual. In this sense, the threat to the singleton's identity in the large group means to "be lost in oceanic feelings of unity or, if the oneness is personified, to be part of a salvationist inclusion" (Turquet, 1974, p. 360). It means to be caught into

> a mental activity in which members seek to join in a powerful union with an omnipotent force, unobtainably high, to surrender self for passive participation, and thereby feel existence, well-being, and wholeness.
>
> (Turquet, 1974, p. 357)

The internal skin, in turn, relates to a "time boundary" (Turquet, 1975, p. 97) created to enable the singleton to differentiate past and present, here-and-now, there-and-then, and future. It gives the singleton a sense of continuity regarding their identity throughout the large-group experience. The individual member is challenged to establish internal and external boundaries that evoke previous experiences of helplessness (Turquet, 1975, p. 124). Turquet called attention to the interdependence between both. Therefore, if on the one hand these boundaries allow separation and detachment from other members to be dealt with, on the other, they may give way to a desire to fuse. Thus, "fusion/separation is an ever-present dynamic, the former leading on to membership individual and the latter leading back to a singleton state" (Turquet, 1975, p. 98). This dynamic is affected by primitive anxieties, such as fear of annihilation, fear of void, and experiences of unfamiliarity, boundlessness, and an overwhelming interplay of projections/introjections.

For Turquet, the singleton's external and internal skin involves an interplay of centripetal and centrifugal forces, a polarity between fusion and separation in the large group. Immediately after joining the large group, a singleton experiences two competing forces: a centripetal force compels them to belong, to fuse with the group as a membership individual; and a centrifugal force makes them pull out of the group, by either alienation or isolation (Turquet, 1975, p. 99). Therefore, the boundaries of the skin-of-my-neighbour are continuously stretched and threatened. They may disrupt under the influence of centrifugal forces, which certainly will cause the "I" to withdraw, but they may also favour the emergence of idiosyncratic and isolated positions in large group interactions (Turquet, 1975, p. 101). Ultimately, the singleton's problem in the large group is how to become and remain an individual member, resisting the large group's attempts to transform their belongingness into participation as a membership individual. This imbalance reveals some of the classic internal struggles carried on by the individuals who long for interactions with the group, but at the same time need to defend their individuality, now threatened by the group's powerful unifying, homogenizing forces.

Turquet (1975) began a discussion on boundaries and skin phenomena in the large group that may clarify some concurring phenomena related to transformations in an individual's behaviour within crowds and masses. Le Bon (1895) understood these phenomena in terms of hypnosis, contagion, and suggestibility, whereas Freud (1921) interpreted them as unconscious processes, libido, regression, and identifications between group members and their leader. Turquet's ideas on threats to individuals' identity in the large group may be enriched by subsequent theoretical psychoanalytic developments, such as research on the organization of narcissistic and borderline personalities (Kernberg, 1975) and on *état-limite* and *double limite* (Green, 2005) in the regular or pathological development of subjectivity. Indeed, large groups deal with regression and situations in which psychotic anxieties are at stake, eliciting powerful mental processes, some of them quite similar to those observed in narcissistic and borderline constellations. Transitional areas and spaces in groups (Winnicott, 1971) are other important fields for research in connection not only with boundaries in large groups, but also with the singleton's different status in the group. Bick's (1968) and Meltzer's (1975) considerations on the skin in early object relations and on the concept of adhesive identification, as well as Anzieu's (1984) work on psychic envelopes in groups and on *Skin Ego* (Anzieu, 1989) are additional contributions to discuss the theory of Oneness.

Turquet (1975) argues that it is probably easier to remain a singleton in the large group, although it means non-adherence to the group and provokes a sense of isolation, inadequacy, or even self-referral, making the singleton less neighbour-oriented. In the movement away from the individual member state, two different states can emerge (Turquet, 1975, p. 103).

The first is described by the term "disarroy", coined by Turquet. It is most likely akin to the French word *désarroi* (Lawrence, 1985, p. 319) to designate a state of bewilderment accompanied by a feeling that the individual member's world is fracturing and falling apart under the overwhelming experience of the large group. Turquet (1975) states that "disarroy" not only describes an experience of change in the large group, but also points to a sense of disintegration, collapse, leading to a wish to return to the *status quo ante* (Turquet, 1975, p. 103). Hopper (2003b) reminds that a state of "disarroy" in the large group may be associated with mental states Bion (1967, p. 41) later called "bizarre objects".

The second state is extreme and describes a situation in which the individual member crosses the intermediate state of "disarroy" and reaches a state of idiosyncrasy expressed by a disconnected, bizarre, and aggressive behaviour. In such cases, although physically present, participants seem no longer to be part of the group. This behaviour helps keep participants inside and outside the group at the same time; however, it has disastrous consequences to the group's dynamics (Turquet, 1975, p. 103), often triggering a state of chaos and multiple splitting characterized by wandering, polarized behaviours, and alienation that hinder the continuation of the group. The member loses their individual member status after the rupture, interference, or deprivation of external boundaries in the relationship with the group and is on their way to become silent, withdrawn, and isolated (Turquet, 1975, p. 104). In fact, in the large group, the bombardment of projective identifications in all directions, discontinuous discussions, and the impossibility of relatedness generate a sense of being ignored, unheard. All these circumstances contribute to the de-skilling of the individual member, depriving them of self-awareness and promoting participation as membership individual or a *lumpenproletariat* state, as Turquet called it (Turquet, 1975, p. 107).

Turquet (1975) considered that a sense of familiarity was fundamental for the singleton, the transitional "I" to create and maintain the state of individual member. Thus, the facilitating differentiation "me/not me", as well as the delimited skin-of-my-neighbour boundaries may help the singleton fight against homogenization and contribute to restoring the weakened boundaries of the "I" by reaffirming the sense of I.M.-ness. However, unable to create familiarity or an experience of a fit or congruency, the "I" defends themselves against alienation and "disarroy" by establishing an "identical response" (Turquet, 1975, p. 112). Therefore, pressed by a quasi-impossibility of establishing a sense of familiarity, time, or safe boundaries, the individual member soon becomes immersed in the group with other individual members, revealing the fear of being lost in each other as member individuals.

Turquet (1975) went further, highlighting the role of violence in large groups. He described the individual's initial and ongoing fears of other members' aggressiveness, loss of control, and violent behaviour, which might emerge in large group situations. Indeed, nameless fears, fear of silence, fantasies, and persecutory feelings haunt large group interactions. Moreover, the size of a large group is frightening, and violence is the outcome of fears and frustrations felt when persons try to express themselves in such situations. One of the strategies to control the emergence of violence in the large group is to create a group/anti-group dichotomy. This is a classical manoeuvre that provides balance to large group interactions; however, it may also trigger polarization and projection of aggressiveness in the other subgroup. Moreover, a subgroup can easily be transformed into an anti-group (Turquet, 1975, p. 134).

For Turquet (1975), the immediate object of violence in a large group is the individual member. The theory of Oneness explores the challenges individuals face when trying to preserve their individuality within large groups. This preservation seems unacceptable in a homogenized large group, because the main tendency points to fusion, and the individual member thus perceives the large group's main goal as the annihilation of their individuality. In this threatening situation, the individual member is driven to seek a state of sociocultural homogeneity characterized by equality, similarity of beliefs and language, no differentiation of roles, and no use of personal authority, and then becomes a member individual (Hopper, 2003b, p. 41). Therefore, the tendency towards homogenization is quite strong as a result of an attempt to encompass violence by neutralizing the threatening effects of the large group on the individual's identity. These processes can be easily observed in large religious-ideological groups or in different communities or tribes where "any simplistic generalization or ideology that permeates the group may be easily transformed into a conviction of absolute truth" (Kernberg, 1998, p. 5). In this situation, pressured by role fixation and by homogenization and fusion, member individuals are at the mercy of leadership. Having lost their individual identities, but being protected by the group, they easily become an undifferentiated mass of followers. In this direction, Turquet's (1975) reflections on violence in large groups give a contemporary outlook to discussions about the role of individuals and the "location of their responsibility" (Turquet, 1975, p. 128) in violent crowds, initially discussed by nineteenth-century criminologists and psychologists (Sighele, 1891; Tarde, 1893; Le Bon, 1895).

The influence of Kleinian ideas on the theory of Oneness is clear. Primary envy seems to fuel the experience of a singleton who becomes a member individual. In this sense, Turquet (1975) states: "Many aspects of the large group can be interpreted as exercises in the force of envy towards this presumed 'richer other'" (Turquet, 1975, p. 141). The tendency towards Oneness in the large group is characterized as a defence against envy, since, for Turquet, aggressiveness in the large group acquires the form of envy – envy of thought, individuality, rationality, and ultimately envy of difference. Turquet's theory, by postulating homogenization as a defence against envy, is connected to

Rickman's Russian experience, in which avoidance of envy preserves the communion of beliefs in a homogenized group or community.

Turquet's investigations into large groups are original and his considerations on homogenization and fusion are similar to developments in the psycho-analytic and group analytic theories of the 1970s. In 1974, Anzieu (1984) carried out large-group experiences in training activities and observed omnipresent regression and primitive processes and defences in unstructured groups. Here, we can see similarities between the process of homogenization described in the theory of Oneness and the phenomenon of group illusion (Anzieu, 1971).

The concept of group illusion refers to "the substitution of the ego ideal of each group member by a common ego ideal" (Anzieu, 1984, p. 145). In group illusion, instead of identifying themselves with the leader, group members identify among themselves (Anzieu, 1984, p. 158). For Anzieu, individual instinctual needs are fused with a conception of the group as a primitive ego ideal equated to a gratifying primary object, the mother of the earliest stages of development. Thus, unlike Freud's proposition, the group faces a collective narcissistic fusion with the image of an omnipotent mother. Therefore, group illusion is a group defence against the phantom of the primal scene (Anzieu, 1984, p. 148). As a collective mental state, it relates to the early stages of development, where "the regressed ego, the id, and the primitive (pre-Oedipal) ego ideal of each individual are fused in the group illusion" (Kernberg, 1998, p. 6).

Group psychology, in this regard, is based on three sets of shared illusions that deny the individual's primal phantom (Anzieu, 1984). The first set concerns the idea that a group is composed of all equal individuals, thus denying sexual differences and castration anxiety. The second, that a group is self-engendered, having been generated by parthenogenesis within the body of a fecund and omnipotent mother, thus satisfying the desire for restoring childhood narcissism. Then, the fused group becomes the substitute for a lost object. The third set relates to the notion that the group, by itself, can heal and repair narcissistic wounds by becoming an idealized breast-mother (Anzieu, 1984; Kernberg, 1998).

Kernberg (1998) points to Janine Chasseguet-Smirgel, who in 1975, building on Anzieu's group illusion, suggests "the fulfilment of the wish for fusion between the ego and the ideal by the most regressive means, those pertaining to the pleasure principle" (Chasseguet-Smirgel, 1984, p. 82). Chasseguet-Smirgel explores the connection between narcissism and the ideal and says that narcissism is a state of archaic wholeness in which the ego occupies the place of its own ideal. The superego would thus be the heir of the Oedipus complex, whereas the ego ideal would be the heir of primary narcissism, the heir of the infantile illusion of omnipotence (Chasseguet-Smirgel, 1984, p. 76). The remembrance of primal oneness – rooted in the separation from the first object of love and in the awareness of the helplessness associated with this experience – would persist in the individual in the form of an ideal, the ego ideal. However, the ego ideal would not be shaped by idealized parental introjects, as

Freud had described; it would relate directly to the fundamental human desire to return to the mother's womb. Idealized parental introjects serve as further reminders of the lost perfection of childhood. Human evolution as a whole would then spring from the nostalgia of a lost paradise, and human beings would be in an endless quest to find it again.

In Chasseguet-Smirgel's analysis of groups under the influence of ideologies, we can see the same wish to fuse the ego and the ego ideal. This wish is related to both regression and illusions. However, these collective formations do not rely on the support of paternal figures or on superego impingements. They are constituted by the "hallucinatory realization of the wish to take possession of the mother by the sibship, through a very regressive mode, that of primary fusion" (Chasseguet-Smirgel, 1984, p. 82). That is, the group has as its major fantasy not the submission to the father's authority, but the fusion with the good breast or the omnipotent mother.

Although not considering it as the father of the primal horde, Chasseguet-Smirgel does not neglect the figure of the leader who conducts the masses. In her analysis, the leader of an ideological group activates the wish for the fusion between the ego and the ego ideal, as in the example of Nazism. Commenting on Chasseguet-Smirgel's ideas, Kernberg (1998, p. 6) suggests that "any group ... tends to select leaders who represent not the paternal aspects of the prohibitive superego but a pseudopaternal 'merchant of illusions'". It means that ideological groups would seek leaders who could provide the group with an ideology, as an illusion to confirm the individual's narcissistic aspirations of fusing with the group as a primitive ego ideal – the all-powerful and all-gratifying pre-Oedipal mother (Chasseguet-Smirgel, 1984). Thus, in groups based on ideologies and strongly identified among themselves, individuals would experience narcissistic restorations and feelings of greatness, omnipotence, and power (Kernberg, 1998). In addition, it is important to notice that, in ideological groups, the superego is completely disdained and its functions are taken up by the ideals. The abandonment of the superego in an ideological group can be observed in the atrocities part of the German society committed under the Nazi ideology. Such considerations point to the fact that ideological groups thirst "less for a leader than for illusions" (Chasseguet-Smirgel, 1984, p. 82).

The phenomenon of homogenization and fusion is crucial to the study of group psychodynamics in the twentieth century, and supports a new psychoanalytic and group analytic comprehension of the nature of cohesion in small, median, and large groups. Some investigations have indeed revealed that homogenization and fusion are primitive defences – although not necessarily connected to primary envy, as Turquet proposed (1975) – that guarantee the survival of the individual in the group. These defences keep sexuality repressed, aggressive impulses projected to the outside, and provide narcissistic restoration. However, as a result of their regressive and illusory features, such defences unveil how groups are vulnerable to unscrupulous leadership, narcissistic personalities, and fundamentalist ideologies.

Turquet brought innovative conceptualizations to large group research. Yet, as a psychoanalyst and group thinker, he was mainly interested on describing the conscious and unconscious behaviour of people in groups, especially in group relations conferences (Lawrence, 1979). In this regard, his work refers mainly "to the relatedness of the individual in the large group rather than to the basic dynamic of the group itself as a group" (Miller, 1998, p. 1500). Turquet's contributions to the psychodynamics of large groups and basic assumptions show important insights and describe group situations that elicit primitive anxieties and defences in groups of any size:

> ... (1) the idealization of the leader in the horde, described by Freud; (2) the idealization of the group ideology and of leadership that promotes narcissistic self-aggrandizement of the group, described by Anzieu (1981) and Chasseguet-Smirgel (1975); and (3) the small group processes described by Bion (1961) ...
>
> (Kernberg, 1998, p. 98)

Turquet's theory of Oneness is currently referred to as classical, although some think it is underpinned by outdated postulates. This criticism is related to three factors. First, it is a theory based on Kleinian intrapsychic postulations that prioritize the innate malignant envy and its role in large-group psychodynamics, although both psychoanalytic and group analytic theory have developed new approaches to the subject, in which theories of emotional development do not prioritize primary envy or its role in forging basic assumptions (Hopper, 2003b, p. 44). Second, it can be considered as a theory inserted in a paradigm that values the idea of the individual, a characteristic of modern individualism. Nevertheless, throughout the singleton's path in the large group, we can glimpse interdependencies (Elias, 1984) influencing the individual's interactions in the group and on its boundaries. It means we can infer some key situations from the Oneness psychodynamics. Situations in which the singleton's intersubjective and trans-subjective figurations influence large-group states. Third, Turquet's theory may no longer be considered as a new basic assumption, since the experience with large groups in different settings indicates that the phenomenon of Oneness is neither ubiquitous nor inevitable in large groups (Hopper, 2003b, p. 43).

Lawrence, Bain, and Gould: the Me-ness theory

After Turquet's (1975) theory of Oneness, which some consider as a fourth basic assumption (baO), further investigations tried to conceptualize new basic assumptions. Writing from their experience as group relations consultants and directors, as well as from their practice as social scientists, organizational consultants, and psychoanalysts, Lawrence, Bain and Gould – following Hopper's preliminary formulation of a new fourth basic assumption in group analysis in 1989 (Hopper, 2003b, p. 48) – proposed a fifth basic assumption in 1996: the Me-ness (baM) theory. By opposing Turquet's Oneness, they formulated another basic-assumption group, emphasizing separateness and refusing the idea of "we". The basic assumption "Me-ness" refers to "Not-oneness", that is, "baM equals ba not-O" (Lawrence, Bain, & Gould, 2000, p. 97).

Following Bion's tradition, influenced by Turquet's work, and having observed individuals from younger generations in the context of small and large groups at group relations conferences, Lawrence, Bain and Gould (2000) propose the fifth basic assumption of Me-ness, in which group members behave as if there was no group – each member is an individual with no connection to the whole. By denying the idea of a group, members protect themselves from the frightening aspects of group life and attune to the modern Western value of individualism.

The fifth basic assumption is hypothesized as a critical view of changes in Western industrialized societies in the 1980s and 1990s. The basic assumption of Me-ness is marked by the influence of sociocultural context transformations on the individual's behaviour. The idea is that life in contemporary societies puts individuality at risk, making individuals withdraw and look for the safety of their inner world. However, rather than explaining the basic assumption of Me-ness through the lens of individual narcissism, Lawrence, Bain and Gould conceptualize it as a cultural phenomenon, a transitional cultural experience engendered by conscious and unconscious social anxieties and fears. Their work is inspired by the social critique of post-industrial society Lasch (1979) explored in *The Culture of Narcissism* and by other authors (Lawrence, Bain, & Gould, 2000, pp. 98–101).

Conceived shortly after the fall of the Berlin Wall, when the European sociopolitical context shifted dramatically, the fifth basic assumption demonstrated that Eastern Europe was undergoing reconfigurations, with new countries and new borders, where the reaffirmation of national identities was once again at the foreground. Economic recession, bankruptcy, homelessness, and the ghost of unemployment were threatening Europe. On the other hand, capitalism was growing stronger, whereas individuals lost confidence in the social structures and eventually returned to their own selves, evidencing what Lawrence, Bain and Gould (2000, p. 99) called a "socially induced schizoid withdrawal". That is, individuals were being led to remit to the inner world of the self as a result of the impact of the dominant sociopolitical situation.

In conferences and consultancies carried out during the 1980s and 1990s, Lawrence, Bain and Gould (2000) observed that the concern with the individual's professional efficiency over collective ideals and teamwork prevailed among participants. A predominant narcissistic culture was leading individuals to isolation, anomie, and resistance to any type of collective project or group work. It was a culture of selfishness, and group participants imagined themselves as self-sufficient individuals willing to consider that the ultimate and unique reality was that of the individual. Therefore, they unconsciously behaved as if the group did not exist, but if it did exist, it was a source of persecuting experiences. In addition, the idea of "group" became associate with fantasies of contamination and impurity (Lawrence, Bain, & Gould, 2000, p. 100). The individuals' basic anxiety seemed to be that, if the group became an unavoidable reality, the individuals would be lost in it, however paradoxically it might seem because they wished to attain magically the status of work group. After all, as professionals, they were required to interact in groups. Basically, the Me-ness culture "is an unconscious system of defence against both the experiences of We and other ba groups" (Lawrence, Bain, & Gould, 2000, p. 101).

In their investigation, Lawrence, Bain and Gould (2000) observe significant differences in the psychodynamics of large groups when compared to the theory of Oneness. They start their analysis based on Turquet's (1975) idea of the singleton and on how the singleton joins the large group as an "I". They notice that, rather than relating to each other and acknowledging each other in a mutual "we-ness", it is the "me" part of the "I" that is mobilized (Turquet, 1975, p. 101). Their working hypothesis is that a new mental activity phenomenon does not allow individuals to enter an I/singleton state. Therefore, "as the opposite of Oneness, we are proposing another basic assumption group that emphasizes separateness and hates the idea of 'we'" (Turquet, 1975, p. 97). Group participants are caught in a me/singleton dynamic in which group experience is rejected. Thus, contrary to the tendency toward homogenization introduced by Turquet (1975), the Me-ness theory postulates that individuals withdraw narcissistically from the group as a defence against the anxiety of being taken by the "we-ness of homogenisation" (Hopper, 2003b, p. 49), typical of the Oneness psychodynamics.

According to Lawrence, Bain and Gould (2000), the idea of Me-ness can be connected with Winnicott's (1988) theory that an individual's development goes through a stage that mobilizes the idea of inside/outside, Me/not-Me. Moreover, they observe the presence of narcissistic and schizoid anxieties in participants. These defences may be explained by different object relations theories. In the Bionian tradition, Lawrence, Bain and Gould (2000) point that it is impossible for participants to rely on the idea of authority and leadership, or to function under the basic assumption of Dependency. There is no possibility of taking on different roles in order to work at the primary task. Their rejection of the idea of group is also connected with attacks on linking (Bion, 1967), where -L (of love) and -K (of knowledge) shape the impossibility of learning from experience with others, because learning is an activity for oneself alone. All these manifestations of Me-ness involve withdrawal, alienation, and aggression against the group-as-a-whole and are socially induced by a threatening social system.

The Me-ness theory represents an attempt to propose a basic assumption that includes the thought of Elias (2001), who "analyses the relationship between changes in the structure of human relations in societies with the concomitant changes in personality structure as part of a societal process" (Lawrence, Bain, & Gould, 2000, p. 117). Instead of limiting the debate to the influences of a narcissistic culture (Lasch, 1979) or to transformations in post-industrial societies, Lawrence, Bain and Gould (2000) underline the dichotomies prevailing in modernity that oppose individual and society. In this regard, they raise the idea of a closed individual, discussed by Elias (2001) in the concept of *Homo clausus*.

Moreover, using examples from philosophy, arts, and literature, they identify a tendency to transform an individual into an autonomous man – *Homo individualis* (Tecglen, 1992 *apud* Lawrence, Bain, & Gould, 2000, p. 118). Lawrence, Bain and Gould reveal in the here-and-now of conferences and consultations the deleterious effects of individualism at the end of the twentieth century. Their hope is that, in the twenty-first century, new figurations will be co-created for individual-group relationships, freeing individuals from the pressures of the narcissistic culture. They believe that a new conceptual basis, such as the *Homines aperti* (open people) proposed by Elias (2001), can be created by linking people as interdependent individuals (Lawrence, Bain, & Gould, 2000, p. 116). Unfortunately, at the dawn of the twenty-first century, individualism seems to be at its apex, and its side effects are manifesting in "the weariness of the self" (Ehrenberg, 2010). That is, feelings of deficiency, insufficiency, isolation, and shame are overshadowing subjects, creating a mass of excluded, "depressed", deprived individuals who personify twenty-first-century forms of personal and social suffering (Penna, 2020).

The Me-ness theory can be understood only in dialectical relation to the theory of Oneness (Hopper, 2003b). We should consider that some of the theoretical differences between them could be credited to shifts in the *Zeitgeist* of the late 1960s and 1990s, when the Oneness and the Me-ness theories were formulated, respectively. Even inadvertently, the theory of Oneness may have been consciously and unconsciously influenced by the effervescence of the sociocultural context of the 1960s, when the ideas of cohesion, homogeneity, democracy, and equality were close to the collective and countercultural values of the time. In a complementary and equally important way, the study of homogeneity and fusion provides clues to a deeper understanding of twentieth-century mass movements.

On the other hand, the Me-ness theory was formulated when the aspired ideal of cohesion in groups was giving place to the traumatic reality of Incohesion processes in the conscious and unconscious life of groups and social systems (Hopper, 2003b). This topic will be explored in Chapter Ten, as a new and ubiquitous fourth basic assumption. Therefore, inserted in the culture of narcissism (Lasch, 1979), in which "the fall of the public man" (Sennett, 1974) was reshaping individual-society interdependencies, an increased individualism and a tendency to withdraw to the safety of the private realm became the reality. That is, at the height of the counterculture and narcissistic culture, both postulations, although intending to be as universal as Bion's basic assumptions reveal in their psychodynamics the restraints and constraints of the social unconscious (Hopper & Weinberg, 2011, 2016, 2017) of participants, conveners, and theorists.

The theory of Oneness and the Me-ness theory have as their starting point observations on the individual's behaviour in group relations conferences and as their background the dichotomy that opposes individual and society, a classic feature of the individualistic paradigm. However, Turquet's considerations are connected mainly with the struggles an individual faces in large group interactions, whereas Lawrence, Bain and Gould highlight the "socially induced" influence of the sociocultural context on the shaping of an individual's behaviour in the large group. In this sense, the fifth basic assumption of Me-ness is one step ahead of Turquet's theory when seen from a perspective that takes into account the figurations between individuals and society. Even though it is impossible to deny the relevance of co-created interdependencies between the large group participants and the society, both theories are trapped in views that prioritize now the individual, now the social in the we-I balance (Elias, 2001). In fact, by exploring basic assumption groups, Turquet (1975) and Lawrence, Bain and Gould (2000) ended up contributing to a deeper understanding of large group psychodynamics in group relations and group analytic settings.

Moreover, it is important to mention that, in Brazil, the Bionian Paulo Sandler, has hypothesized a sixth basic assumption, Hallucionosis of Exclusion/Appertaining:

> … one hallucinates that one appertains to a given group (or subgroup within the group) and/or hallucinates that one is excluded from the given group that one aspires to be positioned with or to be a functional part of.
>
> (Sandler, 2013, p. 231)

Sandler (2013) states that his basic assumption is quite different from Turquet's and Lawrence, Bain and Gould's, both conceived in their experiences in the field of group relations. Sandler's hypothesis is drawn from his work as a psychoanalyst, relying on empirical resources from community psychiatry, as well as observations of intragroup facts and crises in psychoanalytic institutions and in the history of the movement.

It is not possible to examine Sandler's postulation in depth here, especially his contribution to the psychoanalytic study of difficult interrelationships in training institutes. In this book, this brief mention of Sandler's work underlines the importance of Bion's basic assumption group and work group for understanding better primitive mental functioning of persons in institutional/organizational settings and in the wider environment. Moreover, based on Sandler's work, which interweaves Bion's theory of groups and his further work in psychoanalysis, we can capture the importance of Bion's ideas about "caesura" (Bion, 1977), that is, about the paradox of discontinuity that emerges from an underlying continuity. Indeed, acknowledging this paradox is fundamental for studies on groups.

8 Foulkes and group analysis

The development of the theory of the social unconscious

Foulkes and group analysis

As outlined in Chapter Five, the cross-breeding of the theoretical influences with which Foulkes had been in contact in Germany in the 1920s and 1930s enabled him to delineate a specific figuration to conceive small group work at Northfield. Foulkes's use of "small-group principles to a specified large group *per se*" (de Maré, 1983, p. 230) transformed the interactions in the hospital-as-a-whole. A few years later, Foulkes defined group analysis as a "form of Psychotherapy in Small groups and also as a Method of studying Groups and the behaviour of Human Individuals in their social aspects" (Foulkes, 1948, p. vii). The Northfield experiments were fundamental to the development of group work in England. In Chapter Six, we discussed some legacies of Rickman and Bion's first experiment in groups. In Chapter Seven, we focused on advances in group practice – especially from the 1960s onwards – that led to attempts to formulate new basic assumptions in the work with groups. The second experiment, with Tom Main and Harold Bridger, opened the way for the establishment of therapeutic communities in England (Harrison, 2000, 2018; Pearce, & Haigh, 2017) and gave birth to group analysis through the work of S. H. Foulkes.

Foulkes's ground-breaking work replaces the traditional dichotomies between individual and society with a new framework that confers value to their interdependencies (Elias, 1939, 2001) based on the intrinsic relationality of human beings. Indeed, since its inception, group analysis has focused on the social dimension of relationships, improving intersubjective and trans-subjective perspectives in open living systems. Through group analysis, Foulkes (1948) was able to move from a society of individuals to a society of persons – as explored in Chapter Four – by revealing that "the old juxtaposition of an inside and outside world, constitution and environment, individual and society, phantasy and reality, body and mind and so on, are untenable" (Foulkes, 1948, p. 10). For Foulkes, individuals cannot be separated from their context: "We cannot isolate biological, social, cultural and economic factors, except by special abstraction" (Foulkes, 1975b, p. 37), which means that body, mind, and society are interdependent and intertwined. This new perspective allowed Foulkes to

DOI: 10.4324/9780429399534-9

shift from classic psychoanalysis to group analysis by highlighting the individual as part of a network of interactions and communications that comprise the group matrix.

At Northfield, Foulkes could observe the group situation from a wider perspective and improve small-group work. However, before taking part in the "Group Affair" (Foulkes, 1948, p. 21), in an article co-written with Eve Lewis (Foulkes & Lewis, 1944, pp. 33–34), Foulkes had already addressed the relevance of four specific therapeutic factors found in group-analytic groups: (1) the patient is brought out of isolation into a social situation; (2) the patient realizes that other patients have similar anxieties and impulses that act as therapeutic agents – this set of factors is called *mirror reactions*; (3) deep unconscious material stemming from the collective unconscious is activated and acts in the group as a *condenser*; (4) explanations and information are elements of *exchange* between the participants and alter the emotional situation of the group. In 1948, when Foulkes published his first book, *Introduction to Group-Analytic Psychotherapy*, he supplemented these four specific factors with two others: (5) the group as a *forum*, symbolizing the community as a whole; (6) the group as a *support*, pointing to a transformation in the individual transference situation (intragroup transference), which enables the group to absorb what in the individual treatment is focused on the therapist (Foulkes, 1948, pp. 167–168).

We can infer how Foulkes's group-analytical thinking was marked, from the beginning, by a relational perspective in which interpersonal and transpersonal processes were taken seriously. The influence of the Lewinian social field, the Gestalt figure/ground, Goldstein's holistic approach, Elias's sociology, and an *avant garde* intersubjective psychoanalytic perspective is visible on Foulkes's first group-analytic postulations. Patients are immersed in social situations and influenced by their contexts, which means that their "disturbed function is due to disturbance in the equilibrium of the total situation" (Foulkes, 1948, p. 2). Therapeutic factors such as mirroring and exchange are complementary (Zinkin, 2000) and interrelated in multiple dimensions in a group-analytic situation. Both factors reveal how conscious and unconscious processes co-created between the members are crossed by a continuous interplay between sameness and difference, which is not only therapeutic, but fundamentally relational. Exchange implies difference and mirroring sameness. Therefore, the dialectics established between "owning and sharing" (Zinkin, 2000, p. 11), between the interpersonal and transpersonal spheres are vital for development and change in therapeutic groups and for healthier life groups. Moreover, they facilitate new identifications and identity processes. Group-specific factors in groups are also a source of support, socialization, and belongingness to members; they symbolize and provide better interactions for persons.

In addition, a group analytic situation stimulates the release of "deep unconscious material [which] is expressed more readily and more fully. It is as if the 'collective unconscious' acted as a *condenser*" (Foulkes, & Lewis, 1944, p. 34; italics in the original). In this statement, influenced by Lewis – and by the ideas of Karl Mannheim (Scholz, 2017) – Foulkes uses the expression "collective unconscious" to name an important insight that was in his thinking since the beginning of the group-analytic project. Although the idea of collective unconscious – defined as psychic predispositions based on a universal character that manifests in all cultures (Jung, 1936) – had influenced Foulkes, it took him time to disentangle the concept of the social unconscious from the Jungian concept of collective unconscious (Hopper, 2003a, p. 124, Weinberg, 2007; Hopper & Weinberg, 2011). Only years later, especially after the conceptualization of the primordial level of communication in groups - which enhanced the possibility of sharing universal symbols and archetypal images in group communications - was he able to make this fundamental distinction (Nitzgen, 2011, p. 15).

Foulkes bequeathed to his younger colleagues and students the task of clarification and development of the notion of the social unconscious in group analysis. Their identity as group analysts required the consideration of the social nature of human beings, the inevitable tension between psychological and socialization processes, in their search for a broader understanding of group phenomena and the work in group-analytic groups. In this sense, the idea of a socially unconscious mind, which had been part of Foulkes's thinking since his early work as a psychoanalyst in Germany, was transmitted, even in inchoate form, to his followers.

However, although Foulkes referred to the idea of the social unconscious to examine biological, social, and cultural forces people are unaware of, he never discussed the concept systematically or explored it in his clinical work (Hopper & Weinberg, 2011). Yet, it is natural to infer that group analysts were sensible to the existence of unconscious processes beyond the individual's subjectivity. Moreover, since the first group-analytic experiences with large groups (Kreeger, 1975; Foulkes, 1975b), group analysts observed, especially in traumatic contexts, the emergence of unconscious processes that seem to lie beyond the interplay between individuals and their groupings (Hopper, 2003a). In fact, for group analysts, "each human interaction is a group interaction at an unconscious level" (Knauss, 2006, p. 160). Thus, the unconscious mind has always been socially unconscious.

Today, the study of the social unconscious is anchored to group-analytic epistemology. Their philosophical, sociological, psychological, political, and religious dimensions will be discussed in this chapter as an essential bridge for remodelling investigations into crowds, Freudian masses, and for explorations in large groups. But first, it is necessary to follow how these theoretical figurations evolved.

The internalization of the external world and the notion of social unconscious

The concept of unconscious connects with the origins of psychoanalysis in the late nineteenth century. However, before Freud, the unconscious had been part of the vocabulary of magnetizers, philosophers, scientists, and literati throughout Western history (Ellenberger, 1970). Freud (1900, 1915a) revolutionized its conceptualization and, consequently, the way of conceiving human subjectivity.

In Freudian psychoanalysis, discussions about unconscious processes go beyond the individual realm and include the relationship between subject and culture, drive (*Trieb*) and civilization (Freud, 1921, 1923a, 1930a, 1933a), as well as the interconnections between phylogenetic inheritance and ontogenesis and their effects on psychic transmission (Freud, 1913, 1937, 1939). These considerations have undoubtedly brought to the fore the relevance of archaic inheritance and of the unconscious dimensions that transcend the individual experience (Freud, 1937). In this direction, Freud (1923a, 1933a, 1939) draws attention to connections between the unconscious and the history of human-kind, which allow us to glimpse the possibility of a social dimension in the unconscious. However, despite Freud's words – "... and so from the very first individual psychology, in this extended but entirely justifiable sense of the words, is at the same time social psychology as well" (Freud, 1921, p. 69) – the psycho-analytic mainstream took decades to realize the importance of this assertion. Then, before engaging in investigations of the social unconscious, we must highlight a fragment of Freud's thinking that appeals to the imagination: "The hypothesis of there being inherited vestiges in the id alters, so to say, our views about it" (Freud, 1938, p. 299). It is not much, but this fragment opens phylogenetic, ontogenetic, and sociogenetic perspectives – as Foulkes suggested in 1938 in his review of Elias's first volume of *The Civilizing Process* (E. Foulkes, 1990, p. 81) – on the future linked to investigations into the social unconscious.

The notion of the social unconscious is not novel. Hopper (2001) states that the ideas underpinning this concept have been found in Shakespeare, in social philo-sophy, and in the social sciences since Durkheim, Weber, Tönnies, and especially Marx. It means that discussions on topics such as alienation, the sociality of human nature (Hopper, 1982, p. 18), nature *versus* nurture, and the individual or the social *a priori*, even inadvertently, pose questions related to the idea of the social uncon-scious.[1] Investigations into the internalization of the social world and its effects on the unconscious life of persons have been suggested by countless intellectuals and are at the core of the group analytic project.

Early on his career and still in Frankfurt, Foulkes himself was influenced by psychologists, psychoanalysts, philosophers, and sociologists in debates con-cerning the impact of society's class and power structures on personality. However, the scope of these influences varies according to the focus of analysis. On the one hand, orthodox Marxism was entangled with debates on inequal-ity, as well as on the fundamental role of class consciousness and the importance of social justice (Jay, 1973). On the other hand, Foulkes was interested in the investigation of the social *a priori*, in the impact of socialization and theory of socialization on the formation of personality, that is, on "socially created iden-tities" (Hopper, 2020, personal communication), an idea that is close to the notion of the social unconscious. Therefore, because of his closeness to the work of some Freudo-Marxists and Frankfurtians, and because of his sociopsychological quests, Foulkes was immersed in topics that would later be explored in terms of the social unconscious. However, Foulkes views were more connected to the social system as a whole than to Marxist dialectics and the influence exerted by power structures or social class (Nitzgen & Hopper, 2017).

Yet, considering the period Foulkes was working in Frankfurt, we should bear in mind that investigations of the metabolization of social objects – such as those Horkheimer, Adorno, and Fromm[2] conducted in the Institute for Social Research in the early 1930s – are in connection with the social unconscious as well (Nitzgen, 2011, p. 17). Therefore, the link between Foulkes and the social unconscious can be traced back to the same German sources that enabled him to create group analysis: Goldstein's and Gelb's psychological analysis, Freudian psychoanalysis, Freudo-Marxist works, sociology, and cultural anthropology. Therefore "the *idea* of a social unconscious can be found in Foulkes's work from the very beginning of it" (Nitzgen & Hopper, 2017, p. 6; italics in original).

However, as Nitzgen (2011) reveals, it is not easy to track Foulkes's mentions to the notion of the social unconscious. The first was in 1950, in *Group Therapy: Survey, Orientation and Classification*:

> ... the group-analytic situation, while dealing intensively with the unconscious in the Freudian sense, brings into operation and perspective a totally different area of which the individual is equally unaware. Moreover, the individual is as much compelled and modelled by these colossal forces as by his own *id* and defends himself as strongly against their recognition without being aware of it, but in quite different ways and modes. One might speak of a social or interpersonal unconscious.
>
> (Foulkes, 1950, p. 52)

Although Foulkes moves beyond Freud's definition of the unconscious by adding the importance of interpersonal processes (Weinberg, 2007), it seems that, in his first statement, he was still attached to the Freudian unconscious. This allegiance can be observed in Foulkes's recommendations "that the 'translation' of the 'social unconscious' follows the same principles as the translation of Freudian 'repressed unconscious'" (Nitzgen, 2011, p. 5). However, it was clear for Foulkes that the group situation affords the opportunity "for the exploration of what may be called the 'social unconscious'" (Foulkes & Anthony, 1957, p. 42).

Moreover, the group situation reduces censorship to the patient's relationship to others and to the conductor, allowing to approach "the social unconscious, i. e., unconscious social relationships not usually revealed" (Foulkes & Anthony, 1957, p. 56). In this sense, the group-analytic situation, while dealing with the sharing of inner mental processes, reveals interpersonal and multipersonal (Foulkes, 1975b, p. 37) phenomena in groups, enabling the analysis, the translation, and the investigation of various dimensions of conscious and socially unconscious communication among group members. In effect, these inner mental processes were manifest in these interpersonal relations, and vice-versa, but in these processes, the psychological life of persons was changed.

The "social a priori" and the social unconscious

The debate on the origins of the concept of social unconscious, especially regarding processes of internalization and metabolization of social objects, finds in Dalal (1998, 2011) an original thinker. Dalal states that it was not Foulkes's prerogative to point to the social unconscious, for the formulation of the "social *a priori*" is a topic in philosophical and sociological debates. However, he inquires how, in particular times and places, people come to share a view or take things for granted, "things that are not only outside the scope of our consciousness, but *the basis of it?*" (Dalal, 2011, p. 254; italics in original). The "answers" connect to conventions to which the individuals belong from birth to death, and which they thoughtlessly reproduce and reinforce. In this sense, Dalal (2011) explores similarities between the work of important scholars[3] who investigate the "social *a priori*" and the formulation of the concept of the social unconscious in group analysis.

About Foulkes's work, Dalal (2011, p. 250; italics in original) writes, "One name for the social *a priori* is the Foulkesian one of the *social unconscious*". Indeed, Foulkes framed the concept of the social unconscious in terms of a "social *a priori*", highlighting the importance of internalizations of forces operating in the group, in the community to which the person belongs (E. Foulkes, 1990, p. 212). Although Foulkes has always been concerned with the importance of the introjection of external objects, as we can observe in his psychoanalytic paper "On Introjection" (1937), group analysis is not a form of social psychology nor is exclusively focused in the valuation of processes of internalization of social objects. The interweave between the personal, the interpersonal and the transpersonal have always been fundamental for Foulkes. Moreover, group analysts have always realised that the personal matrix would involve individuality and this is also where creativity and charisma might lie (Hopper, 2003a). In this sense, to explore the social unconscious is not to discuss how the social is *in* the unconscious of a person or how they are simply affected by society and culture (Dalal, 1998). To understand the social unconscious, it is fundamental to take into account Elias's (2001, 1984) interdependencies between individual-society and his work on figurations, because "the individual is formed by, and simultaneously informs, the social" (Dalal, 1998, p. 211).

Research on the social unconscious includes what authors have discussed about the cultural unconscious[4]. For Dalal, however, the notion of the social unconscious is the same as that of discourse and includes "power relationships *between* discourses. The social unconscious is a discourse which hierarchically orders other discourses" (Dalal, 1998, p. 212; italics in original). Indeed, each individual is born in a social environment and naturally absorbs the discourses produced within this milieu. Thus, power relations are part of the social unconscious and individual persons are permeated by discourse, ideology, and apparatuses of power (Althusser, 1969; Foucault, 1972; Penna, 2016a). They end up legitimizing "language categories and ideas", as well as "a taxonomy on the world and the mind" and "systems of inclusion and exclusion" (Dalal, 2011, p. 258) that are socially unconsciously created in some societies.

Dalal aligns group analytic debates on the social unconscious with philosophical and sociological perspectives. By highlighting the figuration of social power that "describes the structured network of human existence itself" (Dalal, 1998, p. 212), he puts into perspective the psychic relevance of representations of economic and political structures, joining it with the social through language and symbol in Elias's tradition. However, Hopper and Weinberg (2011) argue that, although social power relations are vital for exploring social unconscious processes, "they are hardly either the only or the most important social objects that are introjected" (p. xxxvi). This comment reveals how the study of the social unconscious, even in the group-analytic milieu, is crossed by multiple influences and may follow different paths.

Dalal's investigations into the social unconscious are connected to the discussion on *Taking the Group Seriously* (1998), where he explores a radical Foulkesian theory – Radical Foulkes – as opposed to a classic Foulkesian theory – Orthodox Foulkes. Dalal reveals how Foulkes's theory – given his dual affiliation to Freudian psychoanalysis and Eliasian sociology – is marked by different paradigms in the conception of the individual and the social, underlining how it carries, embedded in its conceptual scheme, the germ of a radical transformation in the way of seeing individual-society relationships. Indeed, by "taking the group seriously", it is possible to build a post-Foulkesian group analytic theory. It means that, avoiding the pitfalls of prioritizing now the individual, now the social, Dalal (2011) proposes a reflection on figurations to conceive a new group analytic paradigm that would finally give value to "individuals-in-social-relations", as Elias imagined (Dalal, 2011, p. 252). From this perspective, the study of the social unconscious reshapes the debate on the so-called internalization of social objects by taking seriously whole situations and the figurations co-created by persons, groups, and social systems. Next, we explore how the social unconscious study proceeded through these intrinsic interdependencies.

Group analysis and the social unconscious

Group-analytic theory circumscribes the investigation of the social unconscious from its roots in Foulkes's thinking in the 1920s and 1930s in Germany to twentieth-first-century research. Over the last forty years, the study of the social unconscious has evolved and many group analysts have been involved in the research. In 1984, Hopper (1984, 2003a) published an article, reproduced later as book chapters, highlighting the problem of context and its importance to group-analytic psychotherapy. He also advanced investigations of the social unconscious in presentations in workshops and conferences and published his selected papers from 1965 to 2003, organized in the book *The Social Unconscious* (Hopper 2003a). His work in the development of a fourth basic assumption theory (Hopper, 2003b), to be explored in Chapter Ten, is also connected to the study of the social unconscious.

The European Association for Transcultural Group Analysis (EATGA) was set up in 1982 by a group of psychoanalysts and group analysts from different cultures. Through transcultural workshops and work with small and large groups, the team formulated a working hypothesis, proposed by René Kaës, about the existence of "an undifferentiated zone in both individual and collective psyches in every culture, based on the earliest exchanges between mother and infant as well as on cultural codes and rules, but only discernible when confronted by people of another culture" (Brown 1987, p. 238). These workshops became a source for observations of socially unconscious differences in persons, groups, and societies in group analysis. They might also have contributed to the development of Kaës's (2007) works on shared spaces and unconscious alliances.

In 1994, Dennis Brown and Louis Zinkin published *The Psyche and the Social World*, bringing important developments to group-analytic theory. In turn, Dalal (1998), as mentioned earlier in this chapter, discussed the notion of the social unconscious in connection to Norbert Elias's work and Foulkesian group analysis in search of a more consistent group analytic paradigm. In 2007, Haim Weinberg published an article discussing misconceptions and misunderstandings about the social unconscious conceptualization. After that, Hopper and Weinberg started an extensive and fruitful partnership investigating the social unconscious. Together with collaborators from different countries, they edited three volumes – *The Social Unconscious in Persons, Groups and Societies* (Hopper & Weinberg, 2011, 2016, 2017) – with comprehensive introductions and lines of investigation on the topic. A fourth volume, based in clinical work, is being prepared.

On exploring Hopper and Weinberg's trilogy, we can observe shifts and ripening in the theorization of the social unconscious that allowed the definition of its scope and clarification of its meanings in group analysis. The first volume of the series focuses on mapping the theoretical field of the social unconscious, identifying its origins in Foulkes's work (Nitzgen, 2011) and differentiating the notion of similar philosophical, psychological, psychoanalytical, and sociological investigations (Hopper & Weinberg, 2011).[5] It became clear that, despite its similarities with other approaches, the concept of the social unconscious in group analysis provides not only theoretical and empirical inputs, but also a clinical outlook on the investigation of socially unconscious processes. Embedded in group-analytic theory, investigations of the social unconscious plunge into the figurations co-created by persons, groups, and social systems, involving, in open systems, the dimensions of time and space.

However, before discussing the psychodynamics of these interdependencies, it is important to provide a general definition of the social unconscious:

> We use the concept of the social unconscious in order to refer to the
> social, cultural, and communicational constraints and restraints of which
> people are to varying degrees unconscious. The social unconscious
> emphasizes the shared anxieties, fantasies, defences, myths, and memories
> of the members of a social system… The field theory of the social
> unconscious includes its sociality, relationality, transpersonality, transge-
> nerationality, and collectivity.
>
> (Hopper & Weinberg, 2017, p. xxii)

Extracted from the third volume of the trilogy under discussion, this definition
encompasses the evolution of the social unconscious conceptualization
(Hopper, 2001, p. 10; Hopper, 2003a, p. 127; Hopper & Weinberg, 2011,
p. xxx). It enables us to explore entanglements between sociological views –
the unconscious constraints of social objects (social facts and social forces) that
have been internalized – and psychoanalytic views – the various dimensions of
unconscious processes in psychoanalytic theory, as well as restraints based on
Freud's (1930a) view of subjects in opposition to civilization (Hopper, 2003a).

The definition also reveals what happens *in between* the interpersonal persons
Foulkes studied. In this sense, what Winnicott (1971) describes in the transitional paradox lies at the core of the conceptualization of the social unconscious, pointing to an area where socially unconscious processes are co-
invented/co-created (Hopper & Weinberg, 2011). Winnicott's transitional
phenomena in connection to social unconscious processes show the relevance
of the concept of shared reality and of Winnicott's (1971, p. 128) quest for the
location of cultural experience. Then, based on the Winnicottian theory, we
conclude that the social unconscious is not simply a matter of the internalisa-
tion of sociocultural objects, it is intrinsically related to transitional spaces where
interpersonal and transpersonal relations take place (Hopper & Weinberg, 2017,
p. xxvi).

Investigations into the social unconscious explore what Winnicott has
designated as a third area, located in the potential space between the subject
and the environment. They also answer Winnicott's question, "… where is
cultural experience located?" (Winnicott, 1971, p. 139). This finding allows us
to infer that the nature of the intersubjectivity and trans-subjectivity Foulkes
has developed since the 1940s in group analysis, especially the idea of a socially
unconscious mind, is akin to what Winnicott's intersubjective thinking discussed years later in psychoanalysis. This kinship reveals how group-analytic
thinking, still unknown in several psychoanalytic circles, is fundamental for
research on contemporary object relations and relational and field theory in
psychoanalysis.[6] Moreover, as we proceed in our explorations of the social
unconscious theory – as we will do in the next section – we can observe that
group-analytic thinking makes us move beyond Winnicott's and other psychoanalytic investigations of intersubjectivity[7] (Ogden, 1994; Kaës, 2007;
Altman, 2010) in search of "where *in the mind* cultural experience is" (Winnicott,
1971, p. 128; italics mine).

The second volume, published in 2016, connects to investigations into foundation matrices, sociocultural transmission of myths, as well as traumatic experiences and defences co-created by persons and groups in particular social systems. Supported by the first volume investigations of akin theories by Jung, Moreno, and Pichon-Rivière, volume two puts into perspective a field theory, in the Lewinian sense of the term, that enables the emergent Foulkesian theory of the social unconscious to explore the dimensions of sociality, relationality, transpersonality, and collectivity (Hopper & Weinberg, 2016, p. xiii). Moreover, social trauma and intergenerational and transgenerational transmissions are especially relevant. At this point, although transdisciplinary explorations brought important insights about the figurations established in different foundation matrices, it becomes clear that advances in the social unconscious theorization require the re-examination and reconfiguration of the concept of matrix.

This task was undertaken by Nitzgen and Hopper (2017) in the third volume (Hopper, & Weinberg, 2017), leading to the concept of "tripartite matrix". In this regard, we can see that the paths taken by contemporary investigations of the social unconscious interweave and reveal a kinship with the course and evolution of group-analytic theory. Analysing the evolution of the social unconscious theory from its initial explorations, we can see how some core concepts of group analysis have matured. This interplay expresses a deep affinity with the study of the social unconscious and contemporary group analysis, especially through the concept of tripartite matrices. Next, we will examine how this link evolved.

From mind to matrix

The evolution of group-analytic theory shows how Foulkes moved gradually towards an important epistemological shift when, by intertwining psychoanalysis and sociology, he started to see mental processes as multipersonal phenomena and conceived the idea of a socially unconscious mind. Moreover, by replacing the concept of mind with the concept of matrix, he contributed to a fundamental step in contemporary group-analytic research on the social unconscious.

In group analysis, Foulkes explored the concept of mind, transforming classical views. He postulated that the mind consists of interacting processes between closely linked persons in a group (E. Foulkes, 1990, p. 224). For Foulkes, when people meet in a group, a new phenomenon is created, allowing for the emergence of "'transpersonal processes', that is, mental processes which, like X-rays in the bodily sphere, go right through the individuals composing such a 'network'" (E.Foulkes, 1990, p. 224). After this finding, Foulkes stopped confining the idea of mind to an individual organism and started thinking in terms of transpersonal networks, moving in the direction of the idea of group matrix as a "unified mental field" (E. Foulkes, 1990, p. 228). In this sense, Foulkes no longer refers to an individual mind or a group mind, because "the mind is not a *thing* which exists but a series of events, moving and proceeding all the time" (E. Foulkes, 1990, p. 224).

This new observation enabled Foulkes to distance himself from misleading metaphors – such as "the group mind" – based on the Cartesian subjectivity that had prevailed in the study of group formations since the nineteenth century, as observed in the work of Spencer, Le Bon (1895), and others. However, until today, some of these metaphors still pervade certain analyses, creating inappropriate homologies and isomorphisms that use persons' properties to describe the properties of social systems[8] (Hopper, 2003a). This discussion is fundamental to reflect on the social unconscious in group analysis, because it warns us of the fact that we cannot explore *the* social unconscious of a group or social system as if a group or social system were a person with a mind and a brain. This way, we can only refer to the social unconscious of persons in the context of groups inserted in their particular foundation matrices.

The concept of matrix, while encompassing the multiple relational perspectives of what happens within a group, is more appropriate to the study of the social unconscious than the concept of mind. The matrix is defined as

> the hypothetical web of communication and relationship in a given group. It is the common shared ground which ultimately determines the meaning and significance of all events and upon which all communications and interpretations verbal and non-verbal, rest.
>
> (Foulkes, 1964, p. 292)

Foulkes chose the word matrix, which carries multiple and ancient meanings,[9] to name the more and the different that happens in groups. The *Oxford English Dictionary* (www.lexico.com/definition/matrix) states that the word matrix derives from "Late Middle English (in the sense 'womb'): from Latin, 'breeding female', later 'womb', from mater, matr- 'mother'". Today, the word matrix is used in the natural sciences, such as biology and geology, but may also designate the cultural, social, organizational, or political environment in which something develops.

Scholz (2011) states that, with the notion of matrix, Foulkes was trying to find a language – "the common pool of meaning, the network of communication, the matrix of the group" (Foulkes, 1975a, p. 122) – for what he was experiencing in interactions between group members. In this direction, Ormay (2012) explores the concept of matrix by connecting the Lewinian ideas about force-field and systems theory to the idea of matrix, combining both in his own theory of *nos*. For Ormay, a matrix is a network of relationships and has many centres. Persons occupy their nodal points (Ormay, 2012, p. 146). Moreover, a matrix is organized in time and space along vertical and horizontal axes (Ormay, 2012, p. 147), an idea akin to Pichon-Rivière's (1980, Losso, de Setton & Scharff, 2017) group theory. Thus, the matrix is present in time and space in the personal, interpersonal and transpersonal levels of relationships as we are discussing in this chapter. In this sense, the matrix metaphor is manifold and multidimensional, "both broad and vague" (Ahlin, 1996, p. 56), bringing in various associations.

For Foulkes, the group matrix is at the centre of communication in groups. It is not only the basis of all mental processes, but also the matrix of interpersonal relationships in the group. Its lines of force cross right through the "individual members and can therefore be called *a transpersonal network*, comparable to a magnetic field" (Foulkes, & Anthony, 1965, p. 258; italics in original). Therefore, the matrix of a group brings into interaction interrelated persons and not "individuals as if they were closed systems" (Foulkes, & Anthony, 1965, p. 214). This reference connects the group matrix to Elias's (1939) discussions on the concept of *Homo clausus*, enabling us to replace the idea of individual (in all its modern connotations) with the term person, more appropriate to group analytic reflections, as discussed in Chapter Four. This postulation helped group analysts to enter in the "brave new world" of explorations of communication over boundaries, as it were, interpersonal and transpersonal interactions that take place in a group matrix. It means that to explore the matrix of a group is "to approach the known but yet unseen or unheard results of what is not consciously known. It is to enter into the area of paradoxes and to test the limits of thinking" (Ahlin, 1996, p. 55).

To examine the development of the concept of group matrix in connection with the social unconscious project, Nitzgen and Hopper (2017, pp. 8–10) studied Foulkes's work from the late 1940s to the 1960s. Both explored how Foulkes's thinking moved from the idea of "the group matrix as a social network" (Foulkes, 1948, p. 14) to the matrix as a "web of communication and relationship in a given group" (Foulkes, 1964, p. 292), leading to the formulation of a more historical and contextualized view of the matrix as a common shared ground for all group communications in 1970, as the "mother soil in which all dynamic processes take their place" (E. Foulkes, 1990, p. 212).

Here, it is interesting to observe Foulkes's use of the metaphor "mother soil" to describe and ground the concept of matrix. This metaphor applied to group matrix brings about the idea of support, nourishment from the soil, reminding us that the group matrix creates a basis, a stage for the development of a group. In fact, "the group matrix is truly a group-work creation and its aims and shape bear witness not only to the individuals in it but to their ancestors, histories, cultures" (Ahlin, 1996, p. 57). Thus, the group matrix crosses interpersonal and transpersonal boundaries as X-rays, besides displaying the past and the present of its members' interactions. Therefore, as Nitzgen and Hopper (2017, p. 11) conclude in their analysis of the evolution of the concept in Foulkes, "the matrix became firmly *rooted* or *grounded* in both historical time and space, and in *interpersonal* and *transpersonal* space… In other words, the matrix became simultaneously both *social* and *mental*".

This observation reshapes the concept of matrix, introducing to group-analytic theory and clinical work a multidimensional time/space outlook. It gives a four-dimensionality to interdependencies and communication between personal, interpersonal, transpersonal, and transgenerational processes in the group matrix. It confers to group-analytic theory a spatiality in open living systems properly appreciated in studies on the social unconscious (Hopper & Weinberg, 2017; Hopper, 2018b).

Tripartite matrices

The concept of matrix evolved, allowing Foulkes to introduce the notions of foundation matrix and dynamic matrix in the First European Symposium in Group Analysis, held in Lisbon in 1970:

> ... it is possible to claim a firm pre-existing community or communion between the members, founded eventually on the fact that they are all human. They have the same qualities as a species, the same anatomy and physiology, and also perhaps archaic traces of ancient experiences. This pre-existing and relatively static part we call the "foundation matrix". On top of this there are various levels of communication which are increasingly dynamic. They develop under our eyes. This is called the dynamic matrix. In between are levels which in accord with the opinion of the observer are determined either more biologically or more culturally.
>
> (E. Foulkes, 1990, pp. 212–213)

In 1973, in *The Group as Matrix of the Individual's Mental Life*, Foulkes continues:

> I have accepted from the beginning that even this group of total strangers, being of the same species and more narrowly of the same culture, share a fundamental, mental matrix (*foundation matrix*). To this their closer acquaintance and their intimate exchanges add consistently, so that they also form a current, ever-moving, ever-developing *dynamic matrix*.
>
> (E. Foulkes, 1990, p. 228)

At the European Symposium, Foulkes also highlighted the conscious and unconscious levels of transmission of cultural inheritance between the foundation matrix and the dynamic matrix; some levels are more connected to biology, others are more culturally embedded (E. Foulkes, 1990, pp. 213–215). As Scholz (2011, p. 270) suggests, in the beginning, the foundation matrix was based on biology, including the anatomy and physiology of the human species, in a clear reference to Goldstein, but it came to include body, language, culture, education, and class. Double dimensions of culture transmitted to a person throughout a life cycle, intergenerational and transgenerational issues (Le Roy, 2000, p. 182), as well as shared memories, socioeconomic structure (Scholz, 2011, 2017), and power relations (Dalal, 2011) have been added to the analysis. Therefore, the foundation matrix contains all dimensions of communication, including verbal and non-verbal language, gestures, postures, and expressions (E. Foulkes, 1990, p. 213). Scholz (2017, p. 34) brings to the discussion on foundation matrices Deleuze and Guattari's (1987) concept of "rhizome", conferring a post-modern outlook to the investigation of foundation matrices, avoiding a dualistic and binary analysis and favouring the necessary multiplicity of interwoven dimensions that comprise the study of foundation matrices.

Therefore, the multidimensionality of foundation matrices is directly connected to the research on the social unconscious. Its study unveils how socio-cultural structures, *habitus* (Elias, 1939; Bourdieu, 1986), myths, collective memories (Halbwachs, 1925), and social trauma are intergenerationally, trans-generationally transmitted (Hopper, 2003a; Faimberg, 2005; Frosh, 2013a) and co-constructed in some societies (Hopper & Weinberg, 2011, 2016, 2017).

Dynamic matrices are the "theatre of operation of ongoing change" (Foulkes, 1975a, p. 132), enabling us to explore the flow of themes that take place in interpersonal and transpersonal communications in the life of a group, as well as within the different groups and organizations where persons interact in the society.

In addition, albeit in a rudimentary form, Foulkes advances the idea of a personal matrix. On discussing interacting psychological processes in the group matrix at different levels, Foulkes (1975a, p. 130) states that "just as the individual's mind is a complex of interacting processes (personal matrix), mental processes interact in the concert of the group (group matrix)". Powell (2000, p. 13) refers to the personal matrix as "the workings of the individual mind" and connects its domain to the transference and projective levels and spheres Foulkes pointed for the group-analytic group. Foulkes dedicated just a few lines to the concept of personal matrix in his work. Even so, Nitzgen and Hopper (2017, p. 15) argue that the personal matrix is

> based on "culturally embedded values and reactions" (Foulkes, 1975, p. 131) ... *"developed* and *transmitted"* in the process of socialisation, especially in the *nuclear family*, in the *social network, class*, etc., and have been *maintained* or *modified* by the *intimate plexus* in which the person now moves.
> (Foulkes, 1975, p. 132, italics ours; cf. Foulkes & Anthony, 1984, p. 27)

In Portugal, Leal (1968; Neto, & França, 2021) devoted to the study of the group-analytic matrix and developed the concept of "internal relational matrix" (in Portuguese, *matriz relacional interna*) in clinical work. This concept shares similarities with the Foulkesian idea of personal matrix. For Leal (1968), when a person joins a group, they bring their own internal matrix, developed from early object relations. Therefore, treatment in group-analytic groups allows for transforming early attachment patterns, renewing and promoting the development of its members' internal relational matrix. We can thus infer that it is through the group matrix that personal matrices mature and evolve in their intrapersonal, interpersonal, and transpersonal dimensions.

In addition, the Foulkesian idea of personal matrix is close to what the Argentinian psychoanalyst and group analyst Pichon-Rivière[10] (1980) postulates, based on the concepts of "internal group", "link" (*vínculo*), and "conceptual referential operative schema" (CROS) (Tubert-Oklander & Hernández de Tubert, 2004; Losso, De Setton, & Scharff, 2017). Pichon-Rivière's conceptualizations illustrate how persons constitute their "internal group" through internalized linking structures that act dialectically as internal and external networks. Therefore, the notion of link/*vinculo* shares a similar view with the Foulkesian concept of personal matrix.

The conceptualization of personal matrix in group analysis seems to be the missing link in the configuration of the matrix as a multirelational process that interweaves the mind of an individual person (personal matrix) with the context of the collective mind of a grouping (dynamic matrix) and the context of a society (foundation matrix). In this regard, the elements that make up a particular foundation matrix are also unconsciously rooted in time and space in the personal and dynamic matrix of its members. Moreover, the realms of the tripartite matrix can be analysed in terms of the properties of social systems that include patterns of interaction, normation, communication, and styles of thinking and feeling (Nitzgen & Hopper, 2017, p. 15; Hopper, 2018b). This observation reaffirms the connection between explorations into the social unconscious and investigations into Hopper's (2003b) Incohesion theory.

The extension and reconfiguration of the group matrix allow us to explore the figurations that interweave particular foundation, dynamic, and personal matrices encompassing investigations into different social systems that are especially relevant for the study of the social unconscious. The new dimensionality proposed by the study of tripartite matrices can be studied as field theory – from Lewin's (1947) classical field theory to Pichon-Rivière's dialectic spiral process (Pichon-Rivière, 1980; Baranger & Baranger, 2008, 2009; Losso, De Setton, & Scharff, 2017) to contemporary field theory in psychoanalysis (Tubert-Oklander, 2014, 2017).

On the other hand, the social systems theory permits the examination of the tripartite matrix of a particular social system by exploring how foundation, dynamic, and personal matrices interweave (Hopper, 2018b). Additionally, through processes of equivalence[11] (Hopper, 2003a, p. 94), we can observe that what happens in the global sphere may be recapitulated within societies, and societal dynamics may be recapitulated within regions, organizations, families, and dyads. These frames of reference grant multiple possibilities for social unconscious investigations in social systems.

In sum, the conceptualization of tripartite matrix confers a new place to the social unconscious within the general theory of group analysis. It means that "the social unconscious can no longer be *located* in any *one* part of the group matrix. Instead, it has to be *located* in all of them" (Nitzgen and Hopper, 2017, p. 16; italics in original).

Perspectives on the social unconscious and large groups

In a few words, the study of the social unconscious highlights the socially unconscious fantasies, anxieties, defences, myths, and collective memories co-created in tripartite matrices. Besides, by exploring the *habitus* of foundation matrices (Hopper & Weinberg, 2016, 2017), it points to traumatic experiences in the unconscious life of groups and group-like social systems (Hopper, 2003b), allowing us to observe the transgenerational transmission of trauma (Mojovic, 2011; Wilke, 2016), as well as the impact of structural oppression (Penna, 2016a) and totalitarianism (Klímová, 2011; Marlin, 2016) on particular foundation matrices. In this regard, investigations into the social unconscious are vital to bring us in contact with co-constructed psychic and social facts and with a co-constructed psychic and social reality, especially in traumatized contexts (Hopper, 2018b).

However, one of the main difficulties in the investigation of the social unconscious relates to the various possible ways to explore the concept in social systems. These multiple directions and dimensions preclude any attempt to limit the investigation to one single consistent plan, preventing a linear and closed form of analysis. For this reason, research on the social unconscious requires post-modern thinking (Lyotard, 1984) to encompass an interdisciplinary and transdisciplinary approach (Frosh, 2013b) with the group-analytic theory – through the concept of matrix/tripartite matrix – as a benchmark.

Today, the model of tripartite matrices, in association with the social unconscious theory in group analysis, offers new perspectives on the *question du nombre*, remodelling investigations into crowds, Freudian masses, and explorations of large groups in group analysis. Moreover, this model transcends the Freudo-Marxist debate and contributes to develop the Frankfurtian studies on masses, totalitarianism and fascism (Adorno, 1951; Jay, 1973). Investigating the social unconscious using the concept of tripartite matrices allows for reconfiguring socio-historical, philosophical, and political discourses about crowds and masses, providing them with new meanings, temporalities, and translations.

Moreover, investigations into the social unconscious contribute to new theoretical conceptualizations for understanding social and group phenomena, especially in traumatic contexts. In this direction, the study of large groups and transcultural processes in group analytic conferences, workshops, and communities, as well as the work on social dreaming matrices (Lawrence, 1998) have been providing important space for examining socially unconscious processes. In addition, with the COVID-19 syndemic (Horthon, 2020), the study of the social unconscious in group analysis promises to be an invaluable tool to face the challenges of current social trauma and its working-through processes.

In this chapter, we discussed how the Foulkesian group analysis changed individual-society relationships, proposing a different ontology that gives importance to interpersonal and transpersonal processes and to different levels of communication in groups. We explored Foulkes's thinking since its inception, following the development of group analytic theory. In this journey, which covers almost ninety years of thought, we could follow the ongoing creation and a welcome theoretical refinement of group-analytic postulations, especially through the reconfiguration of the concept of matrix. The study of the socially unconscious mind found in the social unconscious project a field for transdisciplinary research in different societies. In this sense, group-analytic methodologies, particularly the work with large groups, proved to be important allies in the investigation of the social unconscious and in the contemporary understanding of the psychodynamics of crowds, masses, and large groups. The study of large groups in group analysis will be explored in the next chapter.

Notes

1   The term "social unconscious" was used for the first time by the American psychoanalyst Trigant Burrow in his article "Social images versus reality". He also coined the term "group analysis", later used by Foulkes (Pertegato & Pertegato, 2013, p. lxxxvi). Foulkes (1948) was aware of Burrow's work and mentioned that he owed him insights on group dynamics, however his "method… was developed into quite different directions" (p. 37). Burrow was attuned with the idea of the internalization of the social world and was influenced by the social sciences, philosophy and biology of the late nineteenth century and early twentieth century (Hopper, 2013, p. xvi). However, Burrow's perspective emphasized biology, to the detriment of the sociocultural and political dimensions of the foundation matrix explored by Foulkes in group analysis (Hopper, & Weinberg, 2017, p. xviii).

2   From 1934, in Germany, Erich Fromm advanced the idea of the social unconscious. In the 1930s, as a psychoanalyst and a member of the Frankfurt Institute for Social Research, Fromm was involved in the social-psychological foundations of character formation (Fromm, 1930, 1932) and empirical research on "Authority and the family" (Horkheimer,1936). Together with his Frankfurtian colleagues, and as a result of their concerns with Hitler's rise to power (Fromm, 1963, p. 122), he explored the authoritarian character (Horkheimer,1936; Fromm, 1941). Fromm was trying to understand how the unconscious mind is shaped by both the body and society. He also regarded society as an "organism" that was characterized by sociocultural, economic, and political structures in connection to libidinal and death instincts (Hopper & Weinberg, 2011, p. xxv). Yet, Fromm associated the idea of social character with the notion of the social unconscious to investigate common areas of repression among the members of the society. In this sense, he aimed to understand how social order and power structures unconsciously influence the individual mind (Fromm, 1962, p. 88).

   Fromm's discussion on "The Revolutionary Character" (1963) enriches the debate on the social unconscious by bringing into perspective the impact of the social unconscious constraints and restraints on the idea of "free will". In this direction, Hopper (2003a) explored in group analysis Fromm's concept of revolutionary character connected with a commitment with ethical living, development of citizenship and maturity in groups.

   In the psychoanalytic milieu, Karen Horney (1937) was the first psychoanalyst to apply the idea of the social unconscious to clinical work regarding social unconscious influences on gender identity and neurotic ambition (Hopper, 2003a, p. 159).

3   In his reflections on the various formulations of social *a priori* in connection with the study of the social unconscious, Dalal (2011) highlights Hegel's (1806) postulations on the concept of *Zeitgeist*, as well as Marx's on the concept of ideology, and Althusser's (1969) on the "unconscious ideology". In addition, Dalal points to Barthes's (1984) discussions about language and power, which explore how the concept of "myth", historically and socially constructed, helps to naturalize certain world views. Also prominent are Elias's (1991) considerations on "symbol" and "*habitus*", examined by Bourdieu (1986) (Dalal, 2011, p. 255). Likewise, we cannot ignore

Dalal's reflections on the social unconscious in Foucault (1972, 1979), especially on concepts such as "episteme" and "discourse", Kuhn's (1962) thoughts on paradigms, and Lacan's (2007) psychoanalytic view of the unconscious structured as language (Dalal, 2011, p. 256). Jameson's (2002) "political unconscious" and Cornelius Castoriadis's (1975, Nitzgen, 2011, pp. 17–18) discussions on the concept of "social imaginary" are also relevant contributions for the debate on the social unconscious.

4 Cultural and social anthropologists began to use the concept of cultural unconscious in investigations into the "personality and culture" of a particular society. Spector-Person (1992), when studying the cultural unconscious, explored the internalization of values and norms of what is usually known as the culture of a particular society. Yet, ambivalent combinations of the unconscious with the social and the cultural predominate in the discussion (Hopper & Weinberg, 2011, p. xxxv).

5 In the first volume of the trilogy, the notion of the social unconscious in Foulkes is distinguished from Jung's (1936) collective unconscious, revealing that its contemporary conceptualization is quite similar to the concept of social unconscious in group analysis. The notion of social unconscious was also compared to the idea of co-unconscious in Moreno and is akin to Pichon-Rivière's (1980) perspectives on the link theory (Hopper & Weinberg, 2011).

Although Pichon-Rivière has never referred to the social unconscious or had contact with Foulkes, both share similar ways of conceiving the unconscious dimension of human beings. For Pichon-Rivière, as for Foulkes, there is no opposition between individual and collective psychology; therefore, the individual and the group are mere illusions (Tubert-Oklander, 2011). Moreover, Pichon-Rivière's epistemology postulates a pluridimensional approach of "man-in-situation" (Pichon-Rivière, 1980, p. xii; translation mine). Foulkes postulates the intrinsic sociality of human nature and the indissolubility of the network co-created between persons and their contexts, as discussed by Hopper (1982). In the same way, Pichon-Rivière writes: "One cannot think in terms of a distinction between the individual and society. It is an abstraction, a reductionism that we cannot accept, because we carry society within us" (*apud* Tubert-Oklander, 2011, p. 61).

6 In this regard, and inspired by object relations, relational and field theory in psychoanalysts, especially in José Bleger's (2016) work with regressive states in bi-personal analysis, published in Argentina in 1967, Tubert-Oklander (2014) reflects on the creation of a new metapsychology that comprises psychoanalysis, group analysis, and socio-analysis, called "syncretic paradigm". Bleger (2016) postulated the existence of a deep, primitive, syncretic level of experience in which there were no differentiations, but a coexistence of all opposites that stand together in a state of fusion, ambiguity. This implies a non-discrimination between subject and object, inner and outer, love and hate, mind and body, self and environment (Tubert-Oklander, 2014, p. 60). For Bleger, there is always an undifferentiated and ambiguous experience of everything, which coexists with the differentiated experience of everyday life. It means that there is an undifferentiated dimension in the individual and in group psychology as well, in institutional and community relationships, and it happens to be the very basis of collective existence. Although human groups are apparently made up of individuals, at the "syncretic" relations level they coexist, interconnected, as communicating vessels (Tubert-Oklander, 2014, p. 67). Bleger's conceptualizations on symbiosis and ambiguity enables the appreciation of the early stages of the development of personality that occur in the individual and in group psychology, also allowing for a deeper comprehension of undifferentiated states in institutional and organizational settings. Therefore, the new paradigm aims to explore an area in the mind where intrapsychic, interpersonal, and transpersonal processes in interdependencies flourish, providing a common matrix for the individual and the group. The development of this paradigm can be of vital importance in the creation of a framework that might integrate the various aspects of the

psychoanalytical study of "the group-as-a subject". It also contributes to Hopper's (2003b) work on the fourth basic assumption in the unconscious life of groups and group-like social systems.

7　In psychoanalysis, developments connected to intersubjectivity have contributed to more integrated views of subject-environment or, as we say in group analysis, persons in context. In France, the work of René Kaës brought new perspectives on intersubjectivity, especially in the exploration of the individual-society relationship. Concepts like "intermediate", as well as the notions of "contract", "denial pact", and "unconscious alliances" are especially important to the creation of common and shared psychic spaces and for the investigation of unconscious psychic transmissions (Kaës, 1975, 2007). Nevertheless, Kaës' perspective differs from the group-analytic approach, because, whereas the former favours the body as the initial source of psychic life, group analysis grants a privilege to society and culture through language as the first source of psychic life (Hopper, 2003a, p. 18). Indeed, in group analysis, "the social takes precedence over the organismic, and, thus, over the psychic as well". Therefore, "although the ego of adaptation precedes the ego of agency, the body-ego does not necessarily precede the society-ego" (Hopper, 2018b, p. 117).

8　Metaphors based on the idea that social systems are like people or that the individual mind/brain can be used metaphorically to describe the group mind/brain or a group-like social system mind/brain (Ormay, 2012) is a fallacy derived from the difficulty in accepting the reality of social facts (Hopper & Weinberg, 2011, p. xli). It means that, although persons have minds and brains, groups and group-like social systems do not have an unconscious mind, but a culture of which their members are unconscious. The only exception to the use of organismic and personalistic homologies relates to the psychodynamics of regressed and traumatized social systems (Hopper, 2003b).

9　The idea of matrix involves mathematical relationships and can be traced back to Chinese philosophers and to the Japanese mathematician Saki. It probably arrived in Europe through the Silk Road, and Leibniz used it in the seventeenth century. Two centuries later, the term "matrix" was associated with the organization of relationships and, in the early twentieth century, James Joseph Sylvester used the Latin word "matrix", meaning "womb", to conceptualize a matrix as a condenser which contains smaller or sub-matrices, foreseeing modern systems theory (Hopper & Weinberg, 2017, p. xviii).

10　Pichon-Rivière's concepts transformed the psychoanalytic theory, revealing how the subject is born and grows within a linking network that supports relationship and socialization processes. For him, the concept of link replaces the notion of instinctual drives and is defined "as a complex structure that includes a subject, an object, and their mutual dialectical interrelations with communication and learning processes" (Pichon-Rivière, 1980, p. xi; translation mine). Therefore, through the link established by the mother-baby relationship "as a mechanism of interaction, as a Gestalt, that are at the same time two-body and three-personal" (Pichon-Rivière, 1980, p. 2; translation mine), the child introjects a "relational structure" that acquires an intra-subjective dimension which will enable them to learn from and about the world and the environment. The link includes, but is not restricted to what we know as object relations. In this sense, "the object relation is the inner structure of the bond [link]" (Tubert-Oklander, 2011, p. 60). It involves the confluence of two psychological fields, the inner field and the outer field:

There is, then, a perpetual dialectics of the inner and the outer, which is the very stuff of human existence. The internal bonds [links] and the external bonds [links] are integrated in a dialectic spiral process, by means of which that which was originally external becomes internal again, and so on. There is fluid interchange between the two fields, which helps to establish the differentiation between the inside and the outside, while at the same time keeping a deep continuity between them. Hence individual and society form an indissoluble unit, a single dynamic field, because we all carry society within us.

(Tubert-Oklander, 2011, p. 61)

11 Harold Kaye characterized in group analysis the phenomenon of equivalence. Equivalence, refers to a particular process based on very primitive interpsychic mechanisms that communicate what has been made unconscious in the group as a result of the anxiety and splitting involved in it (Hopper, 2003a, p. 73). Equivalence, enables us to glimpse the unconscious, the dynamic aspects of how a group creates and maintains a certain theme on its conscious and unconscious life. It means that, not only in groups, but also in different social systems, people are unconsciously prone

"to recreate situations (in terms of actions, fantasies, object relations and affects) that have occurred at another time and space, such that the new or later situation may be taken as 'equivalent' to the old or previous one".

(p. 130)

For Hopper (2003a), equivalence is a function of at least three factors: the extent to which the feelings and fantasies are unconscious and the psychological defences involved are primitive; the severity of the anxiety and guilt associated with these feelings and fantasies; and the extent to which the members of the group are regressed. (p. 100)

9 Large-group psychodynamics in group analysis

The transformative context of the 1960s and 1970s conferred a new *Zeitgeist* for the development of group work in England. The impetus inherited from the Northfield experiments combined with new sociocultural perspectives favoured innovations in healthcare that led to advances in group practice. In this context, we introduced in Chapter Six the early work in group relations at the Leicester Conferences and the A.K. Rice Institute, focusing on the emergence of the study of large groups. In Chapter Seven , we discussed Bion's legacy and his colleagues' attempts to formulate new basic assumptions. Chapter Eight considers the Foulkesian group analysis, exploring the roots and contemporary study of the social unconscious, mainly through the extension and reconfiguration of the concept of matrix (Nitzgen & Hopper, 2017). Some of these developments happened in parallel, broadening the knowledge of group psychodynamics as a whole. However, Foulkes's new epistemology associated with explorations of the social unconscious enabled a further and alternative approach to the study of large groups as an essential tool for the investigation of the *question du nombre*.

Before proceeding, it is important to underscore that, although we can discuss large social formations in society, institutions, organizations, and communities in general, in this chapter we aim to explore the psychodynamics of artificially created large groups[1] "as transitory and non-institutionalised systems" (Hopper & Weyman, 1975) in training institutes, group analytic conferences, and workshops. This enables us to conduct the study of their psychodynamics as if in a laboratory.

Moreover, no matter how large, a group is not the same as an organisation or a society. Not all groupings are the same, and not all groupings should be called groups. For example, groups are not families, although in some respect families are groups (Hopper & Weyman, 1975, p. 177). A social system constitutes a group when it has a simple structure – open to natural, psychological, and social environments – and relatively unstable boundaries. These differentiations are important, because, theoretically speaking, groupings, tribes, gangs, and other group formations may be inadvertently confused with groups and group-like social systems.

From a broader perspective, albeit with new goals, research on large-group psychodynamics reshapes the main tenets of crowd psychology, delving into

DOI: 10.4324/9780429399534-10

the psychoanalytic investigations of masses in connection with social psychology, sociology, philosophy, and history. Here, we must recall Freud's (1930a, p. 106) words in *Civilization and its Discontents*: "We may expect that one day someone will venture to embark upon a pathology of cultural communities". In this sense, the study of large groups can be considered as a new theoretical and technical research tool to broaden the contemporary understanding of the psychodynamics of persons when gathered in large numbers.

Indeed, after Northfield and during the post-war period, large-group work experienced a push, fostered by both the sociocultural context and the claims of a new generation of professionals. In the group analytic field, work with large groups allowed for an in-depth understanding of personal, interpersonal, and transpersonal primitive processes in groups (Kreeger, 1975), pointing to the possibility of humanizing society and developing citizenship through dialogue in large groups as well (de Maré, 2012b). Large groups also offered the opportunity to examine the dynamics of organisations (Hopper, 2012), the social unconscious in tripartite matrices (Hopper & Weinberg, 2017), and to observe Incohesion as a fourth basic assumption (Hopper, 2003b), which will be discussed in Chapter Ten. However, before exploring these developments, it is necessary to discuss different approaches in group analysis, considering its core topics.

Mapping the field

In 1965, Lionel Kreeger was appointed consultant psychiatrist and psychotherapist at the Halliwick Hospital in London where he met Patrick de Maré. De Maré had been trained for Army psychiatry by Rickman and Bion at Northfield and collaborated with Foulkes and Main in the second experiment. After the war, he worked at St George's Hospital and had been involved with the Group Analytic Society since it was set up in 1952. At Halliwick, Kreeger and de Maré worked together using the principles of therapeutic community to establish a new culture in ward and community meetings through the work in groups. In 1966, fascinated with large groups, they introduced this activity in the hospital. In 1967, Kreeger joined the Group Analytic Society and developed into an active group analyst. In 1969, having had considerable experience with Kleinian thinking, he became an Independent Psychoanalyst at the British Psychoanalytic Society (Kreeger, 1975, 2009; de Maré, 2012b).

In 1971, the Institute of Group Analysis in London started to host large-group experiences in its training programs (Skynner, 1975).[2] In the following year, at the Second European Symposium on Group Analysis, held at Maudsley Hospital, Kreeger and de Maré included a three-hour large-group session in the scientific program. The first large group joined over one hundred participants seated in a single circle. It generated great interest and enthusiasm and led to the incorporation of large groups into most symposia and workshops thereafter (Kreeger, 2009, p. 282). In 1984, de Maré started a seminar on large groups and, in 1987, the Large Group Section of the Group Analytic Society was established (de Maré, Piper, & Thompson, 1991). In the following year, a median black-and-white group was started, aiming at fostering dialogue and discuss institutionalized racism among persons from different ethnical backgrounds (Ferron, 1991). Yet, the training of large groups – the "marginal discipline" (Reicher, 2020) – is still challenging in different institutes of group analysis.

In its early days, large-group work was underdeveloped and not integrated into one single perspective. Moreover, group analytic perspectives overlapped with those from the group relations tradition (Skynner, 1975, p. 228). Members of the Group Analytic Society in London, such as Lionel Kreeger, Patrick de Maré, Tom Main, Malcolm Pines, Robin Skynner, Stuart Whiteley, among others, were working in large groups in various hospital settings – day hospitals, wards, therapeutic communities and community meetings (Sharpe, Hopper, Shapiro & Shields, 2002, p. 432). This first large-group cohort in group analysis was influenced by a mixture of Freudian, Kleinian, Bionian, and Foulkesian theoretical perspectives (Wilke, 2003a). However, whereas the group relations field, grounded in Bionian group theories, built a more structured and unified frame for their work, in group analysis there never was just one single group analytic approach to large-group work. Despite their differences, these pioneers cherished a kind of "group analytical" spirit (Hopper, 2021, personal communication), certainly inherited from the innovations brought about by the Northfield experiments, and forged in the scope of the 1960s and 1970s transformative *Zeitgeist*.

In this spirit, in 1975,[3] Kreeger edited in London the first collection of articles on large groups, *The Large Group: Dynamics and Therapy*. In chapters now regarded as classical, different pioneers offered a broad and deep-searching analysis – ranging from training to sociotherapy – of the first attempts to work with large groups (Kreeger, 1975, p. 14). The eclecticism of their contributions is fascinating; however, they reveal a "confusion" concerning the definition of a large group, its purpose, its optimal size, the ecology of the setting, the role of the conductor/convenor, as well as its therapeutic value. As reported by Isobel Jacobs (1973), Kreeger and de Maré were already developing rivalry for leadership and an ambivalent relationship in their theoretical approach to the work in large groups. These controversies, already existing in Kreeger's first book, continue to these days, eliciting ambivalence and theoretical disagreements in group analysis.

To introduce our research, we ask: what is a large group? What are its aims? Does it have therapeutic functions? What is its optimal number of participants? All these questions require careful investigation, perhaps because large groups provide a new and wider dimension of personal experience (Kreeger, 1975, p. 16), uncovering aspects of human relationships that cannot be easily found or are hidden in small-group processes (Hinshelwood, 1987a, p. 14) in need of further examination (de Maré, 2012b).

Size and setting

The literature differs about the optimal number of persons in a large group. In this respect, it is important to explore and locate the transition point from small to large groups (Hopper & Weyman, 1975; Hinshelwood, 1987a). In small therapeutic groups, the number fluctuates between seven and twelve participants(Schneider & Weinberg, 2003).[4] Large groups, in turn, "might involve at least 30 [participants] but more likely between 50 and 100" (Foulkes, 1975b, p. 52), "40 to 100 or more people" (Kreeger, 1975, p. 16) or more. However, depending on the number of participants, a group can no longer be face to face and "the large-group situation cannot be encompassed by any of its members in a single glance" (Turquet, 1975, p. 88). Therefore, as Turquet highlights, from thirty-two members onwards – since this number corresponds to the number of pieces each player has on a chessboard and seems to be the largest number of people that a person can consciously keep in mind at one time (Hopper & Weyman, 1975, p. 325) – participants start to experience the elements of a large-group situation.

In 1975, Foulkes (1975b) discussed the work in large groups and explored important differences between small and large groups. Concerning size and number of participants, Foulkes argues that not much has been established about the optimal size for changing from small to large groups. He asks, "When does a group become 'large'? At what point does it change its character?" (Foulkes, 1975b, p. 51). These questions are of particular importance, because we are not merely dealing with a "large" or "small" group, since "we are moving on a scale on which everything is relative" (Foulkes, 1975b, p. 51). Foulkes's words reveal that the reflection is far more complex than the size of the group, assuming the crucial point is that "quantity becomes quality" (Foulkes, 1975b, p. 51). Nevertheless, he puts it clearly when he asks: "Now where does the large group starts? Nobody knows" (Foulkes, 1975b, p. 52).

De Maré contrasts Foulkesian small groups with larger groups. He states that "large groups can be said to take over where small groups leave off" (de Maré, Piper, & Thompson, 1991, p. 10). De Maré discusses extensively the differences between both structures while developing his theoretical approach to large groups. He suggests that the ideal size for a large group ranges from sometimes twenty, but in general fifty, to a hundred people seated in one or two-tiered circles, an arrangement reminiscent of Greek amphitheatres (de Maré, Piper, & Thompson, 1991, p. 13).

As seen, the ideal number of participants in a large group is difficult to determine. This issue also relates to the group's ecology, which may or may not contribute to creating an optimal setting for conducting large groups. The size and acoustic properties of the room and the layout of chairs – elevated or not, arranged in concentric circles or in spiral – interfere with hearing, seeing, interacting, and even noticing other participants (Sharpe, 2008). If a large group is arranged in concentric circles, it increases closeness among participants. In contrast, participants sitting with their back to the others may produce ambivalence, false hierarchies, and paranoid anxieties (Schneider & Weinberg, 2003).

Large groups have been organized in various settings under different conditions and sometimes, especially in group-analytic conferences, the number of participants increases to four hundred persons or even more. Such circumstances intensify the challenges of organizing and conducting large groups, for they interfere with group frameworks to the point of breaking boundaries or reducing the possibility of containment, interfering in reality testing (Main, 1975; Ahlin, 2010) as well. Above all, the loss of minimal setting conditions for creating large groups, especially regarding size, triggers psychodynamic processes that are similar to those in unstructured large-group situations or in disorganized large groups in which the fear of being in a mob or in a crowd is elicited (Skynner, 1975; Kernberg, 2003).

The larger the group, the higher the anxiety and interpersonal defences, characterizing what Turquet (1975) identified as threats to the identity of individual persons in the large group. Moreover, large groups tend to be traumatogenic and, for this reason, are likely to be characterized by Incohesion: Aggregation/Massification processes (Hopper, 2003b).

Depending on the size of a large group, the possibility of developing face-to-face interactions decreases and precludes intimacy, identifications, or bonding, engendering indifference, anonymity, and alienation (Kreeger, 1975).

Perspectives in group–analytic large groups

Defining a single perspective in large-group work in group analysis is not an easy task. In fact, since its early days, this work has been shaped not only by Foulkes's ambivalence regarding large groups (Wilke, 2003a), but also by the emergence of different theoretical perspectives in the large-group approach.

Foulkes – the "founding father" of Group Analysis – clearly preferred working in small groups, and he was uncertain about the therapeutic potential of large groups (Foulkes, 1975b, p. 56). His ambivalence may have been intuited since his participation in the Northfield experiments, for initially he was concerned with developing a technique for small groups (Hinshelwood, 2007) as a "sociopsychological vaccine" (Wilke, 2003a, p. 87) that "could be an antidote to the 'mass techniques' employed by 'the totalitarian states'" (Nitzgen & Hopper, 2017, p. 4). Even so, as de Maré, Piper and Thompson (1991, p. 11) remind us, Foulkes was aware of the potential of large groups when he wrote that "group therapy is an altogether desirable contribution to their [people's] education as responsible citizens" (Foulkes & Lewis, 1944, p. 21).

Foulkes's fears of mass psychology and the power of its leaders might have spilled over into the possibility of working with large groups. Foulkes (1975b, p. 54) warns about the conductor's awareness of the power of his/her suggestive and hypnotic influence, reminding the conductor to resist the illusion of becoming the leader of the group instead of just leading it. Foulkes's words are a clear reference to the illusory power of mass leaders highlighted by Freud in *Group Psychology and the Analysis of the Ego* (1921) and discussed with his Frankfurtian colleagues Karl Landauer and Heinrich Meng in a joint seminar in the summer of 1932, just before moving to England (Rothe, 1989, p. 408). Foulkes's fears were certainly connected to his experiences in Germany and to totalitarianism in Europe during the twentieth century. In this sense, the idea of a leader has always been problematic for him and other group analysts of the second generation. This ambivalence rests on the dynamic matrix of group analysis as an institution (Wilke, 2003b, p. 78) and, to this day, certainly contributes to the resistance and distrust some group analysts face in their work with large groups, especially when compared to the well-established culture of small-group work.

In "many ways, Foulkes gave impetus to the [large-group] work" (Pines, 1975, p. 293); however, he only wrote one chapter on the theme, leaving the task of building large-group theory to the second generation (Wilke, 2003a). In "Problems of the Large Groups" (Foulkes, 1975b), Foulkes discusses three types of large groups: problem-centred, experience-centred, and therapy-centred (pp. 41–47). His descriptions reveal a concern with small-group work principles, considering the use of large groups in association with the Northfield experiments, with therapeutic communities, and as a form of sociotherapy. In his chapter, Foulkes discusses the importance of total situations in group work, the role of the conductor, and the location of the large group in the total spectrum of psychotherapy, as conceived and displayed in the illustration of his 1948 book (Foulkes, 1948, p. 32). He places the large group in an area called group analysis, moving inwards to psychoanalysis and self-analysis, but also outwards, to open-air psychiatry and life (Foulkes, 1975b, p. 46).

Indeed, based on the contributions to Kreeger's book, we observe how the perspectives regarding large-group work were developing on different fronts. On the other hand, group analysts still had many questions, especially concerning the therapeutic potential of large groups (Kreeger, 1975; Foulkes, 1975b, p. 45). In this direction, we can see that Pines (1975, p. 311) was able to provide an overview, not without caution, of the powerful and unknown forces that were at stake in the early explorations in large groups. Large groups have powerful forces and a "potential use for either good or evil" (Kreeger, 1975, p. 25), for "good or ill" (Skynner, 1975, p. 246). Although developed for creative interactions, thinking, and change, large groups tended towards massive projections, fragmentation, scapegoating, and exclusion processes (Kreeger, 1975, p. 25).

These observations certainly mirror Foulkes's uncertainties about large-group work, as well as his optimistic attitude regarding working possibilities in small groups (Nitsun, 1996, p. 10). Nitsun (1996), in *The Anti-Group*, observed that in the metapsychology of group therapy a series of dichotomies oppose the individual and the group, Bion's and Foulkes's approaches, constructive and destructive forces, pessimistic and optimistic views of group phenomena (Nitsun, 1996, p. 14). In group analysis, this opposition seems to be in a theoretical-conceptual polarization between the Foulkesian idealized view of small groups and the so-called large-group disruptive and destructive potential (Nitsun, 1996; Wilke, 2003a, 2003b).

In fact, in the first experiences in large-group settings, their potential was yet to be determined. The professionals were not attuned with the potential of large groups for sociocultural change, learning from experience, or "repair work" (Pines, 2003). That is, the possibility of working through conscious and unconscious traumatic experiences in communities and societies had not been discovered yet (Hopper, 2003a, 2003b). Moreover, de Maré's (de Maré, Piper, & Thompson, 1991) idea of applying the Foulkesian principles to larger structures, bridging the gap between persons and the sociocultural environment, developing dialogue and *Koinonia* was a territory open to exploration.

Next, we discuss these two different perspectives of the psychodynamics of large-group work, exploring how these tendencies marked theory and practice in group analysis.

The psychodynamics of large groups

Kreeger and other second-generation theorists in group analysis explored the psychodynamics of large groups in depth. Kreeger was an independent psychoanalyst and group analyst. Although both initially Kleinian oriented, Kreeger and Turquet developed an analysis of large-group work that can be understood as "modified Bion". In fact, for Kreeger, the large group was a manifestation of the internal worlds of regressed persons (Hopper, 2003b). These observations were focused mainly on regression, the investigation of psychotic and primitive processes existing in large-group psychodynamics, and the impact of these processes on large-group interactions.

Together, group analysts are inclined to agree that in large groups persons can "learn about primitive defence mechanisms, the fear of psychotic fragmentation, the fragility of communication and the socially divisive and destructive potential in the foundation matrix of each culture" (Wilke, 2003a, p. 86). Indeed, large groups elicit overwhelming emotions that range from threats to identity (Turquet, 1975) to panic and hate (de Maré, Piper, & Thompson, 1991) in face of the unknown. In large-group psychodynamics, psychotic mechanisms and projective processes abound. Experiences of helplessness, difficulty to contain and maintain personal boundaries, broken communication, and primitive anxieties and defences – such as splitting, introjection, and bombardment of projective identifications – make individuals in large groups regress to pre-Oedipal stages (Kreeger, 1975).

For Foulkes (1975b, p. 54), the large group triggers in the individual participant a repetition of the ego development in its early stages. This situation provokes a very rapid regression to these initial stages. Thus, in consonance with this regression, the large group ends up symbolising the all-embracing archaic mother. In addition, Foulkes suggests that in a large group:

> The individual is torn between the mental fear of losing his identity and his very being, and the great fascination this has for him. If we think of a suffering individual with all his cares, worries, anxieties – these are all, as it were, submerged in one go, by diving into the group and disappearing. This is the individual's dilemma.

> (Foulkes, 1975b, p. 54)

Foulkes's observation about regression in the large group evokes Turquet's (1975) debates on homogenization, as well as Chasseguet-Smirgel's (1984) considerations on the human desire to return to the mother's womb, discussed in Chapter Seven. Also, his reflections on the individual's dilemma in the large group are similar to what Bion (1961) discussed about individuals' groupishness. De Maré also contributed to this reflection, stating that in large groups there is a "dialectical tension between the one and the many, recognizing both the autonomy of the individual human subject and the integrity and creativity of the group" (Blackwell, 2000, p. 162).

Threatened in their individuality and personal identities, large-group participants regress, revealing primary processes and early phases of unconscious life. Feelings of chaos and confusion revealed in large-group settings make persons experience a "fear of breakdown" (Winnicott, 1963, p. 87), threats of annihilation – considered by Hopper (2003b) as the primary anxiety in large groups – and even Kohut's (1971) anxiety of disintegration (Schneider & Weinberg, 2003, p. 19). Moreover, large groups may engender in participants a feeling of being dragged by a "large cavernous body without the ability to contain; metaphorically, a womb that is unable to be fertile" (Schneider & Weinberg, 2003, p. 16), or even of being "swollen up with it or taken over by it" (Hinshelwood, 1987b, p. 138).

In large groups, we observe the emergence of power relations, polarization, and interactions between subgroups represented by their "spokesman" rather than between individuals (Skynner, 1975, p. 249). Large groups tend to produce battles for leadership, splitting into subgroups, seen by Kreeger (1975) as a defence against paranoid anxieties that mobilizes large group participants. Awareness of these dynamics is fundamental because large groups tend to break up into smaller groups/subgroups (de Maré, 2012a, p. 59), but not only subgroups, since large groups engender the creation of contragroups, as it was extensively explored by Hopper's Incohesion theory involving the experience of aggregation. Large groups also create role differentiation, specialization and develop hierarchies, which may convert a group into an organization rather than a group (Hopper, 2003b).

Large groups offer opportunities for the study of primitive mechanisms in large-group life, expanding the comprehension that "common defences against mental pain, of denial, splitting and projection into others, have immense social consequences when used by whole groups of individuals" (Main, 1975, p. 63). Participating in a large group allows persons to be "more clearly in touch with the primitive aspects of their own personality development than any other treatment situation" (Kreeger, 1975, p. 16), despite their achievements in their own analytic treatment. It means participation in large groups refers to "self-study" (Turquet, 1975, p. 90) and contributes to broadening the understanding of oneself, enabling persons to learn more about the little-known field of multi-body psychology (Rickman, 2003), that is, to learn from experience about specific figurations and socially unconscious processes co-created by intrapersonal, interpersonal, and transpersonal dimensions. Large-group work enables us to face fundamental questions of human's existence, illuminating "the great myths, legends and religious symbols in new and unexpected ways" (Skynner, 1975, p. 251).

Patrick de Maré's perspectives

As noted earlier in this chapter, de Maré took part in the Northfield experiments and, together with Kreeger, was a pioneer in the work with large groups at the Halliwick Hospital and in the group analytic field. Davis (1977) recorded de Maré's first reports on large groups at St George Hospital, illustrating his early experiences in hospital settings. In 1985, after de Maré's presentation at the S. H. Foulkes Annual Lecture (Blackwell, 2000), while discussing the advent of the large group approach, Harold Behr stated that what de Maré did for large groups was what Foulkes did for the small analytic group in group analysis (de Maré, Piper, & Thompson, 1991, pp. 13–14).

Inspired by ancient Greek amphitheatres, where a large number of persons interact face to face, de Maré glimpsed large-group interactions. This idea has to do with the principle of *Koinonia*, a type of "spiritual-cum-human participation and communion in which people can speak, hear, see, and think freely" (de Maré, Piper, & Thompson, 1991, p. 2). *Koinonia* refers to the development of impersonal fellowship, a culture of togetherness and amity in communion (de Maré, Piper, & Thompson, 1991).

De Maré differentiates large groups from other activities conducted in therapeutic communities, hospitals, and staff meetings. Enthusiastic about the large-group scope, he pointed out the importance of creating a unified field where the psychological, political, economic, and sociocultural contexts would interweave to enable thinking in large-group settings (de Maré, 1975, p. 145). He defines large groups as an "intensive and extensive exploration of large, face-to-face, 'primary' groups *per se*" (de Maré, 1975, p. 146).

Large groups allow for exploring group dynamics in depth, involving here-and-now and there-and-then total situations that encompass "total cultures, climates and value systems with specific ideologies and ethos" (de Maré, 1975, p. 152). A large group covers significant areas, offering a structure or a medium for linking the inner world with sociocultural dimensions in which interpersonal relationships take place. It also provides a setting to explore social myths (social unconscious), bridging the gap between ourselves and the sociocultural environment in a way that the small group simply cannot do (de Maré, Piper, & Thompson, 1991, p. 14).

Differently from some of his colleagues, de Maré (1975) criticized the idea of applying psychoanalysis and small-group psychodynamics to large groups. He stated that it was "like trying to play Ludo on a chess-board" (de Maré, 1975, p. 146) and stressed that the major problem for a small-group member was "how to feel" spontaneously without the intrusion of unconscious factors, whereas for the large-group participant the major difficulty was "how to think" (de Maré, 2012a, p. 57). For de Maré (2012b), the context is central in large groups. In psychoanalysis, the context is relatively unchanging and expresses itself through free associations. In small groups, the family context is relevant to group associations and, in large groups, communication happens through dialogue (de Maré, 2012b, p. 87). In this respect, the large group constitutes a more complex and intricate matrix than the individual or the small group situation. Thus, whereas small group work is an arena for the re-enactment of family psychodynamics, the large group is the re-enactment and analysis of culture and politics (Blackwell, 2000, p. 153). Moreover, de Maré stated that psychoanalysis and small groups are concerned with pre-Oedipal and Oedipal configurations, whereas large groups are involved in post-Oedipal considerations, taking the group as a basic unit inclined to the development of sociocultural awareness through thinking and dialogue (de Maré, Piper, & Thompson, 1991, p. 11).

Nevertheless, the path from monologue to dialogue is an art – "dialogue is something that has to be learnt like a language" (de Maré, Piper, & Thompson, 1991, p. 17) – that involves transforming the chaos of mindlessness and hate into mindfulness and human communion (de Maré, Piper, & Thompson, 1991). It means that, in large groups, the major difficulty relates to consciousness and mindlessness, because the experience brings to interactions all sorts of pressure and coerciveness, which eventually block the communicational network and undermine dialogue. In this sense, for large-group work, "the *social matrix* is a useful concept because it involves the growth of a communicational network" (de Maré, 2012a, p. 57). When a network is rudimentary, for instance in the early phases of large-group processes, emotions as panic, rage, splitting, displacement, and projection prevail. Therefore, given the opportunity to organize large-group meetings regularly, the large group evolves a network, and the group dictum could certainly be, "Where chaos was, there shall matrix be!" (de Maré, 2012a, p. 57).

Large groups undeniably trigger strong emotions and frustrate libidinal needs by eliciting primitive and psychotic mechanisms. Kreeger, Turquet, Hopper, and others have investigated these topics extensively, but de Maré took a different path, as we can see in his reinterpretation of some postulations of the Freudian psychoanalytic theory. In his reinterpretation, hate turned into a key concept (de Maré, Piper, & Thompson, 1991). De Maré moved away from the idea of the destructive potential of hate by observing it as a natural response to frustration. For him, hate has a psychic energy that carries the potential for both destructive and constructive transformation. Hate unites, and its energy can be actively transformed into a group's driving force for communication. In the large group, the emergence of dialogue transforms hate into endopsychic energy, mobilizing thinking, learning and further dialogue (de Maré, Piper, & Thompson, 1991, p. 37). It means group dialogue – as "a lateral, affiliative, and non-hierarchical mode of communication" (Blackwell, 2012, p. 162) – transforms mindlessness into understanding and, then, into meaning. Therefore, even threatened in their individuality, large-group members can express themselves and be heard in a rare experiential way, moving from frustration and hate to dialogue and a genuine horizontal relationship with their peers.

However, out of dialogue, primitive subcultures emerge first, then micro-cultures appear as specific features of the large-group psychodynamics. They enable us to examine both the subcultural and macrocultural assumptions existing in society. Moreover, large-group microcultures end up constituting a counter-culture (de Maré, Piper & Thompson, 1991, p. 4). In the large group, subcultures, microcultures, and macroculture are self-regulatory feedback systems; however, when they meet, they form a structure that introduces transformations (de Maré, Piper & Thompson, 1991, p. 7). In this respect, the evolving microcultures in the large group allow participants to expand consciousness, distancing themselves from the transposition of former family and cultural contexts, getting in contact with a wide range of new meanings. For de Maré, the essence of the large group is exactly the development of a micro-counter-cultural dimension created from interactions. This means that dialogue and change will emerge from the transformations that take place in large-group subcultures and microcultures. However, we wonder if the tendency of creating subgroups in large-group processes can reinforce the maintenance of subcultures, microcultures, and aggregation in the service of promoting new meanings and real transformation in the large group.

De Maré shifted from his initial interest in large groups to the principle of *Koinonia* in groups. From 1975 on, during this process of change, and based on his experience with large groups at the Institute of Group Analysis, that ended up evolving into a median group – which involves eighteen to twenty participants – de Maré developed the metastructure of the work in median groups as a bridge between small and large groups (de Maré, Piper, & Thompson, 1991, p. 13). For de Maré, median groups allow for a non-hierarchical and reflective dialogue, which, in smaller and more contained settings, enables exactly what he had glimpsed for large-group interactions: a space for personal engagement and thinking that can transform hate into reflective dialogue and impersonal fellowship (de Maré, Piper, & Thompson, 1991, p. 24).

Working with large groups is not an easy path to take. As Blackwell (2012, p. 162) highlights, large groups reveal psychotic anxieties and elicit powerful political anxieties:

> They begin with the fear of the "mob", no longer under the control of clear social hierarchies and structures. But behind this fear, we find deeper anxieties about the possibilities of dialogue.

Indeed, as de Maré states, the intensive and rigorous application of the large-group technique has not been seriously theorized yet and, until today, large-group phenomena demand deeper understanding (de Maré, 2012a, 2012b; Blackwell, 2000, p. 153). This difficulty is certainly connected to the powerful anxieties elicited in large groups, as well as to the chaotic and unpredictable nature of the work. However, as Blackwell (2012) emphasizes, it is also related to its political and ideological transformative potential. It is only in large groups that microcultures, social cultures, and social unconscious constraints and restraints can be observed in different ways. In this way, through social insight, or outsight, communication and dialogue can emerge, fostering a *koinoniac* spirit and change. However, this potentiality challenges the *status quo* in the social world.

Challenges in group-analytic large groups

Conducting/convening large groups

Just as it is complex to discuss different large-group traditions in group analysis, it is challenging to debate the role of conductor(s)/convenor(s), because "too little has been written about the role and the style of the large group conductor" (Wilke, 2003b, p. 70). At different moments of his career, Foulkes was clear about the role of the small-group conductor (Foulkes, 1948, p. 143; Foulkes, 1964, p. 54; Foulkes, 1975a, p. 157). It involves the conductor's ability to work as an analyst, a dynamic administrator, and a translator (Foulkes, 1964). However, for large groups, Foulkes (1975b, p. 55) didn't say much besides recommending that a team of conductors should meet regularly to discuss immediate reactions, the optimal level of intervention, and keep the elicited tension and anxiety at a tolerable level to enable a more constructive work, an approach Hopper (1993) later termed a "Prime Ministerial" model.

To contain different degrees of anxiety and premature dropouts, Skynner (1975, p. 250) pointed out that conductors/convenors of large groups need to abandon classic analytic postures and become more active and directive in order to control their interventions than it is usually necessary in small groups. Skynner's recommendation connects to his experience with deprived and disturbed patients at Maudsley Hospital in London and reflects his observations of different stages in the training of large groups, especially regarding the tendency to create subgroups and scapegoating processes.

For some large-group pioneers, such as Kreeger (1975), leading a large group resembles St George fighting the dragon, given the mobilization of deep affections – psychotic and projective phenomena that exhaust the conductor/convenor who carries out the difficult tasks of creating a safe environment, maintaining the boundaries of the large group, developing and widening communication through the creation of a group culture. In this direction, Kreeger had a holding and containing style of conducting/convening that gave a strong emphasis on starting and ending the large group sessions (Wilke, 2003b, p. 71).

The conductor/convener of the large group attracts a myriad of projections and transferences and is "always spot-lighted as the individual who serves as a focal point in a sea of uncertainty" (Behr & Hearst, 2005, p. 187). However, considering Adorno's (1951) work on mass psychology, discussed in Chapter Three, we wonder if part of the difficulties involved in conducting/convening large groups is associated with the unconscious dyad (Wilke, 2003b, Shaked, 2003) established between the conductor/convener and the large-group members who mirror socially unconscious fantasies and fears regarding the leadership/followership engraved in the tripartite matrices of Western societies.

Recently, Knott (2012, p. 290) discussed large groups exploring the challenges a conductor/convener faces at work. He highlights the anxiety and loneliness of the conductor/convener stressing how they oscillate between processes of integration and disintegration, paranoid-schizoid and depressive states during a session. Knott warns of the multiple skills required from a conductor/convener who "has to bring together, translate, unite, analyse resistance, and interpret… [while] he has to take hold of the group's *unconscious* fantasies" (Knott, 2012, p. 297). In this regard, Knott's considerations remind Kreeger's (1975) metaphor of St George fighting the dragon; however, as he states, the conductor's/convener's ability to make use of countertransference and of his negative capability (Bion, 1970) is crucial for good work.

For de Maré (de Maré, Piper, & Thompson, 1991), the emphasis on the large group relates to the sociocultural dimension, not to psychotherapy *per se*. In a large group, the group itself constitutes the canvas on which the participant's superego is projected and the "conductor" – more appropriately named in de Maré's approach as a convener – supports the participants and interprets sociocultural pressures, encouraging freedom of dialogue (de Maré, Piper, & Thompson, 1991, p. 35). Moreover, on discussing median groups, de Maré says that a convenor does not lead the group and, although they can assume leadership, the attitude is non-directive. The convenor does not set tasks, topics, or goals for interaction and is not even concerned with the idea of doing a good work with the group (de Maré, Piper, & Thompson, 1991, p. 15).

As a psychoanalyst and group analyst, Malcolm Pines has introduced an eclectic and benign style of facilitating, fostering communication in large-group matrices. This attitude might be described as typical of the group analytic field. Indeed, as Tubert-Oklander and Hernández de Tubert (2014b) explored while comparing the British and Latin American styles of conducting/convening large groups, Pines's style seems to be a good example of the group analytic/British tradition. The British work more as convenors than as conductors, therefore, it "determines a more passive and self-effacing stance" (Tubert-Oklander and Hernández de Tubert, 2014b, p. 338) when asserting their trust in group processes. On the other hand, in the Latin American tradition, conductors act as coordinators, conceived as co-thinkers. Their attitude is more active in containing and holding group interactions, contributing to group development through the use of interpretations. Nevertheless, "in both [styles] the aim of the large group is, as Patrick de Maré suggested, thinking together and developing a group thought" (Tubert-Oklander & Hernández deTubert, 2014b, p. 338).

Indeed, there are different possibilities and styles of conducting/convening interventions, but some "are more analytical and others are more supportive" (Hopper, 2021, personal communication). A good-enough balance between both attitudes is required; however, this balance between different options relates not only to different approaches to large-group processes, but also to the context of its use. Hopper states that the supportive model is more characteristic of the group-analytic field and today we can see a slow trend towards a style that might be called "informed facilitation" (Hopper, 2021, personal communication), which perhaps mirrors – not without difficulties – "the group analytic spirit".

On the other hand, Wilke (2003a, p. 87) says that, although group analysts "have sat easy with a Winnicottian style of working with the group as transitional object and the group process as a transitional space (Winnicott 1971)", they are reluctant to transpose an optimistic attitude regarding the working possibilities of "the good small group" to what is still perceived as "the bad large group" (Nitsun, 1996; Wilke, 2003a).

Despite the challenges posed by large-group work, this tool seems to have left to subsequent generations an ambivalence concerning the theory, technique, purpose, and styles of conducting/convening. We can thus imply, following Wilke's (2003a, 2003b) analysis, that two different large-group approaches took shape in group-analytic tradition. One is connected to Kreeger's (1975) tradition and the other, to de Maré's (1975, 2012a, 2012b; de Maré, Piper, & Thompson, 1991; Blackwell, 2000) postulations. That is to say that "Foulkes's unclear legacy led to the emergence of two related but radically different positions in the second generation of the group analytic thinkers on the large group" (Wilke, 2003a, p. 88).

> The second generation of Foulkesian large group conductors were split between overly optimistic and pessimistic views of large group work. Kreeger and de Maré accepted their group analytic inheritance, consolidated it and developed a large group tradition beyond the father. They ended up in the roles of competing siblings and have handed the current generation a clear choice: to attach to de Maré's model of using large groups to help deepen and widen democracy and fellowship in society; to follow Kreeger in his quest to work more consciously with the pathology that is part of the unconscious interactions within society.
>
> (Wilke, 2003a, p. 89)

This statement is important to understand the questions group analysts ask in the study of large groups. Splitting is disguised, especially when group analysts get together in large groups during group-analytic symposia. Some of the challenges in conducting/convening large groups, mainly in transcultural contexts (Ahlin, 2010; Von Sommaruga Howard, 2011), can be an enactment of this not always acknowledged split/polarization (Wilke, 2003a, 2003b). However, these ambivalences are engraved in the group-analytic edifice and lie at the heart of group-analytic practice with large groups.

Moreover, in group-analytic symposia, most of the participants are group analysts who have developed microcultures, prejudices, problems regarding confidentiality and "memories" of their participation in previous large groups. These experiences update social unconscious processes, theoretical controversies, and power relations, which, as traumatic experiences not yet worked through, resonate in large-group settings and the tripartite matrices of the group analytic field. They also mirror, through equivalence, the disputes that take place in the outside world. In this direction, we wonder if, in other contexts and different matrices, independently from the size of the group or the ecology of the setting, large-group work may find fewer struggles, rejection, rivalry, and more horizontal cooperation and understanding (Island, 2010) in interpersonal and transpersonal relationships. This is a topic for further exploration.[5]

Therefore, we understand that creating large groups poses many challenges related to interpersonal and transpersonal interactions among large numbers of persons. In this sense, performing a good work in large groups links the conductor's/convenor's attunement to social unconscious processes and to their theoretical orientation, technique, style, personality, and skills. It concerns their ability to offer containment (Bion, 1962) and holding (Winnicott, 1965), as well as boundaries, which – as psychic envelopes (Anzieu, 1984), psychic skins (Bick, 1968), or folds (Deleuze, 1993) – would enable group members to face catastrophic anxieties (Meltzer, 1975) and the fear of annihilation (Hopper, 2003b) in the large group.

Experiences in large groups in group analysis

Like Foulkes, second-generation group analysts were traumatized by fascism and World War II. Although distrustful or reticent of the new endeavour, they were willing to create new therapeutic possibilities for group work. They cherished the idea of co-creating safer spaces that would contribute to preventing new forms of fundamentalist thinking, as de Maré wrote: "The only answer to mass violence is collective dialogue" (de Maré, Piper, & Thompson, 1991, p. 31). Perhaps, de Maré's assertion epitomizes that generation's socially unconscious wish, materialized in group analysis through the large-group project. We can thus infer that their motivations were profoundly influenced by a desire to use large groups to encourage democratic thinking, peer leadership, and mature citizenship (Hopper, 2000). Moreover, the large group slowly became an instrument to treat transgenerational wounds and deal with intergroup conflicts in a sociopolitical context. In this regard, it seems that the ghost of the Cold War combined with the Western transformative impetus of the 1960s and 1970s in a group-analytic battle to prevent the fear of the return of totalitarianism through large-group work.

Large-group work pioneered the working-through of traumatic collective processes in group analysis. In 1979, under the auspices of the Group Analytic Society, Hopper, Kreeger, Garland, and a group-analytic staff (Hopper, 2003a, p. 72) organized the Survival Syndrome Workshop, an experience that gathered together participants from different traumatized backgrounds, including Shoah survivors. The workshop was an attempt to experience, clarify, and possibly start to mourn painful feelings associated with massive collective trauma that participants still had to work through. Large groups were used experientially as containers for primitive social and psychological processes, especially those associated with repressed and split-off cognitive and emotional experiences within other substructures of the workshop (Hopper, 2003a, p. 83). The large-group sessions revealed not only the workshop's main content, but also similarly unconscious processes that exist in society, bringing into perspective – as parallel processes – processes of equivalence (Hopper, 2003a, p. 94). It means that, in the workshop, unconscious feelings, fantasies, and primitive interpsychic mechanisms communicated what had been made unconscious in the group and by the group as a result of personal and collective trauma.

The Survivor Syndrome Workshop was a pioneering initiative in group analysis and large-group work with traumatized persons. It was in consonance with the first psychoanalytic efforts that, from the 1980s on, investigated traumatic experiences and their working-through processes, and interfered with and treated the effects of transgenerational psychic transmissions as well (Abraham, & Torok, 1995; Faimberg, 2005; Hopper, 2003a). Therefore, from the 1980s, the association between collective trauma and large-group work forged new fields of investigation, together with research on the social unconscious (Hopper, & Weinberg, 2011, 2016, 2017).

Moreover, the experiences undertaken at the Survivor Syndrome Workshop revealed that through equivalence large groups tend to recapitulate, to enact social unconscious processes that exist in their contextual societies. Consequently, processes of equivalence allow for the observation of figurations between past and present traumatic experiences in the unconscious life of tripartite matrices, helping to unveil total situations and the psychodynamics of unconscious processes in crowds and masses.

Contemporary experiences in group-analytic large groups

Since its early years, large-group work has faced challenges in providing spaces for interaction and reflection at the interface of the private and public spheres. It is not by chance that, as of the 1970s, Richard Sennett (1974) has been denouncing a decline in the public sphere that made room for an inflated private life/realm. Moreover, the culture of narcissism (Lasch, 1979) strengthened individualism in all its forms, which eventually weakened collective goals. In contrast, in the last decades, the work with large groups continues to develop in different fronts through what Pines had earlier glimpsed as "community and communication, these are the two foci of this work" (Pines, 1975, p. 292). Indeed, large-group work is vital for exploring spaces in which private and societal public realms intercept, that is, in spaces where tripartite matrices spiral dialectically.

Large-group work has been applied in numerous settings, such as hospitals, training institutes, organizations, conferences, workshops, traumatized organizations and communities. It has evolved in group analysis, group relations and through other traditions based on psychoanalytical and sociological theories, as well as on basic-assumption theory, general systems theory, living human systems, and field theory (Agazarian, & Carter, 1993). The theoretical postulations of skilled professionals not directly connected to group analysis, such as Agazarian (1997), Agazarian and Gantt (2000), Joseph Shaked (2003), and, Kernberg (1998, 2003), have contributed to improve thinking and work in large groups.

However, despite this plurality, it is still difficult to find interwoven views in large-group practices in group analysis. Perspectives to foster a better equilibrium between the destructive forces and the creative potential of large-group work are yet to be found. Perhaps, transcultural research associated with transdisciplinary views may facilitate a continuous and necessary dialogue between psychoanalytical, group-analytic, sociocultural, and political "languages" in the large group.

Contemporary group analysis points to transdisciplinary perspectives that, mirroring post-modern thinking (Brown & Zinkin, 2000, p. 251; Frosh, 2013b), reveal not-so-smooth paths to deconstruct illusions and certainties regarding academic disciplines and bodies of knowledge. By promoting encounters of "lines of flight" (Deleuze & Guattari, 1987) – described as lines of intensity that do not have a closed-form, move in various directions, open and close, spread and disappear, construct and deconstruct without a defined connection – the analysis gets complex. Large-group work points exactly to "lines of flight" that tangle and untangle encounters of multiple traditions, dimensions, sizes, and boundaries co-created by tripartite matrices.

It is remarkable how, at the turn of the twenty-first century, large-group theory and work experienced a new push, incorporating the contributions of transdisciplinary thinking, but mainly helping to diminish the fears regarding large-group applications. Apparently, a third generation of professionals had to be born to integrate and freely combine the work inherited from the pioneers (Wilke, 2003b) by cross-fertilizing these legacies in the light of contemporary group analytic theory.

The transmission of this inheritance was gradual. The second, third, and even the fourth generation of large-group practitioners remain aligned with the pioneers' conscious and socially unconscious claims when creating experiences in large groups. Indeed, the group analysts who were in close contact with Kreeger and de Maré kept alive their enthusiasm with the work, improving explorations in large groups. Meg Sharpe was one of these early professionals. In connection to de Maré's tradition and spirit, she convened large groups at Shrodells Hospital and other organizations. She was also responsible for training in Norway and Denmark. In 1977, in a visit to a psychiatric service in France, Sharpe (2008, p. 293) conferred to large-group work a special place within the hospital working context, as well as within the sociopolitical sphere.

Hopper (2003b) has been connected to work in large groups since the early years. Initially, he was interested in the study of the properties of large groups, distinguishing groups of any size from highly institutionalized entities (Hopper & Weyman, 1975). Throughout the years, following Bion's work, as well as

Turquet and Kreeger's insights, Hopper's approach to large groups was modified by his work on trauma in association with his sociological background (Hopper, 2003b). Over the years, he has convened large groups in various organizations and training settings. Göran Ahlin (1996, 2010), building on his knowledge of Foulkesian theory, brought to the fore a style of practice in large groups grounded on his work in training and Karolinska Hospital in Sweden. Wilke (2014) developed his practice as a large group consultant and created his own style of working with large groups. He brought to the debate the role of social sciences combined with psychoanalytical thinking in investigations of large-group work.

In the last thirty years, group analysis has developed in various countries in Europe and in Israel, and large-group work found new conductors/conveners involved in various ways in the large-group practice and research. Today, professionals of the third generation have engaged in the idea of fostering collective spaces for working through societal traumas and exploring social unconscious influences on large groups (Hopper, & Weinberg, 2011, 2016, 2017). Therefore, experiences combining working-through traumatic processes and dialogue with "the other" have been encouraged in public spaces, using creative combinations between small, median, and large groups, frequently about a specific topic.

Conversations between professionals and laypersons in communities in conflict, as well as German-Jewish dialogues, are taking place in Israel under Robi Friedman's (2019) leadership. Workshops for "Reflective Citizens" are being organized by Marina Mojovic (2020) and collaborators in Serbia and other countries. In Greece, Vassilis Menoutis (2000) described an interesting application of median and large groups to explore identity issues in future officers of the Naval Academy. In Iceland, Einar Gudmundsson (2014) and colleagues used large-group work in the school system "to increase elementary school students' ability to experience and comprehend democratic processes and the high level of freedom of speech" (Gudmundsson et al., 2014, p. 548). Both experiences reveal how large-group work can creatively foster communication and develop citizenship in different spheres of society.

Large group work is also an important tool for training new group analysts. In Norway, as Thor Island (2003, 2010) describes, slow open long-term large groups have been offered for the training community since 1984. These large groups have provided space for the personal growth of trainees and staff. They also revealed that many fears traditionally attributed to large-group work could be overcome through carefully shared leadership and intensive "learning from experience" through regular participation in large groups. Teresa Von Sommaruga Howard (2012) and other colleagues keep de Maré's tradition in large groups accessible to younger generations through the creation of training workshops, nurturing "large group dialogue in organisations and society".

Pines (2003) seems to have captured the contemporary group-analytic spirit when he stated that "the marketplace is the group-analytic community" (Pines, 2003, p. 54) and "large group meetings are becoming 'second nature' in the group-analytic movement" (Pines, 2003, p. 55). This is a shared ideal and perhaps this is why it is so important for group analysts to create/re-create containing spaces for renewed social fabric in the public sphere – by "repopulating agoras" (Scanlon, 2018, p. 80) – where fellowship and citizenship may flourish; spaces in which the *zoon politikon* can lead a *vita activa* (Arendt, 1958) through collectivity, plurality, dialogue, and action (Penna, 2016b).

In 2020, with the emergence of the syndemic[6] (Horthon, 2020) of Covid-19, and the need for social distancing between people, face-to-face large-group meetings were interrupted, being replaced with virtual "settings" worldwide. It is not possible yet to define in which ways these new experiences represent significant changes in theory, technique, and styles of leadership in large groups, or whether a new type of work in large group is being conceived. It is too early to imagine how the situation will evolve, but the idea of creating spaces where a large number of people meet, even virtually, in the interface of the private and public spheres, remain alive. Perhaps, we will need to learn from these new experiences (Weinberg & Rolnick, 2020) how disembodied individual persons can occupy "virtual agoras", fostering dialogue and mature citizenship through virtual large groups.

In the next and last chapter of this book, our research continues with a discussion on an important development in group-analytic theory. Hopper's (2003b) formulation of a fourth basic assumption – Incohesion: Aggregation/ Massification – encompasses explorations in basic-assumption theory, large groups, and social unconscious processes in tripartite matrices, proposing a contemporary framework to investigate traumatic experiences in the unconscious life of groups and group-like social systems.

Notes

1 For decades, using a psychoanalytic approach, Volkan (1997, 2004, 2006, 2013) has been researching the psychodynamics of ethnic, religious, national, and ideological large groups. His work is fundamental for understanding intergroup relations, intractable conflicts, social trauma, transgenerational transmissions, and collective identity in societies. Volkan defines large groups as groups composed by millions of persons who share a common ethnic-national identity: "Large group identities are the end result of a historical continuity, geographical reality, a myth of a common beginning, and other shared events; they evolve naturally" (Volkan, 1997, p. 22). Therefore, in Volkan's approach, the expression large group replaces a specific social system, that is, people or nations. However, Hopper's sociological background brings an important theoretical differentiation between Volkan's approach to the study of large groups and those studied by group-analytic and group-relations scholars. This differentiation prevents confusion in the use of the expression "large group" and encompasses the investigation discussed in this book, although we must acknowledge that some group analysts and some colleagues who take a group relations approach share Volkan's definition of "large groups".

2 In France, Didier Anzieu (1984) introduced large groups in training. His observations, connected to primitive anxieties and aggression in unstructured groups, contributed to the development of the French theory of groups. Pines (2003) states that Anzieu's work exerted a powerful influence on the British pioneers; however, large-group work in France has not developed as in England.

3 Ten years earlier, Kreeger had contributed the chapter "The Large-Group Event" to the book on group relations edited by Rice (1965).

4 Gosling (1981) discusses very small groups with five members. Curiously, in Brazil, the very first small analytic group, held by the psychoanalyst Alcyon Baer Bahía in 1951 "remained alive" with one single participant in "mind interaction" with those members who had unexpectedly left the group. In subsequent sessions, Bahía sustained "the group process" until selecting new patients (Martins, 2017). In Bahía's group, it is interesting to observe how the group matrix was introjected by the patient on his personal matrix, his "inner group" (Mello Franco, 2015, p. 275). Moreover, the transference/countertransference co-created by the dyad patient/ group and analyst kept the small-group matrix alive. In this example, some of Hopper and Weyman's (1975) considerations, based on Simmel's (1908) postulation on dyads as the elemental structures of all groups, acquire meaning, as it happened in Bahía's endeavour. In this sense, small groups form the elemental structure of large groups (Simmel, 1908, p. 185).

5 In this regard, Tubert-Oklander and Hernández de Tubert (2014a, 2014b, 2014c) bring different perspectives on large-group work connected to the Latin American and Pichon-Rivière's approaches. Their investigation highlights theoretical and technical differences, a different style of conducting/convening, holding and containing large-group sessions that reveal the influence of the context, but also social unconscious processes related to the tripartite matrices in which the large group takes place. Their experience shows how large-group psychodynamics differ in various foundation matrices and how transcultural explorations in large groups are relevant to the development of theory and practice in large groups.

6 The notion of a syndemic was first conceived by Merrill Singer, an American medical anthropologist, in the 1990s. Syndemics are characterized by biological and social interactions between conditions and states, interactions that increase a person's susceptibility to harm or worsen their health outcomes. In the case of SARS-CoV-2, two categories of disease interact within specific populations. These conditions cluster within social groups according to patterns of inequality embedded in our societies. The combination of these diseases on a background of socioeconomic disparity exacerbates the adverse effects of each separate disease (Horton, 2020, p. 874).

10 Traumatic experience in the unconscious life of social systems

Earl Hopper's theory of the fourth basic assumption of Incohesion: Aggregation/ Massification or (ba) I: A/M

Introduction

In previous chapters, we explored the history of analytic group work in England. In Chapter Nine, we discussed how the work with large groups in group analysis brought new perspectives to the interpersonal and transpersonal relations of a large number of persons, contributing to a more contemporary understanding of the psychodynamics of the crowd and the mass. In this chapter, we move further, introducing Earl Hopper's theory of Incohesion: Aggregation/Massification as a fourth basic assumption in the unconscious life of groups and group-like social systems. Hopper prepared this latest version of his theory of Incohesion, especially for this book. It is followed by my critical commentary on the importance of his theory for an in-depth exploration of social formations in contemporaneity.

Before delving into Hopper's presentation of his theory, it is important to trace his professional journey. Earl Hopper (2003a) started his career as a sociologist in 1962, working with Norbert Elias as an Assistant Lecturer in Sociology at the University of Leicester, and then as a Lecturer in Sociology at Cambridge University and later as a Lecturer at the London School of Economics. After becoming a member of the Group Analytic Society and The Institute of Group Analysis (London), he trained as a psychotherapist with the British Association for Psychotherapy and as a psychoanalyst with the British Psychoanalytical Society. Hopper has an extensive clinical practice focused on traumatized patients – including survivors of social trauma – and traumatized organizations. His investigations show the development of his thinking as a sociologist, group analyst, and psychoanalyst whose interdisciplinary education makes him a leading author in the study of group processes – not only in large-group work, but also in contemporary research on the social unconscious, which interconnects with his formulation of a fourth basic assumption theory.

In 1989, at the Royal College of Psychiatrists, through the lens of Group Analysis, Hopper introduced an early version of his theory of the fourth basic assumption. Since then, he has developed an encompassing theory that revolutionized the notion of cohesion, giving rise to the study of Incohesion processes in groups and group-like social systems. Many of his publications on the topic are cited in his paper in this chapter. The most relevant are Hopper 2003a, 2003b,

DOI: 10.4324/9780429399534-11

2012, 2018, and 2019, which include extensive references to the relevant litera-ture. In this respect, from the perspective of Incohesion processes, the study of the psychodynamics of crowds and masses, as well as investigations of group analysis, group analytic psychotherapy, and group dynamics point to what I regard as a shift in the main paradigm that governs current research on group formations.

From Cohesion to Incohesion

In his study on social cohesion, Hopper discussed social formations with an emphasis on the differences between "simple" and "complex" societies and their implications for the understanding of social systems (Hopper, 1965, 1981; Hopper & Weyman, 1975). He stated that all social formations, from primitive social aggregates to complex nation-states, could and should be understood as social systems (Hopper, 2003b).

The notion of cohesion has been relevant for a wide range of disciplines in the natural and social sciences. The definition of Incohesion varies, depending on the field of study and the context. In social psychology and in the work with groups, the idea of cohesion pervaded twentieth-century reflections, underlining the importance of proximity, similarity, solidarity, identification, bonding, identity, connectedness, valency, group size, tasks, and common goals (Hopper, 2003b). In psychoanalysis, concepts such as holding (Winnicott, 1971) and containment (Bion, 1967) in the dyad have been applied to the investigation of social cohesion in small groups, and social cohesion, in the psychosocial sphere of families, organizations and societies.

By the end of the twentieth century, deep transformations were affecting post-industrial Western culture, and knowledge was going through a radical change, especially in the way it was produced, discussed, and legitimized (Lyotard, 1984), leading to a reconfiguration of boundaries in the social sciences (Richards, 2018) and to new paths on critical social theory (Honneth, 1996). These transformations have provided the context in which discourse formations (Foucault, 1972) were co-created in the work with small and large groups. However, it was Hopper's (2003b) postulation of a fourth basic assumption, shifting the focus of analysis from Cohesion to Incohesion processes in social systems, that pointed to a "perspective reversal" that deconstructs modern certainties, narratives, and discourse analysis (Foucault, 1972; Lyotard, 1984).

Hopper's research (2003b) unveils the dichotomies between the individual and society discussed in Chapter Four and advances the idea that the understanding of social phenomena requires transdisciplinary efforts and interdependent visions to acknowledge the social nature of persons in the context of their groups as dynamic open systems. This statement is akin to the principles of group analysis and takes into account social facts and social forces people are not aware of, pointing out their social unconscious as well. They allow for tackling the issue of inter-dependencies between society, community, organizations, family, and persons, contextualizing in time and space the figurations they co-create, especially in contexts marked by traumatic experiences. Therefore, we can say that Hopper's basic assumption connects Elias's process sociology with group-analytic tripartite matrices, systems theory, and psychoanalysis, providing new perspectives on Bion's basic assumption study and enriching contemporary critical theory (Honneth, 1996). Hopper's theory thus underlines the relevance of failed dependency and traumatogenic processes by means of co-created figurations in tripartite matrices, as we can follow in his contribution to this chapter.

Another obstacle to bridging the gap between these disciplines is the misleading idea that in the analysis of social formations, persons, groups, and social systems are isomorphic, as highlighted in Chapter Eight. Although many psychoanalysts, group analysts, and social scientists imagine that social systems can be broadly investigated as groups, this correlation is not necessarily true (Hopper, 2003b). Based on discussions that range from Marxist and Durkheimian theories to systems theory, as well as on his clinical experience, Hopper says that it is only when a social system – a society, a city, a village – is traumatized that it shows processes that may be described as a regression from the complex to the simple and analysed as a group: "Traumatized societies become like groups, and traumatized groups become like people" (Hopper, 2003b, p. 18). Therefore, it is only under these circumstances that an isomorphism between persons, groups, and social systems can be postulated.

The analysis of Cohesion and Incohesion in groups begins with Hopper's (1981) investigations of tensions between integration and disintegration, or between order and disorder in various human social systems. Previously, in the field of group relations, group psychotherapy and group analysis, psychological and sociological studies focused on and even favoured the study of cohesion, integration and solidarity of social systems to the detriment of the study of Incohesion or disintegration processes, except when pointing to significant social changes or moments of social instability. In classical Freudian psychoanalysis, integration (or maturation) is based on imitation, identification, and empathy, when the ego ideal of the members of a social system is projected onto the leader (Freud, 1921) or onto the group itself (Anzieu, 1971). In turn, disintegration is explained in terms of the dilution of mutual identifications, self-destruction associated with the "death instinct" and transgenerational Oedipal struggle (Hopper, 2003b, p. 21). From these perspectives, the social context is taken for granted and the constraints of the social unconscious and the variety of social systems are neglected. Hopper's (1984; 2003a) analysis resembles some of Lukács's remarks about Freud's non-critical and a-historical approach to mass psychology, mentioned in Chapter Three.

The fourth basic assumption theory was developed between the end of the twentieth century and the beginning of the twenty-first century – from the end of the Cold War to the recrudescence of ethnic conflicts, terrorism, racism, immigration, fundamentalist thinking, and the intensification of socioeconomic problems – when expectations regarding an idealized, globalized, and democratic world diminished, stressing uncertainty, fragmentation, and fear. Hopper's thinking captured exactly these psychosocial fractures, these cracks, these conscious and unconscious traumatic experiences, enabling the postulation of a broad, all-encompassing, and ubiquitous basic assumption.

In the last decades of the twentieth century, we experienced the inflation of the private realm to the detriment of personal participation in the public sphere (Sennett, 1974), the prevalence of a narcissistic culture (Lasch, 1979), and the exacerbation of individualism (Ehrenberg, 2010). Today, life in society is facing the escalation of neoliberal policies, displacements on Foucauldian biopower (Foucault, 1979), and the emergence of necropolitics (Mbembe, 2003). We witness millions of persons daily submitted to humiliation, shame, disrespect, exclusion, and other forms of systemic and subjective violence (Gilligan, 1996).

Contemporaneity is thus forging new dimensions of traumatic experiences that characterize an increase in Incohesion: Aggregation/Massification processes in tripartite matrices. In this sense, the weariness of the selves (Ehrenberg, 2010), a precarious life (Butler, 2015), and a burnout society (Han, 2015) have contributed to reinforcing the discourses of identity (Taylor, 1994; Richards, 2018) in an attempt to cope with new sources of personal and social suffering (Akhtar, 2014). Nevertheless, perhaps as a sign of personal and collective resistance, we are also witnessing the emergence of new struggles for recognition (Honneth, 1996), demands for dignity, and politics of identity (Fukuyama, 2018). In this direction, public and performative assemblies (Butler, 2015) and attempts to work through collective wounds (Soreanu, 2018), such as the movement "Black Lives Matter", are suggesting glimpses of hope for persons, groups, and societies. This makes the study of Hopper's theory crucial for a detailed investigation of the discontinuities and challenges posed by twenty-first century incohesive social systems. Moreover, as Hopper states, the acronym for "Incohesion: Aggregation/Massification" is I: A/M, which can also be read as "I am", "an assertion of personal identity when identity is felt to be threatened" (Hopper, 2012, p. xli). In this sense, "Incohesion is especially pertinent to working with the vicissitudes of social identity" (Hopper, 2019, p. 9). These ideas are considered in Hopper's (2003a) conceptualization of various forms of instrumental adjustment, and in his later theory of "mature hope" as the ability and willingness to exercise the transcendent imagination.

Therefore, in order to help the reader to grasp the importance of Hopper's fourth basic assumption in this investigation, we introduce his personal contribution to the debate. It will be followed by my commentary on the relevance of his theory to examine current struggles for recognition and today's politics of identity.

"Notes" on the Theory and Concept of the Fourth Basic Assumption in the Unconscious Life of Groups and Group-like Social Systems: Incohesion: Aggregation/Massification or (ba) I: A/M

by Earl Hopper© 2021

I will outline my theory and concept of Incohesion: Aggregation/Massification of (ba) I: A/M as the fourth basic assumption in the unconscious life of groups and group-like social systems, especially those in which trauma is prevalent. An outline of a theory about a complex topic is necessarily very condensed. However, I have tried to develop and clarify my thinking about Incohesion in a series of publications that contain clinical and empirical illustrations of the theory and extensive bibliography, which I will cite here as appropriate.[1]

I – Basic assumption processes: general considerations

I assume that whereas it is not necessary to summarize the theory of basic assumption processes, the literature about these processes, and the data that have been used to illustrate these ideas, it is necessary to provide some general introductory information about this theory, which was first conceptualized by W.R. Bion (1961), and later developed by his colleagues, who have always focused more on the study of groups than on using them for the provision of psychotherapy. According to my understanding of this Bionian theory:

1

All groups are characterized by their "work group" structures and by their "basic assumption group" configurations. There are many kinds of work-group defined in terms of their conscious intention in order to do some work or to carry out what we call primary and secondary tasks. Within a group who meets for the purpose of psychotherapy, the mutual reflection takes place within the work group, at least ideally; but in practice, mutual reflection is deeply influenced by basic assumption processes.

2

Basic assumptions are configurations of relational defences against various psychotic anxieties which arise as a function of the regression of groups and group-like social systems: Pairing as an expression of sexuality used as a defence against depressive position anxieties (Pairing can be "normal" or "perverse", the latter based on the sexualization of hatred); Fight/Flight as an expression of paranoid and persecutory anxieties associated with denigration as an expression of one part of envy; and Dependency as an expression of idealization as a defence against the other part of envy. These basic assumptions have been discussed in terms of many different frames of reference, but this is how I have conceptualized them. At any given time, a basic assumption group is likely to be characterized by a particular basic assumption or combination of them.

3

Although they vary in their intensity, basic assumptions are ubiquitous and omnipresent. The metaphor of the work group floating like a cork on the Sea of Basic Assumptions is entirely apposite. Although it is better for the three men in the tub to navigate rather than merely float, this implies that they think that they know where they are going.

4

Basic assumptions can impede work as well as facilitate it. The three men in the tub are sometimes able to make creative use of psychotic anxieties and their expression in basic assumption processes.

5

Basic assumptions are associated with roles that are typical of each of them. People vary in their vulnerability to the suction power of these roles, their valence for enacting them, and/or their compulsion to personify them. Taking such roles supports the skins of identity that people in various states of regression need in order to survive the anxieties associated with regression. Whereas these personifications are usually discussed in terms of "leadership", in fact "followership" is a better description of them. Real leadership is associated with work-group processes and the ability and willingness to take roles rather than to be sucked into the enactment of them.

6

Given the close connections of their genotypical structures with their underlying psychotic anxieties, basic assumptions can be understood in terms of the classical Jungian concept of the collective unconscious, which is a property of the species of Homo sapiens, and is, therefore, universal. However, in their phenotypical manifestations, basic assumptions take on local colouration and expression, and, therefore, can also be understood in terms of the "social unconscious", located within the socio-cultural parts of the foundation matrix. For example, the basic assumption of Fight/Flight in California looks rather different from Fight/Flight in the Middle East, although their underlying dynamics are the same.

II – *Traumatic experience and the fear of annihilation in personal matrices in the development of the fourth basic assumption of Incohesion: Aggregation/ Massification*

In terms of a Bionian perspective, it is virtually impossible to conceptualize a fourth basic assumption, because in order to do so it is necessary to privilege the understanding of helplessness in terms of failed dependency, and to relegate the assumption of innate malign envy. (This might be why Pierre Turquet argued that the study of trauma was not psychoanalytical as much as it was sociological, and that "Oneness" was not really a fourth basic assumption). However, my theory of Incohesion as a fourth basic assumption draws heavily on the perspective developed by S.H. Foulkes, who was the founder of Group Analysis as a clinical discipline. He was not particularly interested in the study of basic assumptions, primarily because they were assumed to be "innatist" and what is nowadays termed "essentialist", whereas the group analytic perspective is based on the study of the social unconscious, and draws especially on socio-logical ideas. From the point of view of Foulkesian Group Analysis, basic assumptions in the unconscious life of groups and group-like social systems are expressed and manifest in each and all of the sub-matrices of the tripartite matrix, including the foundation matrix of the contextual society, the dynamic matrix of the social system in question, and the personal matrices of each of the participants in it, including the personifications of roles that are typical of each of the basic assumptions (Hopper, 2018a, 2018b, 2020).

1

I will now outline the first part of my theory and concept of Incohesion. In the 1970s, working in the tradition of Winnicott and others associated with the Group of Independent Psychoanalysts of the British Psychoanalytical Society, rather than in the tradition of Klein and others associated with the Kleinian group, I studied the fear of annihilation. I came to think that this anxiety was caused not by innate malign envy, but by profound helplessness associated with the traumatic experience of failed dependency through inadequate holding and insufficient containment. Moreover, I argued that envy was an emergent defence against the pain of profound helplessness, and was directed towards whoever was perceived as able to be of help but who either would not or could not do so. I outlined the phenomenology of the fear of annihilation in terms of psychotic anxieties associated with psychic fission and fragmentation, such as the terror of exploding into bits and pieces, falling for ever, and/or of becoming invisible, in oscillation with psychotic anxieties associated with rela-tional fusion and confusion of parts of the self with what can be found among parts of the lost and abandoning object, such as the terror of suffocation, being eaten alive and/or being utterly controlled by another person.[2] Traumatized people who get stuck in states of fission and fragmentation tend to develop crustacean character structures, in which their vulnerability is hidden beneath a protective shell; and traumatized people who get stuck in states of fusion and confusion tend to develop amoeboid character structures, in which their strength is hidden beneath a protective cloak of vulnerability (Hopper, 1981, 2003a, 2003b).[3]

2

When psychotic anxieties are so great that one cannot think, and when con-nections have been broken between body and mind, and between and among people, it becomes extremely difficult to communicate through narratives, which require symbolization and language. Words fail those who have been severely traumatized, perhaps because when they were in extreme distress, words were all that were offered to them. This is the world of the body rather than the mind, of atonal music rather than rhythm and harmony, and the world of borygmie (stomach rumbles) rather than stories of hunger (Solomon, 2007). Without access to the power of symbolization and verbalization in the context of relations with others who might listen, hear, and convey a sense of understanding, the body becomes an instrument of communication through enactments, as well as through projective and introjective identification involving a narrative of signs and sensations (Pines, 1998; Green, 1983; Nitzgen, 2013; Grossmark, 2017).

3

I (Hopper, 1965) have argued that aggressive feelings are a product of frustration and low self-esteem within a specific socio-cultural-political context; that the relationship between aggressive feelings and aggression is regulated by various normative orientations towards the expression of feelings in general and aggressive feelings in particular; that aggressive feelings and aggression can be displaced from sources of frustration towards a variety of persons and their property, as well as towards internal representations of them; and that aggressive feelings and aggression can be directed toward removing the sources of frustration as well as towards retaliation and revenge against them (Hopper, 1965). Aggressive feelings are a necessary but insufficient source of aggression. Many factors regulate the expression of aggressive feelings in actual aggression.[4] I have also argued that discussions of aggression should distinguish its targets from its forms and functions (Hopper, 2003c).

Violence is an extreme form of aggression. It is intended to cause extreme harm to another person who is motivated to avoid such harm. The main cause of violence is the perpetrator's desire to avoid feelings of shame and humiliation, perhaps by making the victim feel what the perpetrator wishes not to feel as well as what the victim actually does feel (Gilligan, 1996). The severely traumatized feel compelled to pervert the Golden Rule that they should do unto others as they *would* be done by; instead, they feel compelled to do unto others as they *have been* done by.

Consistent with their tendency to communicate through somatization and enactments, the traumatized use their bodies as "narrative weapons" against both other people and themselves. However, even these processes occur within a social context. As Biran (2015) has argued, not only is the compulsive projection of beta-elements the primary form of communication, it is also a primary form of violence towards the object who is perceived to have failed dependency needs or as a displacement from this object. I would add that the body can also be the least expensive weapon available.

4

Positive and negative encapsulations are the main intra-psychic dissociative defenses against the fear of annihilation and the painful phenomenology of it. A positive encapsulation is like a haven from the poisonous, malignant and toxic processes within the whole person; and a negative encapsulation is like a depository of such processes from which the whole person is protected. In the former, what is encapsulated is protected from what is not; and in the latter, what is not encapsulated is protected from what is. Encapsulation has also been discussed in terms of *encystment*, as well as *entombment* and *encryptment* (Abraham & Torok, 1995).

5

Variations in resilience greatly influence the short and long term sequalae of traumatic experience. The many determinants of resilience range from properties of the organism to properties of the situation in which people are located. The responses of others to those who have been traumatized are one of the main determinants of the sequalae of their experience. This is especially true for "betrayal trauma".

6

Based on my work with Shoah survivors and their children, and on my work with drug addicts, I conceptualized a "trauma syndrome" that involves addiction, somatization, sadistic perversions, risk taking, delinquency and criminality, which could just as well have been called an "addiction syndrome", because in my clinical experience the elements of the one are more or less identical to the elements of the other (Hopper, 1995, 2003a, 2003b). These associations and co-morbidities are based on the sexualization of aggression as an attempt to escape the painful anxieties associated with it, and on the compulsive and defensive seeking of excitement (Limentani, 1989). They are also based on traumatophilia, the compulsive desire to enact traumatic experience (Abraham, 1907).

III – The Manifestations of the Intra-Psychic Phenomenology of the Fear of Annihilation in the Incohesion of the Tripartite Matrix of Groups and Group-Like Social Systems

I will now outline the second part of my theory of Incohesion. In the 1980s, I began to study the phenomenology of trauma in the context of the structures and processes of social systems. I focused on processes of what I came to call "Incohesion: Aggregation/Massification". Drawing from sociological and anthropological studies of the cohesion of social systems, I argued that processes of Incohesion are an expression and a manifestation of the phenomenology of the fear of annihilation as a consequence of traumatic experience, and that these processes of Incohesion are likely to be recursive, that is, to lead to further traumatic experience. I also argued that Incohesion should be regarded as a fourth basic assumption in the unconscious life of groups and group-like social systems, and as such might be denoted as (ba) I:A/M. My argument followed from the axiom that trauma and the fear of annihilation are primary, and the emergence of envy is secondary and in essence defensive. In the same way that the phenomenology of the fear of annihilation and the defences against it can be considered as the "core complex" of persons (Glasser, 1979), the basic assumption of Incohesion can be considered as the core complex of groups and group-like social systems.

1

The members of traumatized social systems are likely to feel that their leaders have failed their reasonable dependency on them, and have in effect betrayed them. Social systems in which traumatic experience is prevalent can be considered as traumatized social systems, for example: *societies* characterized by events such as natural disasters, wars, rampant inflation, sudden changes in political policies, the assassination of political leaders, high rates of unemployment, large influx of refugees, mass migration, very closely contested elections, rapid shifts in the occupational structure with respect to the ratio of what used to be called "blue collar" and "white collar" jobs, etc; *organizations* characterized by events such as sudden changes in the cost of raw materials, extreme volatility in the value of a national currency that leads to the unpredictability of the cost of imports and exports, hostile and unplanned company takeovers and mergers, patterns of sexual harassment, patterns of corruption in career advancement, etc; *organizations concerned with the professional practice of psychotherapy and training for it* characterized by the development of increasingly effective drugs, effective brief therapies, a proliferation of trainings, change in the ratio of men and women in the profession, and change in the ratio of medical and non-medical practitioners, etc; *families* characterized by incest, physical abuse, multiple divorces, etc; *groups generally* characterized by events such as the unreliability of their leaders, the failures of contextual organizations to provide goods and services that the group needs in order to function, etc; and even clinical groups who meet for the purpose of providing therapy for their members who are characterized by events such as the abrupt departure of one of their members can be considered as a traumatized therapy group.

On the basis of patterns of projective and introjective identification and other forms of externalization and internalization, traumatic experience in the foundation matrix of the society is likely to be recapitulated in the dynamic matrices of its constituent groupings, and in the personal matrices of their members, and to a degree vice-versa. For example, high rates of unemployment are likely to give rise to unstable family structures in which there is a higher rate of child abuse, or a new member of a therapy group is likely to generate a response that is typical of how a society responds to immigrants. Organizations in which personal trauma are prevalent are also likely to develop patterns of Incohesion. For example, prisons and mental hospitals can be considered in these terms. It is often difficult to know where a trauma has been initiated, and where traumatogenic processes are located. In other words, traumatogenic processes are almost always recursive, and manifest in the tripartite matrix as-a-whole.

2

Traumatogenic events are, of course, various and numerous. However, events that cause people to experience a sense of failed dependency through inadequate containment and insufficient holding can be considered in terms of stress, cumulative, and/or catastrophic traumatogenic processes. This is always a function of both the security and stability of the social system, and the severity of the failures involved.

3

The size of a group is an important source of traumatic experience for the members of it. The larger the group, the more likely is it that the participants in it will feel anonymized, invisible, unheard, and so on, and in general unrecognized (Main, 1975; Turquet, 1975). In other words, participation in large groups is itself likely to be traumatic. However, this depends on the ecology of the setting of the group and the communication technology that is available to all members of the group. Good acoustics and good technology contribute to the very meaning of *large* and *larger*.

In general, however, the larger the group, the more likely it is that the alien nature of the "Neighbor" will come to the fore. The neighbor can be understood as the "Other" who has the power to transform a person into an "interrupted subject". Although the neighbor is close, he/she is also unknowable. However, each individual identifies with others, and each feels what the other feels. My love and yours are entwined, but so is our hate! Although dislocated from ourselves we become connected to others in erotically heightened and dizzyingly discomforting ways (Frosh, 2008).

An increase in the size of a social system tends in itself to be traumatic. Societies in which there has been a rapid increase in the size of their population are often characterized by increased competition for resources that are perceived to be limited and even scarce. Without careful management organizations that experience a rapid increase in the number of their participants can become bureaucratic. New siblings can disrupt the authority structure of a family and create a sense of deprivation within it. However, we do not really know much about the consequences of an increase in the size of a group, which partly depend on the size of the group before the increase occurs. For example, the effects of an increase of one member in a group of eight might be more obvious and disruptive than an increase of one member in a group of thirty-five, and so on (Hopper, 1975, 2003a).

4

Traumatized social systems are likely to regress in their structures. However, we no longer think about regression and progression in terms of simple, biologically based lines of development, not even in the case of an organism.

Regression and progression do not follow "natural" lines of development characterized by linear and secular stages or phases of maturation. Instead, these processes must be understood in terms of various dimensions of social systems, and in the context of the "life-trajectories" that are typical of them (Hopper, 1981). For example, with respect to patterns of interaction, shifts occur from complexity to simplicity with respect to role specialization and differentiation. Moreover, traumatized societies are likely to become like bureaucratic organizations, and organizations are likely to become like groups and group-like social systems. Herein lies a paradox in that the development of a group into an organization involves both progression and regression simultaneously: on the one hand, the group is likely to be able to deal with its tasks more effectively and efficiently, but, on the other hand, the precious and vulnerable balance between the me-ness and the we-ness of the group is likely to be destroyed (Lawrence, Bain, & Gould, 2000).

5

Groups and group-like social systems tend to be characterized by basic assumption processes generally. When they have been traumatized and/or when traumatic experience is prevalent within them, groups and group-like social systems regress into a liminal space in which they do not exist as groups but as social aggregates in oscillation with social masses. However, in the context of traumatogenic processes large groups tend to become characterized by Incohesion: Aggregation/Massification.

6

Incohesion is bi-polar. Aggregation is the primary form of Incohesion. A socio-cultural aggregate is a grouping of what Turquet (1975) called singletons, who are likely to be in envious competition with one another, excessively detached from one another, and to have crustacean character structures. An aggregate can also be a grouping of dysfunctional sub-groups and contra-groups that cannot relate to one another in constructive and productive ways. With respect to societies, such dysfunctional sub-groups and contra-groups tend to be based on various socio-cultural-political constructs such as race, gender and ethnicity, which by definition have little or no connection with institutionalized activity, especially economic productivity. In effect, such groups are populist, and they are sub-institutional (Hopper, 2005b).

Massification is the second form of Incohesion. It is defensive against the anxieties and difficulties associated with Aggregation, and polar to it. A socio-cultural mass is a grouping of what Turquet (1975) called *membership individuals,* who are likely to be involved in personal and collective merger with a shared and idealized object. They tend to cling to one another, and to have ameboid character structures. They attempt to obliterate all distinctions and differences among themselves. Although Massification masquerades as cohesion, it is as incohesive as Aggregation, especially in the longer term.

7

There are many metaphors for aggregates and masses. For example, an aggregate is like a handful of gravel, and a mass is like a piece of basalt. Colleagues in Ireland like to say that more organically an aggregate is like a bowl of boiled potatoes, each of which maintains its identity as an individual potato, and a mass is like a bowl of mashed potatoes in which it is impossible to identify any particular individual potato. Also apposite is a bowl of whitebait in contrast to *quenelle de brochet*, as is a piece of carp in contrast to a nice piece of gefilte fish.

8

As in the development of the paranoid/schizoid and the depressive positions, which in the first instance are stages or phases of maturation, but in the second instance are positions which tend to oscillate with each other, Aggregation and Massification are in the first instance stages or phases of socio-cultural responses to the fear of annihilation, but, in the second instance, are socio-cultural positions which tend to oscillate with each other. It is important to remember that, despite appearances to the contrary, Aggregation and Massification are equally incohesive.

Oscillation between Aggregation and Massification does not derive only from the externalizations of the psychotic anxieties associated with the fear of annihilation and its phenomenology of fission and fragmentation, and fusion and confusion. Aggregation is also highly unstable. It is very difficult for an aggregated group to work effectively and efficiently, especially to find ways to cooperate. Similarly, Massification is highly transitory and non-adaptive to environmental challenges and diversity. It is very difficult for a massified group to work effectively and efficiently, and to take advantage of the diverse skills of its participants and to make long term plans.

9

The dynamics of Incohesion are traumatogenic in themselves. Incohesion tends, therefore, to be self-perpetuating. It is very difficult for a social system characterized by Incohesion to recover and to rebuild its work groups, and for them to become effective and efficient. It is almost impossible for people in social systems characterized by Incohesion to function as what Turquet called "individual members" of them, and accordingly to engage in effective and efficient work. For example: with respect to societies, it is difficult for people to function as engaged but rational citizens (Hopper, 2000); with respect to families, for the members of them to individuate from one another; with respect to organizations, for people to take their work roles with a sense of discipline and willingness to maintain boundaries, that is, to become "organizational citizens"; and with respect to groups generally, it is difficult for the participants in them to get the balance right between too much "me-ness" and too much "we-ness".

10

The constituent groupings of a social system which is characterized by Incohesion tend themselves to become incohesive, and to oscillate between states of Aggregation and states of Massification. Whereas aggregated groupings are the basis for competition and conflict rather than cooperation, massified groupings become like cults and tend to become contra-groupings. These sub-groupings and contra-groupings can become fractals of the society as-a-whole, and are likely to carry important information about it.

IV – Incohesion as a property of the tripartite matrix

As is true of all basic assumptions, Aggregation and Massification are manifest in the various dimensions of the tripartite matrix. With respect to patterns of interaction (or interpersonal relations), the basic assumption group of Incohesion is in a state of unintegration or disintegration: when Aggregation prevails, the group tends to become a collection of singletons, sub-groups, and contra-groups; and when massification prevails, the group tends to become a coalition or conglomeration of membership individuals and their sub-groups and contra-groups. With respect to patterns of normation (values, norms, and beliefs), the basic assumption group of Incohesion is in a state of "insolidarity": in states of Aggregation, various forms of anomie prevail; and in states of Massification, various forms of "nomie" prevail (Hopper, 1981). With respect to patterns of communication (verbal and non-verbal), the basic assumption group of Incohesion is in a state of incoherence: in states of Aggregation, various forms of "bureaucratese" prevail; and in states of Massification, various forms of "cult-speak" prevail.

Similar distinctions can be made with respect to other dimensions of the tripartite matrix, such as styles of technology; styles of leadership, followership, and bystandership; styles of thinking and feeling; and etc.

These dimensions of the tripartite matrix in states of Aggregation and Massification are summarised in Table 10.1 and Table 10.2.

These conceptual distinctions enable us to discuss such phenomena with an appropriate degree of precision and theoretical support. For example, one of the many reasons why it is important to distinguish patterns of interaction from patterns of normation is that in complex social systems cohesion is derived from the integration of the interaction system, whereas in simple social systems cohesion is derived from the solidarity of the normative system.

Table 10.1 Some dimensions of a tripartite matrix and the socio-cultural states of
Cohesion and Incohesion of social systems

Dimensions: Examples	Socio-cultural states	
	Cohesion: the work group	Incohesion: the basic assumption group
Patterns of interpersonal relationships (the interaction system)	Integration	Unintegration
Patterns of values, norms and beliefs (the normation system)	Solidarity	Insolidarity
Verbal and non-verbal communication	Coherence	Incoherence

Table 10.2 Some properties of the socio-cultural states of Incohesion: Aggregation/
Massification of social systems in terms of some dimensions of the tripartite
matrix

Dimensions: Examples	Socio-cultural states of Incohesion	
	Aggregation	Massification
Patterns of Interaction: Patterns of interpersonal relationships (the interaction system) **UNINTEGRATION/ DISINTEGRATION**	• Market exchange • Many Isolates and singletons	• Anonymization • Many "Membership individuals"
Patterns of Normation: Patterns of values, norms and beliefs (the normation system) **INSOLIDARITY**	• Anomie (forms of) • Low Morale Diversity of cultural products	• Nomie (forms of) • Pseudo-Morale • Homogenization of signifiers (a bagel is only a roll with a hole)
Patterns of verbal and non-verbal communication: **INCOHERENCE**	• "Bureaucratese" • Jargon • Experimental music	• Cult speak • Speaking in tongues • Celebratory identity music

V – Incohesion and patterns of aggression

Each basic assumption is characterized by distinctive amounts and patterns of
aggression. In Incohesion aggressive feelings and aggression are prevalent. They
are characterized by the following patterns:

1

In the context of Aggregation, aggression ranges from indifference, hostility and
withdrawal from relationships to more open hatred and conflict in which each

person is against each person, and each subgroup is against each subgroup. In contrast, in the context of massification aggressive feelings are more focused. It is essential to eliminate the group father and "his" parts that are perceived to block access to the group "mother" (Schindler, 1966), and that may prevent a merger with "her" (Chasseguet-Smirgel, 1984). In general, the development and maintenance of Massification as a defence against Aggregation involves attempts to create a perfect womb-like group with no imperfections, followed by attempts by the members of the group to merge with it. Such processes of fatal purification involve the obliteration of all imperfections, and the obliteration of all obstacles to merger. The hallucinated merger with a perfect maternal object of safety is associated with the hallucinated annihilation of the forbidding paternal object of boundary maintenance, rules and regulations, and the exercise of authority and power in general. However, whereas merger is always expressed through hallucination, the annihilation of paternal obstacles to this merger can be expressed through many forms of actual aggression and of actual violence.

Many targets of aggression are defined as pseudo-species (Erikson, 1968), who are denigrated as "different", "strange", "inferior", and "dirty", and, therefore, as a source of pollution. This process of pseudo-speciation is used to justify various kinds of sadistic attacks on the members of these pseudo-species (Hopper, 2003c).

2

Those who are at the centre of the group develop and maintain an attitude of "moral superiority" towards those who are at the periphery of it (Hopper, 1981). This is maintained through the manipulation of the norms that regulate moral judgements (absolute rather than relative; and stringent rather than lenient) so as to ensure that those who are at the periphery of the group are defined as deviant, immoral and criminal. These judgements are then used to justify and to mobilize pressures to conform, to participate in various public rituals, and comply with the expectations of those in authority.

3

Processes of "anonymisation" (Main, 1975) are developed and used to regulate any member of the group who attempts to assert his personal identity. Anonymization reduces the assignment of personal responsibility for thought, feeling and deed. Action is felt to originate in a specific role and not in the mind of a unique person who interprets the role. This eliminates the possibility of giving credit to individuals for their contributions. This is sometimes known as the "tall poppy syndrome" or the "tall sunflower syndrome" in which any flower that is seen to be taller than the others must be cut down to size. Paradoxically, although anonymization is a form of aggression towards individuals, it also reduces the envy of individuality, and, hence, it helps to dilute aggressive feelings and aggression towards people who are able to retain their "names".

People also anonymize themselves in order to pre-empt envy from others (Kreeger, 1992).

4

The assassination of people and their characters ceases to be shocking. Obviously actual assassination occurs less often than character assassination, and actual assassination is unlikely to occur within the context and frame of reference of organizations and groups. However, both the central persons of the basic assumption of Incohesion and the leaders of the work group which is associated with it are especially vulnerable to character assassination.

Within most societies an assassination of a leader violates expectations about personal and public life, and it becomes extremely difficult to maintain the morale of the work group. The loss of a leader involves a loss of social glue. Anomie with respect both to social goals and the means for achieving them is likely to arise. The isolation, subgrouping and contra-grouping of Aggregation become ubiquitous. Moreover, an assassination is very difficult to mourn. Although it might seem to unite people in their public grief, an assassination is likely to delay the protective shift from Aggregation to Massification, and the development of work group functioning.

VI – Incohesion and the development of social psychic retreats

Based on positive and negative intra-psychic encapsulations, Incohesion is often associated with the development and maintenance of social psychic retreats, as seen in the formation of ghettos and enclaves (Mojovic, 2011). These social psychic retreats can be partial or total, and positive or negative. The boundaries of social psychic retreats are not fixed and stable, but vulnerable to becoming rigid and brittle, broken, ruptured, dissolved, rent, etc. Some social psychic retreats can be defined geographically, and the boundaries of them maintained and enforced legally.

VII – Role suction, valence and personification of the roles that are typical of Incohesion

1

The roles generated by Aggregation include those of the "lone wolf" and the "space cadet"; and the roles generated by massification include those of the "cheerleader" and especially the "charismatic leader".

Aggregation roles tend to be personified by crustaceans, and massification roles by amoeboids.

2

The roles generated through Incohesion are personified by people who are particularly vulnerable to the suction power of these roles, or who have a valence for the enactment of the demands of them. People with crustacean and amoeboid character structures, who are especially unable to find words for their feelings, and who tend to communicate through actions and enactments, tend to personify roles that offer them opportunities for the enactment of their various impulses, which are often based on sensations rather than feelings and thoughts. I (Hopper, 1995) have emphasized the importance of the trauma/ addiction syndrome in those who are likely to personify the roles of Incohesion. Such traumatized people are also prone to suicide following murder, and to the murder of others either intentionally or accidentally through suicide.

Charismatic narcissistic leaders are always projectively identified with their groupings. Malignantly charismatic leaders of massification processes are especially dangerous (Kernberg, 2020). Volkan (2006) has emphasized that although charismatic leaders tend to be destructive, some of them can be reparative, driven to make creative use of their own traumatic experience.

3

The dynamics of these personifications, which carry intensified and condensed messages about their contextual matrices, have often been explored in literature and drama. For example, it is well worth referring to *Julius Caesar* (Hopper, 2003b; Garland, 2010). The analysis of the political cell who rebelled against the power and authority of Caesar suggests that the dynamics of Incohesion underpin those of the more obvious patterns of Oedipal and sibling rivalry, and that particular roles tend to be generated by Incohesion. The list of characters reads like a list of these roles, which have more generally come to be known in terms of the names of the characters who took on the roles. For example, consider: Brutus, who was really an ineffectual man of compromise. The "godly" epilepsy of Caesar can hardly be overlooked. The crustacean Cassius, who had a lean and hungry look was not regarded as entirely trustworthy; and the amoeboid Casca, who is likely to have had a cognitive disability and who had difficulty making friends with the other boys at school, was extremely biddable.

It seems that Shakespeare also understood that Incohesion is likely both to generate assassination and to be generated by it. He also understood the relevance of the addiction/trauma syndrome in those who are vulnerable to the suction power of the roles generated by Incohesion.

VIII – Fundamentalism and scapegoating in the context of Incohesion

As a defence against the development and maintenance of Aggregation as a consequence of social trauma, massification is supported by fundamentalism, based on social category thinking and feeling, as a characteristic of the habitus of the social system in question. However, when fundamentalism dissipates, massification is supported by scapegoating processes involving those forms of aggression that are typical of Incohesion, such as anonymization, pseudo-speciation, and assassination.

The further discussion of fundamentalism and scapegoating as the twin pillars of massification is beyond the scope of this outline[5].

Summary

The steps from failed dependency to the development of the trauma syndrome can be summarised as follows:

1

Various events that cause the experience of inadequate containment and insufficient holding that can be characterized in terms of failed dependency;

2

The fear of annihilation characterized by intra-psychic fission and fragmentation and various psychotic anxieties associated with this, in oscillation with relational fusion and confusion with what is left of and with what can be found in the other, and various psychotic anxieties associated with this, based on seeking protection against the psychotic anxieties associated with each of the two polarized conditions;

3

The development of crustacean and amoeboid character structures, and of negative and positive encapsulations, encystment, and/or encrypment;

4

The propensity towards the enactment of aggressive feelings in aggression and violence based on traumatophilia, i.e. based on the sexualization of aggressive feelings and on the use of sexuality as a defence against depressive anxieties, as seen in the development of the trauma syndrome involving addiction, somatization, sadistic perversion, risk taking, delinquency, and criminality.

The hypotheses that comprise the theory of the basic assumption of Incohesion: Aggregation/Massification or (ba) I: A/M in groups and group-like social systems can be summarised as follows

1

Incohesion is a manifestation and an expression of the intra-psychic phenomenology of the fear of annihilation and relational forms of defensive protection against the pain of this experience. This can be seen in the primary development of the socio-cultural state of Aggregation and in the secondary development of the socio-cultural state of Massification, and then in the defensive oscillations between them. These socio-cultural states are manifest in those patterns of relations, normation, communication, and styles of thinking and feeling, as well as in patterns of aggression, that are typical of them.

2

Incohesion is associated with the development of social psychic retreats such as ghettos and enclaves which are often based on sub-groupings and contra-groupings associated with social identities. The sub-groupings and contra-groupings within a contextual society characterized by Incohesion are likely themselves to become characterized by Incohesion and the dynamics of it.

3

Incohesion is characterized by the development of roles that are typical of Aggregation and Massification.

4

Traumatized people are especially vulnerable to the suction power of these roles, and, in turn, they are likely to personify them.

The theory of Incohesion has been useful in our attempts to understand traumatogenic processes within societies, such as those in which terrorism has occurred (Hopper, 2020), and those which are characterized by various kinds of political and economic crises (Griffiths & Hopper, *in press*; Levine, 2018). It has also been useful in consultations to organizations, especially those in which traumatic experience is ubiquitous, such as hospitals and prisons, and in those in which traumatic experience is acute, such as commercial organizations threatened by bankruptcy (Hopper, 2012).

The theory of Incohesion has been helpful clinically in psychoanalysis and psychoanalytical psychotherapy as well as in group analysis, especially with difficult patients, such as drug addicts and delinquents (Hopper, 2003a, 2003b), not only in terms of countertransference, but also in the sense that they have suffered the deepest traumatic experience (Hopper, 2005a). Having a valence for the roles associated with (ba) I: A/M, suffering a vulnerability for being sucked into them, and/or feeling driven to personify them, enables such a member of a group to become the focus of the group's attention and activity. This enables a group to provide a highly traumatized patient with specific help and insight. However, this can also provoke powerful enactments of unconscious traumatic experience, which in turn provoke failed dependency and a repetition of traumatogenic processes throughout the tripartite matrix of the group. In other words, as is the case for all basic assumption processes, those of Incohesion can both facilitate and impede our clinical work, but there can be no doubt that processes of Incohesion are extremely challenging.

Comment on Hopper's "*Notes*" on the Theory and Concept of the Fourth Basic Assumption in the Unconscious Life of Groups and Group-like Social Systems: Incohesion: Aggregation/ Massification or (ba) I: A/M

Hopper has been developing his Incohesion theory for decades, broadening ideas, defining and refining concepts about traumatic experience in the unconscious life of groups, which seem to acquire more and more relevance in the contemporary world. I will now comment on his contribution to this chapter, focusing on its connection to the study of identity and politics of identity.

"*A fourth basic assumption*"

After Hopper's fourth basic assumption theory, it became impossible to deny the figurations between persons, groups and their contexts, as well as the influence of social unconscious processes on tripartite matrices. Hopper's fourth basic assumption enables investigations in large group settings and the work on traumatized organizations, contributing to clinical work with traumatized patients. It also promotes a broader understanding of sociological and political processes in society, providing insights into the current examination of the psychodynamics of crowd and mass movements.

The theory of Incohesion: Aggregation/Massification involves a paradigm shift in the study of basic assumptions proposed by Bion (1961) and contributions from the study of large groups by authors such as Turquet (1975) and Lawrence, Bain and Gould (2000). Hopper's theory of Incohesion proposes a theoretical shift from postulations based on a Kleinian/Bionian model of mind that derives from the death instinct and favours primary envy. In this drive theory, it is impossible to conceptualize an anxiety more primitive than the schizoid. Consequently, if innate malign envy reflects the action of the death instinct, one cannot postulate basic assumptions that are more primitive than Dependency. However, making use of a group analytical relational perspective, we can conceptualize a fourth basic assumption. However, in order to do so, we need to understand helplessness in terms of failed dependency, abandoning the assumption of an innate malignant envy (Hopper, 2003b). Indeed, for Hopper (2020, p. 29), "trauma is more basic than envy. I regard envy as a defence against the profound helplessness that follows trauma, rather than as an expression of the death instinct". Trauma and the fear of annihilation are thus primary and the emergence of envy, secondary and, in essence, defensive against horrible anxieties. Therefore, Hopper's fourth basic assumption should be regarded as the first of the four basic assumptions, prior even to Dependency (Hopper, 2003b, p. 183). Moreover, as Hopper observes, "Bion's theory of basic assumptions is a theory of incohesion" (Hopper, 2003b, p. 29).

Hopper's postulations build on the possibility Bion (1970) mentioned of a fourth basic assumption "as a manifestation of illusions of fusion and oneness based on an infant's need to protect against anxieties associated with birth" (Hopper, 2003b, p. 40), later studied by Turquet (1975). A fourth basic assumption points to primitive anxieties associated with a protomental level described by Bion (1961) as the most undifferentiated dimension of symbolic experience. In this sense, Hopper's basic assumption is akin to psychoanalytic research on primitive undifferentiation, preceding the paranoid-schizoid position undertaken by Bleger's (2016) glischro-caric position and by Ogden's (1989, 1994) autistic-contiguous position, both mentioned in Chapter Six and in Hopper's "*Notes*" in this chapter.

In fact, by conferring to a basic assumption theory an intersubjective and relational approach, grounded on Foulkesian group analysis, Hopper innovates, pointing to the ubiquitous role of trauma, helplessness, and experiences of failed dependency in association with the vicissitudes of the fear of annihilation manifested in the realms of tripartite matrices. This observation is meaningful for the conceptualization of a basic assumption theory, because, when it highlights introjection instead of projective processes, and the pivotal influence of the context, Hopper's theory confers a different status to the vicissitudes of the "addiction/trauma syndrome" and to the expression of aggressive feelings, aggression and violence (Hopper, 2003c, 2020). The intersubjective perspective for a basic assumption allows new frames of reference to explore current intrapersonal, interpersonal, transpersonal, and transgenerational traumatic experiences.

Bi-polar sociocultural states of Incohesion and the dialectics without synthesis in tripartite matrices

Investigating Hopper's theory of Incohesion: Aggregation/Massification is challenging not only because he has built a complex theory that crosses disciplines, but also because his theoretical innovations stir acceptance and admiration by some, and rejection, denial and indifference by others. Understanding Hopper's theoretical contributions require attention and a good dose of negative capability (Bion, 1970) to delve into the maze of new ideas and concepts, as well as on the uncertainty of incohesive paths that reveal more than a new basic assumption.

The study of the fourth basic assumption favours the examination of the Incohesion theory as a property of the tripartite matrix. Aggregation and Massification sociocultural states of Incohesion manifest in the various dimensions of tripartite matrices. In this respect, patterns of interaction (interpersonal relationships), normation (values, norms, and beliefs), communication (verbal and nonverbal), technology, styles of thinking and feeling, and styles of leadership, followership, and bystandership, along with patterns of aggression under Incohesion enable a rich, detailed, and all-encompassing analysis of the psychodynamics of groups, especially the traumatized (Hopper, 2003b, 2003c, 2019). The inadvertent researcher risks being trapped in the ubiquity of Hopper's fourth basic assumption, either as a person amidst the multiple stimuli of a crowd or as a member of a mass following a leader who introduces them to a theory that, as a new *Weltanschauung* (Freud, 1933b), would enable a deep understanding of the psychodynamics of groups and group-like social systems. This choice seduces followers of those typically modern schools of thought that, through a closed system, long for a metanarrative (Lyotard, 1984) as a safe theoretical path. However, when Hopper built his transdisciplinary theory, based on Incohesion processes and non-dialectic oscillations between Aggregation and Massification sociocultural states, he designed a fourth basic assumption and a post-modern theory about figurations (Elias, 1984) that, as lines of flight (Deleuze, & Guattari, 1987), can be explored through the cracks of personal, group, and societal "trans spaces" (Frosh, 2013b).

Using non-dialectic oscillations between the Aggregation and Massification, Hopper demonstrates what Merleau-Ponty's (1968) phenomenology conceptualizes as dialectics without synthesis. From a Hegelian perspective, Merleau-Ponty postulates the notion of "hyper-dialectical", that is, the dialectics without synthesis in which a critical attitude accentuates a move to go beyond, to transcend rigid polarities, deconstructing every positive final synthesis. For Merleau-Ponty, the relation between contradictory and inseparable thoughts reveals a tension and an ambiguity that indicate the indeterminacy of human existence: "We have left Plato's dialectical universe for the fluid universe of Heraclitus" (Merleau-Ponty, 1969, p. 145). As in Heraclitus, dialectics without synthesis

> is neither the simple sum of opposed movements nor a third movement added to them, but their *common meaning*, the two-component movements visible as one sole movement, *having become* a totality.
>
> (Merleau-Ponty, 1968, p. 91)

This is exactly what Hopper's oscillations between Aggregation and Massification sociocultural states in tripartite matrices try to unveil: phenomena revealing figurations in open systems that will never have a closed or single form or direction.

Incohesion oscillates between Aggregation and Massification sociocultural states whose traumatogenic dynamics tend to be self-perpetuating (Hopper "*Notes*" in this chapter), forging a dialectics without synthesis in open systems. Reflecting on oscillations between Aggregation and Massification, subgrouping characterizes the first phase of a shift from Aggregation to Massification, whereas contragrouping marks the shift from Massification back to Aggregation. Consequently, the creation of subgroups and contragroups or even microcultures (de Maré, Piper, & Thompson, 1991) are attempts to purify the system-as-a-whole (Hopper, 2012). Here, we must underline that the achievement of the ideal of purity connects bi-polar oscillations with the Freudian economic point of view about group formations discussed in Chapter Two. It means that, although being manifestations of Incohesion, shifts between Aggregation and Massification states are under in-group and out-group pressures that affect their dynamic equilibrium. In the same vein, aggression and aggressive feelings relate to oscillations between subgroups and contragroups and contribute to the balance and psychodynamics of the socio-cultural states of Aggregation and Massification.

Oscillations between Aggregation and Massification states bring light to the investigations of the psychodynamics of societies and their dysfunctional subgroups and contragroups, which tend to be based on several social, cultural and political constructs, such as gender, race, or ethnicity (Hopper "*Notes*" in this chapter). In this sense,

> These social categories are, so to say, "good for nothing". However, they are the basis for various forms of social identity and as such are available for subgrouping and contragrouping.
>
> (Hopper, 2019, p. 17)

A social category is a collection of people who have at least one characteristic in common, which is not unlike, with respect to race, what Rustin called an "empty category" (Rustin, 1991, p. 67). In this respect, they are a receptacle for a myriad of projective processes that can display a destructive and powerful facade, but, at the same time, facilitate the creation of social groups based on social identities. In fact, Hopper's theory suggests many questions about contemporary collective movements based on the development and maintenance of social identities (Butler, 2015; Fukuyama, 2018; Richards, 2018; Soreanu, 2018).

Personification in Incohesion processes

The fourth basic assumption theory reveals how important personification is in Incohesion processes and basic assumptions in general. Hopper identifies typical roles that function as new skins of identity for traumatized persons who have experienced the fear of annihilation and developed protective encapsulations in order to survive to anxieties associated with regression. These persons are unconsciously vulnerable, through valence and/or role suction (Redl, 1942; Kernberg, 2003), to personifications of roles associated with Aggregation and Massification. People who experience the fear of annihilation need the holding and containment that such roles provide, for they offer skins of identity that can replace those that have been threatened, fragmented, or lost.

Personifications can be pathological, especially when associated with compulsive identity substitutions in connection with social categories. Traumatized people and people with addiction/trauma syndrome take on and personify roles that offer them the opportunity to enact unprocessed, non-symbolized experiences in tripartite matrices (Hopper, 2003b, pp. 91–92). The personification of Aggregation or Massification may promote a "multi-generational cycle of perversion in which victims become perpetrators, and vice versa, and the majority collude as bystanders" (Hopper, 2003b, p. 96).

Personifications involve projective and introjective identifications in traumatized persons, but are mainly sociocultural processes that encompass the interdependencies between persons and their groupings in a specific context. The concept of personification is fundamental in Hopper's fourth basic assumption. First, because it interconnects sociology (using the concepts of figuration and identity), psychoanalysis (based on the relevance of trauma, failed dependency and the fear of annihilation, and the defences associated with them) and group analysis (through collusions, collective enactments, and social unconscious processes). Second, because, through personifications, we can observe how the tripartite matrices interweave.

Personifications are closely connected to the concepts of identity and social identity, in particular. In this respect, group analytic theory, especially through Hopper's fourth basic assumption and investigations on the social unconscious in tripartite matrices, allows for exploring the figurations co-created by personal identities, social identities, collective identities, identity politics, and national identities in the incohesive social world. Therefore, by investigating personification processes and oscillations between subgroups and contragroups, we can identify what is being enacted/acted out in contemporary social systems through identity processes.

Indeed, Hopper's use of the notion of personification reveals and exemplifies how particular figurations are involved and displayed in tripartite matrices. It means that the individual participants of a social system are unconsciously inclined to get sucked into a role or to have a valence for a particular role in Aggregation or Massification sociocultural states. They interpret the demands for a certain role in terms of their own personality and sensitivity features. This observation allows us to recognize the importance of the personal and interpersonal sub-matrix as a component of the tripartite matrix. Hopper (personal communication) prefers to use the notion of personification as an alternative or perhaps a complement to the ideas of role suction (Redl, 1942) or valence when he discusses the Incohesion theory in tripartite matrices.

Identity, social identity, and recognition in the Incohesion theory

The study of identity is important in social theory and social critical theory, especially in contemporaneity, or "late modernity" (Hall, 1992) when transformations regarding the idea of identity and the subjective experience of identity took place. Throughout history three different concepts of identity have been associated with individual subjects: the Enlightenment sovereign subject, fully centred, with a unified identity during the course of life; the sociological subject, characteristic of the first half of the twentieth century, aware of the fact that the inner core is not autonomous or self-sufficient, but formed in the relationship with "significant others"; and the post-modern subject, with a decentred, fragmented, and plural identity (Hall, 1992, p. 275).

Identity seems to be a limit-concept. It can be defined psychologically and sociologically, bridging the intrapsychic and intersubjective realms. Identity is highly influenced by interpersonal and transpersonal processes (Erikson, 1950). It contains aspects of the self related to autonomy and belongingness, and is anchored in processes of recognition and relatedness in family and society (Bohleber, 2010). Hopper (2009a) defines identity "as a systemic figuration of internal and external objects within a social-psychological space in relationship to one another and to their various environments" (Hopper, 2009a, p. 407). Therefore, constancy and adaptation are involved in forging an identity, "always a function of a person's 'location' within his primary, secondary and foundation matrices" (Hopper, 2009a, p. 407).

In contemporaneity, deconstructed and contradictory identities prevail. Identities are becoming open, more fluid, acquiring different meanings, "in some cases referring simply to social categories or roles, in others to basic information about oneself" (Fukuyama, 2018, p. 9). Identities seem to have acquired a "protean" quality, "drifting" (Bohleber, 2010, p. 50) in incohesive social systems, oscillating between individuation and merger in Aggregation and Massification sociocultural states, respectively.

Identity gained importance in connection to demands for recognition and became the basis of contemporary politics, as well as the driving force behind nationalism movements in politics (Taylor, 1994; Volkan, 2006; Fukuyama, 2018). In the same direction, struggles for recognition opened new streams of inquiry in contemporary critical social theory (Honneth, 1996). Discourses on identity have been built intersubjectively, and identity has been partly shaped by recognition or the absence of it (Taylor, 1994). In this sense, "nonrecognition or misrecognition can inflict harm, and be a form of oppression, imprisoning someone in a false, distorted, and reduced mode of being" (Taylor, 1994, p. 25). It means that recognition is vital to the development of human beings and the continuous co-creation of personal and social identity. Moreover, it means that non-recognition is traumatic and likely to generate a sense of shame that can be mainly personal or mainly social.

The connection between identity and recognition dates back to modernity, in association with the collapse of social hierarchies, which used to be the basis for the idea of honour in a world where inequalities prevailed. To replace the notion of honour, the ideal of dignity emerged, built in terms of universalist and egalitarian values. This new premise legitimized the dignity of human beings, making citizens' dignity an inherent value, equally guaranteed to people (Taylor, 1994). This right is connected to the emergence of a democratic society in association with the individualistic premises (Simmel, 1989) discussed in Chapter One. Therefore, a new understanding of the individual identity developed associated with the growth of romanticism and ideas such as moral sense, pride, "sentiment of being" (Rousseau). These processes revealed a "subjective turn in modern culture, a new form of inwardness" (Taylor, 1994, p. 29), where each person has an inner-self that demands respect and recognition (Fukuyama, 2018). These new styles of thinking and feeling supported the development of the modern ideal of authenticity related to individualistic goals of self-fulfilment and self-realization (Honneth, 1996).

Discourses on recognition can be seen in private and public realms. In the intimate sphere, identity is formed in a continuing dialogue with significant others. In the public sphere, the understanding of identity and authenticity is forged in open dialogue, valuing politics of equal recognition to people (Taylor, 1994, p. 37). In contrast, the modern notion of identity has fed a politics of difference linked to the individualism of uniqueness (Simmel, 1989), conferring value to the recognition of individual persons in terms of the uniqueness of their identity. The "right" of being unique thus ended up confused with the recognition of the human command of equality and dignity for all, connected to the individualism of singleness (Simmel, 1989). Moreover, the violation of egalitarian rights is an indelible reality in the socioeconomic and political sphere, as well as in civil society. In this regard, the guarantee of equality eventually creates a "difference blindness" (Taylor, 1994, p. 40) for persons and social identity formations, becoming "a cardinal sin against the ideal of authenticity" (Taylor, 1994, p. 38). This state of affairs becomes more complex when the "difference blindness", based on the politics of equal dignity and respect, is associated with power relations and hegemonic cultures that impose their values on minority groups and/or cultures.

To challenge the Hobbesian teleological conceptions of humankind, drawing on the struggle for individual's self-preservation, Honneth (1996) conceives a critical social theory based on Hegel's early Jena-period (1801–1806) model of "struggle for recognition" and on G. H. Mead's (1972) symbolic interactionism. In this way, Honneth (1996) brings to critical theory the historical importance of intersubjective thinking, highlighting the idea that the basis of interaction is the social conflict and that its "moral grammar is the struggle for recognition" (Honneth, 1996, p. 10).

Taking into account conflicts originated by experiences of social disrespect and interweaving philosophy, sociology, psychology, and psychoanalysis, Honneth (1996) develops a critical theory of society that identifies ethical and intersubjective conditions to restore mutual recognition and respect. Consequently, self-realization would depend on the creation of ethical relationships of reciprocal recognition. Instead of focusing on the self-realization of the isolated individual, he trusts in the development of three different spheres of recognition. In this sense, human flourishing can only be achieved through the creation of ethical relationships with others, in which love, law and rights, and solidarity can be fostered. Accordingly, the development and maintenance of self-confidence, self-respect, and self-esteem could only be acquired through mutual recognition. These accomplishments would encompass not only the development of good-enough relationships of love and self-confidence, established since early childhood (Winnicott, 1971), but also experiences in which dignity and respect for human rights, guaranteed by law and the State, when fulfilled, would bring self-respect to persons. These include situations in which bonds of solidarity and shared community values can foster the development of ethical and stable self-esteem within society (Honneth, 1996; Penna, 2020).

Social movements reached their apex in the 1960s, when demands for recognition of discriminated or marginalized social groups – feminist and civil rights movements – were connected to identity claims, giving birth to the "modern identity politics" (Fukuyama, 2018, p. 107). These claims started to be seen from a new perspective, although they had already been historically present in nationalist and religious identity movements. The identity movements of the 1960s had a choice between claiming equal recognition by the society or asserting a separate identity for its members when demanding respect exactly for being "different" from the mainstream (Fukuyama, 2018, p. 107). Therefore, multiculturalism and the growing consciousness of minorities rights helped to legitimize and intertwine personal and social identities in a particular cultural lived experience and in particular styles of being, thinking, and feeling. By that time, the work in analytic groups, especially in large groups (Kreeger, 1975; de Maré, 2012b) developed substantially, as pointed out in Chapters Seven and Eight.

Today, fifty years after May 1968, individualism seems to have reached its peak (Penna, 2020), and personal and social disillusionment within the sociopolitical sphere has increased. Fukuyama (2018) points that, twentieth-century politics have been organized "along a left-right spectrum defined by economic issues, the left advocating for more equality and the right demanding more freedom" (Fukuyama, 2018, p. 6). However, in the second decade of the twenty-first century, the focus turned again to identity issues. The left leaned over the rights of marginalized and excluded groups and the right showed an intensified concern for the protection of national identities. Since Marx, political struggles have been considered as reflections of economic conflicts; however, human beings are also motivated by psychosocial determinants, which include what Fukuyama named as the "politics of resentment" (Fukuyama, 2018, p. 7), an important force in the claims of democratic societies. The politics of resentment is connected to experiences of inequality and indignity in social life and triggers claims for personal and social identity recognition that are tantamount to the struggles for recognition explored by Honneth (1996).

"Recognition forges identity" (Taylor, 1994, p. 66) in the interpersonal and transpersonal dimensions built through the social categories available in the social world. Fukuyama (2018) states that *thymos* is the part of the soul that seeks recognition and dignity. In this direction, a demand for recognizing one's identity is a quest that unifies what is happening at the personal and social levels and in global contemporary politics. In Fukuyama's words (Fukuyama, 2018, p. xvi):

> The rise of identity politics in modern liberal democracies is one of the chief threats that they face, and unless we can work our way back to more universal understandings of human dignity, we will doom ourselves to continuing conflict.

Considering both Honneth's (1996) discussions on the struggles for recognition in history and Fukuyama's (2018) works on identity and the politics of resentment, Hopper's Incohesion theory adds new perspectives to this trans-disciplinary debate.

The phenomenology of contemporary struggles for recognition points to an increase in experiences of failed dependency in tripartite matrices and to their impact on identity politics. Therefore, they are pervaded by Incohesion: Aggregation/Massification processes. Then, we can infer from Hopper's theory that the precarious contemporary bonds and experiences of failed dependency have been pushing people – through valency and/or role suction – to personify roles associated with Aggregation and Massification sociocultural states. In response to social trauma, people would end up "privileging social identities over other ways of being in the world. Identity is being taken from a social category rather than personal identity" (Hopper, personal communication). Personifications guarantee survival, providing "new" personal identities, and forge social identities for traumatized people in Incohesion. So, personification exposes and confines people to the illusory containment and protection these personal or social identities offer.

However, what seems to be new in the discussion is not the potential for autonomy, belongingness, and recognition offered by a social identity, but the fact that fragile personal identities tend to coalesce into a social identity or various social identities that might function as "identity prostheses". It means that contemporary identities may operate as prêt-à-porter social categorizations that are "good for nothing", an "empty category" that facilitates through personification the enactment of powerful anxieties and defences. Through social identity, people would be inclined to develop patterns of interaction, normation, and communication, as well as styles of thinking and feeling and styles of leadership, followership, and bystandership to guarantee either a pseudo-individuation in Aggregation states or the tendency to a merger in Massification states.

Indeed, identity and social identities oscillate between Aggregation and Massification. In a discussion of fundamentalism, Hopper (2022) argues:

> When aggregation prevails, the boundaries of each cultural category and social formation associated with it in such a way that both the category and the formation become a collection of the properties of the individual members of it. Individual identities are privileged over social identities, which are denied and disavowed. However, when massification prevails, the opposite occurs: all social classifications and formations are collapsed into one, and social identities are privileged over individual identities.

Social identity formations might also be based on positive and negative intra-psychic encapsulations, protected by positive or negative social psychic retreats (Mojovic, 2011). A positive social psychic retreat can offer a harbour and protection to identities and social identities under personal, social, or national threat. It can develop a negative facade as well, similar to a ghetto or an enclave with the features of a massification sociocultural state.

In the Aggregation states, identity and social identities reflect the fragmentation of the social world and the atomization of life in Western societies over the last decades. Individualism (Lipovetsky 1983; Ehrenberg, 2010), narcissism (Lasch, 1979), impoverished attachment, tendency to isolation, withdrawal and detachment (Lawrence, Bain, & Gould, 2000), intellectualization, anomie, competition, and conflict are experienced by persons as a collection of Turquet's singletons (Hopper, 2019). Crustacean character structures and roles as truth-teller, anti-hero, stable-cleaner, lone wolf, and space cadet give persons personal/social identities that mirror the cold and alienated detachment characteristic of personifications in an Aggregation sociocultural state (Hopper, 2003b, p. 95).

However, in the first decades of the twenty-first century – perhaps due to the exhaustion of the individualistic perspectives, that is, "too much me-ness" (Hopper, "*Notes*" in this chapter), as well as to increased experiences of failed dependency, as feelings of the weariness of the self (Ehrenberg, 2010), abandonment, isolation, and deprivation in the social world – we can see a shift from an Aggregation to a Massification sociocultural state that provides defence and an "illusory protection" against the fission and fragmentation anxieties characteristic of the Aggregation state. Mirroring the impossibility to meet the increasing demands for socioeconomic performance in the Western "achievement society" (Han, 2015, p. 30), persons and groups fail and eventually experience a burnout condition. The "burnout society" described by Han (2015) leads persons to experience the consumption of their own souls, blurring the "Hegelian master-slave dialectics, by transforming subjects into masters and slaves of themselves" (Han, 2015, p. 60). Therefore, feeling exhausted, errant, and non-engaged, singletons are being role-sucked to personify identities or engage in social identity groups as membership individuals (Turquet, 1975). Moreover, amoeboid character structures and the roles of hero, jester, whistle-blower, magician, cheerleader, and especially different kinds of charismatic personalities and/or leadership are available to people in the Massification states (Hopper, 2003b, p. 94).

In Massification, identity and social identities run the risk of searching for uniformity of beliefs and develop fundamentalist psychodynamics characterized by "too much we-ness" (Hopper, "*Notes*" in this chapter), displaying properties specific to the sociocultural state of Massification (Hopper, 2003b, p. 71; also "*Notes*" in this chapter). Hopper's (2020, p. 32) discussion of fundamentalism and scapegoating processes emphasizes that both are the twin pillars of Massification. Fundamentalism is based on the development of a style of thinking and feeling marked by social categories, characterized by a tendency to create the binary classifications typical of the paranoid-schizoid position functioning. Facing real or imaginary threats of annihilation, people develop polarized thinking in terms of "either/or". In this sense, the tendency of making binary classifications could easily lead to the creation of social categorizations. Therefore, sociocultural classifications are the basis to form social identities (Hopper, 2022).

Social identity in Massification sociocultural states reveals a minimal degree of differentiation, adhesive identification (Bick, 1968; Meltzer, 1975), homogeneity, nomie, pseudo-morale, and styles of communication, feeling and thinking, resembling cults and contragroups (Hopper, 2003b) or negative social psychic retreats. Transformed in Turquet's membership individuals, the persons evince a tendency to merge by sharing an idealized self-object. As a "safe womb-like group" (Hopper, 2020), a social identity may provide an illusion of personal and/ or social cohesion for membership individuals, guaranteeing recognition, identity, containment, and the pseudo-safety that the Massification sociocultural state offers. Through fusion and confusion, Massification avoids a shift back to anxieties e defences connected to an Aggregation sociocultural state. Moreover, the optimal balance in Massification requires continuous aggression regulation and scapegoating processes (Hopper, 2003c, 2020).

In addition, identity and social identity are connected to ethnic movements and national identities. Research on ethnic movements shows that individual self-esteem is also measured in relation to one's national or religious identity, revealing how the political affects the personal (Fukuyama, 2018, p. 107). The research illustrates how personal and social struggles for recognition (Honneth, 1996) are linked to the resurgence of nationalism and modern identity politics. Personal, social, and national identities are intermingled in tripartite matrices, claiming for dreamt equality and recognition in the private and public spheres. Moreover, new social movements (Butler, 2015) represent the struggles of people who have been hitherto suppressed and invisible in the public sphere, but started to claim for the public recognition of their inner worth. The claims of today's social categories unveil how modern identity politics is connected to collective reactions against experiences of failed dependency and threats of annihilation in different dimensions of tripartite matrices.

Some further implications of the theory of (ba) I: A/M

As Hopper's theory demonstrates, the history of the twentieth century discloses how the Incohesion theory underpins and legitimizes the Aggregation processes associated with individualism and narcissism and the Massification processes related to fundamentalism, totalitarianism, and fascism, bringing in pervasive forms of aggression and scapegoating, as observed in totalitarian ideological groups. Philosophers, historians, sociologists, psychoanalysts, and group theoreticians have discussed these topics in depth; however, Hopper's theory, by examining the unconscious, traumatizing, and transgenerational perspectives of these processes, explores their traumatic psychoanalytical and social roots, unveiling the core of their psychodynamics in tripartite matrices. Moreover, when Hopper reveals the consequences of traumatic experiences in countries devastated by collective trauma and natural disasters, such as the syndemic of COVID-19, his work points to the role of unmourned traumas and psychic transmission in the social unconscious of various social systems. This assigns to his theory a status of basic assumption and, consequently, the ubiquity of oscillations between the Aggregation and Massification sociocultural states, which magnifies the importance of work done in the past and calls attention to transdisciplinary research on Incohesion processes in the future. Notwithstanding, the unconscious life of such traumatic experiences is frightening and discouraging, for it directs attention to repetition compulsion and new cycles of failed dependency.

Incohesion: Aggregation/Massification processes highlight the relevance of identity and social identities, especially when both are threatened by experiences of failed dependency. Personal, social, and national identities offer identification, recognition, cohesion, ideals, and illusions to persons, groups, and social systems. However, groups can develop pathological forms of cohesion, characterizing "too much me-ness" in Aggregation states or "too much we-ness" in Massification processes (Hopper, "*Notes*" in this chapter). Certainly, an optimal degree of cohesion – as in Freud's use of Schopenhauer's porcupine metaphor (Freud, 1921) – facilitates and enhances life in groups and society, enabling the creation of what Bion (1961) described as a work group. The idea of optimal cohesion in groups and in social life involves the fine equilibrium posed by the "dilemma of the individual" (Bion, 1961, 1970) regarding the person's struggle between their narcissism (egocentric) and socialism (sociocentric). This dilemma has been a challenge to modern and post-modern schools of thought in human sciences (Simmel, 1908; Freud, 1921, 1930a; Rickman, 1938, 2003; Elias, 1939, 1984, 2001; Bion, 1961, 1970; Foulkes, 1948, 1964, 1975a; Turquet, 1975; Kreeger, 1975; Pichon-Rivière, 1980; de Maré, 1972; Sennett, 1974; Chasseguet-Smirgel, 1984; de Maré, Piper, & Thompson, 1991; Dalal, 1998; Hopper, 2003b, 2012, 2019, 2020; Blackwell, 2000; Armstrong, 2005; Tubert-Oklander, 2014) in its attempt to determine an optimal figuration to the we-I balance (Elias, 2001) in individual-society relations.

The reflections in this book were guided by the examination of these theories, perhaps as an illusory effort to grasp where "the one and the many" meet in their dialectics without synthesis, or even to find the optimal cohesion in a work group. In this regard, Hopper's Incohesion theory enables the researcher to refrain from illusions and explore the psychodynamics of various social formations. Yet, we wonder if it is possible to create an optimal balance between "too much me-ness" and "too much we-ness" not only in group analytic work, especially in large groups, but also in life groups (Foulkes, 1948).

Throughout his work, Hopper (2003a) explores hope. He distinguishes several expressions of hope from mature hope, which, as he highlights, is the human ability to mourn losses adequately and, at the same time, to develop trust and optimism and, consequently, a better personal and collective life. However, mature hope is only possible when a group is characterized by what Hopper considers as "authentic cohesion" (Hopper, 2003a, p. 193), and not when it is caught in the dialectics without synthesis of Incohesion processes in response to traumatic experiences. Therefore, without getting caught up in the idealizations, illusions, and utopias encompassed in the study of groups, but insisting on the wish for an authentic cohesion and on the idea of mature hope at the same time as we face Incohesion processes, we ask: is it possible to promote "authentic cohesion" in groups? What influence do past and social unconscious processes exert on contemporary groups and social systems? And the future? We will certainly not find "the" answer, but research will continue to raise challenging questions about the twenty-first-century collective phenomena.

Notes

1 For example, see the following publications: Scapegoating within the context of Incohesion as seen in terrorism and terrorists: A brief note. IAGP Forum, online, 2020; "'Notes' on the theory of the fourth basic assumption in the unconscious life of groups and group-like social systems: Incohesion: Aggregation/Massification or (ba) I: A/M", *Group* (2019); *Trauma and Organizations* (ed.) (2012); The theory of the basic assumption of Incohesion: Aggregation/Massification or (ba) I:A/M. *British Journal of Psychotherapy* (2009b); *The Social Unconscious: Selected Papers* (2003a); *Traumatic Experience in the Unconscious Life of Groups* (2003b).

2 This was akin to what Ogden (1994) later called the anxieties of the autistic/contiguous position, which developmentally precedes those associated with the paranoid/schizoid position. In terms of the theory of the Oedipus complex, this was also akin to what has been called the fear of a "father death" by violence, as opposed to a "mother death" through relinquishing life (Hopper, 2003b).

3 The work of Tustin (1981) was of vital importance in the development of my thinking. It is relevant to recognize that the features of the internal worlds of those who have been traumatized have recently been outlined and illustrated by Bradley and Kinchington (2018), who draw extensively on the work of Winnicott about unintegration/disintegration, and of Bowlby about various kinds of disordered and disrupted attachments. See also the work of Meloy and Yakeley (2014).

4 It is worth noting that Freud's theory of the *death instinct* as the main source of aggression was taken further by Klein's hypothesis that the death instinct is the source of envy, which, because it is so threatening, requires deflection outward, which, in turn, makes the individual fearful of attacks by others. Although it is generally accepted that, unconsciously, hate is as basic to our make-up as love, Kohut (1971) linked the origins of hatred to the universal *narcissistic wound*. However, Fairbairn (1952) held that, in the context of relationships, frustration fosters hatred.

5 For this project, see Hopper (2022).

Epilogue

The dichotomies that have shaped modern thinking over the last centuries transformed the idea of the individual into the keystone of Western societies. Not only classic – such as Simmel (1908), Dumont (1981), and Elias (1939, 1984, 2001) – but also contemporary authors – Sennett (1974) and Lasch (1979), for instance – have pointed to the difficulties the individualistic paradigm brought to the study of life in society. Simmel's and Elias's process sociology sought to escape the polarities that oppose individual and society by developing more interdependent ways of thinking about these relations. However, despite their attempts and the studies on the "weariness" of the individualistic paradigm today (Lipovetsky, 1983; Ehrenberg, 2010; Han, 2015), the idea of the individual remains deeply rooted in Western thought, especially in the current neoliberal outlooks.

In psychoanalysis, from Freud's inaugural words in *Group Psychology and The Analysis of the Ego* (Freud, 1921, p. 69) to contemporary intersubjective developments, it is still difficult to take into account what in group analysis Foulkes (1948) considered to be the social nature of persons, and what Hopper (1982) called the "sociality of human nature". That is, the shift of focus from "*the* individual (e.g., Klein, Freud), or *the* individual-in-relation with another individual (e.g., Winnicott, Fairbairn), or with individual*s* in relation (e.g., Foulkes, Mitchell)" to a new paradigm that considers "individuals-in-*social*-relation (e.g., Elias)" (Dalal, 2011, p. 252) remains a challenging undertaking.

Semprún (2002, p. 20) wrote that "since Aristotle, the problem of the *demos* (people) and of the *pletos* (the superabundance, the multitude, the plethora) has been fundamental to political science"; however, after the French Revolution mobs, the *question du nombre* started to be taken into consideration, favouring the transformation of "numbers" – that is, persons – into political subjects. Moreover, the French Revolution and its enshrining of the Rights of Man, as well as the importance Western societies conferred on Hegelian ideas of universal recognition, slowly contributed to the shift of focus in the analysis of collective phenomena in the nineteenth century (Semprún, 2002). Thus, the nineteenth-century turbulent crowds and the twentieth-century totalitarian masses and their leaders called in question the investigation of the topic, revealing an enigma about their psychology that is yet to be deciphered. In this

DOI: 10.4324/9780429399534-12

sense, we ask: what is the psychodynamics of crowds and masses? How did Tarde and Le Bon's conservative views on nineteenth-century crowd psychology become the twentieth-century Freudian mass psychology studied by left-wing theorists?

Initially, social-historical explanations seemed to answer these questions, albeit partially. Likewise, the concept of *Zeitgeist* allowed researchers to reflect on different perspectives on crowds and masses, pointing in their investigations to "texts inserted in contexts" (Mucchielli, 1998). So, the "spirit of the times" – that is, the *genius seculi* (Herder, 1769 *apud* Hegel, 1830) – seemed to be of paramount importance to understand the psychodynamics of social formations, especially collective phenomena, at different times.

The Frankfurtians and other twentieth-century intellectuals have conducted studies that developed an interdisciplinary understanding of the early crowd psychologists' main concerns and also favoured the analysis of how human beings, converted into masses, are led to commit atrocities on behalf of a leader or ideology. However, their investigations could never provide "answers" to some of the impossible questions posed to humankind in the twentieth century (Adorno, 1947; Arendt, 1948).

In this respect, the postulation of the concept of social unconscious (Hopper, 2003a; 2018b; Hopper & Weinberg, 2011, 2016, 2017) allows for recontextualizing the research by identifying, in tripartite matrices in time and space, the unconscious restraints and constraints and the transgenerational psychic transmissions co-created in these processes. Not only fears, defences, myths, and fantasies, but also *habitus* and collective memories in different foundation matrices seem to have shaped distinct views about crowds and masses since the nineteenth century. In addition, ideology, power relations, and the discourses typical of each historical period contributed to several outlooks and analyses of these phenomena.

The political-intellectual movement that took over the investigations into mass psychology after World War II did not fade. The work with analytical groups grew stronger, reaching a breakthrough in the 1960s, a decade that witnessed the emergence of important sociocultural transformations in liberal democracies to guarantee the civil rights of oppressed minorities and triggered the sexual revolution and the feminist movement. These social achievements highlighted the idea of identity and social identities, promising equality, self-esteem, recognition, and dignity to individuals (Taylor, 1994; Fukuyama, 2018), together with freedom and a project for individual self-realization (Honneth, 1996).

This new panorama made transformations easier in psychoanalytic and group analytic theory, enabling the investigations of group theory to shift their analysis from Oedipal to pre-Oedipal configurations and to enhance the importance of regression and illusion in groups. However, even exploring the role of primitive defences, the analysis of group formations still revolved around the importance of cohesion, which had been vital for the study of social formations during the first half of the twentieth century. Moreover, it was also from the

1960s onwards that the work with large groups gained weight in both group relations conferences and group analytic settings. The sociopolitical and cultural transformations that took place in the period provided a context where group initiatives flourished, fostering more horizontal and democratic relationships in the social sphere.

Indeed, for group analytic professionals, the work with groups, especially with large groups, was more than a legacy from wartime. It became a conscious and socially unconscious project able to function as "an antidote against social massification" (de Maré, Piper, & Thompson, 1991, p. 18). An inquiring spirit, the exploration of new basic assumptions, the working through of collective traumas, the prevention of warlike scenarios, and the desire to improve communication and dialogue within groups seem to have motivated these professionals. Therefore, by fostering thinking and dialogue in large group settings, they could transform the powerful unconscious collective processes that had previously been displayed as thoughtless behaviour in nineteenth-century crowds or blind followership into twentieth-century totalitarian masses. De Maré expresses these wishes clearly:

> Dialogue has an enormous thought potential: it is from dialogue that ideas spring to transform the mindlessness and massification that accompany social oppression, replacing it with higher levels of cultural sensitivity, intelligence, and humanity.
>
> (de Maré, Piper, & Thompson, 1991, p. 17)

In this direction, and capturing the same transformative spirit – and interestingly initiating his postulations in 1989, the same year of the fall of the Berlin Wall – Hopper (2003b) proposed a fourth basic assumption, bringing forth an important group analytic contribution to the post-modern study of the twenty-first-century analytic group psychodynamics.

The fall of the Berlin Wall marked the end of the Cold War. In 2002, Semprún (2002) stated that, just as the 1920s and 1930s, the early years of the twenty-first century can be considered "a post-war period, with all the consequences that imply for the countries of the old Soviet empire" (Semprún, 2002, p. 20). We could then argue that the beginning of the twenty-first century was not just a time when European borders gained new contours and the collective working-through of the traumatic experiences lived in the twentieth-century world wars and totalitarian regimes found a new push; it was also a moment of *interregnum*, as defined by Bauman (2012, p. vii):

> … when the old ways of doing things no longer work, the old learned or inherited modes of life are no longer suitable for the current *conditio humana*, but when the new ways of tackling the challenges and new modes of life better suited to the new conditions have not as yet been invented, put in place and set in operation.

These changes pointed to the emergence of new psychosocial problems, liquid modernity (Bauman, 2012), and new frames for investigating Western social formations.

Semprún's analysis in association with Bauman's considerations on the idea of *interregnum* allows us to infer that today we are no longer involved in the threats of nineteenth-century crowd psychology or exclusively immersed in the classical model of twentieth-century mass psychology. We are dealing with new interdependencies in the sociocultural and political spheres, in which twentieth-century traumatic legacies and their psychosocial consequences for the social systems play an important role. Unmourned losses – intergenerationally and transgenerationally transmitted – have been conducting to the repetition compulsion of conscious and unconscious traumatic experiences, fostering Incohesion processes, new cycles of failed dependency and the phenomenology of fear of annihilation and defences against it (Hopper, 2019). In that respect, enactments of non-symbolized traumatic experiences are leading persons, groups, and social systems in the early twenty-first century to reproduce regression, pain, and violence at smaller or larger scales.

Today, society expects professionals, especially in the human sciences, to take a stand on issues concerning relationships between individuals, groups, and society and on topics related to violence, terrorism, racism, collective traumas, and the politics of identity and exclusion. Group analysis seems to be engaged in this endeavour when it proposes transdisciplinary approaches to tackle the challenges posed by contemporary "individuals-in-*social*-relation" (Dalal, 2011, p. 252). The post-Cold War period and the *interregnum* discussed by Semprún (2002) and Bauman (2012), respectively, are giving space to new contours in the psychosocial sphere of Western societies.

Foucault's (1972, 1979) concepts of "biopower" and "biopolitics" allowed for understanding modern "disciplinary society". In contemporaneity, Agamben (2005) and Mbembe (2003) say that Foucault's analysis needs to move further, because we are witnessing the creation of Schmitt's "states of exception", as well as "zones of anomie" and "zones of exclusion" (Agamben, 2005) beyond human rights, in which the right to expose other people to social or civil death prevail over the right to live (Mbembe, 2003, p. 39). Contemporary forms of subjugating life are no longer related only to Foucauldian "biopower", they are related to "necropower" (Mbembe, 2003, p. 40) and forms of social coexistence in which human life is not important anymore. What Mbembe's (2003) analysis shows is directly connected to the essence of Hopper's Incohesion theory, which includes references to his previous work on anomie and anomogenic processes (Hopper, 1981), as discussed in Chapter Ten.

Recently in the political scene, things changed dramatically and polarization between the Right and the Left divided people, promoting intolerance and politics of exclusion against socially identified minorities. Fundamentalist thinking (Hopper, 2020, 2022) and populist nationalism (Fukuyama, 2018) are also triggering massification processes and radicalism in association to national identities. Moreover, the neoliberalism of recent decades, together with the "market model of consumer sovereignty" (Armstrong and Rustin, 2012, p. 17) and the "casino culture" in politics (Yates, 2015), contributed to reducing democratic leadership in organizations and especially in the political sphere. Therefore, after the spreading of World War II anxiety – for fear of the return of authoritarianism – and the strong mobilization of people for democratic causes, in the current political arena, fundamentalist thinking and "states of exception" (Agamben, 2005) are again challenging the *locus* of human beings.

In addition, the emergence of the Covid-19 syndemic Horthon in 2020 reveals disconcerting perspectives that point not only to the "end" of the *interregnum* period, but also to profound transformations in the life of humankind (Horthon, 2020). It seems too early to predict the traumatic impact of the Covid-19 syndemic – a "crowd disease" – on populations. What can we expect? This crisis foreshadows unknown sociocultural, political, economic, ecological, medical, ethical, and psychological figurations for the twenty-first century. We hope that the historical and theoretical discussions outlined in this book can contribute to exploring the new challenges life will pose after the syndemic of Covid-19.

Throughout its ten chapters, this book combined an inquiry into the enigma of crowds and mass psychology with the history of group analytic and group relations' advances in the study of group formations. From the knowledge gained in this research and revisiting some of the questions raised in the Introduction, we ask: after almost two centuries of investigations into collective processes, were we able to advance in the research on social formations? What happened to the threatening power of crowds? What is the impact of "democratic recession" (Armstrong & Rustin, 2012), the resurgence of right-wing politics, and the populist surge (Fukuyama, 2018) on the unconscious life of groups? What is the relationship between the new sociopolitical and economic reality and the increase of Incohesion processes in association to identity politics? Can the theories discussed in this book clarify the psychodynamics of some of these contemporary collective processes?

The study of social formations and large-group psychodynamics in group relations and group analysis have brought about new theoretical, technical, and clinical viewpoints for understanding the psychodynamics of a large number of persons. Group analytic theory – by interweaving explorations into the social unconscious of tripartite matrices, Incohesion theory, and the work with large groups – revealed what has been denied, encapsulated, silenced in the unconscious life of persons, groups, and social systems. These theories allowed professionals to intervene in, contain, and interrupt repetition compulsion by promoting the working through of traumatic experiences in groups. Moreover, through the Incohesion theory, in association with studies on social identity and politics of recognition, we discussed the psychosocial consequences of the failure of modern promises on acknowledging people's equality, that is, their "sameness to other people" (Fukuyama, 2018, p. 104).

Furthermore, we realize that the early twenty-first-century figurations – even after the communication and technology revolution of the last decades – was not followed by other "civilizing process" achievements (Elias, 1939; Mennell, 1997). The disillusionment regarding civilization's accomplishments – nurtured by Freud (1915b, 1921, 1927, 1930a) and late nineteenth and early twentieth-century intellectuals – seems to be again a source of surprise and concern among scholars of the early twenty-first century (Han, 2015; Reckwitz, 2021). Today, difficult forms of psychosocial coexistence prevail, as well as inadequate leadership (Kernberg, 2020) and the idealization of Anderson's (1983) imagined communities/nationalisms. In this sense, we remain trapped in the illusory nature of group formations and the demands of the individualistic paradigm.

Differently from nineteenth-century "frightening" crowds, we observed – from the joyful crowd celebrations after the fall of the Berlin Wall in 1989 to the Tahrir Square demonstrations in Egypt in 2011 – a foreshadowing of new figurations for collective phenomena. Unfortunately, some of these movements evolved in unexpected directions, as witnessed in the Arab Spring. Today, social movements (Tilly, Castañeda, & Wood, 2020), social identity revindications, and worldwide climate demonstrations call attention to the renewed power of crowds and to people's engagement in public assemblies and alliances in the streets (Butler, 2015). They reveal new possibilities of social participation that may be slowly "re-populating agoras" (Scanlon, 2018), re-occupying the public sphere. These "new crowds" emerged from social movements, and social identity groups' struggle for recognition have been fostering popular sovereignty, *zoon politikon*, and "action" (Arendt, 1958) through collective engagement. They also have allowed for the co-creation of new figurations for persons, groups, and societies in the twenty-first-century tripartite matrices.

Still, at the core of "new crowds" demonstrations, in social movements and in social identity claims, we can identify not only the role of illusions highlighted by Lebonian "group mind" and by Freudian mass psychology, but also the vicissitudes of Incohesion processes and social unconscious psychodynamics as we discussed in this book. Nevertheless, the new possibilities brought about by collective movements also open an invaluable space for sharing the ideals and hopes that populate and renovate conscious and unconscious yearnings for a better life in society.

These fraternal collective longings have built history in large-group work in group analysis. Now, the study of the unconscious life of groups and the large-group psychodynamics seems crucial to face contemporary challenges, because large groups do provide unique spaces for working through traumatic experiences, and to foster dialogue in the public sphere. Yet, given the contemporary socioeconomic and psychosocial hardships, for some, the idea of working with group analytic large groups leads to ambivalence and disbelief at the possibility of using the large group as a tool to humanize society and transform relationships among a large number of persons. Indeed, the idea of learning from experience in large groups or developing a koinoniac spirit seems to be just a little sparkle of "togetherness" amidst the uncertain fellowship witnessed in the increasing Incohesion processes of the twenty-first century.

At this point, considering the current panorama and the transformations triggered by the Covid-19 syndemic, we wonder if the fellowship envisaged by large-group work will find the strength to "face" the struggles posed by a new post-syndemic world. What will be the future of crowds and masses psychodynamics in the twenty-first century? This uncertainty finds a harbour when it meets the different definitions of the word "epilogue".[1] That said, this epilogue allows us to navigate new and still unknown paths for future reflections on the psychodynamics of crowds.

Žižek (2020, p. 7) brings to our reflections on the Covid-19 syndemic the old Mao Zedong's motto of "Trust the people!". Foulkes's motto of "Trust the group!" immediately comes to the fore as "an act of faith" (Nitsun, 1996, p. 22) in the encounters provided by group work. In both "mottoes", the word "trust" reminds us that today, despite all complexities in tripartite matrices psychodynamics, we need to develop "an extra trust, an extra sense of solidarity, an extra sense of goodwill" (Žižek, 2020, p. 10) to foster global cooperation based on values as trust and hope.

Therefore, it seems necessary to find in a recondite, and sometimes almost forgotten area of the soul, a space to develop enduring creativity, transcendent imagination and mature hope (Hopper, 2003a). To find this inner space, we sought inspiration in Pier Paolo Pasolini's "visit" to the twenty-sixth canto of Dante's *Inferno*, where the poet noticed the "tiny light" from fireflies:

> The poet is observing the eighth bolgia of hell, a political bolgia if ever there was one, since we can recognize a few eminent citizens of Florence gathered there … all under the same condemnation as evil counselors.
>
> (Didi-Huberman, 2018, p. 1)

In an outspoken article, "The Vacuum of Power", also known as "L'articolo delle Lucciole" ("The article of fireflies"), initially published in the *Corriere della Sera* in 1975, Pasolini analyses the decline of old fascism and the rise of a "permissive" neofascism in Italy in the 1960s and 1970s. To develop his critique, Pasolini used as a metaphor the sudden disappearance of fireflies from the fields of Italy due to air pollution.

Years later, based on Pasolini's metaphor, the historian Didi-Huberman wrote *Survival of the Fireflies* (2018) to discuss, building on authors such as Walter Benjamin, Giorgio Agamben and Amy Warburg, the importance of the survival of experience as a form of political resistance in dark times in a broad sense. Didi-Huberman inquires:

> But first, have the fireflies truly disappeared? Have they *all* disappeared? Do they still emit − but from where? − their wondrous intermittent signals? Do they still seek each other out somewhere, speak to each other, love each other in spite of all, *in spite of all* the machine − in spite of the murky night, in spite of the fierce spotlights?
>
> (Didi-Huberman, 2018, p. 21)

We might imagine that, because of their fragility, their passing pulsating light, the fireflies would be certainly condemned to disappear. However, as Didi-Huberman highlights, the live firefly dance can take place only in the middle of the darkness, where it creates a dance of desire that forms a community, a community of survival, a community of resistance. Therefore, from a more positive perspective, Didi-Huberman states that "the ability to recognize a resistance in the smallest firefly [becomes] a light for all thought" (Didi-Huberman, 2018, p. 33).

Throughout Didi-Huberman's book, it is clear how the metaphor of the "surviving fireflies" describes precisely the relevance and meaning of the group analytic endeavour from the heroic times at the Northfield Hospital to the contemporary large group experiences. As different species of fireflies, group relations and group analytic professionals' attitudes and experiences, especially through large-group work, represent sparkling lights of understanding and thinking to face the darkness before contemporary personal and social suffering. Almost as if day-dreaming (Bion, 1962), we wonder if, like "tiny human-fire-flies", we could develop a bioluminescent skill to illuminate the paths of persons, crowds and masses in the darkness of the twenty-first-century struggles.

Note

1 Used as a piece of writing at the end of a work of literature, an epilogue enables the writer to: (1) satisfy the readers' curiosity by telling them about the fate of characters after the climax; (2) cover the loose ends of the story; (3) suggest a sequel or next instalment of the story (https://en.wikipedia.org/wiki/Epilogue).

References

Abraham, K. (1907). On the significance of sexual trauma in childhood. In: C, Hilda, & M. Abraham, (Eds.). *Clinical Papers and Essays on Psycho-Analysis*. London: The Hogarth Press, 1955.

Abraham, N., & Torok, M. (1995). *The Shell and the Kernel*, Volume I. Chicago: University of Chicago Press.

Adorno, T. (1946). Anti-semitism and fascist propaganda. In: E. Simmel (Ed.). *Anti-Semitism: A Social Disease* (pp.125–138). New York: International Universities Press.

Adorno, T. (1947). Education after Auschwitz. Retrieved from https://josswinn.org/wp-content/uploads/2014/12/AdornoEducation.pdf.

Adorno, T. (1951). The Freudian theory and the pattern of fascist propaganda. In: A. Arato & E. Gebhardt (Eds.). *The Essential Frankfurt School Reader* (pp. 118–137). New York: Continuum, 2005.

Adorno, T., Frenkel-Brunswik, E., Levinson, D., & Sanford, R. (1950). *The Authoritarian Personality*. New York: John Wiley, 1964.

Agamben, G. (2005). *State of Exception*. Chicago: University of Chicago Press.

Agazarian, Y. (1997). *Systems-centred therapy for groups*. London: Karnac.

Agazarian, Y. & Carter, F. (1993). Discussions on the large group. *Group* 17 (4): 210–234.

Agazarian, Y. & Gantt, F. (2000). *Autobiography of a Theory: Developing a Theory of Living Human Systems and its Systems-Centred Practice*. London: Jessica Kingsley.

Ahlin, G. (1996). *Exploring Psychotherapy Group Cultures: Essays on Group Theory and the Development of Matrix Representation Grid*. Stockholm: Karolinska Institutet.

Ahlin, G. (2010). Notations about the possibilities in large groups. *Group Analysis*, 43 (3): 253–267.

Akhtar, S. (2014). *Sources of Suffering*. London: Karnac.

Althusser, L. (1969). *For Marx*. London: New Left.

Althusser, L. (1971). *Ideology and Ideological State Apparatuses*. London: New Left.

Anderson, B. (1983). *Imagined Communities: Reflections on the Origin and Spread of Nationalism*. London: Verso.

Altman, N. (2010). *The Analyst in the Inner City: Race, Class, and Culture Through Psychoanalytic Lens*. New York: Routledge.

Anzieu, D. (1971). L'illusion groupale. *Nouvelle Revue de Psychanalyse*, 4: 73–93.

Anzieu, D. (1984). *The Group and the Unconscious*. London: Routledge & Kegan Paul.

Anzieu, D. (1989). *The Skin Ego*. London: Karnac.

Arendt, H. (1948). *The Origins of Totalitarianism*. New York: Harcourt, Brace, Jovanovich, 1973.

Arendt, H. (1958). *The Human Condition*. Chicago: University of Chicago Press, 1998.

Ariès, P. & Duby, G. (1992). *History of Private Life*. Cambridge: Harvard University Press.

Armstrong, D. (2005). *Organization in the Mind: Psychoanalysis, Group Relations, and Organizational Consultancy*. London: Karnac.

Armstrong, D. & Rustin, M. (2012). What happened to democratic leadership? *Soundings*, 50:59–71.

Baranger, M. & Baranger, W. (2008). The analytic situation as a dynamic field. *International Journal of Psychoanalysis* 89: 795–826.

Baranger, M. & Baranger, W. (2009). *The Work of Confluence. Listening and Interpreting in the Psychoanalytic Field*. London: Karnac.

Barthes, R. (1984). *Mythologies*. London: Paladin.

Bauman, Z. (2012). Foreword to the 2012 Edition: Liquid Modernity Revisited. In: Z. Bauman. *Liquid Modernity*. Cambridge: Polity.

Behr, H. (2018). Captain Alfred Dreyfus: a case study in the group dynamics of scapegoating. *Group Analysis*, 51 (4): 515–530.

Behr, H. & Hearst, L. (2005). *Group Analytic Psychotherapy: A Meeting of Minds*. London: Whurr.

Bettelheim, B. (1956). *Freud's Vienna & Other Essays*. London: Vintage, 1991.

Bick, E. (1968). The experience of skin in early object relations. *International Journal of Psychoanalysis*, 49: 484–486.

Billow, R. (2003). *Relational Group Psychotherapy: From Basic Assumptions to Passion*. London: Jessica Kingsley.

Bion, W. (1948). Psychiatry in a time of crisis. *British Journal of Medical Psychology*, 21 (2): 81–89.

Bion, W. (1961). *Experiences in Groups*. London: Routledge, 1991.

Bion, W. (1962). *Learning from experience*. London: Karnac.

Bion, W. (1965). *Transformations*. London: Heinemann.

Bion, W. (1967). *Second Thoughts: Selected Papers on Psycho-Analysis*. London: Routledge.

Bion, W. (1970). *Attention and Interpretation*. London: Tavistock.

Bion, W. (1977). *Two Papers: The Grid and Caesura*. London: Karnac.

Biran, H. (2015). *The Courage of Simplicity: Essential Ideas in the Work of W. R. Bion*. London: Karnac.

Birman, J. (2013). Os paradigmas em psicanálise são comparáveis? Sobre o mal-estar, a biopolítica e os jogos de verdade. [Are psychoanalytic paradigms comparable? On malaise, biopolitics and truth games]. *Tempo Psicanalítico*, Rio de Janeiro, 45(1): 147–178.

Blackwell, D. (2012). Epilogue. In: R. Lenn & K. Stefano (Eds.). *Small, Large, and Median Groups* (pp. 161–169). London: Karnac.

Blackwell, D. (2000). And Everyone Shall Have a Voice: The Political Vision of Pat de Maré. *Group Analysis*, 33 (1): 151–162.

Bléandonu, G. (1994). *Wilfred Bion: His Life and Works, 1897–1979*. London: Free Association.

Bleger, J. (2016). *Symbiosis and Ambiguity*. J. Churcher & L. Bleger (Eds). London: Routledge.

Bohleber, W. (1995). The presence of the past: xenophobia and rightwing extremism in the Federal Republic of Germany: psychoanalytic reflections. *American Imago*, 52: 329–344.

Bohleber, W. (2010). *Destructiveness, Intersubjectivity, and Trauma: The Identity Crisis of Modern Psychoanalysis*. London: Karnac.

Bourdieu, P. (1986). *Distinction: A Social Critique of the Judgement of Taste*. London: Routledge.

Bradley, C. & Kinchington, F. (2018). *Revealing the Inner World of Traumatised Children and Young People*. London: Jessica Kingsley.

Bridger, H. (1990). The discovery of the therapeutic community: The Northfield Experiments. In: E. Trist & H. Murray (Eds.). *The Social Engagement of Social Science: A Tavistock Anthology*, Vol. 1 (pp. 68–87). London: Free Association.

Brown, D. (1985). Bion and Foulkes: Basic assumptions and beyond. In: M. Pines (Ed.). *Bion and Group Psychotherapy* (pp. 192–219). London: Jessica Kingsley.

Brown, D. (1987). Context, content and process: inter-relationships between small and large groups in a transcultural workshop. *Group Analysis*, 20: 237–248.

Brown, D. & Zinkin, L. (2000). *The Psyche and the Social World*. London: Jessica Kingsley.

Butler, J. (2015). *Notes Toward a Performative Theory of Assembly*. Cambridge: Harvard University Press.

Canetti, E. (1960). *Crowds and Power*. New York: Farrar, Straus and Giroux.

Carlyle, T. (1980). *Thomas Carlyle: Selected Writings*. London: Penguin.

Carone, I. (2012). A personalidade autoritária: estudos frankfurtianos sobre o fascismo [The authoritarian personality: Frankfurtian studies on fascism]. *Sociologia em Rede*, 2 (2): 14–21.

Castoriadis, C. (1975). *The Imaginary Institution of Society*. Cambridge: Polity.

Chasseguet-Smirgel, J. (1984). *The Ego Ideal: A Psychoanalytic Essay on the Malady of the Ideal*. New York: W.W. Norton.

Clark, T. (2010). *Gabriel Tarde: On Communication and Social Influence: Selected Papers*. Chicago: University of Chicago Press.

Consolim, M. (2008a). Gabriel Tarde e as ciências sociais francesas [Gabriel Tarde and the French Social Sciences]. *Revista Mana*, 14 (2): 15–28.

Consolim, M. (2008b). Posfácio [Afterword]. In: G. Le Bon. *Psicologia das Multidões* [Crowd Psychology] (pp. 193–217). São Paulo: Martins Fontes.

Costa, J. F. (1989). *Psicanálise e Contexto Cultural [Psychoanalysis and Cultural Context]*. Rio de Janeiro: Campus.

Dalal, F. (1998). *Taking the Group Seriously: Towards a Post-Foulkesian Group Analytic Theory*. London: Jessica Kingsley.

Dalal, F. (2011). The social unconscious and ideology: in clinical theory and practice. In: E. Hopper & H. Weinberg (Eds.). *The Social Unconscious in Persons, Groups, and Societies. Vol. 1. Mainly Theory* (pp. 243–263). London: Karnac.

Davis H. (1977). Three Years of Large Group Therapy. *Group Analysis*, 10 (2): 122–126.

de Maré (1983). Michael Foulkes and the Northfield Experiment. In: M. Pines (Ed.). *The Evolution of Group Analysis* (pp. 218–230). London: Jessica Kingsley.

de Maré (1985). Major Bion. In: M. Pines (Ed.). *Bion and Group Psychotherapy* (pp. 108–113). London: Jessica Kingsley, 2000.

de Maré, P. (1972). *Perspectives in Group Psychotherapy*. London: Allen & Unwin.

de Maré, P. (1975). The politics of the large groups. In: L. Kreeger (Ed.). *The Large Group: Dynamics and Therapy* (pp. 145–158). London: Karnac.

de Maré, P. (2012a). Large group psychotherapy: a suggested technique. In: R. Lenn & K. Stefano (Eds.). *Small, Large, and Median Groups* (pp. 55–59). London: Karnac.

de Maré, P. (2012b). Large group perspectives. In: R. Lenn & K. Stefano (Eds.). *Small, Large, and Median Groups* (pp. 79–98). London: Karnac.

de Maré, P., Piper, R. & Thompson, S. (1991). *Koinonia: From Hate Through Dialogue to Culture in the Large Group*. London: Karnac.

de Tocqueville, A. (1835). *Democracy in America*. New York: Harper Collins, 2006.

Deleuze, G. & Guattari, F. (1987). *A Thousand Plateaus: Capitalism and Schizophrenia*. Minneapolis: University of Minnesota Press.

Deleuze, G. (1993). *The Fold*. London: Continuum.

Didi-Huberman, G. (2018). *Survival of the Fireflies*. Minneapolis: University of Minnesota Press.

Dumont, L. (1981). *Homo Hierarchicus: The Caste System and its Implications*. Chicago: University of Chicago Press.

Dumont, L. (1986). *Essays on Individualism: Modern Ideology in Anthropological Perspective*. Chicago: University of Chicago Press.

Dunning, C. & Mennell, S. (1996). Preface. In: N. Elias. *The Germans*. Cambridge: Polity.

Durkheim, E. (1893). *The Division of Labor in Society*. New York: Free Press, 1997.

Durkheim, E. (1895). *The Rules of Sociological Method*. New York: Free Press, 1982.

Durkheim, E. (1912). *The Elementary Forms of the Religious Life*. London: Allen & Unwin, 1915.

Ehrenberg, A. (2010). *The Weariness of the Self: Diagnosing the History of Depression in the Contemporary Age*. Montreal: McGill-Queen's University Press.

Eizirik, C. (2001). Freud's group psychology, psychoanalysis, and culture. In: E. Spector-Person (Ed.). *On Freud's "Group Psychology and the Analysis of the Ego"* (pp. 155–173). London: Analytic Press.

Elias, N. (1939). *The Civilizing Process*. New York: Blackwell, 2000.

Elias, N. (1983). *The Court Society*. Dublin: University College Dublin Press.

Elias, N. (1984). *What is Sociology?* New York: Columbia University Press.

Elias, N. (1989). *The Germans*. Cambridge: Polity.

Elias, N. (1991). *The Symbol Theory*. London: Sage.

Elias, N. (1993). *Mozart: Portrait of a Genius*. Berkeley: California University Press.

Elias, N. (2001). *The Society of Individuals*. London: Continuum.

Ellenberger, H. F. (1970). *The Discovery of the Unconscious: The History and the Evolution of Dynamic Psychiatry*. New York: Basic Books.

Engels, F. (1908). Socialism: utopian and scientific. In: K. Marx & F. Engels. *Selected Works*, Vol. 3 (pp. 95–151). London: Progress, 1970.

Enriquez, E. (1990). *Da Horda ao Estado: Psicanálise do Vínculo Social* [From the Horde to the State: The Psychoanalysis of the Social Bond]. Rio de Janeiro: Zahar.

Erikson, E. (1950). *Identity and the Life Circle*. New York: W.W. Norton.

Erikson, E. (1968). *Identity, Youth and Crisis*. New York: W.W. Norton.

Faimberg, H. (2005). *The Telescoping of Generations: Listening to the Narcissistic Links Between Generations*. London: Routledge.

Fairbairn, R. (1952). *Psychoanalytic Studies of the Personality*. London: Tavistock.

Federn, P. (1919). De la psychologie de la révolution: la société sans père. *Revue de Psychanalyse*, 5: 153–173, 2000.

Fenichel, O. (1934). Psychoanalysis as the nucleus of a future dialectical-materialistic psychology. *American Imago*, 24 (4): 290–311, 1967.

Ferenczi, S., Abraham, K., Simmel, E., Jones, E. & Freud, S. (1921). *Psychoanalysis and War Neuroses*. London: International Psychoanalytic Press.

Fernández, A. M. (2006). *O Campo Grupal: Notas para uma Genealogia* [The Group Field: Notes for a Genealogy]. São Paulo: Martins Fontes.

Ferron, E. (1991). The Black and White Group. *Group Analysis*, 24: 201–210.

Figueira, S. A. (1981). *O Contexto Social da Psicanálise* [The Social Context of Psycho-analysis]. Rio de Janeiro: Francisco Alves.

Figueiredo, L. C. (1999). Acerca do que Freud infelizmente considerou alheio ao seu interesse naquele momento [About what Freud unfortunately considered foreign to his interest at that time]. *Psicanálise e Universidade* 9–10: 35–47.

Foucault, M. (1972). *The Archaeology of Knowledge*. New York: Vintage.

Foucault, M. (1979). *Microfísica do Poder* [Microphysics of Power]. Rio de Janeiro: Paz e Terra.

Foulkes, E. (Ed.). (1990). *S. H. Foulkes: Selected Papers: Psychoanalysis and Group Analysis*. London: Karnac.

Foulkes, S. H. (1937). On Introjection. In: E. Foulkes (Ed.). *S. H. Foulkes: Selected papers* (pp. 57–78). London: Karnac, 1990.

Foulkes, S. H. (1946). On Group Analysis. *International Journal of Psychoanalysis*, 27: 46–51.

Foulkes, S. H. (1948). *Introduction to Group-Analytic Psychotherapy*. London: Karnac, 1983.

Foulkes, S. H. (1950). Group therapy: survey, orientation, and classification. In: S. H. Foulkes. *Therapeutic Group Analysis* (pp. 47–54). London: Karnac, 1964.

Foulkes, S. H. (1964). *Therapeutic Group Analysis*. London: Karnac.

Foulkes, S. H. (1975a). *Group Analytic Psychotherapy: Methods and Principles*. London: Karnac, 2002.

Foulkes, S. H. (1975b). Problems of the large groups. In: L. Kreeger (Ed.). *The Large Group: Dynamics and Therapy* (pp. 33–56). London: Karnac.

Foulkes, S. H. & Anthony, E. J. (1957). *Group Psychotherapy: The Psychoanalytic Approach*. London: Karnac, 2014.

Foulkes, S. H. & Anthony, E. J. (1965). *Group Psychotherapy: The Psychoanalytic Approach*. 2nd Edition. Harmondsworth: Penguin.

Foulkes, S. H. & Lewis, E. (1944). Group Analysis: Studies in the Treatment of Groups on Psychoanalytical Lines. In: S. H. Foulkes. *Therapeutic Group Analysis*. (pp. 20–37). London: Karnac,1964.

Frankfurt Institute for Social Research (1956). *Aspects of Sociology*. Preface by Max Horkheimer and Theodor W. Adorno. London: Heinemann Educational, 1973.

Freud, S. (1900). *The Interpretation of Dreams*. S.E., 4 and 5. London: Hogarth.

Freud, S. (1905). *Psychical or Mental Treatment*. S.E., 7: 283–304. London: Hogarth.

Freud, S. (1907). *Creative Writers and Day-dreaming*. S.E., 9: 141–154. London: Hogarth.

Freud, S. (1913). *Totem and Taboo*. S.E., 13: 1–164. London: Hogarth.

Freud, S. (1914). *On Narcissism: An Introduction*. S.E., 14: 67–102. London: Hogarth.

Freud, S. (1915a). *The Unconscious*. S.E., 14:161–215. London: Hogarth.

Freud, S. (1915b). *Thoughts for the Times on War and Death*. S.E., 14: 275–300. London: Hogarth.

Freud, S. (1917). *Mourning and Melancholia*. S.E., 14: 237–258. London: Hogarth.

Freud, S. (1919a). *Introduction to Psychoanalysis and the War Neurosis*. S.E., 17: 205–211. London: Hogarth.

Freud, S. (1919b). *The Uncanny*. S.E., 17: 217–252. London: Hogarth.

Freud, S. (1920). *Beyond the Pleasure Principle*. S.E., 18: 7–64. London: Hogarth.

Freud, S. (1921). *Group Psychology and the Analysis of The Ego*. S.E., 18: 67–143. London: Hogarth.

Freud, S. (1923a). *The Ego and the Id*. S.E., 19: 3–66. London: Hogarth.

Freud, S. (1923b). *Preface to Max Eitingon Reports on the Berlin Psychoanalytical Policlinic*. London: Hogarth.

Freud, S. (1927). *The Future of an Illusion*. S.E., 21: 3–56. London: Hogarth.

Freud, S. (1930a). *Civilization and Its Discontents*. S.E., 21: 64–145, London: Hogarth.

Freud, S. (1930b). Letter from Sigmund Freud to Arnold Zweig, November 26, 1930. *The International Psycho-Analytical Library*, 84: 21–22.

Freud, S. (1933a). *The Dissection of the Psychical Personality. New Introductory Lectures on Psycho-Analysis*. S.E., 22: 71–100. London: Hogarth.

Freud, S. (1933b). *The question of a Weltanschauung. New Introductory Lectures on Psycho-Analysis*. S.E., 22: 195–225. London: Hogarth.

Freud, S. (1933c). *Why War? (Einstein and Freud). New Introductory Lectures on Psycho-Analysis*. S.E., 22: 197–218. London: Hogarth.

Freud, S. (1935). Postscript. Freud (1925[1924]). *An Autobiographical Study*. S.E., 20: 7–76. London: Hogarth.

Freud, S. (1937). *Constructions in Analysis*. S.E., 23: 255–270. London: Hogarth.

Freud, S. (1938). *Shorter Writings. Findings, Ideas, and Problems. July 20th*. S.E, 23: 299–300. London: Hogarth.

Freud, S. (1939[1934–1938]). *Moses and Monotheism*. S.E., 23: 3–140. London: Hogarth.

Freud, S. (1955[1920]). *Addendum: Memorandum on the electric treatment of war neuroses*. S. E., 17: 211–216. London: Hogarth.

Friedman, R. (2019). *Dreamtelling, Relations, and Large Groups*. London: Routledge.

Fromm, E. (1930). *The Working Class in Weimar Germany: A Psychological & Sociological Study*. Cambridge: Harvard University Press, 1984.

Fromm, E. (1932). *Psychoanalytic characterology and its relevance for social psychology. In: The Crisis of Psychoanalysis* (pp. 164–187). Greenwich: Fawcett, 1971.

Fromm, E. (1941). *Escape from Freedom*. New York: Farrar & Rinehart.

Fromm, E. (1962). The Social Unconscious. In: *Beyond the Chains of Illusion: My Encounter with Marx and Freud*. New York: Continuum.

Fromm. E. (1963). The Revolutionary Character. In: *The Dogma of Christ* (pp.122–139). New York: Holt, Rinehart and Winston.

Frosh, S. (1999). *The Politics of Psychoanalysis: An Introduction to Freudian and Post-Freudian Theory*. New York: New York University Press.

Frosh, S. (2002). The other. *American Imago*, 59 (4): 389–407.

Frosh, S. (2008). *Desire, Demand and Psychotherapy: On Large Groups and Neighbours, Plenary Lecture in Dublin. Publishes in Psychotherapy and Politics International* 6 (3): 185–197.

Frosh, S. (2013a). *Hauntings: Psychoanalysis and Ghostly Transmissions*. London: Palgrave Macmillan.

Frosh, S. (2013b). Transdisciplinary tensions and psychosocial studies. *Enquire*, 6 (1): 1–15.

Fukuyama, F. (2018). *Identity: The Demand for Dignity and the Politics of Resentment*. New York: Farrar, Straus, and Giroux.

Gampel, Y. (2001). Group psychology, society, and masses. In: E. Spector-Person (Ed.). *On Freud's "Group Psychology and the Analysis of the Ego"* (pp. 129–152). London: Analytic Press.

Garcia, C. & Penna, C. (2010). O trabalho do negativo e a transmissão psíquica [The work of the negative and psychic transmission]. *Arquivos Brasileiros de Psicologia*, 62 (3): 68–79.

Garcia, C. (2007). O conceito de ilusão em psicanálise [The concept of illusion in psychoanalysis]. *Estudos de Psicologia*, 12 (2): 169–175.

Garrigou, A. & Lacroix, B. (1997). *Norbert Elias, la politique et l'histoire*. Paris: La Découverte.

Garland, C. (2010). *The Groups Book: Psychoanalytic Group Therapy: Principles and Practice*. London: Karnac.

Gay, P. (2006). *Freud: A Life for Our Time*. New York: W.W. Norton.

Gilligan, J. (1996). *Violence: our Deadliest Epidemic and its Causes*. New York: Grosset /Putnam.

Glasser, M. (1979). Some aspects of the role of aggression in the perversions. In: I. Rosen (Ed.). *Sexual Deviation*. (pp. 278–305). Oxford: University Press.

Gosling, R. (1981). A study of very small groups. In: J. Grotstein (Ed.). *Do I Dare Disturb the Universe?* (pp. 633–646). London: Karnac.

Green, A. (1974). The analyst, the symbolization and absence in the analytic setting. In: A. Green. *On Private Madness* (pp. 30–59). London: Karnac, 2005.

Green, A. (1983). *The Work of the Negative*. London: Free Association.

Green, A. (1988). *Life Narcissism, Death Narcissism*. London: Free Association.

Green, A. (2005). *On Private Madness*. London: Karnac.

Griffiths, F. & Hopper, E. (In Press). The basic assumption of Incohesion in societies and groups within them: Clinical and empirical illustrations. In E. Hopper & H. Weinberg (H). (Eds.). *The Social Unconscious in Persons, Groups, and Societies*, Volume 4. London: Karnac.

Grinberg, L., Langer, M. & Rodrigué, E. (1957). *Psicoterapia del Grupo*. Buenos Aires: Paidós.

Grossmark, R. (2017). Narrating the unsayable: Enactment, repair and creative multiplicity in group psychotherapy. *International Journal of Group Psychotherapy*, 67 (1): 27–46.

Grotstein, J. (1981). *Do I Dare Disturb the Universe?* London: Karnac.

Gudmundsson, E. et al. (2014). Managing School Atmosphere Through Large Groups: A Five-Session Trial. *International Journal of Group Psychotherapy*, 64 (4): 547–563.

Halbwachs, M. (1925). *On Collective Memory*. Chicago: University of Chicago Press, 2003.

Hall, S. (1992). The question of cultural identity. In: S. Hall, D. Held & T. McGrew. *Modernity and its Futures* (pp. 274–323). Cambridge: Polity.

Han, B. C. (2015). *The Burnout Society*. California: Stanford University Press.

Harrison, T. (2000). *Bion, Rickman, Foulkes and the Northfield Experiments: Advancing on a Different Front*. London: Jessica Kingsley.

Harrison, T. (2018). Social fields, battle fields, and Northfield: the legacy of the "Northfield Experiments". *Group Analysis*, 51 (4): 442–454.

Hegel, F. (1806). *Phenomenology of Spirit*. Oxford: Oxford University Press, 1976.

Hegel, F. (1830). *Filosofia da História* [Philosophy of History]. Brasília: UnB, 1996.

Heinich, N. (2002). *La Sociologie de Norbert Elias*. Paris: La Découverte.

Hinshelwood, R. (1987a). *What Happens in Groups: Psychoanalysis, the Individual and Community*. London: Free Association.

Hinshelwood, R. (1987b). Large group dynamics and the nuclear threat. *Group Analysis*, 20: 137–146.

Hinshelwood, R. (1999). How Foulkesian was Bion? *Group Analysis*, 32: 469–488.

Hinshelwood, R. (2000). Foreword. In: T. Harrison. *Bion, Rickman, Foulkes and the Northfield Experiments: Advancing on a Different Front* (pp. 7–10). London: Jessica Kingsley.

Hinshelwood, R. (2003). Group mentality and having a "mind". In: R. Lipgar & M. Pines (Eds.). *Building on Bion: Roots* (pp. 185–197). London: Jessica Kingsley.

Hinshelwood, R. (2007). Bion and Foulkes: the group-as-a-whole. *Group Analysis*, 40 (3): 344–356.

Hinshelwood, R. (2018a). Northfield for ever. *Group Analysis*, 51 (4): 434–441.

Hinshelwood, R. (2018b). John Rickman behind the scenes: the influence of Lewin's field theory on practice, countertransference, and W. R. Bion. *International Journal of Psychoanalysis*, 99 (6): 1409–1423.

Hobsbawm, E. (1975a). *The Age of Revolution 1789–1848*. London: Weidenfeld & Nicolson.

Hobsbawm, E. (1975b). *The Age of Capital 1848–1875*. London: Weidenfeld & Nicolson.

Honneth, A. (1996). *Struggle for Recognition: The Moral Grammar of Social Conflicts*. Cambridge: Polity.

Hopper, E. (1965). Some effects of supervisory style: A sociological analysis. *British Journal of Sociology*, 16 (3) 189–205. Reprinted in Hopper, E. (2003a). *The Social Unconscious: Selected Papers*. London: Jessica Kingsley.

Hopper, E. (1981). *Social Mobility: A Study of Social Control and Insatiability*. Oxford: Blackwell.

Hopper, E. (1982). A comment on Professor. M. Jahoda's "Individual and Group". In: M. Pines & L. Rafaelsen (Eds.). *The Individual and the Group: Boundaries and Interrelations* (pp.17–27). New York/London: Plenum Press.

Hopper, E. (1984). Group Analysis: The Problem of Context. *International Journal of Group Psychotherapy*, 34 (2): 173–199.

Hopper, E. (1991). Encapsulation as a defence against the fear of annihilation. *International Journal of Psychoanalysis*, 72 (4): 607–624.

Hopper, E. (1993). "Comment" on the Large Group of the European Conference in Heidelberg of the Group Analytic Society. *Contexts*, 1: 22–27.

Hopper, E. (1995). A psychoanalytical theory of drug addiction: Unconscious fantasies of homosexuality, compulsions and masturbation within the context of traumatogenic processes. *International Journal of Psychoanalysis*, 76 (6): 1121–1142.

Hopper, E. (2000). From objects and subjects to citizens: group analysis and the study of maturity. *Group Analysis*, 33 (1): 29–34.

Hopper, E. (2001). The social unconscious: theoretical considerations. *Group Analysis*, 34 (1): 9–27.

Hopper, E. (2003a). *The Social Unconscious: Selected Papers*. London: Jessica Kingsley.

Hopper, E. (2003b). *Traumatic Experience in The Unconscious Life of Groups*. London: Jessica Kingsley.

Hopper, E. (2003c). Aspects of aggression in large groups. In: S. Schneider & H. Weinberg (Eds.). *The Large Group Re-visited: The Herd, Primal Horde, Crowds and Masses* (pp. 58–72). London: Jessica Kingsley.

Hopper, E. (2005a). Countertransference in the context of the fourth basic assumption in the unconscious life of groups. *International Journal of Group Psychotherapy*, 55 (1): 87–114.

Hopper, E. (2005b). Response to Vamik Volkan's Plenary Lecture "Large Group Identity, Large Group Regression and Massive Violence". *Group Analytic Contexts*, 30: 27–40.

Hopper, E. (2009a). Building bridges between psychoanalysis and group analysis in theory and clinical practice. *Group Analysis*, 42 (4): 406–425.

Hopper, E. (2009b). The theory of the basic assumption of Incohesion: Aggregation/ Massification or (ba) I: A/M. *British Journal of Psychotherapy*, 25 (2): 214–229.

Hopper, E. (2012). Introduction. In: E. Hopper (Ed.). *Trauma and Organizations* (pp. xxxi–li). London: Karnac.

Hopper, E. (2013). Series Editor Foreword. In: E. Pertegato & G. Pertegato (2013). *From Psychoanalysis to Group Analysis: The Pioneering Work of Trigant Burrow* (pp. xv–xviii). London: Karnac.

Hopper, E. (2018a). The development of the concept of the tripartite matrix: a response to "four modalities of the experience of others in groups" by Victor Schermer. *Group Analysis* 51 (2): 197–206.

Hopper, E. (2018b). "Notes" on the concept of the social unconscious in group analysis. *Group*, 42 (2): 99–118.

Hopper, E. (2019). "Notes" on the theory of the fourth basic assumption in the unconscious life of groups and group-like social systems – Incohesion: Aggregation/ Massification or (ba) I: A/M. *Group*, 43 (1): 9–27.

Hopper, E. (2020). The tripartite matrix, the basic assumption of Incohesion and Scapegoating in Foulkesian Group Analysis: Clinical and empirical illustrations, including terrorism and terrorists. *IAGP Forum*, 8: 26–40.

Hopper, E. (2022). "Notes" on Processes of Fundamentalism and Scapegoating in the Context of the Basic Assumption of Incohesion: Aggregation/Massification or (ba) I: A/M. In: A. Berman & G., Ofer (Eds.). *Socio-Cultural and Clinical Perspectives of Tolerance: Hope and Pain of Meeting the Other*. London: Routledge.

Hopper, E. & Weyman, A. (1975). A sociological view of large groups. In: L. Kreeger (Ed.). *The Large Group: Dynamics and Therapy* (pp. 159–189). London: Karnac.

Hopper, E. & Weinberg, H. (2011). Introduction. In: E. Hopper & H. Weinberg (Eds.). *The Social Unconscious in Persons, Groups, and Societies, Vol. 1. Mainly Theory* (pp. xxii–lv). London: Karnac.

Hopper, E. & Weinberg, H. (2016). *The Social Unconscious in Persons, Groups, and Societies, Vol. 2: Mainly Foundation Matrices*. London: Karnac.

Hopper, E. & Weinberg, H. (2017). Introduction. In: E. Hopper & H. Weinberg (Eds.). *The Social Unconscious in Persons, Groups, and Societies, Vol. 3: The Foundation Matrix Extended and Re-configured* (pp. xv–xxxv). London: Karnac.

Horkheimer, M. (1936). Authority and the family. In: M. Horkheimer. *Critical Theory: Selected Essays* (pp. 47–128). New York: Continuum, 2002.

Horkheimer, M. & Adorno, T. (1944). *Dialectic of Enlightenment*. California: Stanford University Press, 2007.

Horney, K. (1937). *The Neurotic Personality of Our Time*. New York: W.W. Norton.

Horthon, R. (2020). Offline: COVID-19 is not a pandemic. *The Lancet*, 396 (10255): 874, September.

Island, T. (2003). The large group and leadership challenges in a group analytic training community. In: *Group Re-visited: The Herd, Primal Horde, Crowds and Masses* (pp. 201–213). London: Jessica Kingsley.

Island, T. K. (2010). Desintegration oder Dialog? Die Bedeutung von Grossgruppen im Kontext. [Disintegration or Dialogue? The Significance of the Large Group in Context]. In: W.M. Roth, J. Shaked &, H. Felsberger (Eds.). *Die Analytische Grossgruppe, Festschrift zu Ehren von Josef Shaked*. Wien: Facultas Verlags-und Buchhandels AG.

Jacobs, I. (1973). Report on the Large Group at the European Workshop on Group Analysis, No. 1. *Group Analysis (G.A.I.P.A.C)* 1 (3): 26–28.

Jacoby, R. (1983). *The Repression of Psychoanalysis: Otto Fenichel and the Political Freudians*. New York: Basic Books.

Jameson, F. (2002). *The Political Unconscious*. London: Routledge.

Jaques, E. (1955). Social systems as a defense against persecutory and depressive anxiety. In: M. Klein, P. Heimann & R. Money-Kyrle (Eds.). *New Directions in Psycho-Analysis* (pp. 478–498). New York: Basic Books.

Jay, M. (1973). *The Dialectical Imagination: A History of the Frankfurt School and the Institute for Social Research, 1923–1950.* Boston: Little Brown.

Judt, T. (2006). *Postwar: A History of Europe Since 1945.* London: Penguin.

Jung, C. G. (1936). The concept of the collective unconscious. *Journal of St Bartholomew's Hospital, London,* XLIV.

Kaës, R. (1975). *Le Group et le Sujet du Groupe.* Paris: Dunot, 2000.

Kaës, R. (2007). *Linking, Alliances and Shared Spaces.* London: Routledge.

Kernberg, O. (1975). *Borderline Conditions and Pathological Narcissism.* New York: Jason Aronson.

Kernberg, O. (1998). *Ideology, Conflict, and Leadership in Groups and Organizations.* New Haven: Yale University Press.

Kernberg, O. (2003). Socially sanctioned violence: the large group and society. In: S. Schneider & H. Weinberg (Eds.). *The Large Group Re-visited: The Herd, Primal Horde, Crowds and Masses* (pp. 125–149). London: Jessica Kingsley.

Kernberg, O. (2020). Malignant Narcissism and Large Group Regression. *Psychoanalytic Quarterly,* 89 (1): 1–24.

King, P. (2003). Introduction. In: P. King (Ed.). *No Ordinary Psychoanalyst: The Exceptional Contribution of John Rickman* (pp. 1–68). London: Karnac.

Klímová, H. (2011). The false we/The false collective self. In: E. Hopper & H. Weinberg (Eds.). *The Social Unconscious in Persons, Group, and Societies, Vol. 1. Mainly Theory* (pp. 187–207). London: Karnac.

Knauss, W. (2006). The group in the unconscious: a bridge between the individual and society. *Group Analysis,* 39 (2): 159–170.

Knott, E. (2012). On Analysing Large Groups. *Group Analysis,* 45 (3): 289–309.

Kohut, H. (1971). *The Analysis of the Self: A Systematic Approach to the Psychoanalytic Treatment of Narcissistic Personality Disorders.* New York: International Universities Press.

Kreeger, L. (1975). Introduction. In: L. Kreeger (Ed.). *The Large Group: Dynamics and Therapy* (pp. 13–29). London: Karnac.

Kreeger, L. (1992). Envy pre-emption in small and large groups. *Group Analysis,* 25 (4): 391–408.

Kreeger, L. (2009). Introduction to large groups. *Group Analysis,* 42 (3): 282–285.

Kuhn, T. (1962). *The Structure of Scientific Revolutions.* Chicago: University of Chicago Press.

La Boétie, E. (1577). *The Politics of Obedience: The Discourse of Voluntary Servitude.* New York: Free Life, 1975.

Lacan, J. (2007). *Écrits.* New York: W.W. Norton.

Laplanche, J. & Pontalis, J. B. (1973). *The Language of Psycho-Analysis.* London: Routledge.

Lasch, C. (1979). *The Culture of Narcissism.* New York: Warner Books.

Lawrence, W. G. (1979). Introductory essay: exploring boundaries. In: W. G. Lawrence. *Exploring Individual and Organizational Boundaries* (pp. 1–19). London: Karnac.

Lawrence, W. G. (1985). Beyond frames. In: M. Pines. *Bion and Group Psychotherapy* (pp. 306–329). London: Jessica Kingsley.

Lawrence, W. G. (1998). *Social Dreaming @ Work.* London: Karnac.

Lawrence, W. G., Bain, A. & Gould, J. (2000). The fifth basic assumption. In: W. G. Lawrence. *Tongued with Fire: Groups in Experience* (pp. 92–119). London: Karnac.

Leal, M. R. (1968). Transference neurosis in group analytic treatment. *Group Analysis* 1 (2): 101–1109.

Le Bon, G. (1895). *The Crowd*. New Brunswick: Transaction, 1995.

Le Roy, J. (2000). Group analysis and culture. In: D. Brown & L. Zinkin (Eds.). *The Psyche and the Social World* (pp. 180–201). London: Karnac.

Levine, D. (Ed.) (1971). *Georg Simmel: On Individuality and Social Forms*. Chicago: University of Chicago Press.

Levine, R. (2018). A group analyst's perspective on the Trump-Clinton election and aftermath. *International Journal of Group Psychotherapy*, 69 (2):192–220.

Lewin, K. (1947). *Field Theory in Social Sciences*. New York: Harper & Brothers.

Limentani, A. (1989). *Between Freud and Klein: The Psychoanalytical Quest for Knowledge and Truth*. London: Free Association.

Lipgar, R. (2003). Re-discovering Bion's *Experiences in Groups*. In: R. Lipgar & M. Pines (Eds.). *Building on Bion: Roots* (pp. 29–58). London: Jessica Kingsley.

Lipovetsky, G. (1983). *L'ère du vide: Essais sur l' individualisme contemporain*. Paris: Gallimard.

Losso, R., de Setton, L. & Scharff, D. (2017). *The Linked Self in Psychoanalysis: The Pioneering Work of Pichon-Rivière*. London: Routledge.

Löwenberg, P. (1996). *Decoding the Past: The Psychohistorical Approach*. New Brunswick: Transaction.

Löwenthal, L. & Guterman, N. (1949). *Prophets of Deceit: A Study of the Techniques of the American Agitator*. New York: Harper & Brothers.

Lukács, G. (1922). Freud's psychology of the masses. In: G. Lukács. *Reviews and Articles from "Die Rote Fahne"* (pp. 33–36). London: The Merlin Press, 1983.

Lukács, G. (1923). *History and Class Consciousness: Studies in Marxist Dialectics*. London: The Merlin Press.

Lukes, S. (1973). *Émile Durkheim, His Life and Work*. London: Allen Lane.

Lyotard, J. (1984). *The Postmodern Condition*. Minneapolis: University of Minnesota Press.

Main, T. (1975). Some psychodynamics of large groups. In: L. Kreeger (Ed.). *The Large Group: Dynamics and Therapy* (pp. 57–86). London: Karnac.

Main, T. (1983). The concept of the therapeutic community: variations and vicissitudes. In: M. Pines (Ed.). *The Evolution of Group Analysis* (pp. 197–217). London: Jessica Kingsley.

Marlin, O. (2016). Psychoanalytic view of the totalitarian mentality: the case of the Czech experience. In: E. Hopper & H. Weinberg (Eds.). *The Social Unconscious in Persons, Groups, and Societies, Vol. 2: Mainly Foundation Matrices* (pp. 81–96). London: Karnac.

Martins, R. (1986). Contribuições de Freud à psicoterapia de grupo [Freud's contributions to group psychotherapy]. In: L. Osório (Ed.). *Grupoterapia Hoje [Group Psychotherapy Today]* (pp. 43–56). Porto Alegre: ArtMed.

Martins, R. (2017). Memória: Alcyon Baer Bahía, Walderedo Ismael de Oliveira e uma aplicação quase esquecida da psicanálise [Memory: Alcyon Baer Bahía, Walderedo Ismael Oliveira and an almost forgotten apllication of psychoanalysis]. *Revista Brasileira de Psicanálise*. Special Edition 221–231.

Marx, K. (1847). *Karl Marx and Frederick Engels, Collected Works*, Vol. 6. New York: International Publishers, 1975.

Mbembe, A. (2003). Necropolitics. *Public Culture* 15 (1):11–40.

McClelland, J. S. (1989). *The Crowd and the Mob: From Plato to Canetti*. London: Routledge.

McDougall, W. (1920). *The Group Mind: A Sketch of the Principles of Collective Psychology*. New York: Putnam's Sons, 2010.

Mead, G. H. (1972). *Movements of Thought in the Nineteenth Century*. Chicago: University of Chicago Press.

Mello Filho, J. (2000). *Grupo e Corpo: Psicoterapia de Grupo com Pacientes Somáticos* [Group and Body: Group Psychotherapy with Somatic Patients]. Porto Alegre: ArtMed.

Mello Franco, O. (2015). Psicoterapia analítica de grupo: a trajetória de uma ideia e de uma práxis. [Group analytic psychotherapy: the trajectory of an idea and of a praxis]. *Jornal de Psicanálise*, 48 (88): 271–285.

Meltzer, D. (1975). Adhesive identification. *Contemporary Psychoanalysis*, 11 (3): 289–310.

Meloy, R. & Yakeley, J. (2014). The Violent True Believer as a "Lone Wolf" – Psychoanalytic Perspectives on Terrorism. *Behavioral Sciences and the Law, 32(3)*. Retrieved http://drreidmeloy.com/wp-content/uploads/2015/12/2014_TheViolent True.pdf.

Menoutis, V. (2000). Median and large group-analytic groups in a naval academy. *Group Analysis*, 33 (1): 49–61.

Mennell, S. (1997). L'envers de la médaille: les processus de décivilisation. In: A. Garrigou & B. Lacroix (Eds.). *Norbert Elias, la Politique et l'histoire* (pp. 213–238). Paris: La Découverte.

Menzies-Lyth, I. (1961). A case-study in the functioning of social systems as defence against anxiety. *Human Relations*, 13: 95–121.

Menzies-Lyth, I. (1981). Bion's contribution to thinking about groups. In: J. S. Grotstein (Ed.). *Do I dare disturb the universe?* (pp. 661–666). London: Karnac.

Merleau-Ponty, M. (1968). *The Visible and the Invisible*. Evanston: Northwestern University Press.

Merleau-Ponty, M. (1969). *Humanisme and Terror*. Boston: Beacon Press.

Mezan, R. (1985). *Freud, Pensador da Cultura* [Freud: A Thinker of the Culture]. São Paulo: Companhia das Letras.

Miller, E. (1990). Experiential learning in groups I. In: E. Trist & H. Murray. *The Social Engagement of Social Science: A Tavistock Anthology*, Vol. 1 (pp. 165–183). London: Free Association.

Miller, E. (1998). A note on the protomental system and "groupishness": basic assumptions revisited. *Human Relations*, 51(12): 1495–1508.

Mitscherlich, A. & Mitscherlich, M. (1975). *The Inability to Mourn*. New York: Grove.

Mojovic, M. (2011). Manifestations of psychic retreats in social systems. In: E. Hopper & H. Weinberg (Eds.). *The Social Unconscious in Persons, Group, and Societies, Vol. 1. Mainly Theory* (pp. 209–232). London: Karnac.

Mojovic, M. (2020). The Balkans on the Reflective Citizens Couch unravelling social-psychic-retreats. In: A. Zajenkowska & U. Levin (Eds.). *A Psychoanalytic and Socio-Cultural Exploration of a Continent*. (pp.175–187). London: Routledge.

Moraes Filho, E. (1983). Formalismo sociológico e a teoria do conflito [Sociological formalism and the conflict theory]. In: E. Moraes Filho (Ed.). *Georg Simmel: Sociologia*. (pp. 7–44). São Paulo: Ática.

Moreno, J. L. (1961). Interpersonal therapy and co-unconscious states: a progress report in psychodramatic theory. *Group Psychotherapy*, 14: 234–241.

Moscovici, S. (1985). *The Age of the Crowd: A Historical Treatise on Mass Psychology.* Cambridge: Cambridge University Press.

Mucchielli, L. (1998). *La Découverte du Social: Naissance de la Sociologie en France, 1870–1914.* Paris: La Découverte.

Mucchielli, L. (2000). Tardomania: reflexions sur les usages contemporaines de Tarde. *Revue d'Histoire des Sciences Humaines,* 3:161–184.

Musse, R. (1999). *As raízes marxistas da Escola de Frankfurt* [The marxist roots of the Frankfurt School] (pp. 15–27). Lecture delivered on July 14, 1997, at the Law School of the Federal University of Paraná, Brazil.

Neiburg, F. & Waizbort, L. (2006). Apresentação [Foreword]. In: N. Elias. *Norbert Elias: Escritos e Ensaios 1: Estado, Processo, Opinião Pública* [Writings and Essays 1: State, Process, Public Opinion] (pp. 7–20). Rio de Janeiro: Zahar.

Neri, C. (2013). Notes on Bion's basic-assumption. *Rivista di Psicoanalisi,* XXVII (3–4): 749–757.

Neto, I. M. & França, M. (2021). *The Portuguese School of Group Analysis: Towards a Unified and Integrated Approach to Theory research and Clinical Work Research.* London: Routledge.

Nitsun, M. (1996). *The Anti-Group: Destructive Forces in The Group and Their Creative Potential.* London: Routledge.

Nitzgen, D. (2008). The Group Analytic Movement Sixty Years On: Revisiting *Introduction to Group Analytic Psychotherapy* by S.H. Foulkes. *Group Analysis,* 41 (4): 325–346.

Nitzgen, D. (2011). The concept of the social unconscious in the work of S. H. Foulkes. In: E. Hopper & H. Weinberg (Eds.). *The Social Unconscious in Persons, Groups, and Societies, Vol.1. Mainly Theory* (pp. 3–21). London: Karnac.

Nitzgen, D. (2013). Symboltheoretische Perspektiven der Gruppenanalyse, *Psychosozial* 36 (1): 19–42.

Nitzgen, D. (2014). Lost in Translation? Reading Foulkes Today. *Group Analysis,* 47 (3): 213–226.

Nitzgen, D. & Hopper, E. (2017). The concepts of the social unconscious and of the matrix in the work of S. H. Foulkes. In: E. Hopper & H. Weinberg (Eds.). *The Social Unconscious in Persons, Groups, and Societies, Vol. 3: The Foundation Matrix Extended and Re-configured* (pp. 3–25). London: Karnac.

Nye, R. (1995). Introduction. In: G. Le Bon. *The Crowd* (pp. 1–25). New Brunswick: Transaction.

Ogden, T. H. (1989). On the concept of an autistic-contiguous position. *The International Journal of Psychoanalysis,* 70 (1): 127–140.

Ogden, T. H. (1994). The analytic third: working with intersubjective clinical facts. *International Journal of Psychoanalysis,* 75 (1): 3–19.

Ormay, T. (2012). *The Social Nature of Persons. One Person is No Person.* London: Karnac.

Ortega y Gasset, J. (1930). *The Revolt of the Masses.* New York: W.W. Norton, 1994.

Ortiz, R. (2016). Escola de Frankfurt e a questão da cultura [The Frankfurt School and the question of culture]. *Sociologia em Rede,* 6 (6): 203–242.

Pasolini, P. P. (1975). The Vacuum of Power in Italy. Retrieved from http://cittapasolini. blogspot.com /2016/09/the-vacuum-of-power-il-vuoto-del-potere.html.

Pearce, S. & Haigh, R. (2017). *The Theory and Practice of Democratic Therapeutic Community Treatment.* London: Jessica Kingsley.

Penna, C. (2016a). Reflections upon Brazilian social unconscious. In: E. Hopper & H. Weinberg (Eds.). *The Social Unconscious in Persons, Groups, and Societies, Vol. 2: Mainly Foundation Matrices* (pp. 139–158). London: Karnac.

Penna, C. (2016b). Homo Clausus, Homo Sacer, Homines Aperti: Challenges for Group Analysis in the 21st-Century. *Group Analysis*, 49 (4): 357–369.

Penna, C. (2019). Psychosocial approaches to mass hysteria phenomena: a case study in Mozambique. *Journal of Psychosocial Studies*, 12 (1–2): 157–169.

Penna, C. (2020). From 'Cultural Revolution' to the Weariness of the Self: New Struggles for Recognition. *Free Associations*, 78, June: 33–49.

Pertegato, E. & Pertegato, G. (2013). *From Psychoanalysis to Group Analysis: The Pioneering Work of Trigant Burrow*. London: Karnac.

Pichon-Rivière, E. (1980). *O Processo Grupal* [The Group Process]. São Paulo: Martins Fontes.

Pick, D. (1989a). *Faces of degeneration: A European disorder*. Cambridge: Cambridge University Press.

Pick, D. (1989b). Thousands of little white blobs. *London Review of Books*, 11 (22): 20–22.

Pick, D. (1995). Freud's "Group Psychology" and the history of the crowd. *History Workshop Journal*, 40: 39–61.

Pines, M. (1975). Overview. In: L. Kreeger (Ed.). *The Large Group: Dynamics and Therapy* (pp. 291–311). London: Karnac.

Pines, M. (1983). *The Evolution of Group-Analysis*. London: Jessica Kingsley.

Pines, M. (1998). *Circular Reflections: Selected Papers on Group Analysis and Psychoanalysis*. London: Jessica Kingsley.

Pines, M. (1999). Forgotten pioneers: the unwritten history of the therapeutic community movement. *The International Journal for Therapeutic and Supportive Organizations*, 20 (1): 23–42.

Pines, M. (2003). Large groups and culture. In: S. Schneider & H. Weinberg (Eds.). *The Large Group Re-visited: The Herd, Primal Horde, Crowds and Masses* (pp. 44–57). London: Jessica Kingsley.

Pines, M. (2009). The matrix of group analysis: a historical perspective. *Group Analysis*, 42 (1): 5–15.

Powell, A. (1994). Towards an unifying concept of the group matrix. In: D. Brown & L. Zinkin. *The Psyche and the Social World*. (pp 11–26). London: Jessica Kingsley.

Rank, O. (1927). *The Double: A Psychoanalytic Study*. Chapel Hill: University of North Carolina Press, 1971.

Reckwitz, A. (2021). *The End of Illusions: Politics, Economy, and Culture in Late Modernity*. London: Polity.

Redl, F. (1942). Group emotion and leadership. *Psychiatry: Journal for the Study of Interpersonal Processes*, 5: 573–596.

Reich, W. (1933). *The Mass Psychology of Fascism*. London: Souvenir Press, 1997.

Reicher, E. (2020). Approaching the Mountain: A journey into the wilderness of large group thinking. *Group Analysis* 53 (3): 420–439.

Reynié, D. (1988). Théories du nombre. *Hermès: Masses et Politique*, 2: 95–104.

Reynié, D. (2005). Introdução [Introduction]. In: G. Tarde. *A Opinião e as Massas* [*The Opinion and the Masses*] (pp. VII–XXXIV). São Paulo: Martins Fontes.

Rice, A. K. (1965). *Learning from Leadership. Interpersonal and Intergroup Relations*. London: Routledge.

Richards, B. (2018). *What holds us together? Popular Culture and Social Cohesion.* London: Karnac.

Rickman, J. (1938). Does it take all kinds to make a world? Uniformity and diversity in communities. In: P. King (Ed.). *No Ordinary Psychoanalyst: The Exceptional Contributions of John Rickman* (pp. 159–183). London: Karnac, 2003.

Rickman, J. (2003). *No Ordinary Psychoanalyst: The Exceptional Contributions of John Rickman.* Compiled and Edited by Pearl King. London: Karnac, 2003.

Rioch, M. (1970a). Group Relations: Rationale and technique. *International Journal of Group Psychotherapy,* 20: 340–355.

Rioch, M. (1970b). The Work of Wilfred Bion in Groups. *Psychiatry,* 33: 56–66.

Rioch, M. (1983). Reflections: Wilfred Bion: an appreciation and some reminiscences. *Group Analysis,* 16 (3): 252–257.

Rouanet, S. P. (1986). *Teoria Crítica e Psicanálise* [Critical Theory and Psychoanalysis]. Rio de Janeiro: Tempo Brasileiro.

Roudinesco, E. & Plon, M. (1997). *Dicionário de Psicanálise* [Dictionary of Psychoanalysis]. Rio de Janeiro: Zahar.

Rothe, S. (1989). The Frankfurt School: An Influence on Foulkes' Group Analysis? *Group Analysis* 22: 405–415.

Rudé, G. (1964). *The Crowd in History: A Study of Popular Disturbances in France and England, 1730–1848.* New York: John Wiley & Sons.

Rustin, M. (1991). *The Good Society and the Inner World.* London: Verso.

Rustin, M. & Armstrong, D. (2019). Psychoanalysis, social science and the Tavistock tradition. *Psychoanalysis, Culture and Society* 24 (4): 473–492.

Sandler, P. C. (2013). A sixth basic assumption? In: P. C. Sandler. *Verbal and Visual Approaches to Reality. A Clinical Application of Bion's Concepts,* Vol. 3 (pp. 229–266). London: Karnac.

Scanlon, C. (2018). 'Practicing disappointment'. From reflection to action in organizations and communities. In: C. Thornton (Ed.). *The Art and Science of Working Together: Practising Group Analysis in Teams and Organizations* (pp. 76–84). London: Routledge.

Sharpe, M. (2008). Styles of Large Group Leadership. *Group,* 32 (4): 89–301.

Sharpe, M., Hopper E., Shapiro, E. & Shields, W. (2002). Reader's Forum. *International Journal of Group Psychotherapy,* 52 (3):431–440.

Schindler, W. (1966). The role of the mother in group psychotherapy. *International Journal of Group Psychotherapy,* 16, 198–200.

Schlapobersky, J. (2016). *From the Couch to the Circle: Group-Analytic Psychotherapy in Practice.* London: Routledge.

Schneider, S. & Weinberg, H. (2003). Introduction. In: S. Schneider & H. Weinberg (Eds.). *The Large Group Re-visited: The Herd, Primal Horde, Crowds and Masses* (pp. 13–26). London: Jessica Kingsley.

Schnerb, R. (1968). *Le XIXe siècle: l'apogée de l'expansion européenne (1815–1914).* 5th ed. Paris: PUF.

Scholz, R. (2011). The foundation matrix and the social unconscious. In: E. Hopper & H. Weinberg (Eds.). *The Social Unconscious in Persons, Groups, and Societies, Vol.1.: Mainly Theory* (pp. 265–288). London: Karnac.

Scholz, R. (2017). The fluid and the solid – or the dynamic and the static: some further thoughts about the conceptualisation of foundation matrices, processes of the social unconscious, and/or large group identities. In: E. Hopper & H. Weinberg (Eds.). *The*

Social Unconscious in Persons, Groups, and Societies. Volume 3: The Foundation Matrix Extended and Re-configured (pp. 27–46). London: Karnac.

Segal, H. (1997). Silence is the real crime. In: H. Segal. *Psychoanalysis, Literature, and War: Papers 1972–1995* (pp. 117–128). London: Routledge.

Semprún, J. (2002). A witness to the 20th century. *International Psychoanalysis*, 11 (1): 19–22.

Sennett, R. (1974). *The Fall of the Public Man.* New York: W.W. Norton.

Shaked, J. (2003). The large group and political process. In: S. Schneider & H. Weinberg (Eds.). *The Large Group Re-visited: The Herd, Primal Horde, Crowds and Masses* (pp. 150–161). London: Jessica Kingsley.

Sher, M. (2003). From groups to group relations. In: R. Lipgar & M. Pines (Eds.). *Building on Bion: Branches* (pp. 109–144). London: Jessica Kingsley.

Shils, E. (1975). *Centre and Periphery: Essays in Macrosociology.* Chicago: University of Chicago Press.

Sidis, B. (1903). *The Psychology of Suggestion.* New York: Appleton & Co., 1927.

Sighele, S. (1891). *The Criminal Crowd and Other Writings on Mass Society.* Toronto: University of Toronto Press, 2018.

Silva, E. P. (2008). As concepções de subjetividade em Gramsci e Lukács e a práxis educacional [Conceptions of subjectivity in Gramsci and Lukács and the educational praxis]. *Trabalho & Educação*, 17 (2): 89–102.

Simmel, G. (1903). The metropolis and mental life. In: G. Simmel. *The Sociology of Georg Simmel* (pp. 409–424). New York: Free Press, 1950.

Simmel, G. (1908). *The Sociology of Georg Simmel.* Glencoe: Free Press, 1950.

Simmel, G. (1964). *Conflict and The Web of Group-Affiliations.* New York: Free Press.

Simmel, G. (1971). Freedom and the individual (Posthumous). In: D. Levine (Ed.). *Georg Simmel on Individuality and Social Forms* (pp. 217–226). Chicago: University of Chicago Press.

Simmel, G. (1989). L'individualisme. In: G. Simmel. *Philosophie de la Modernité* (pp. 251–259). Paris: Payot.

Skynner, R. (1975). The large group in training. In: L. Kreeger (Ed.). *The Large Group: Dynamics and Therapy* (pp. 227–251). London: Karnac.

Solomon, H. (2007). *The Self in Transformation.* London: Karnac.

Soreanu, R. (2018). *Working-Through Collective Wounds: Trauma, Denial, Recognition in the Brazilian Uprising.* London: Palgrave Macmillan.

Spector-Person, E. (1992). Romantic love: at the intersection of the psyche and the cultural unconscious. In: T. Shapiro & R. Emde (Eds.). *Affect Psychoanalytic Perspectives* (pp. 383–411). Madison: International Universities Press.

Spink, M. J. P. (2011). Pessoa, indivíduo e sujeito: notas sobre efeitos discursivos de opções conceituais. In: M. J. P. Spink, P. Figueiredo & J. Brasilino (Eds.). *Psicologia social e pessoalidade* (pp. 1–22). Rio de Janeiro: Abrapso.

Stackelberg, R. (1999). *Hitler's Germany: Origins, Interpretations, Legacies.* London: Routledge.

Steiner, J. (1993). *Psychic Retreats.* London: Routledge.

Sutherland, J. D. (1985). Bion revisited: group dynamics and group psychotherapy. In: M. Pines (Ed.). *Bion and Group Psychotherapy* (pp. 47–86). London: Jessica Kingsley.

Swanson, G. (2014). Collectivity, human fulfilment and the 'force of life': Wilfred Trotter's concept of the herd instinct in early 20th-century Britain. *History of the Human Sciences*, 27 (1): 21–50.

Tarde, G. (1890). *The Laws of Imitation.* London: Read Books, 2013.

Tarde, G. (1893). As multidões e as seitas criminosas [Crowds and criminal sects]. In: G. Tarde. *A Opinião e as Massas* [*Opinion and the masses*] (pp. 141–199). São Paulo: Martins Fontes, 2005.

Tarde, G. (2005). O público e a multidão [The public and the crowd]. In: G. Tarde. *A Opinião e as Massas* [*Opinion and the masses*] (pp. 5–58). São Paulo: Martins Fontes.

Taylor, C. (1994). The politics of recognition. In: C. Taylor (Ed.). *Multiculturalism: Examining the Politics of Recognition* (pp. 25–75). Princeton: Princeton University Press.

Thorner, H. A. (1946). The treatment of psychoneurosis in the British army. *International Journal of Psychoanalysis*, 27 (1–2): 52–59.

Tilly, C., Castañeda, E. & Wood, L. (2020). *Social Movements, 1768–2018*. London: Routledge.

Tönnies, F. (1887). *Community and Society*. Mineola: Dover Publications, 2011.

Torres, C. E. (2007). A multidão religiosa de Lourdes em Zola e Huysmans [The religious crowds at Lourdes in Zola and Huysmans]. *Análise Social*, 184: 733–755.

Torres, N. (2003). Gregariousness and the mind: Wilfred Trotter and Wilfred Bion. In: R. Lipgar & M. Pines (Eds.). *Building on Bion: Roots* (pp. 85–117). London: Jessica Kingsley.

Trist, E. (1985). Working with Bion in the 1940s: the group decade. In: M. Pines (Ed.). *Bion and Group Psychotherapy* (pp. 1–46). London: Jessica Kingsley.

Trist, E., & Murray, H. (1990). *The Social Engagement of Social Science: A Tavistock Anthology, Vol. 1: The Socio-Psychological Perspective*. Philadelphia: University of Pennsylvania Press.

Trotter, W. (1919). *Instincts of the Herd in Peace and War*. London: Fisher Unwin.

Tubert-Oklander, J. (2011). Enrique Pichon-Rivière: the social unconscious in the Latin-American tradition of group analysis. In: E. Hopper & H. Weinberg (Eds.). *The Social Unconscious in Persons, Groups, and Societies. Volume 1: Mainly Theory* (pp. 45–70). London: Karnac.

Tubert-Oklander, J. (2014). *The One and the Many*. London: Karnac.

Tubert-Oklander, J. (2017). Field theories and process theories. In: K. Montana., R. Cassorla. R. and G. Civitarese (Eds.). *Advances in Contemporary Psychoanalytic Field Theory. Concept and future development* (pp. 191–200). New York, London: Routledge.

Tubert-Oklander, J. & Hernández de Tubert, R. (2004). *Operative groups: The Latin-American Approach to Group Analysis*. London: Jessica Kingsley.

Tubert-Oklander, J. & Hernández de Tubert, R. (2014a). The Social Unconscious and the Large Group Part I: The British and the Latin American Traditions. *Group Analysis*, 47 (2): 99–112.

Tubert-Oklander, J. & Hernández de Tubert, R. (2014b). The Social Unconscious and the Large Group Part II: A Context that Becomes Text. *Group Analysis*, 47 (3): 329–344.

Tubert-Oklander, J. & Hernández de Tubert, R. (2014c). The Social Unconscious and the Large Group Part III: Listening to the Voices in the Wind. *Group Analysis*, 47 (4): 420–435.

Turquet, P. (1974). Leadership: the individual in the group. In: G. Gibbard, J. Hartman & R. Mann (Eds.). *Analysis of Groups* (pp. 349–371). San Francisco: Jossey-Bass.

Turquet, P. (1975). Threats to identity in large groups. In: L. Kreeger (Ed.). *The Large Group: Dynamics and Therapy* (pp. 87–144). London: Karnac.

Tustin, F. (1981). *Autistic States in Children*. London: Routledge & Kegan Paul.

Van Ginneken, J. (1992). *Crowds, Psychology & Politics, 1871–1899*. Cambridge: Cambridge University Press.

Vandenberghe, F. (2005). *As Sociologias de Georg Simmel* [The Sociologies of Georg Simmel]. Bauru: EDUSC.

Visentini, P. & Pereira, A. L. (2008). *História do Mundo Contemporâneo: Da Pax Britânica do Século XVIII ao Choque das Civilizações do Século XXI* [History of the Contemporary World: From the 18th Century Pax Britannica to the 21st Century Clash of Civilizations]. Petrópolis: Vozes.

Volkan, V. (1997). *Bloodlines: From Ethnic Pride to Ethnic Terrorism*. New York: Farrar, Straus, and Giroux.

Volkan, V. (2004). *Blind Trust: Large Groups and Their Leaders in Times of Crisis and Terror*. Charlottesville: Pitchstone.

Volkan, V. (2006). *Killing in the Name of Identity. A Study of Blood Conflicts*. Charlottesville: Pitchstone.

Volkan, V. (2013). *Enemies on the Couch: A Psychopolitical Journey Through War and Peace*. Durham: Pitchstone.

Von Sommaruga Howard, T. (2011). The Architecture of Domination: Reflections on Conducting the Symposium Large Group in Dublin. *Group Analysis*, 44 (3): 328–341.

Von Sommaruga Howard, T. (2012). To Stand Sitting! Bi-Cultural Dilemmas in a Large Group in Aotearoa New Zealand. *Group Analysis*, 45 (2): 219–243.

Waizbort, L. (2000). *As Aventuras de Georg Simmel* [The Adventures of Georg Simmel]. São Paulo: Editora 34.

Waizbort, L. (2001). Elias e Simmel. In: F. Neiburg et al. (Eds.). *Dossiê Norbert Elias* (pp. 89–112). São Paulo: Edusp.

Weinberg, H. (2007). So, what is this social unconscious anyway? *Group Analysis* 40 (3): 307–320.

Weinberg, H. & Rolnick, A. (2020). *Theory and Practice of Online Therapy. Internet-delivered Interventions for Individuals, Groups, Families, and Organizations*. New York: Routledge.

Wilke, G. (2003a). Chaos and order in the large group. In: S. Schneider & H. Weinberg (Eds.). *The Large Group Re-visited: The Herd, Primal Horde, Crowds and Masses* (pp. 86–97). London: Jessica Kingsley.

Wilke, G. (2003b) The large group and its conductor. In: R. Lipgar & M. Pines (Eds.). *Building on Bion: Branches* (pp. 70–105). London: Jessica Kingsley.

Wilke, G (2014). *The Art of Group Analysis in Organizations*. London: Karnac.

Wilke, G. (2016). The German social unconscious: second-generation perpetrators symptoms in organizations and groups. In: E. Hopper & H. Weinberg (Eds.). *The Social Unconscious in Persons, Groups, and Societies, Vol. 2: Mainly Foundation Matrices* (pp. 61–80). London: Karnac.

Winship, G. (2003). The democratic origins of the term 'Group Analysis': Karl Mannheim's third way for psychoanalysis and social science. *Group Analysis* 36 (1): 37–51.

Winnicott, D. W. (1952). *Anxiety associated with insecurity. Collected Papers: Through Pediatrics to Psycho-Analysis*. London: Hogarth.

Winnicott, D. W. (1963). Fear of breakdown. In: C. Winnicott, R. Shepherd & M. Davis (Eds.). *Psycho-Analytic Explorations* (pp. 87–95). Cambridge: Harvard University Press, 1989.

Winnicott, D. W. (1965). *The Maturational Processes and the Facilitating Environment*. London: Karnac.

Winnicott, D. W. (1971). *Playing and Reality*. London: Tavistock.

Winnicott, D. W. (1975). *Collected Papers: Through Pediatrics to Psycho-Analysis*. London: Hogarth.

Winnicott, D. W. (1988). *Human Nature*. Philadelphia: Brunner/Mazel.

Whiteley, J. S. (1975). The large group as a medium for sociotherapy. In: L. Kreeger (Ed.). *The Large Group: Dynamics and Therapy* (pp. 193–211). London: Karnac.

Whiteley, J. S. & Gordon, J. (1979). *Group Approaches in Psychiatry*. London: Routledge.

Yates, C. (2015). *The Play of Political Culture, Emotion, and Identity*. London: Palgrave Mcmillan.

Zaretsky, E. (2004). *Secrets of the Soul: A Social and Cultural History of Psychoanalysis*. New York: Vintage.

Zimerman, D. (1993). *Fundamentos Básicos das Grupoterapias* [Foundations of Group Therapies]. Porto Alegre: ArtMed.

Zinkin, L. (1983). Malignant mirroring. *Group Analysis*, 16 (2): 113–126.

Zinkin, L. (2000). Exchange as a therapeutic factor in group analysis. In: D. Brown & L. Zinkin (Eds.). *The Psyche and the Social World* (pp. 99–117). London: Karnac.

Žižek, S. (2020). *Pandemic! Covid-19 Shakes the World*. New York/London: Or Books.

Index

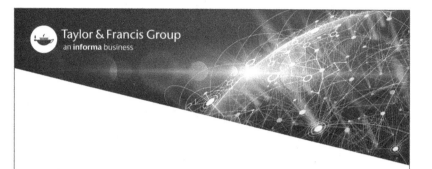